W9-CHK-851

LANDS AND PEOPLES

1 AFRICA

2 ASIA · AUSTRALIA
NEW ZEALAND · OCEANIA

3 EUROPE

4 EUROPE

5 NORTH AMERICA

6 CENTRAL and
SOUTH AMERICA
FACTS AND FIGURES
INDEX

LANDS AND PEOPLES

AFRICA

Volume 1

GROLIER
INCORPORATED
DANBURY, CONN.

Library of Congress Cataloging-in-Publication Data

Lands and peoples.

    p. cm.
   Includes bibliographical references and index.
   Contents: v. 1. Africa; v. 2. Asia, Australia, New
Zealand, Oceania; v. 3–4. Europe; v. 5. North Amer-
ica; v. 6. Central and South America, Facts and fig-
ures, Index.
   1. Geography—Juvenile literature. [1. Geography]
I. Grolier Incorporated.
G133.L3   1993   910—dc20   92-17742
ISBN 0-7172-8016-0

PREFACE

Never in history has there been so crucial a need for people of the world to know one another. Modern technological advances in transportation and communication have made all people neighbors. The distances that kept people apart in the past are swiftly vanishing.

With the turn of a dial or the touch of a button, events and people thousands of miles away come into our awareness with immediacy and impact. We see or hear, almost as if we were indeed participants, a devastating tidal wave in Asia, an earthquake in Peru, a student demonstration in Paris, a tense political meeting in Addis Ababa. The inescapable truth is that each one of us is a citizen of an immense and complex community: the world.

Yet persisting ignorance about other peoples and other lands keeps alive the embers of fear and prejudice that so often burst into flames of hatred and conflict. Every day as we see these flames flare up in different parts of our world, we are reminded that the science that made us a world neighborhood has also produced the weapon with which this neighborhood can annihilate itself.

The task of achieving better understanding among people is a difficult one. A vital part of this task is to provide—especially for young people—accurate, interesting, readable information about every land, its people, its way of life. Hopefully, LANDS AND PEOPLES will fulfill this need.

LANDS AND PEOPLES should appeal to a wide range of readers, from elementary school students to adults at home and to the many who travel every year to other lands to visit other peoples. All will find a wealth of information on the geography, history, and economy of the countries of the world. They will also acquire clear insights into the lives of the people of these countries, their life styles, their beliefs, their work, and their play. A very deliberate effort was made to select content that develops those concepts and attitudes basic to a good understanding of the interaction among people and their social, their cultural, and their physical environment.

The basic principle of the editorial policy underlying LANDS AND PEOPLES is the presentation of fact, not opinion. Bias, subtle propaganda, value words, or the slightest hint of stereotype is scrupulously avoided.

The articles in this set of books were written by scholars and experts. Many of the authors' names will be readily recognized as prominent in the life of the people they write about. Articles are reviewed by authorities of proven competence. Every article, picture, and map was submitted to a staff of skilled researchers who checked information against primary sources wherever possible. Where authorities disagree or information is not known, the reader is so informed.

To facilitate the locating of information, the contents of LANDS AND PEOPLES are organized by continents. Within each volume the countries of a particular continent are arranged geographically. The tables of contents list the countries in alphabetical order. The final volume of the set includes general statistical information and the Index.

LANDS AND PEOPLES offers its readers an exciting learning experience. It combines an unusually readable and authoritative text with color photographs presented in the most modern possible format. The illustrations, although beautiful, are not used merely as decoration but as a vivid editorial device. They have been chosen carefully to evoke, visually, the essence of the lands they illustrate and the reality of the lives of the people. The editors believe that LANDS AND PEOPLES makes an especially valuable contribution to understanding because of this interplay of the written word with the visual image.

In a world beset by difficulties that often seem insurmountable, tolerance and understanding frequently give way to hostility and ignorance. Anger replaces thoughtful deliberation and insensitivity supplants compassion. Only by means of knowledge of each other can people ever hope to achieve a saner world. It is the sincere hope of the editors that these volumes will help to bring constructive new ideas to solve the problems of the changing world.

The Editors

CONSULTANTS

CONTRIBUTORS AND REVIEWERS

AL-HAMMAMI, Abdallah
Permanent Mission of the Yemen Arab Republic to the United Nations
YEMEN

AMERASINGHE, H.S.
Permanent Representative of Sri Lanka to the United Nations
SRI LANKA

ARCINIEGAS, Germán
Colombian Ambassador to Venezuela; Author, *Latin America: A Cultural History*
COLOMBIA

ASHCRAFT, Norman
Acting Chairman, Department of Anthropology, Adelphi University
BELIZE

ATWOOD, Evangeline
Staff Historian, *Anchorage Daily Times*; Author, *Anchorage: All-America City*
ALASKA

BAILEY, Norman A.
Professor of Political Science, Queens College of the City University of New York; Co-author, *Portuguese Africa* ANGOLA

BALDAIA, Raul Sergio Pinto
Former Chief of the Cabinet, São Tomé and Príncipe
SÃO TOMÉ AND PRÍNCIPE

BARTON, Thomas Frank
Professor of Geography, Indiana University
PAPUA NEW GUINEA

BATES, Margaret L.
Associate Professor of Government, Smith College TANZANIA

BENEDICT, Burton
Professor of Anthropology, University of California at Berkeley; Author, *Mauritius: Problems of a Plural Society; People of the Seychelles*
MAURITIUS; SEYCHELLES

BIGELOW, Ross Edgar
Assistant in Geography, Michigan State University; Consultant, Regional Office for West Africa, the Ford Foundation, Lagos, Nigeria
IVORY COAST

BORGES, Jorge Luis
Director, Biblioteca Nacional, Argentina; Author, *Book of Imaginary Beings; Aleph and Other Stories; Dreamtigers*
ARGENTINA: AN INTRODUCTION

BRACE, Richard M.
Professor of History, Oakland University, Rochester, Michigan; Author, *Ordeal in Algeria; Morocco, Algeria, Tunisia*
MOROCCO

BROADFOOT, Barry
Feature Writer, *Vancouver Sun*, Vancouver, British Columbia
BRITISH COLUMBIA; PRAIRIE PROVINCES

BROOKS, Hugh C.
Director, Center for African Studies, St. John's University; Fellow, Royal Geographical Society; Founding Member, African Studies Association; Co-author, *Refugees South of the Sahara*
CONGO; GAMBIA, THE; GUINEA-BISSAU; NAMIBIA; SOUTH AFRICA; WESTERN SAHARA; ZAMBIA

BULLIET, Richard W.
Professor of History, Middle East Institute, Columbia University
SOUTHWEST ASIA; TURKEY; CYPRUS; SYRIA; LEBANON; ISRAEL; JORDAN; SAUDI ARABIA; YEMEN; OMAN; UNITED ARAB EMIRATES; BAHRAIN; QATAR; KUWAIT; IRAQ; IRAN; AFGHANISTAN

BUSTIN, Edouard
Associate Professor of Government, Boston University; Professor Extraordinary, African Studies Center, National University, Lubumbashi
ZAÏRE

BUTWELL, Richard
President, California State University, Dominguez Hills; Author, *Southeast Asia Today—and Tomorrow; The Changing Face of Southeast Asia; Southeast Asia, A Political Introduction*
BRUNEI; CAMBODIA; INDONESIA; MALAYSIA; MEKONG RIVER; PAKISTAN; PHILIPPINES; SINGAPORE; SOUTHEAST ASIA; VIETNAM

CABOT, Jean
Faculté de Géographie, Université de Paris-Vincennes; Author, *Le Bassin du Moyen Logone; Les Lits du Logone* CHAD

CARLSON, Lucile
Associate Professor of Geography and Chairman of the Department of Geography, Case Western Reserve University; Author, *Africa's Lands and Nations* MALI; BURKINA

CASTAGNO, Alphonso A.
Director, African Studies Center, Boston University; Author, *Somalia*
SOMALIA

CASTAGNO, Margaret F. SOMALIA

CASTEDO, Leopoldo
Chairman, Department of Art, State University of New York at Stony Brook; Author, *Historia de Chile* CHILE

CHENG, Tao
Associate Professor of Political Science, Trenton State College, New Jersey; Author, *Communist China and the Law of the Sea*
MONGOLIA; TIBET

CHINCHILLA AGUILAR, Ernesto
Professor of History, State University of New York at Stony Brook; Director of the National Archives of Guatemala; Author, *La Inquisición en Guatemala; El Ayuntamiento de la ciudad de Guatemala* GUATEMALA; NICARAGUA

CHOISIT, Paul
Consulat Général de Monaco, New York MONACO

CHOMCHAI, Prachoom
Professor and Head, Department of Public Finance and Economy, Chulalongkorn University, Bangkok; Author, *Chulalongkorn the Great* THAILAND

CHRISTIANSEN, Ulla
Danish Information Office, New York GREENLAND

CLEAVER, Charles G.
Professor of English, Grinnell College; Fulbright Visiting Lecturer, Tokyo National University, Sendai JAPAN

COLLINS, Robert O.
Associate Professor of African History, University of California at Santa Barbara; Author, *The Southern Sudan, 1883–1898*; Co-author, *Egypt and the Sudan* SUDAN

COMMAGER, Henry Steele
Professor of History and American Studies, Amherst College; Author, *The Heritage of America; The American Mind* UNITED STATES: AN INTRODUCTION

COWAN, L. Gray
Director, Institute for African Studies, Columbia University; Author, *Local Government in West Africa: Dilemmas of African Independence; Transition in Africa* TOGO

CSICSERY-RÓNAY, István
Associate Librarian, University of Maryland; Author, *First Book of Hungary* HUNGARY

DE BOINVILLE, David
Information Department, British Embassy, Washington, D.C. ENGLAND

DELZELL, Charles F.
Professor of History, Vanderbilt University; Author, *Italy in the Twentieth Century, Mediterranean Fascism, Mussolini's Enemies* ITALY

DE WARREN, Réginald
Counselor of Embassy, French Embassy, Washington, D.C. PARIS

DIOGO, Innocent A.
Diplomatic Attaché, Permanent Mission of Benin to the United Nations BENIN

DIRVIN, Rev. Joseph I.
Assistant to the President, St. John's University; Author, *Mrs. Seton, Foundress of the American Sisters of Charity* VATICAN CITY

DOCTOROFF, Mark
Director, Soviet Elite Database Project, W. Averell Harriman Institute, Columbia University CENTRAL AND NORTH ASIA; MONGOLIA

DUCCI, Carlos
Second Secretary, Permanent Mission of Chile to the United Nations EASTER ISLAND

DUFEK, George J.
Rear Admiral, U.S. Navy (Ret.); Director, The Mariners Museum, Newport News, Virginia; Author, *Heroes of Polar Exploration* ANTARCTICA; ARCTIC

DURÓN, Jorge Fidel
Rector, University of Honduras; Author, *The Laws of Honduras* HONDURAS

DZIEWANOWSKI, M.K.
Professor of History, Boston University POLAND

EDOHO, Edoho Bassey
Professor of African History, State University of New York at Albany NIGERIA; RWANDA

EL-AYOUTY, Yassin
St. John's University; Fellow, African Studies Association; Fellow, the Middle East Association of North America; Author, *The Afro-Asians and the Concept of Self-Government Under the UN Charter* EGYPT; JORDAN; NILE RIVER; SOUTHWEST ASIA; SUEZ CANAL; TIGRIS AND EUPHRATES RIVERS

ENVELA-MAKONGO, Gustavo
Ambassador, Permanent Mission of Equatorial Guinea to the United Nations EQUATORIAL GUINEA

FAYACHE, M.L.
First Secretary, Permanent Mission of Tunisia to the United Nations TUNISIA

FEHRENBACHER, Don E.
Coe Professor of American History, Stanford University; Author, *A Basic History of California; The Era of Expansion, 1800–1848* PACIFIC STATES

FERGUS, Howard
University of the West Indies (Montserrat) ANTIGUA AND BARBUDA; SAINT KITTS-NEVIS

FERNÁNDEZ, J.W.
Associate Professor of Anthropology, Dartmouth College; Fellow, African Studies Association BENIN

FIGUERES, José
Former President of Costa Rica COSTA RICA

FISCHER-GALATI, Stephen
Professor of History, University of Colorado; Editor, *Romania*; Author, *The New Rumania: From People's Democracy to Socialist Republic* ROMANIA

FISHER, John W.
President, John Fisher Enterprises Ltd.; Former Commissioner, Canadian Centennial Commission ONTARIO

FISKE, John
Former Cultural Affairs Officer, United States Embassy, Reykjavik, Iceland ICELAND

FITZGERALD, Thomas

Assistant Chief Inspector (retired), Department of Education, Dublin, Ireland; Author, *Justinian*
IRELAND; NORTHERN IRELAND

FREEDMAN, Paul

Foreign Trade Editor, *The Journal of Commerce;* Author, *German Parliament in Action; Elections and Political Parties in Germany; Documents on German Unity*   GERMANY

FRENCH, Karen Elizabeth

Graduate Department, Bryn Mawr College   LIBERIA

FREYRE, Gilberto

Author, *The Masters and the Slaves; New World in the Tropics; Mother and Son; Mansions and Shanties*   BRAZIL

FRIEDBERG, Judith

Senior Editor, *Travel and Leisure* Magazine
LONDON; SCOTLAND

FRIEDLAND, William

Professor of Community Studies and Sociology, University of California at Santa Cruz; Author, *Unions and Industrial Relations in Underdeveloped Countries;* Co-editor, *African Socialism*
GUINEA

FULLER, Charles Edward

Chairman, Sociology and Anthropology Department, St. John's University; Consultant to Christian Council of Botswana; Former Director, Study-Service Seminar in Botswana
BOTSWANA; BURUNDI

GALAR, Alberto Fernández

Governor, Las Palmas, Canary Islands   CANARY ISLANDS

GERTEINY, Alfred G.

Associate Professor of African and Middle Eastern History and Politics, University of Bridgeport; Author, *Mauritania; Islam in Africa*   MAURITANIA

GHORRA, Edouard

Former Ambassador and Permanent Representative of Lebanon to the United Nations   LEBANON

GODENSCHWEGER, Ingeborg

German Information Center, New York   RHINE RIVER

GOKHALE, B.G.

Professor of History and Director, Asian Studies Program, Wake Forest University; Author, *Ancient India; The Making of the Indian Nation*   GANGES RIVER; INDIA; INDUS RIVER

GOUAMBA, Philippe

Secretary (Press) of the Embassy, Permanent Mission of the People's Republic of Congo to the United Nations   CONGO

GRAYSON, George W.

John Marshall Professor of Government and Citizenship, College of William and Mary; Author, *The Politics of Mexican Oil, The United States and Mexico: Patterns of Influence*
PORTUGAL; SPAIN

GRENIER, Suzanne

Ministry of International Relations, Quebec, Canada   QUEBEC

GUNTHER, John

Author, *Inside South America; Inside Europe; Inside USA;* Editor, *Mainstream of Modern World History Series*
CENTRAL AND SOUTH AMERICA: AN INTRODUCTION

HACHEME, Abdou O.

Second Secretary, The Permanent Mission of Mauritania to the United Nations   MAURITANIA

HALLMUNDSSON, Hallberg

Translator and Editor   FINLAND

HARSCH, Joseph C.

Chief Editorial Writer and Columnist, *Christian Science Monitor;* Commander, the Order of the British Empire (Hon.); Author, *Pattern of Conquest; The Curtain Isn't Iron*
LONDON; UNITED KINGDOM; SCOTLAND

HASSAN, Sir Joshua

Chief Minister of Gibraltar   GIBRALTAR

HASSELRIIS, Caspar Henrik Wolfsen

Former Director, Danish Information Service, New York; Commander of the Order of Dannebrog   DENMARK

HATCH, John

Author, *The Dilemma of South Africa; New from Africa; Everyman's Africa; Africa Today and Tomorrow; A History of Post War Africa; Africa: The Re-Birth of Self-Rule*   AFRICA

HAYS, H.R.

Formerly, Associate Professor of Humanities, Long Island University; Author, *From Ape to Angel; In the Beginning; The Kingdom of Hawaii*   HAWAII

HELLY, Dorothy O.

Assistant Professor of History, Hunter College of the City University of New York   SENEGAL

HELMREICH, J.E.

Professor of History, Allegheny College; Author, *Belgium and Europe: A Study in Small Power Diplomacy, Gathering Rare Ores: The Diplomacy of Uranium Acquisition, 1943–54*
BELGIUM; LUXEMBOURG

HERZ, Ulrich

Secretary General, International Peace Bureau, Geneva
SWEDEN

HOLLON, W. Eugene

Ohio Regents Professor of History, Emeritus, University of Toledo; Author, *The Southwest Old and New; The Great American Desert*   SOUTHWESTERN STATES

HU, C.T.

Professor of Comparative Education, Teachers College, Columbia University; Co-author, *China, Its People, Its Society, Its Culture;* Author, *Chinese Education Under Communism*
CHINA; YANGTZE RIVER; YELLOW RIVER

HUNT, Donald Wayne

Editor, The Scribner Desk Dictionary of American History
PACIFIC STATES

IMMONEN, Mikko

Former Consul, Consulate General of Finland, New York
LAPLAND

JARDIM, Anne

Deputy Permanent Representative, Guyana Mission to the United Nations   GUYANA

JOUGHIN, Jean T.

Professor of History, The American University, Washington, D.C.; Author, *The Paris Commune in French Politics, 1871–1880; The History of the Amnesty of 1880*   FRANCE

KALB, Marvin

Diplomatic Correspondent, Columbia Broadcasting System News; Author, *Eastern Exposure; Dragon in the Kremlin; The Volga—A Political Journey Through Russia*   VOLGA RIVER

KALIS, William H.

Chief of Government Information Services, Bahamas News Bureau   BAHAMAS

KARAN, P.P.

Professor and Chairman, Department of Geography, University of Kentucky; Author, *The Himalayan Kingdoms; Bhutan, Sikkim, and Nepal; Nepal: A Physical and Cultural Geography; Bhutan: A Physical and Cultural Geography*
          BHUTAN; BANGLADESH; HIMALAYAS; KASHMIR

KHALID, Ali

Delegate of the Sudan Mission to the United Nations   SUDAN

KIRCHHERR, Eugene C.

Professor of Geography, Western Michigan University; Author, *Abyssinia to Zona al Sur del Draa: An Index to the Period 1951– 1967*   NIGER

KIRK, George

Professor of History, University of Massachusetts; Author, *A Short HIstory of the Middle East; The Middle East in the War, 1939–45; The Middle East 1945–50; Contemporary Arab Politics*
          BAHRAIN; MIDDLE EAST; OMAN; QATAR;
          UNITED ARAB EMIRATES

KITCHEN, Helen

Former Editor in Chief, *Africa Report;* Author, *A Handbook of African Affairs; Footnotes to the Congo Story;* Editor, *The Press in Africa; Africa and the United States; Images and Realities; The Educated African*   MOZAMBIQUE

KLEIN, Philip S.

Professor of American History, Pennsylvania State University; Author, *Pennsylvania Politics 1817–1832: A Game Without Rules; President James Buchanan, A Biography;* Co-author, *History of the United States*
          NORTHEASTERN STATES: MIDDLE ATLANTIC STATES

KLINE, Hibberd V.B., Jr.

Professor and Chairman, Department of Geography, and Chairman, African Studies Program, University of Pittsburgh
          ZIMBABWE

LAI, David Chuenyan

Department of Geography, University of Victoria (Canada); Author, *Arches in British Columbia;* Co-author, *The Small Industrial Unit in Hong Kong: Patterns and Policies*   HONG KONG

LANGAKER, Lars

Cultural Attaché, Information Service, Royal Norwegian Embassy, Washington, D.C.   NORWAY

LANUZA, José Luis

Vice-President, Argentine Society of Writers; Author, *Una historia de la raza africana en el Río de la Plata*   ARGENTINA

LeBAR, Frank M.

Research Associate, Human Relations Area Files, Inc.; Co-editor, *Laos, Its People, Its Society, Its Culture*   LAOS

LEKONGA, Augustin N.

First Secretary, Permanent Mission of the Republic of Zaïre to the United Nations   CONGO RIVER

LENCEK, Rado L.

Associate Professor, Department of Slavic Languages, Columbia University; Author, *A Bibliographical Guide to the Literature on Slavic Civilizations; An Outline of the Course on Slavic Civilizations*   BULGARIA

LENGYEL, Emil

Professor of History, Fairleigh Dickinson University; Author, *Turkey; The Changing Middle East*   TURKEY

LE VINE, Victor T.

Associate Professor of Political Science, Washington University, St. Louis; Author, *The Cameroons from Mandate to Independence; Political Leadership in Africa*   CAMEROON

LEWIS, William H.

Associate Professor of Political Science, George Washington University, Washington, D.C.; Co-author, *Modern Middle East and Muslim Africa; New Forces in Africa; Emerging Africa; French-Speaking Africa; Islam in Africa*   ETHIOPIA

LLEWELLYN, Richard

Captain, the Welsh Guards; Author, *How Green Was My Valley* and other books   WALES

LOGORECI, Anton

Political Commentator and Scriptwriter, British Broadcasting Corporation, European Services   ALBANIA

LOURENÇO, Leão

Permanent Mission of Portugal to the United Nations   MACAU

MAKONNEN, Tassew

Acting Consul, Ethiopian Consulate, New York   ETHIOPIA

MALDONADO, Alex W.

Associate Editor, *El Mundo,* San Juan, Puerto Rico
          PUERTO RICO

MALE, John

Former Chief, Advisory Services, Division of Human Rights, United Nations; Journalist and Broadcaster, New Zealand
          NEW ZEALAND

MALEFIJT, Annemarie de Waal

Professor of Anthropology, City University of New York; Author, *The Javanese of Suriname*   SURINAME

MARCOPOULOS, George J.

Associate Professor and Deputy Chair, Department of History, Tufts University   GREECE

MASITHELA, J.L.

First Secretary, Embassy of the Kingdom of Lesotho to the United States, Washington, D.C.   LESOTHO

MATHEWS, Thomas
Association of Caribbean Universities and Research Institutes
DOMINICA; SAINT VINCENT AND THE GRENADINES;
SAINT LUCIA

MAZRUI, Ali A.
Professor of Political Science, Makerere University College,
Uganda; Author, *Towards a Pax Africana; The Anglo-African
Commonwealth; On Heroes and Uhuru Worship;* Co-editor,
Protest and Power in Black Africa UGANDA

McLEOD, Norma
Associate Professor of Anthropology, Tulane University; Fellow,
African Studies Association MADAGASCAR

McVEY, Ruth T.
School of Oriental and African Studies, University of London;
Author, *The Rise of Indonesian Communism;* Editor, *Indonesia,
Its People, Its Society, Its Culture* INDONESIA

MEDINA, José Ramon
Professor of Literature, Universidad Central de Venezuela,
Caracas VENEZUELA

MENDÈS-FRANCE, Pierre
Former Premier of France and Minister of Foreign Affairs; Officer of the Legion of Honour; Author, *A Modern French Republic*
and other books FRANCE: AN INTRODUCTION

MIERS, Earl Schenck
Author, *Golden Book of American History; Golden Book History
of the United States; The Bill of Rights; Emancipation;* and many
other books on American history UNITED STATES

MILES, John A.
Senior Political Affairs Officer, United Nations; Former Senior
Lecturer in Pacific History, Australian School of Pacific
Administration FIJI; NAURU; OCEANIA;
TONGA; WESTERN SAMOA

MILNE, Robert Scott
Former Staff Editor, *Encyclopedia Americana;* Member, Society
of American Travel Writers UNITED STATES CITIES

MIRANDA, Hernany
Vice-Consul, El Salvador Consulate, New York EL SALVADOR

MOHAMOUD, Abdurahman Hussein
Counselor, Embassy of the Somali Republic, Washington, D.C.
SOMALIA

MONTES DE OCA, Antonio
University of Mexico; Author, *Pliego de testimonio; Delante de
la luz cantan los pájaros; Cantos al sol que nos alcanza; Funda-
ción de entusiasmo; La vendimia del juglar; Pedir el fuego*
MEXICO

MOORE, Clement Henry
Assistant Professor of Political Science, University of California
at Berkeley; Author, *Tunisia Since Independence: The Dy-
namics of One-Party Government;* Co-author, *Tunisia: The Politics of Modernization* TUNISIA

MORRISON, Joseph L.
Professor of Journalism, University of North Carolina, Chapel
Hill; Author, *W.J. Cash: Southern Prophet; Josephus Daniels,
The Small-d Democrat; Josephus Daniels Says*
SOUTHEASTERN STATES

MOSCOTE, Rafael E.
Head, Department of History, Universidad de Panama; Author,
Aspectos de la civilización occidental PANAMA

MOWER, Jack H.
Lecturer in African Studies, School of Advanced International
Studies, Johns Hopkins University KENYA

MURRAY, John J.
Professor and Chairman of the Department of History, Coe College, Iowa; Editor, *The Heritage of the Middle West;* Author, *An
Honest Diplomat at The Hague; Amsterdam in the Age of Rem-
brandt;* and other books NORTH CENTRAL STATES

NOWOTNY, Thomas
Information Service, Austrian Consulate General, New York
DANUBE RIVER

OCHSENWALD, William
Professor of History, Virginia Polytechnic Institute and State Uni-
versity; Author, *Religion, Society and the State in Arabia; The
Hijaz Railroad* SAUDI ARABIA

OLDENBURG, Philip
Adjunct Professor of Political Science, Columbia University;
Member, Southern Asia Institute
SOUTH ASIA; PAKISTAN; INDIA; NEPAL; BHUTAN;
BANGLADESH; SRI LANKA; MALDIVES

OLSON, Robert W.
Department of History, University of Kentucky IRAQ; SYRIA

OUEDRAOGO, Louis-Dominique
First Counsellor, Permanent Mission of Burkina Faso (Upper
Volta) to the United Nations BURKINA

OUELLET, Jo
Editor and Publisher, *Le Quebecker;* Author, *Instant French*
QUEBEC

OUSSEINI, Soumana
Permanent Mission of the Republic of Niger to the United
Nations NIGER; NIGER RIVER

PACHAI, Bridglal
Professor of History, University of Malawi; Author, *History of
Indian Opinion: Life and Work of Mahatma Gandhi in South
Africa* MALAWI

PALMARO, Marcel A.
Consulat Général de Monaco, New York MONACO

PAREJA DIEZCANSECO, Alfredo
Former Professor of History, University of Miami; Universidad
Central del Ecuador; Author, *Historia del Ecuador; Hombre sin
tiempo; Los nuevos años; Los poderes omnimodos* ECUADOR

PAZHWAK, Abdur-Rahman
Former Ambassador and Permanent Representative of Afghanistan to the United Nations; Former President of the United Nations General Assembly AFGHANISTAN

PERETZ, Don

Professor of Political Science and Director, South West Asia-North Africa Program, State University of New York at Binghamton; Author, *Israel and the Palestine Arabs; The Middle East Today;* Co-author, *The Middle East*   JERUSALEM

PERLÈS, Alfred

Author, *Sentiments Limitrophes; Le Quatuor en Ré-Majeur; The Renegade; Alien Corn; Round Trip; My Friend Henry Miller; My Friend Lawrence Durrell*   CYPRUS

PONCE-LUQUE, José G.

Minister-Consul General of Ecuador, New York
GALÁPAGOS ISLANDS

PORTISCH, Hugo

Editor in Chief, Austrian Television and Radio Corp.; Author, *Eyewitness in Russia, Africa and South America; Eyewitness in Red China; Siberia*   AUSTRIA

PRATT, Bruce W.

Editorial Director, *The Australian Encyclopedia*   AUSTRALIA

PYLE, Fergus

Paris Correspondent, the *Irish Times;* Co-editor, *1916–The Easter Rising*   NORTHERN IRELAND

QURESHI, I.H.

Vice-Chancellor, University of Karachi; Author, *The Pakistani Way of Life; The Muslim Community of the Subcontinent of India and Pakistan; The Struggle for Pakistan*   PAKISTAN

RADDALL, Thomas H.

Awarded Gold Medal for distinguished contribution to Canadian Literature (1956); Author, *His Majesty's Yankees; West Novas; Halifax, Warden of the North; Footsteps on Old Floors;* and many other books   ATLANTIC PROVINCES

RE, Charles

Consul of San Marino, New York   SAN MARINO

RIDGELL, Reilly

Assistant Professor, Guam Community College; author, *Pacific Nations and Territories*
AUSTRALIA AND NEW ZEALAND; AUSTRALIA; NEW ZEALAND; OCEANIA; MICRONESIA; FEDERATED STATES OF MICRONESIA; MARSHALL ISLANDS; NAURU; KIRIBATI; MELANESIA; PAPUA NEW GUINEA; SOLOMON ISLANDS; VANUATU; FIJI; POLYNESIA; TONGA; WESTERN SAMOA; TUVALU

RODMAN, Selden

Author, *Renaissance in Haiti; Haiti: The Black Republic; Quiqueya: A History of the Dominican Republic;* Editor, *A New Anthology of Modern Poetry*   HAITI

RODRÍGUEZ MONEGAL, Emir

Professor of Latin American Literature, Yale University; Author, *Literatura uruguaya; El viajero inmóvil; Introducción a Pablo Neruda; El desterrado; Borges par lui-même*   URUGUAY

ROFF, William

Professor of History, Columbia University; Member, Southern Asia Institute.
SOUTHEAST ASIA; MYANMAR; THAILAND; LAOS; CAMBODIA; VIETNAM; MALAYSIA; SINGAPORE; INDONESIA; BRUNEI; PHILIPPINES

ROLVAAG, Karl F.

Former United States Ambassador to Iceland; Former Governor of Minnesota   ICELAND

ROSS, Harold M.

Chairman, Division of Social Sciences, St. Norbert College
KIRIBATI; SOLOMON ISLANDS; TUVALU; VANUATU

ROTHKOPF, Carol Z.

Author, *The First Book of Yugoslavia; The First Book of East Europe; The First Book of the Red Cross; Leo Tolstoy; Jean and Henry Durant; The Opening of the Suez Canal*   YUGOSLAVIA

ROWEN, Herbert H.

Professor, Rutgers University, New Brunswick; Author, *The Princes of Orange; The Stadholders in the Dutch Republic*
NETHERLANDS

RYBACEK, Irina

Executive Director, American Czech-and-Slovak Education Fund
ARMENIA; AZERBAIJAN; BELARUS; BOSNIA AND HERZEGOVINA; CROATIA; CZECH REPUBLIC; ESTONIA; GEORGIA; KAZAKHSTAN; KYRGYZSTAN; LATVIA; LITHUANIA; MACEDONIA; MOLDOVA; SLOVAKIA; SLOVENIA; TAJIKISTAN; TURKMENISTAN; UKRAINE; UZBEKISTAN; YUGOSLAVIA

SAMBATH, Huot

Former Permanent Representative of Cambodia to the United Nations   CAMBODIA

SANCHEZ, Luis Alberto

Former Rector of San Marcos University, Lima, Peru; President of the Union of Latin American Universities; Former President of the Senate of Peru; Author, *El Pueblo en la revolución americana; Examen espectral de América Latina; La universidad no es una isla; Historia de la literature peruana; Balance y liquidación del novecientos; Historia de América; La reforma universitaria*
PERU

SCHILLER, Edward H.

Associate Professor of History and Director of International Studies, Nassau Community College, New York; Fellow, African Studies Association; Fulbright Fellow in West Africa
GAMBIA, THE; GHANA; NIGERIA

SHAMMAS, Sami Y.

Counsellor and Chargé d'Affaires, Permanent Mission of the State of Kuwait to the United Nations   KUWAIT

SHERLOCK, Sir Phillip

Former Vice-Chancellor, University of the West Indies; Secretary-General, Association of Caribbean Universities; Author, *Land and People of the West Indies; Belize, A Short History*
BARBADOS; JAMAICA; TRINIDAD AND TOBAGO

SHESKIN, Ira M.

Associate Professor, University of Miami   ISRAEL

SHIBATA, Thomas

Professor of Economics, Tokyo Metropolitan University; Director, Department of General Planning and Coordination, Metropolis of Tokyo; Author, *Tokyo—Its Socio-Economic Analysis; Comparative Study on World Cities*   JAPAN

SHULMAN, Colette

Research Associate, School of International Affairs, Columbia University; Editor, *We The Russians*
UNION OF SOVIET SOCIALIST REPUBLICS

SMITH, Frank E.

Director, Tennessee Valley Authority; Author, *The Yazoo River; Congressman From Mississippi; Look Away From Dixie; The Politics of Conservation;* Co-author, *Mississippians All*
SOUTH CENTRAL STATES

SMYTHE, Hugh H.

Former United States Ambassador to Malta   MALTA

SNOW, C.P. (Baron Snow)

Former Parliamentary Secretary, British Ministry of Technology; Former Fellow, Christ's College, Cambridge; Former Regents Professor, University of California at Berkeley; Former Rector, University of St. Andrews; Author, *Strangers and Brothers*
UNITED KINGDOM: AN INTRODUCTION

SORIA, Mario T.

Professor and Chairman of the Department of Modern Languages, Drake University; Author, *Armando Chirveches: novelista boliviano*
BOLIVIA

SPAAK, Paul-Henri

Former Foreign Minister and Premier of Belgium; First President of the United Nations General Assembly; President of the Consultative Assembly of the Council of Europe, 1949–51; Chairman of the International Council of the European Movement, 1950–55; Secretary-General of the North Atlantic Treaty Organization (NATO), 1957–61
EUROPE: AN INTRODUCTION

SPADA, Nello

Author, *Garibaldi and the Red Shirts; Dante's Divine Comedy*
ROME

SPADA-BALLUFF, Dorothea

Editor in Chief, International Edition, *Abitare*
LIECHTENSTEIN; SWITZERLAND

SPITZER, Leo

Instructor in History, Dartmouth College; Associate of the Institute of African Studies, Fourah Bay College, Freetown, Sierra Leone
SIERRA LEONE

SPITZER, Manon L.
SIERRA LEONE

STANLEY, William R.

Associate Professor of Geography, University of South Carolina; Fellow, African Studies Association
LIBERIA

STEINBERG, David I.

Representative, The Asia Foundation, Washington, D.C.; Author, *Korea: Nexus of East Asia;* Translator, *In This Earth and in That Wind: This is Korea*
KOREA

STEVENS, Richard P.

Chairman, Department of Political Science, and Director, African Studies Program, Lincoln University; Author, *Lesotho, Botswana and Swaziland: The Former High Commission Territories in Southern Africa*
LESOTHO; SWAZILAND

SZULC, Tad

Diplomatic Correspondent, *The New York Times* Washington Bureau; Author, *Twilight of the Tyrants; Cuban Invasion; Winds of Revolution; Latin America; Dominican Diary*
CUBA

TAYLOR, Alan R.

Associate Professor of International Relations, School of International Service, The American University, Washington, D.C.; Member, Middle East Institute; Author, *Prelude to Israel*
JORDAN

TRAGER, Frank N.

Professor of International Affairs, New York University; Author, *Burma From Kingdom to Republic; Building a Welfare State in Burma; Marxism in Southeast Asia*
MYANMAR

TUMA, Ginette M.

Press Attaché, Chief, Documentation Division, French Embassy
FRENCH GUIANA

VAKHIL, Mehdi

Former Ambassador and Permanent Representative of Iran to the United Nations
IRAN

VAN DONGEN, Irene S.

Assistant Professor, Department of Geography and Earth Science, California State College, California, Pennsylvania
CENTRAL AFRICAN REPUBLIC

VAN EVERY, Dale

Author, *The American Frontier; Westward the River; The Shining Mountains; Men of the Western Waters; The Voyagers; Forth to the Wilderness; A Company of Heroes; Ark of Empire; The Final Challenge;* and many other books
MOUNTAIN STATES

VARLEY, Paul

Director, Donald Keene Center of Japanese Culture; Professor of History and Acting Chairman, Department of East Asian Languages and Cultures, Columbia University
EAST ASIA; CHINA; HONG KONG; MACAU; TAIWAN; NORTH KOREA; SOUTH KOREA; JAPAN

VELEZ MAGGIOLO, Marcio

Director de Extensión Cultural de la Universidad Autónoma de Santo Domingo; Author, *El sol y las cosas; El buen ladrón; Intus; El prófugo; Creonte; Judas; La vida no tiene nombre; Los angeles de hueso*
DOMINICAN REPUBLIC

WAGLEY, Charles

Franz Boas Professor of Anthropology and Former Director, Institute of Latin American Studies, Columbia University; Author, *Introduction to Brazil; The Latin American Tradition*
CENTRAL AND SOUTH AMERICA

WALKER, Edward W.

Visiting Scholar, Columbia University's Harriman Institute
ALBANIA; ARMENIA; AZERBAIJAN; BELARUS; BOSNIA AND HERZEGOVINA; BULGARIA; CROATIA; CZECH REPUBLIC; ESTONIA; GEORGIA; HUNGARY; KAZAKHSTAN; KYRGYZSTAN; LATVIA, LITHUANIA; MACEDONIA; MOLDOVA; POLAND; ROMANIA; RUSSIA; SLOVAKIA; SLOVENIA; TAJIKISTAN; TURKMENISTAN; UKRAINE; UZBEKISTAN; YUGOSLAVIA

WARMAN, Henry J.

Dean, School of Geography, Clark University
AMAZON RIVER; ANDES; APPALACHIAN MOUNTAINS; MISSISSIPPI RIVER; ORINOCO RIVER; RIO DE LA PLATA BASIN; ROCKY MOUNTAINS; SAHARA

WATSON, J. Wreford

Professor of Geography and Head of the Department of Geography, University of Edinburgh; Former Chief Geographer, Canada; Former Director of the Geographical Branch, Canadian Department of Mines and Technical Surveys; Author, *North America: Its Countries and Regions; Canada: Problems and Prospects*
NORTH AMERICA

WAUGH, Alec

Author, *Island in the Sun; Sugar Islands; A Family of Islands; A Spy in the Family;* and many other books
CARIBBEAN SEA AND ISLANDS

WEBB, Richard E.

British Information Service, New York
FALKLAND ISLANDS

WECHSBERG, Joseph

Foreign Correspondent, *The New Yorker*; Author, *The Voices; Vienna, My Vienna; Journey Through the Land of Eloquent Silence*; and other books CZECHOSLOVAKIA

WEINSTEIN, Brian

Assistant Professor of Political Science, Howard University; Fellow, African Studies Association; Author, *Gabon: Nation-Building on the Ogooué* GABON

WILBER, Donald N.

Editor, *The Nations of Asia*; Author, *Afghanistan, Its People, Its Society, Its Culture; Contemporary Iran; The Land and People of Ceylon; Pakistan, Its People, Its Society, Its Culture*
ASIA; NEPAL

WILGUS, A. Curtis

Professor of Hispanic-American History and Director Emeritus, School of Inter-American Studies, University of Florida; Author, *The Caribbean; Contemporary Trends; The Caribbean: Its Role in the Hemisphere; Historical Atlas of Latin America*
PANAMA CANAL AND CANAL ZONE

WILLIAMS, Richard A.

Coordinator of East Asian Studies, Central Connecticut State University TAIWAN

WINDER, VIOLA H.

Author, *The Land and People of Lebanon* LEBANON

WOODCOCK, George

Editor, *Canadian Literature*; Former Associate Professor of English, University of British Columbia; Author, *The Crystal Spirit: A Study of George Orwell; The Doukhobors*
YUKON AND NORTHWEST TERRITORIES

YNSFRAN, Pablo Max

Professor Emeritus of Spanish and Portuguese, The University of Texas at Austin; Author, *La expedición norteamericana contra el Paraguay; El Paraguay contemporáneo; Papeles de D. Valentín Gómez Farias* PARAGUAY

YOUNG, J. Cromwell

Executive Editor, *Encyclopedia Canadiana* CANADIAN CITIES

ZACEK, Joseph Frederick

Professor of History, State University of New York, Albany; Author, *Palacky: The Historian as Scholar and Nationalist* EUROPE

ZARTMAN, I. William

Professor of Political Science, New York University; Author, *Government and Politics in Northern Africa; International Relations in the New Africa* ALGERIA

ZIADEH, Nicola A.

Professor of Modern Arab History, The American University of Beirut; Author, *Urban Life in Syria Under the Early Mamluks; The Modern History of Libya; Syria and Lebanon* LIBYA

ILLUSTRATORS AND PHOTOGRAPHERS

ATKESON, Ray

Portrait, industrial, news, and advertising photographer; One-man shows, Eastman Kodak (Rochester, New York), International Photographic Exposition (New York)

BERNHAUT, Andy

Free-lance photographer specializing in travel; Contributing photographer, *Life*

BERNHEIM, Marc and Evelyne

Husband and wife photography team: Co-authors, *From Bush to City*

BUCTEL, George

Designer of maps and book jackets; Illustrator of numerous books for children; Exhibitor, *Washington Times-Herald Art Show*, Graphic Arts Division

BURRI, Rene

Contributing photographer, *Look, Life, Paris Match*; Represented in *The Photographer's Eye* and *Photographer at Mid-Century*

CAPA, Cornell

Photographer and picture editor; Contributing photographer, *Life*; Photographer of U.S. presidential campaigns (1952, 1956, 1960)

CARTIER-BRESSON, Henri

Photographer, *The Decisive Moment, From One China to Another, People of Moscow, The Europeans*; Recipient, Overseas Press Club Award (three times), Art Directors Club Award (two times), French Photographic Society Award

COOKE, Jerry

Contributing photographer to national and European magazines; Exhibitor, Museum of Modern Art (New York) and Metropolitan Museum of Art; Contributor, *The Family of Man*

CRUMP, Frank

Illustrator, Bookmakers Inc.

DONOVAN, Jere

Editorial artist and cartographer, *Time*; Exhibitor, Weyhe Gallery, Society of Illustrators, "Air Force Program" and "America Observed"; Member, Society of Illustrators

ENGLEBERT, Victor

Free-lance photographer and writer; Contributor, *Venture, Paris Match*, and *Modern Photography*; Contributing writer and photographer, *National Geographic*; Author and photographer for children's books

ERGENBRIGHT, Eric L. and Ric

Father and son photography team; Leaders of photo expeditions in Europe and South America

ERWITT, Elliot

Magazine and advertising photographer; Exhibitor in one-man shows at Museum of Modern Art and The Smithsonian

FORMAN, Harrison

Photographer; Senior Editor, *McCall's*; Former foreign correspondent, *The New York Times*; Former foreign correspondent, NBC; Technical Director, *Lost Horizon* (Academy Award winning motion picture)

FRANK, Carl

Photographer specializing in travel with emphasis on South

America and Africa; Contributor, *The Family of Man, Modern Photography Annual*

FRANK, Jerry

Free-lance photographer; Contributor, *Life en Español, Forbes, Venture, U.S. Camera Annual, Modern Photography Annual*; Exhibitor, International Photo Exhibition (New York)

FRISTEDT, Herbert

Documentary, advertising, and portrait photographer; Exhibitor, Board of Social Affairs (Stockholm, 1970)

GOLDMAN, Louis

Free-lance photographer and cinematographer specializing in the field of travel

HALIN, Ray

Photographer specializing in travel and human interest; Exhibitor, Kodak displays in many different countries

HARRINGTON, Alfred Earle

Free-lance photographer and lecturer

HEDIN, Sven-Erik

Photographer-journalist specializing in travel photography

HEILMAN, Grant

Photographer specializing in agriculture and science; Contributor to farm publications in the United States, Canada, and Europe; Recipient of several Art Director Club awards

HENLE, Fritz

Free-lance photographer; Photographer, *Holiday in Europe, Fritz Henle's Figure Studies, The Caribbean: A Journey with Pictures*, and other books.

HOLLYMAN, Tom

Former photographer and editor, *Holiday;* Cinematographer and head photographer, *Lord of the Flies*

HOLTON, George

Free-lance photographer specializing in wildlife, archeology, primitive people, and travel; Contributor, *Life, Time, Newsweek, Venture, Holiday, National Geographic*; Exhibitor, Limelight Gallery (New York) and Photokina (Germany, 1970)

HORTENS, Walter

Free-lance illustrator; Recipient, Honolulu Academy of Art Award, Paris Beaux-Arts Award, Vienna Museum School Award; Exhibitor in Algeria and New York; Member, Society of Illustrators

JANGOUX, Jacques

Documentary motion picture photographer and editor; Still photographer specializing in education and (in Latin America and Africa) anthropology

JEANMARIE, Hrefna Hannesdottir

Free-lance photographer

KARLSON, Gloria

Free-lance photographer; Contributor, *Modern Photography*; Exhibitor, Image Gallery (New York)

KOSLOW, Howard

Artist specializing in industry, travel, and aeronautics; Exhibitor in one-man shows; Paintings for NASA in National Gallery of Art

and Smithsonian Institution; Member (and officer), Society of Illustrators

LATTA, Jane

Free-lance photographer and picture editor, specializing in the United States and Latin America

MANLEY, Ray

President, Ray Manley Commercial Photography Inc.; Recipient, Master of Photography 1960 by Professional Photographers Association of America; Exhibitor, the Eastman Kodak Show (New York)

McCARTNEY, Susan

Illustration and advertising photographer; Contributor, *Infinity, Life*

McKEOWN, Wesley B.

Artist, illustrator, and photographer; Exhibitor, Illustrators '66, '67, U.S.A.F. Exhibition (1964, 1965), Illustrator's Book Show; Member (and past president), Society of Illustrators

MORENILLA, José Mateu

Amateur travel photographer; Winner of Spanish national photo awards

PHILLIBA, Allan A.

Free-lance photographer and art director-designer; Contributor, *Holiday, Town and Country, Travel and Camera, Auction*; Exhibitor, Art Directors' Club of New York

RIBOUD, Marc

Contributing photographer, *Look, Epoca*, and *Paris Match;* One-man show, Chicago Art Institute; Exhibitor, permanent photography collections of the Metropolitan Museum of Art and the Museum of Modern Art (New York)

SCHWARZ, Frank

Designer and illustrator for books and magazines

SCHWITTER-HAMILTON, Norma

Travel photographer specializing in Europe, Asia, and Africa; Owner and manager of photographic library

SILVERSTONE, Marilyn

Photographer based in India; Reporter of the Asian and Near Eastern scene for magazines and newspapers

SPRING, Bob and Ira

Travel photography team; Co-authors, *High Adventure, This is Washington, Japan, Scandinavia, Alaska, Pioneer State*, and *North Cascades National Park*

STAGE, John Lewis

Contributing photographer to national magazines and advertising campaigns; Recipient, Art Directors Gold Medal for editorial photography

TURNER, Pete

Industrial and fashion photographer; Contributor, *Look, Time, Esquire, Venture*; Recipient, Art Directors' Annual Award every year from 1961 to 1970; Exhibitor in many one-man shows

VACCARO, Michael A.

Free-lance photographer; Contributor, *Life, Esquire, Venture, Holiday, Ladies' Home Journal, McCall's;* World War II combat photographer; Photography instructor, Syracuse University and Cooper Union College (New York)

THE WORLD

CONTENTS
AFRICA
Volume 1

Africa: An Introduction	1	Mali	140
Africa	4	Mauritania	134
Algeria	71	Mauritius	378
Angola	341	Morocco	61
Benin	212	Mozambique	363
Botswana	351	Namibia (South-West Africa)	347
Burkina	191	Niger	146
Burundi	328	Niger River	144
Cameroon	232	Nigeria	217
Canary Islands	58	Nile River	120
Cape Verde	152	Réunion	384
Central African Republic	247	Rwanda	324
Chad	241	Sahara	55
Comoros	383	São Tomé and Príncipe	239
Congo	258	Senegal	154
Congo River	273	Seychelles	339
Djibouti	298	Sierra Leone	173
Egypt	97	Somalia	301
Equatorial Guinea	237	South Africa	394
Ethiopia	286	Sudan	124
Gabon	253	Suez Canal	119
Gambia, The	161	Swaziland	385
Ghana	196	Tanzania	332
Guinea	168	Togo	207
Guinea-Bissau	166	Tunisia	81
Ivory Coast	186	Uganda	316
Kenya	306	Western Sahara	132
Lesotho	390	Zaïre	263
Liberia	180	Zambia	275
Libya	89	Zimbabwe	355
Madagascar	369		
Malawi	281	Illustration Credits	407

FLAGS OF AFRICA

MOROCCO

ALGERIA

TUNISIA

LIBYA

EGYPT

SUDAN

MAURITANIA

MALI

NIGER

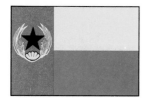
CAPE VERDE

SENEGAL

GAMBIA

GUINEA-BISSAU

GUINEA

SIERRA LEONE

LIBERIA

IVORY COAST

BURKINA

FLAGS OF AFRICA (continued)

GHANA

TOGO

BENIN

NIGERIA

CAMEROON

EQUATORIAL GUINEA

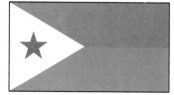

SÃO TOMÉ AND PRÍNCIPE

CHAD

CENTRAL AFRICAN REPUBLIC

GABON

CONGO

ZAIRE

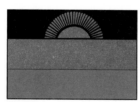

ZAMBIA

MALAWI

ETHIOPIA

DJIBOUTI

SOMALIA

KENYA

FLAGS OF AFRICA (continued)

UGANDA

RWANDA

BURUNDI

TANZANIA

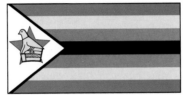

SEYCHELLES

ANGOLA

BOTSWANA

ZIMBABWE

MOZAMBIQUE

MADAGASCAR

MAURITIUS

COMOROS

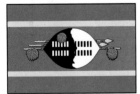

SWAZILAND

LESOTHO

SOUTH AFRICA

NAMIBIA

AFRICA: AN INTRODUCTION

One of the most significant phenomena of the period following World War II has been the "wind of change" that has altered the political map of the Third World out of all recognition. In Africa the transformation, in political terms, has been dramatic. Instead of only four independent countries, as before World War II, there are now dozens of such countries in the continent and its adjoining islands. Even the last stronghold of white minority rule, South Africa, is now in the process of monumental change. The articles of this volume tell the story of Africa as it has been transformed in consequence.

Generalization is always a hazardous exercise. It is difficult to generalize about a whole nation; it is much more so in relation to Africans as a whole. References here to Africans or the African are therefore made with considerable diffidence and should be taken with equal reservation. In the first place, Africa is not one territorial unit ruled by one government—Africa is many countries inhabited by diverse peoples under different governments with their varied problems and policies. Yet almost all of these countries have passed through the experience of being a colonial possession, open or covert, of some metropolitan non-African power, with consequences for good or ill that will be longstanding. Practically all of them won or regained their independent national identity since World War II. Most Africans firmly believe in, and are working for, greater continental unity. Despite their differences, they feel that they belong together and will sink or swim together.

The political record of African countries in the decades immediately following independence was often disappointing. There were violent takeovers in many African countries—in some, coup after repeated coup. In others, civil war raged—in some cases for decades. Insofar as political ideologies are concerned, Africa can be said to be still in search of a plant suitable to its particular soil. Many countries that began as multiparty democracies at independence later became one-party states, on the theory that a single party could serve as the glue holding together the diverse ethnic groups often found in countries with boundaries drawn by European powers ignorant of such distinctions. Without opposition, the heads of such single-party states were tempted to remain in office rather than retire and resume the status of ordinary citizens. Often leaders who had seized power in military takeovers legitimatized their rule by establishing one-party states dominated by the military.

In the late 1980s and early 1990s, however, the same wave of democratic reform sweeping Eastern Europe and the former Soviet Union also swept Africa. The end of the Cold War accelerated the peace process in war-torn Angola, and socialist economic policies were discredited. Dictators could no longer count on a steady flow of foreign aid and military protection simply because they supported one or the other superpower in the Cold War. Official corruption, human rights abuses, and economic stagnation or decline sparked widespread demands for political change.

In country after country, dictators were overthrown or voted out of office; multiparty constitutions became the norm, rather than the exception. Economically troubled Zambia, for example, held its first multiparty elections in nearly 20 years in 1991. Kenneth Kaunda, who had led the nation since independence, was voted out of office. The expectations for Zambia's new government and Africa's many other fragile new democracies are high—perhaps unrealistically so. If people do not see immediate improvements in their declining standards of living, they may again take to the streets in protest. In the absence of strong central governments, some ethnically diverse African nations might break apart, as did Yugoslavia in Europe. Economic problems, under which the poor suffer the most, may tempt people to follow new demagogues. Alternately, the army might again seize power to avert chaos. There is a need to develop strong institutions like courts to bolster democracy and ensure the stability needed to encourage economic investment.

Much of Africa's second wave of democracy has been fueled by social progress. Initially, many of Africa's newly-independent nations experienced encouraging social and economic growth. As education became more widespread and health facilities extended to rural areas, a large part of the population in most countries was brought more rapidly into participation at all levels of the society than was the case in colonial days. This social progress produced a new generation of well-educated and talented individuals prepared to shape the future of the continent. Drastic reductions in expenditures on health, education, and other social programs in the 1980s only served to increase the demands for political change.

The other spur to political change was economic. Today most Africans are poorer than they were at independence. Unfortunately, in many countries much of the new wealth generated by economic development in the 1960s and 1970s remained in the hands of too few, and in some countries priority was given to economic ventures of doubtful viability. State-run enterprises were often inefficient and corrupt. Drought and civil war disrupted agriculture and led to widespread famine. Even under ordinary circumstances, the vital agricultural sector was frequently neglected. Many farmers moved to the city, and improvements in health care led to rapid population growth. Thus, there were more and more mouths to be fed by fewer and fewer farmers. Often, these farmers produced less and less due to soil depletion and deforestation caused by poor farming practices. Food imports rose, increasing foreign debt. Rising oil prices for the majority of African nations that were oil importers also increased debt, as did borrowing to pay for prestige projects that contributed little or nothing to the general well-being of the people. Increased debt payments and the diversion of scarce resources to military spending left less money for social and economic development. Also, most African countries remained dependent for foreign exchange upon a few agricultural or mineral exports that were at the mercy of world prices. The prices for many of these commodities fell in the 1980s, contributing to economic woes.

Africans today must deal with economies wrecked by civil war and mismanagement, complicated by an AIDS epidemic that has decimated the middle class in many countries. Today the continent has the highest infant mortality rate, the lowest literacy rate, and the highest rate of population growth in the developing world. Less than half of the people living in African countries south of the Sahara have access to basic health care, and nearly two-thirds lack access to safe drinking water. Life expectancy is about 52 years, as opposed to a world average of 63 years. Even though 104 of every 1,000 children born in Africa die before their first birthday, some 46 percent of the population is less than 15 years of age. Civil wars and drought have caused hundreds of thousands of people to leave their homes and created a refugee burden most countries lack the resources to solve. In many cases the structural adjustment programs instituted across Africa in response to the demands of international lending institutions, which cut social spending and eliminated subsidies for basic foodstuffs, removed the only social safety net of the poor and contributed to civil unrest.

In an effort to improve this bleak record, many African governments are dissolving inefficient state-run corporations, investing in the vital agricultural sector, and actively seeking foreign investment. As an aid to economic growth, they are asking governments and international lending agencies to help them in this process by forgiving or restructuring their burdensome foreign debts. Realizing that trade is critical to development, they are also working to further the regional cooperation that is an essential part of the key to the continent's future. The nations of North Africa, for example, have established a common market to develop trade and other forms of cooperation. Kenya, Tanzania, and Uganda agreed to renew the regional economic and social cooperation they had had before the 1977 collapse of the East African Community. South Africa, the only industrialized nation in sub-Saharan Africa, has moved to improve its trade links with the rest of Africa as it moves to end white rule at home. The Organization of African Unity (OAU) has still not fulfilled the highest expectations of its founders. But the OAU has not been a failure. It has made a great contribution to African solidarity, which has been valuable for the relations of Africa with the outside world, and it is taking a more active role in solving regional conflicts. In early 1992, a number of former African presidents founded a council of African elders designed to help settle conflicts within Africa.

Africa today faces great challenges. But the picture is not entirely grim. Where less than 20 percent of the people were immunized against serious diseases in the early 1980s, nearly 60 percent were immunized only 10 years later. Average life expectancy, primary school enrollment, and other health and social measurements rose between 1960 and 1990 to levels that took the industrialized nations a century to achieve. Most important, Africa is a continent rich in human and natural resources. If harnessed, these resources could change the economic face of Africa dramatically over the next few decades. The same desire for change that is currently altering the political face of the region gives cause for hope. Africans today are working to retain the best in African values and culture and conserve the valuable environmental benefits that nature has given them while making the most they can of the benefits of modern technology, modern political and administrative techniques, and relations with the non-African world.

Animals graze on a game reserve near the base of Kilimanjaro.

AFRICA

Many people think of Africa as a land of humid steamy jungles, waterless sandy deserts, and sweltering equatorial forests. So it is; but it is also a continent of massive peaks snowcapped all year round and long, sweeping savannas, of cold misty rain and bitter frosty nights. The people of Africa are usually thought of as black. Many of them are, though there are various shades of black. But some other African peoples are brown, yellow, or white.

Africa is a huge continent of infinite variety. It is the second largest continent in the world. Only Asia is larger in area. Africa is so vast that the landmasses of the United States, Europe, India, and Japan could fit into it and there would still be plenty of empty space left.

It is about 5,000 miles (8,050 kilometers) long from north to south, and, at its widest points, over 4,600 miles (7,400 km.) from east to west. For such a large area—one fifth of all the earth's land surface—its inhabitants are comparatively few. There is about 12 percent of the world's total population living on the entire continent.

Unlike continents such as Asia and Europe, Africa has relatively few densely populated regions. The fertile valley of the Nile River supports a large population, and Africa does have many large cities. However, vast areas of the continent are uninhabited, mainly because of poor soil unsuitable for cultivation or because of insect pests that carry disease to people and cattle.

Modern Africa is reflected in these new buildings in Nairobi, Kenya.

Africa contains much mineral wealth. There are diamonds, gold, and uranium mined in South Africa, gold and diamonds in Ghana and Tanzania, and tremendous deposits of copper in the Republic of Zaïre and Zambia. There are great stores of oil in the west and the north and large deposits of iron and coal in several regions. However, many of the continent's resources have scarcely been developed, and it seems almost certain that more riches still lie under the ground, waiting to be discovered. Africa also produces many agricultural goods, such as cotton, tea, coffee, cacao, rubber, cloves, and tobacco.

Although there are some very wealthy people in Africa, they are mostly Europeans and a few Asians. Very few Africans have acquired riches from the wealth of their continent, and most Africans are very poor, probably earning an average annual income of no more than $200. However, it is very difficult to calculate living standards in terms of money, because many Africans grow their own food and build their own houses, hardly using money at all.

Great numbers of Africans are illiterate. Many have never been to school. A multitude of tropical diseases brings despair and death. A large number of infants die before the age of 5. Those who grow into adulthood can only expect to live to the age of about 40 years.

First Home of Man

There are people who still think of Africa as a continent only recently discovered. But Africa was probably one of the birthplaces of man, perhaps his first birthplace. In 1967 a jawbone fragment of one of man's early ancestors was discovered in Kenya by a team of Harvard

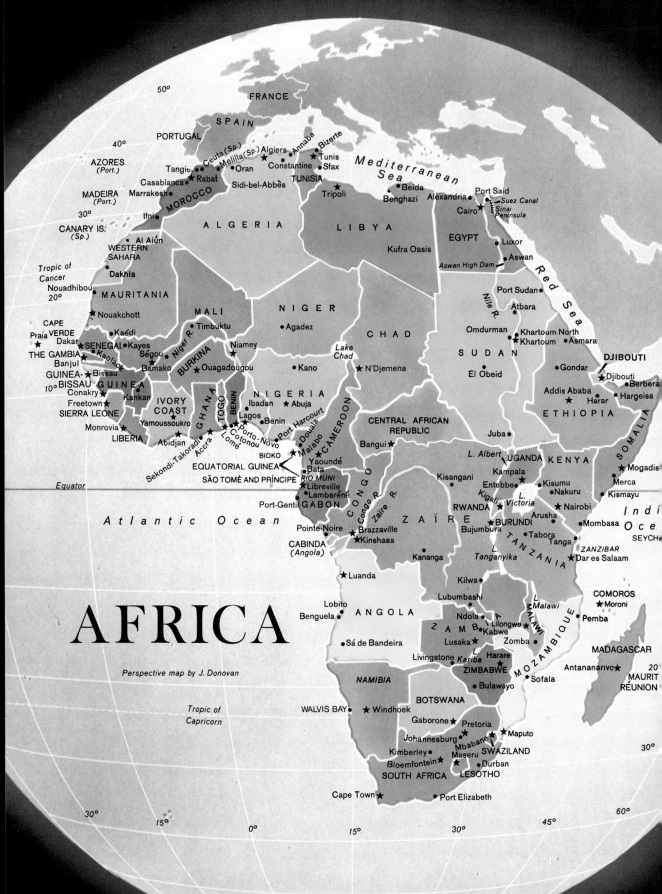

AFRICA

Perspective map by J. Donovan

FRANCE

SPAIN

PORTUGAL

AZORES
(Port.)

MADEIRA
(Port.)

CANARY IS.
(Sp.)

Tropic of
Cancer

WESTERN
SAHARA

Mediterranean
Sea

Tangier ★ Ceuta (Sp.) Melilla (Sp.) Algiers ★ Annaba Bizerte
Casablanca ● Rabat ● Oran ● Constantine Tunis ★ Sfax
Marrakesh ● TUNISIA
Sidi-bel-Abbès ● Tripoli ★
Ifni ●

MOROCCO

ALGERIA

LIBYA

EGYPT

Beida ●
Benghazi ● Alexandria ● Port Said
Cairo ★ Suez Canal
Sinai
Peninsula

Luxor ●
Aswan ●
Aswan High Dam

Al Aiún ●

Dakhla ●

Nouadhibou
20°

MAURITANIA

MALI

NIGER

CHAD

Kufra Oasis ●

SUDAN

Red Sea

Nile R.

Port Sudan ●
Atbara ●

Omdurman ●
Khartoum North ●
El Obeid ● Khartoum ● Asmara ●
Gondar ●

DJIBOUTI

Djibouti ●
Berbera ●
Hargeisa ●

Addis Ababa ★
Harar ★

ETHIOPIA

SOMALIA

CAPE
VERDE
Praia ★
Dakar ●
SENEGAL
THE GAMBIA
Banjul ★
GUINEA-★ Bissau
BISSAU
Conakry ★
Freetown ★
SIERRA LEONE
Monrovia ★
LIBERIA

Nouakchott ★

Kaédi ●
Kayes ●
Kaolack ★
Ségou ●
Bamako ★

GUINEA

Kankan ●

IVORY
COAST

Yamoussoukro ★

Abidjan ●

Timbuktu ●

Niger R.

BURKINA

Niamey ★

Ouagadougou ★

GHANA

Sekondi-Takoradi ●
Accra ★

TOGO
BENIN

Lomé ★

Agadez ●

Kano ●

N'Djemena ★

NIGERIA

Ibadan ● Abuja ★
Lagos ● Benin ●
Porto-Novo ★
Cotonou ●
Porto Harcourt ●
Douala ●
Malabo ●
CAMEROON
BIOKO

EQUATORIAL GUINEA
SÃO TOMÉ AND PRÍNCIPE

Lake
Chad

CENTRAL AFRICAN
REPUBLIC

Bangui ★

Juba ●

UGANDA

L. Albert

Kampala ★
Entebbe ●

KENYA

Kisumu ●
Nakuru ●

Mogadishu ★

Merca ●
Kismayu ●

Equator

Atlantic Ocean

Yaoundé ★
Bata ●
RIO MUNI
Libreville ★
Lambaréné ●
Port-Gentil ●

GABON

CONGO

Congo R.

Kisangani ●

Zaïre R.

ZAÏRE

Kananga ●

L. Victoria

Kigali

RWANDA

Bujumbura ★

BURUNDI

Pointe-Noire ●
Brazzaville ★
Kinshasa ★
CABINDA
(Angola)

Luanda ★

Lobito ●
Benguela ●

ANGOLA

Sá de Bandeira ●

NAMIBIA

Tropic of
Capricorn

WALVIS BAY ●

Kananga ●

Lubumbashi ●

ZAMBIA

Ndola ●
Lusaka ★
Kabwe ●

Livingstone ●

Nairobi ★

Arusha ●

Mombasa ●

TANZANIA

Tabora ●
Tanga ●

L.
Tanganyika

Kilwa ●

L.
Malawi

MALAWI

Lilongwe ★
Zomba ★

Kariba

Harare ★

ZIMBABWE

Bulawayo ●

Sofala ●

MOZAMBIQUE

Indian
Ocean

SEYCH.

ZANZIBAR
Dar es Salaam ●

COMOROS

Moroni ★

Pemba ●

MADAGASCAR

Antananarivo ★

MAURIT.
RÉUNION

BOTSWANA

Windhoek ★

Gaborone ★

Johannesburg ★
Kimberley ●
Bloemfontein ★

SOUTH AFRICA

Cape Town ★

Pretoria ★
Mbabane ★ Maputo ★
Maseru ★ SWAZILAND
Durban ●

LESOTHO

Port Elizabeth ●

50°

40°

30°

20°

10°

30°

15°

0°

15°

30°

45°

60°

20

30°

FACTS AND FIGURES

LOCATION: Africa is bounded by the Mediterranean Sea, the Red Sea, the Gulf of Aden, the Indian Ocean, and the Atlantic Ocean.

AREA: 11,711,000 sq. mi. (30,331,000 sq. km.).

POPULATION: 672,142,000 (1991).

PHYSICAL FEATURES: Highest point—Mount Kilimanjaro, Tanzania (19,340 ft.; 5,895 m.). **Lowest point**—Lake Assal, Djibouti (552 ft.; 168 m. below sea level). **Chief rivers**—Nile, Congo, Niger, Zambezi, Orange, Senegal, Limpopo. **Major lakes**—Victoria, Nyasa, Tanganyika, Chad, Volta.

COUNTRIES AND TERRITORIES OF AFRICA

COUNTRY	AREA (sq. mi.)	(sq. km.)	POPULATION (1991 estimate)	CAPITAL
Algeria	919,591	2,381,740	26,022,188	Algiers
Angola	481,351	1,246,700	8,668,281	Luanda
Benin	43,483	112,620	4,831,823	Porto-Novo
Botswana	231,803	600,370	1,258,392	Gaborone
Burkina	105,868	274,200	9,359,889	Ouagadougou
Burundi	10,745	27,830	5,831,233	Bujumbura
Cameroon	183,568	475,440	11,390,374	Yaoundé
Canary Islands	2,808	7,273	1,456,474	Las Palmas, Santa Cruz de Teñerife
Cape Verde	1,556	4,030	386,501	Praia
Central African Republic	240,533	622,980	2,952,382	Bangui
Chad	495,753	1,284,000	5,112,467	N'Djamena
Comoros (including Mayotte)	838	2,170	476,678	Moroni
Congo	132,046	342,000	2,309,444	Brazzaville
Djibouti	8,494	22,000	346,311	Djibouti
Egypt	386,660	1,001,450	54,451,588	Cairo
Equatorial Guinea	10,830	28,050	378,729	Malabo
Ethiopia	471,776	1,221,900	53,191,127	Addis Ababa
Gabon	103,347	267,670	1,079,980	Libreville
Gambia, The	4,363	11,300	874,553	Banjul
Ghana	92,100	238,540	15,616,934	Accra
Guinea	94,927	245,860	7,455,850	Conakry
Guinea-Bissau	13,946	36,120	1,023,544	Bissau
Ivory Coast	124,502	322,460	12,977,909	Yamoussoukro, Abidjan
Kenya	224,961	582,650	25,241,978	Nairobi
Lesotho	11,718	30,350	1,801,174	Maseru
Liberia	43,000	111,370	2,730,446	Monrovia
Libya	679,359	1,759,540	4,350,742	Tripoli
Madagascar	226,656	587,040	12,185,318	Antananarivo
Malawi	45,745	118,480	9,438,462	Lilongwe
Mali	478,764	1,240,000	8,338,542	Bamako
Mauritania	397,953	1,030,700	1,995,755	Nouakchott
Mauritius	718	1,860	1,081,000	Port Louis
Morocco	172,413	446,550	26,181,889	Rabat
Mozambique	309,494	801,590	15,113,282	Maputo
Namibia	318,259	824,290	1,520,504	Windhoek
Niger	489,189	1,267,000	8,154,145	Niamey
Nigeria	356,668	923,770	122,470,574	Abuja
Reunion	969	2,510	597,823	Saint-Denis
Rwanda	10,170	26,340	7,902,644	Kigali
São Tomé and Príncipe	371	960	128,499	São Tomé
Senegal	75,749	196,190	7,952,657	Dakar
Seychelles	108	280	68,932	Victoria
Sierra Leone	27,699	71,740	4,274,543	Freetown
Somalia	246,200	637,660	6,709,161	Mogadishu
South Africa	471,444	1,221,040	40,600,518	Pretoria, Cape Town, Bloemfontein
Sudan	967,494	2,505,810	27,220,088	Khartoum
Swaziland	6,703	17,360	859,336	Mbabane
Tanzania	364,900	945,090	26,869,175	Dar es Salaam
Togo	21,927	56,790	3,810,616	Lomé
Tunisia	63,170	163,610	8,276,096	Tunis
Uganda	91,135	236,040	18,690,070	Kampala
Western Sahara	102,703	266,000	196,737	Al Aiún
Zaïre	905,563	2,345,410	37,832,407	Kinshasa
Zambia	290,583	752,610	8,445,724	Lusaka
Zimbabwe	150,803	390,580	10,720,459	Harare

The Zimbabwe ruins, seat of the 15th century Monomotapa kingdom, in Zimbabwe.

University anthropologists. After extensive work and research, the University announced in 1971 that this bone fragment dates back 5,000,000 years. In Olduvai Gorge in northern Tanzania, excavations have uncovered the fossilized bones of creatures, probable ancestors of early man, who lived between 1,500,000 and 1,750,000 years ago. These are the earliest creatures known to have made their own tools. Then in 1978 human-like footprints about 3,590,000 years old and made by a creature about 4 feet (1.2 meters) tall were discovered at Laetolil, Tanzania.

It is only fairly recently that scholars have been able to piece together the history of Africa. With a few exceptions, such as the Egyptians who used hieroglyphics and the later peoples who used Arabic, most African communities did not develop written languages until a relatively short while ago.

All regions of Africa have been inhabited by organized communities from very early times. Some of them played important roles in the history of the Mediterranean lands. Others were important in the trading communities of the Indian Ocean.

The "Dark Continent"

There is a myth that Africa is a "dark continent" that was first discovered and explored by Europeans. However, Africans were trading across the Indian Ocean with Arabs, Indians, and even some Chinese as far back as the 1st century A.D. Gold and leather crossed the Sahara to be sold in Europe, but very few of the buyers had any idea where these products came from. In the late Middle Ages, Timbuktu was a city of great learning. It was one of the many centers of Islamic scholarship. However, Europeans knew little or nothing about this city of western Africa.

The Early Societies

People moved about in Africa more than they did in Europe. Only certain areas were fertile, and the search for productive land led whole communities, or the more intrepid members of them, to seek new opportunities. Most Africans have always been farmers, growing crops to feed their families. Throughout the centuries Africans have worked as communities to perform many social tasks, such as making paths and building roads and bridges.

People co-operated with their neighbors or members of their families to build their houses, harvest their crops, or tend their cattle. Historically, the community as a whole participated in entertainment, music making or dancing, or in religious rites. Even now in many areas this is still true.

Each community had its own form of decision making, which centered on a chief, on a group of elders or some sort of council, or on a method of achieving general agreement among all members. Very few African societies have been authoritarian. Even where there was a chief, his powers were almost always limited. Participation by all adult men in decision making was a widespread African tradition.

Each society evolved its own customs according to the needs of its members—for example, the need for protection against aggression or for the marketing of special products. When the cohesion of the community needed strengthening, more power was concentrated at the

Granite obelisks at Aksum, Ethiopia, a major religious center of ancient times.

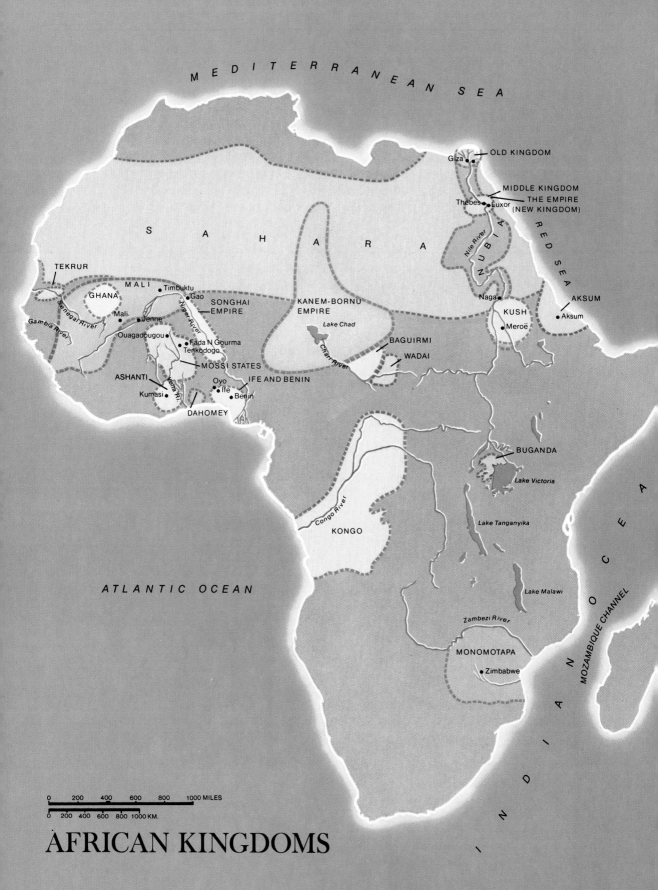

MEDITERRANEAN SEA

S A H A R A

Giza • —— OLD KINGDOM

MIDDLE KINGDOM
THE EMPIRE
(NEW KINGDOM)

Thebes • • Luxor

N U B I A

Nile River

R E D   S E A

TEKRUR

M A L I

GHANA

Timbuktu •
• Gao

SONGHAI
EMPIRE

Mali •

• Jenne

Senegal River

Gambia River

Ouagadougou •

• Fada N Gourma
• Tenkodogo

—— MOSSI STATES

Niger River

ASHANTI

Kumasi •

Volta Ri.

Oyo •
• Ife
• Benin

IFE AND BENIN

DAHOMEY

KANEM-BORNU
EMPIRE

Lake Chad

Chari River

BAGUIRMI

WADAI

Naga •

KUSH

• Meroë

AKSUM

• Aksum

BUGANDA

Lake Victoria

Congo River

KONGO

Lake Tanganyika

I N D I A N   O C E A N

Lake Malawi

ATLANTIC OCEAN

Zambezi River

MONOMOTAPA

• Zimbabwe

MOZAMBIQUE CHANNEL

0   200   400   600   800   1000 MILES

0 200 400 600 800 1000 KM.

AFRICAN KINGDOMS

center. If life was peaceful and undisturbed, people were able to make more decisions within the smaller family units.

In Africa, as everywhere, societies merged with each other, fragmented and joined others, and then moved off to form new groups. These processes brought new customs. Government, law, language, religion and family relations were all constantly affected in this way.

African communities have always been affected by the character of the region where they are situated. It is difficult to attempt to draw definite boundaries between the various regions of Africa. The northern coastal countries have always had contact with the Mediterranean lands. The people of these countries are mostly Muslim and Arab. The inhabitants of the east coast of the African continent have had many centuries of experience in trading with Arabia, India, and the East Indies. Africa's west coast has had the longest direct contact with Europe and was the scene of most of the slave trade. The south was colonized by Europeans from the 17th century onward. All of these different factors inevitably affected the way different countries or communities developed.

The period of European colonial rule in Africa is but a tiny fragment of the continent's history and experience. It was only during the last quarter of the 19th century that the Europeans partitioned Africa among themselves. Until then almost all the peoples of Africa had governed themselves. And by most accounts, they did so quite capably.

Throughout most of the continent, African societies made their own laws according to customs and tradition. With few exceptions, the Europeans usually kept to the coastal settlements where goods—particularly slaves—were brought to them from the interior. Until late in the 19th century, European countries had no desire to colonize African lands and so become responsible for the government of the people.

To many Africans the period following the end of World War II, in 1945, appears less as an era of independence than of regained self-government. At various times in Africa's history, kingdoms were established. Africans look back to these lost kingdoms as their rich heritage. When the Gold Coast became independent in 1957, for instance, it took the name of Ghana, an ancient West African kingdom. Once independent, Africans turned their minds to creating new nations that would combine the best of old African tradition with the best of the New World.

THE PEOPLE

Virtually all Africans are descended from some form of combination of the original Bushmanoid with Negroid and Caucasoid stocks, constantly adapting to their local environments. Caucasoid peoples spread over North Africa and down into the east during an early period. The Negroids migrated throughout most of West Africa. The Caucasoids met Negroid peoples and through intermarriage produced the varieties seen among many Africans of today.

The Diffusion of Culture

The common assumption that Africa is divided by the Sahara is without foundation. Although the Sahara did cut off Africans south of it from direct contact with Europe and western Arabia, it has always been a highway of trade and communications. Cultural contact—as evidenced early between Egypt and the kingdom of Nubia—through the Lower Nile

Berber children of Tunisia.

A mother makes up her daughter for one of the Ivory Coast's many festivals.

A woman and child in Adiaké, a village in the southeastern part of the Ivory Coast.

Funeral dance musicians perform in a small village in the Ivory Coast.

INDEX TO AFRICA MAP

Abidjan **B4**	Cairo **F1**	Guardafui, Cape **G3**	Malabo **C4**	Port Said **F1**
Abuja **C4**	Cameroon Mt. **C4**	Guinea, Gulf of **C4**	Malange **D5**	Pretoria **E7**
Accra **B4**	Cape Town **D8**	Harare **F6**	Malawi, Lake **F6**	Rabat **B1**
Addis Ababa **F4**	Casablanca **B1**	Hargeisa **G4**	Maputo **F7**	Ras Dashan **F3**
Aden, Gulf of **G3**	Chad, Lake **D3**	Ibadan **C4**	Marrakesh **B1**	Red Sea **F2**
Agadez **C3**	Colomb-Bechar **B1**	Johannesburg **E7**	Maseru **E7**	Sofala **F6**
Agulhas, Cape **E8**	Conakry **A4**	Kampala **F4**	Massawa **F3**	Stanley Falls **E4**
Al Aiún **A2**	Constantine **C1**	Kananga **E5**	Mbabane **E7**	Suez Canal **F1**
Albert, Lake **F2**	Dakar **A3**	Kano **C3**	Mediterranean Sea . . . **D1**	Tabora **F5**
Alexandria **E1**	Dakhla **A2**	Kenya, Mt. **F5**	Meru, Mt. **F5**	Tahat **C2**
Algiers **C1**	Dar es Salaam **F5**	Khartoum **F3**	Mogadishu **G4**	Tana, Lake **F3**
Annaba **C1**	Delgado, Cape **G6**	Khartoum North **F3**	Mombasa **F5**	Tanganyika, Lake **E5**
Antananarivo **G6**	Djibouti **G3**	Kigali **F5**	Monrovia **A4**	Tangier **B1**
Aswan **F2**	Durban **F7**	Kilimanjaro, Mt. **F5**	Moroni **G6**	Timbuktu **B3**
Azizia **D1**	East London **E8**	Kimberley **E7**	Mozambique Channel **G6**	Tlemcen **B1**
Bab el Mandeb **G3**	Edward, Lake **E5**	Kinshasa **D5**	Nairobi **F5**	Tripoli **D1**
Bamako **B3**	Elgon, Mt. **F4**	Kisangani **E4**	N'Djemena **D3**	Tunis **D1**
Bangui **D4**	El Obeid **F3**	Lagos **C4**	Niamey **C3**	Turkana, Lake **F4**
Benghazi **E1**	Emi Koussi **D3**	Libreville **C4**	Nouadhibou **A3**	Verde **A3**
Benguela **D6**	Entebbe **F4**	Lilongwe **F6**	Nouakchott **A2**	Victoria Falls **E6**
Bissau **A3**	Fez **B3**	Lome **C4**	Omdurman **F3**	Victoria, Lake **F5**
Bizerte **C1**	Freetown **A4**	Lopez, Cape **C5**	Oran **B1**	Walvis Bay **D7**
Bloemfontein **E7**	Gaborone **E7**	Luanda **D5**	Ouagadougou **B3**	Windhoek **D7**
Brazzaville **D5**	Ghadames **C1**	Lubumbashi **E6**	Palmas, Cape **B4**	Yamoussoukro **B4**
Bujumbura **E5**	Gibraltar, Strait of **B1**	Lusaka **E6**	Pemba **G6**	Yaounde **D4**
Bulawayo **E7**	Good Hope, Cape of . **D8**	Majunga **G6**	Port Elizabeth **E8**	Zomba **F6**
			Porto Novo **C4**	

Valley and across the Sahara has always existed between the Caucasoid Arab peoples of North Africa and the Negroid peoples south of the desert.

One of the most important cultural exports from the north to the south was that of the techniques of food growing and cattle rearing. The discovery of these techniques was probably made in West Asia and spread to North Africa and then up the Nile Valley. With the knowledge of agriculture, larger populations could be sustained. People began to expand their communities and to move about in search of better land. Some groups specialized in cattle. Today the Masai in Kenya and Tanzania are examples of those who still maintain this tradition. But most societies combined agriculture with cattle raising.

A further factor that encouraged the diffusion of African communities was the introduction of staple foods from other continents. Only millet and sorghum are native to Africa. Their cultivation provided the opportunity for settlement of large communities in the savanna country of the northwest, the south, and the east. It was the importation of rice, yams, and bananas from Asia, probably by traders to the east coast, that allowed the forest areas to be settled. Some of the early great African states were established in West Africa—Ghana, Mali, Songhai, and Kanem-Bornu. Meanwhile, in the 1st century A.D., the great migration of the Bantu people had begun. They spread from either the west or the center, or both, across eastern, central, and southern Africa, mixing with the people already there who spoke Khoisan or Cushitic languages. Later, in the slave era, plants from America, such as maize (corn), sweet potato, and cassava, were brought to West Africa to feed the slaves awaiting shipment and were adopted by African farmers, again providing sustenance for larger communities.

As a result of these widespread movements of peoples and communities, Africa today has hundreds of ethnic groups and nearly 1,000 different languages. Arabic in the north, Swahili in the east, and Hausa in the west are the African languages used by the largest numbers of people.

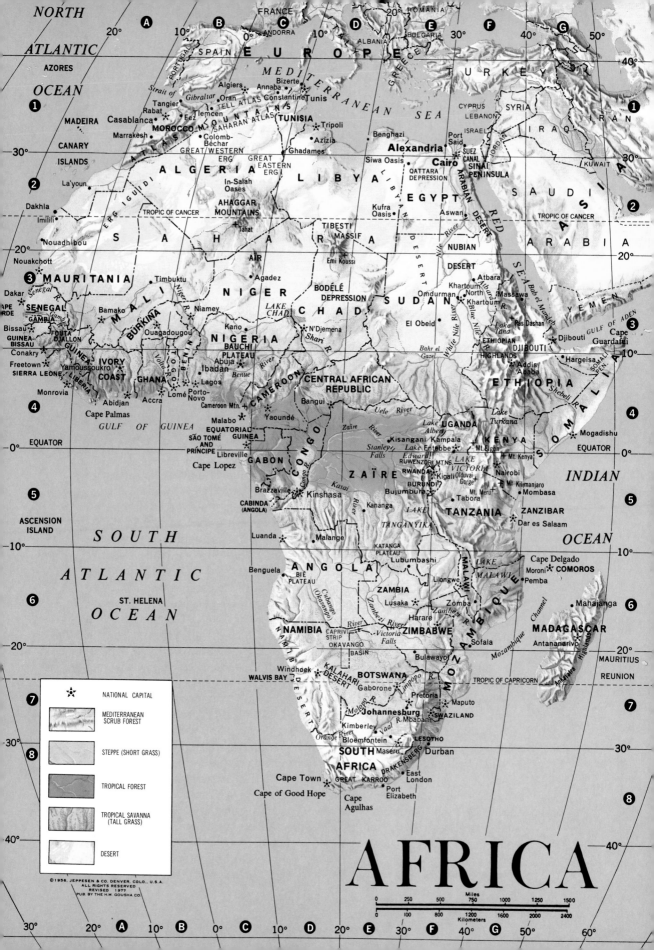

AFRICA

NATIONAL CAPITAL ★

MEDITERRANEAN SCRUB FOREST

STEPPE (SHORT GRASS)

TROPICAL FOREST

TROPICAL SAVANNA (TALL GRASS)

DESERT

Since the advent of European colonialism, however, English, French, and, to a lesser extent, Portuguese, have become more widely used than any single African tongue. The complexity of ethnic varieties and language forms shows how difficult it is to make a detailed study of each African community. The descriptions given in this article must therefore be accepted as no more than generalizations.

THE LAND

The physical features of any territory strongly influence the lives of its inhabitants. This is especially the case in Africa, for most of the continent remains untouched by modern technology. In many areas of Africa roads are scarce, and there are few railways. Only recently has a start been made in the use of fertilizers, tractors, irrigation, and animal husbandry. Thus many Africans still have to rely on the natural qualities of the land unchanged by mechanical devices. They must, by their own unaided efforts, meet the hazards of their local environment—deserts, swollen rivers, drought, tropical rainstorms, mountains, or forests. In addition, medicine has far to go before it can effectively combat the widespread diseases among people and cattle.

Topography

In relief, Africa resembles an upturned soup plate. Much of the continent consists of a high plateau whose sides fall sharply to a narrow, low coastal belt. The plateau varies in elevation between about 1,000 and 8,000 feet (305–2,440 meters), but is not generally mountainous. The main exceptions are mounts Kilimanjaro, Meru, Kenya, and Elgon in the east; the Ruwenzori range between Zaïre and Uganda; the Drakensberg range in South Africa; and the Atlas Mountains in the north.

In general, the southern and eastern areas of the continental plateau form a region of land higher than that in the west and north. This difference in elevation has an important effect on settlement. Much of Ethiopia, for example, is above 8,000 feet (2,440 m.), while the highlands of Kenya also form an extensive area above 8,000 feet (2,440 m.). Johannesburg, the gold-mining and financial center of South Africa, has an altitude of close to 6,000 feet (1,830 m.). Most Europeans have settled in the areas of high altitudes, where temperatures are moderate and disease-carrying pests, such as mosquitos, are rare. Indeed, one African political party in West Africa used to carry an emblem portraying the mosquito as a symbol of the factor that had saved them from the problems brought by white settlers.

The most distinctive features of Africa's topography are the rift valleys in the east. These were formed by volcanic activity and faulting in the earth. There are two of them—the western and eastern—joined together rather like a chicken's wishbone. These rifts can be traced from Lake Malawi: the eastern one extends northward up to and including the Red Sea; the western one extends through lakes Tanganyika, Kivu, Edward, and Albert. Most of these lakes have surfaces well above sea level, but their floors fall well below sea level. Lake Tanganyika is one of the deepest lakes in the world, with a depth of 4,708 feet (1,433 m.). Lake Victoria, the third largest lake in the world, lies between the two rift valleys and, in contrast to its neighbors, is very shallow. One of the consequences of this physical phenomenon for the area's inhabitants is that some of the

The picturesque Fish River canyon in Namibia.

volcanic mountains that line the edges of the rift valleys provide fertile soil that can support comparatively large populations. Another is that the lakes formed in these valleys supply large quantities of fish, the most plentiful source of Africa's protein.

Most of the beaches of Africa are either guarded by surf or backed by shallow, mangrove-forested lagoons. There are few bays offering haven to visiting ships. Many of Africa's rivers cascade over cataracts near the coast. A number of the rivers wind through inland swamps finally to reach the sea, where they form dangerous deltas or obstructing sandbars. Thus the usual methods of penetrating an unknown land were not possible in Africa. European explorers were also stopped by the Sahara. It was not until the mid-19th century that serious contact was made from the outside with the interior peoples of the continent.

"A Stagnant Backwater"

There were not many apparent attractions to induce people from the outside world to try to overcome these natural hazards. Until late in the 19th century the continent was considered by the leading European nations as a stagnant backwater. They thought of Africa as being largely inhabited by peoples who had few of the materials that had drawn Europeans to other lands. There was no evidence of quantities of the gold, silver, and precious jewels that had taken the Spaniards to South and Central America, nor of the fertile land, spices, and hoards of gems that had attracted Europeans to Asia. The slaves that formed the chief export commodity of interest to Europeans were bought on the shores of the continent, captured and sold by Africans themselves. Although gold had been mined in parts of West and Central Africa from ancient times, few outsiders knew of its source. In the west it was exchanged, usually for salt, across the Sahara with North Africans, who then traded it across the Mediterranean to Europe. In the east it was carried from what is now Zimbabwe to the coast, and there traded with Arab or Indian merchants. Copper and iron also followed this trade route from Central Africa. Some of the copper and iron were bought by merchants from Arabia to be sold in India.

New Resources

In the main, the exchange of these valuable materials took place on the shores of Africa. It was not until diamonds and then gold were discovered in South Africa in 1867 and 1884 that the continent attracted hordes of seekers of wealth. At about the same time the marketing of rubber began in the region now known as Zaïre. Ivory had been sought in East Africa throughout the century, but this was a luxury trade. Palm oil was also exported from West Africa. Cacao from the Gold Coast, cloves from Zanzibar, and copper from Katanga in present-day Zaïre, and the nearby copper belt of northern Rhodesia (now Zambia) also gained some importance. But, with the exception of the minerals, these commodities were never of major importance to the nations that were becoming industrialized. They did lead an increasing number of Europeans into the interior of the African continent. But to the outside world it was the gold and diamonds of South Africa and the copper of present-day Zambia and Zaïre that were really important.

Today so much of Africa is still unexplored geologically that many undiscovered valuable materials may lie below the ground. Recently oil has been found in several areas—Libya, Algeria, and Nigeria especially—and has become a profitable export of these countries.

Cultivation

For the mass of the African population it is the fertility of the soil that determines where they can live. With few exceptions the soil of the continent is poor. It was once thought that because much of tropical Africa has dense vegetation, fertile land would be revealed once the forest was removed. This theory has been disproved. Tropical soils are of lower quality and more easily destroyed than those of the temperate zones. Once the land is cleared of its wild vegetation the soil quickly degenerates. The balance that results from self-fertilization through the decomposition of leaves and branches and the action of insects is destroyed. Heavy rains wash away the thin layer of topsoil, and serious erosion quickly develops. Moreover, many tropical soils are infertile because they contain a large quantity of laterite, a form of rock that colors the soil red. Laterite is useful for making roads and some buildings, but it makes the soil useless for agriculture.

Throughout their history most African communities have been accustomed to practice what is known as shifting cultivation. They can only grow food or graze their cattle in a particular area for a limited number of years. When the land is exhausted they move on to another district, leaving the original one to lie fallow until it has recovered its fertility. This practice is not as common now as in the past. Colonial governments effectively discouraged it. Efforts have also been made by independent African governments to persuade communities to settle in one area, and

Mounds of refuse from gold mines located outside Johannesburg, South Africa.

Natural gases are burned off oil wells deep in the desert of Algeria.

modern fertilizers are supplied to enable them to do so. But even the most modern techniques have not yet overcome the problems of the poverty of African soil. In some cases these very techniques have made things worse by the destructive impact of machines on the fragile soil.

The Shortage of Water.   There are other factors connected with the land that limit the African's choice of habitation and reduce his ability to increase the production of food. It is estimated that over three quarters of the area south of the Sahara is short of water. The countries most affected in recent years have been Ethiopia, Mauritania, Senegal, Mali, Burkina, Niger, and Chad, which have suffered from a prolonged drought. This has led to widespread famine, destruction of livestock and farmland, and to the migration of peoples from their homelands.

Disease.   The great prevalence of disease has been an African problem for centuries. In addition to the sicknesses that attack most poor communities, tropical Africa suffers from its special diseases. Malaria, sleeping sickness, yellow fever, and bilharzia all flourish in many parts of the continent. One of the most serious of these diseases is sleeping sickness, carried by the tsetse fly. Over a huge belt of equatorial Africa, stretching from the western bulge to the Tanzanian coast, tsetse are prevalent, making the areas unfit for habitation by men or animals.

Inevitably the effects of disease produce a vicious cycle. Sickness and early death reduce production, low output creates poverty, and poverty induces increased disease.

COMMUNITY LIFE

In Africa land has almost always been cultivated for the sole purpose of providing food for the cultivating community. This method is called subsistence farming. The people eat what they grow. For centuries African

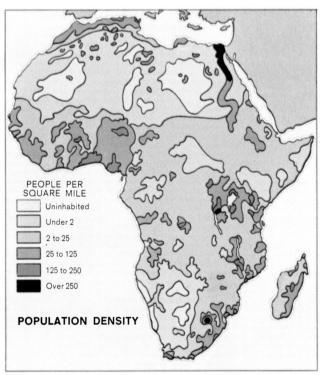

PEOPLE PER
SQUARE MILE
Uninhabited
Under 2
2 to 25
25 to 125
125 to 250
Over 250

POPULATION DENSITY

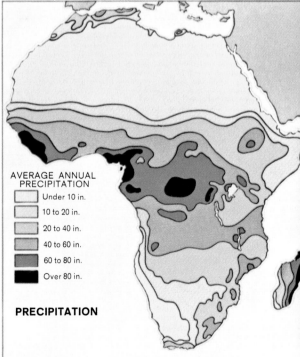

AVERAGE ANNUAL
PRECIPITATION
Under 10 in.
10 to 20 in.
20 to 40 in.
40 to 60 in.
60 to 80 in.
Over 80 in.

PRECIPITATION

farming communities have been small. They have been capable of moving frequently in order to exploit whatever fertile areas they could find. Nearly three quarters of the cultivated land in tropical Africa is farmed in this manner. Thus the majority of Africans live in a self-sufficient community, selling practically nothing of what they produce and therefore accumulating nothing. Thus they are unable to save or to enjoy the use of goods acquired by exchanging with other communities. Inevitably, they are heavily dependent in all aspects of their lives on the community of which they are the members.

The African regards land differently from the way the European or American does. In the Western world land is owned either privately or by corporations or public authorities. It is real estate, marketable, defined by boundaries. A town, village, parish, or homestead consists of a community of people living on a clearly designated area of land bounded by some kind of frontier.

An African's land rights are derived not from purchase or inheritance but from membership in his community. The land is there as is the air. If the community decides to clear the bush or forest in a particular place, the heavy work will be performed by the people. The plots will be allocated to members of the community, usually in family units. The family will farm the plot, co-operating with other families in the larger tasks, until the community decides to move elsewhere and leave the original area to recover. The right to use this land derives from membership in the community. That membership also entails duties. Roads and paths must be built, bridges constructed, marketplaces established and maintained.

This is work done by all, and so responsibility for participating in decisions must be accepted by all. These duties and many other tradi-

A medical assistant prepares for a blood test at a village dispensary in Cameroon.

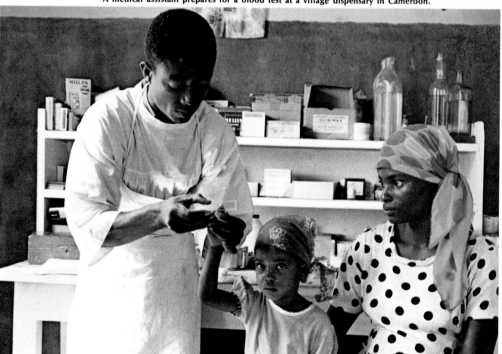

tional customs form essential elements in membership of the community. If membership lapses by the member leaving, perhaps to work in a town, or if a member is expelled, he loses his right to farm the community land.

It was this entirely different concept of land that often led to serious misunderstandings during the 19th and early 20th centuries when European prospectors thought they had "bought" land from African chiefs. To the African it was inconceivable that land could be "sold." The most that could be done was to lease its use. The great resentment felt by many African communities as a result of such misunderstanding often led to political or armed conflicts.

It is evident that the community is all-important to African life. This applies to town-dwellers as well as rural dwellers. Although communal ties are easier to maintain in country village settlements than in towns, the customs and traditions that African boys and girls learn early in life still persist even when they go to the towns and cities. Thus one always finds clan and family groups organized in African towns. These groups do their best to provide the kind of social security that such communities supply to their members in the rural areas.

The Family

It is difficult to convey the depth of this attachment to the community, for it differs fundamentally from any Western concept.

In the first place the African family is much larger than that of the European or the American. In many rural African societies men marry two or more wives. There are therefore more children related to each other and a larger number of adults within the same family unit. The family relationship extends beyond brothers, sisters, half-brothers and half-sisters to co-wives, cousins, aunts, and uncles. In most communities the wife joins her husband's family group on marriage, only returning to her own if the marriage breaks up. Often if she is widowed, she retains her place in her husband's group, at times marrying one of his brothers. Each wife usually has her own hut, and her children live with her in it. Children are looked after by other relatives if their father or mother or both die. The old, the sick, and the crippled are similarly cared for by the group.

All members of the family participate in the work of growing food and tending cattle. Much of the farm work is traditionally the responsibility of the women, while the men look after the cattle. But this custom is changing as cultivation becomes more complicated. From an early age children take part in this work.

The children are also brought up to understand the mysteries, traditions, and etiquette of their clan and group. It is the task of their elders, at first the mother, then the men and women of the clan, to teach children how to behave toward each member of their community, how to conduct themselves when eating, speaking, or playing. It is in the family, too, that children learn the skills needed for their work. Later, in the early teens, they participate with other members of their age group in learning the rites, customs, and responsibilities of membership in their community. Thus social relations are given a primary value in African society, and social learning is the most important aspect of a child's upbringing.

The family is only the inner core of a series of groups of which the

African is a member. Kinship plays various roles in different African societies, sometimes through the father, at other times through the mother, and in some cases through other relatives. But in each case families are linked to larger communities, clans, and ethnic groups. Thus every African is associated for life with others of his kind—with relatives and friends in a variety of communal groups. This cohesive nature of African life is of supreme importance to Africans. Through it most economic activity is organized, local governments are determined, personal and communal life is arranged, and artistic feelings are expressed.

The Towns and Cities

Although traditional rural life, now slowly changing through the impact of new productive methods, remains widespread throughout Africa, increasing numbers of Africans are leaving it to work and live in towns and cities. The populations of the urban centers have steadily grown over the past 100 years, but in more recent times the increase has been enormous. Two examples of the expansion of the cities will illustrate the extent to which Africans have been flocking into urban areas. Since 1940 the population of Cairo, the capital of Egypt and the largest city in Africa, has increased by five times. The population of Johannesburg, at the other end of the continent in South Africa, has doubled since 1940.

It is important to note that there were fair-sized African communities many centuries before the Europeans arrived. About 450 B.C. Herodotus, the Greek historian, wrote of a "big city named Meroe, said to be the capital city of the Ethiopians." Ibn-Batuta, a Muslim traveler of the 14th century A.D., wrote of a port city on the east coast: "Kilwa is one of the most beautiful and well-constructed cities in the world. The whole of it is elegantly built." Leo Africanus, a Spanish Moor, described Timbuktu at the beginning of the 16th century in these words: "Here in

Lagos, the largest city and chief port of Nigeria, is one of Africa's most cosmopolitan cities.

Timbuktu there are great stores of doctors, judges, priests, and other learned men. . . . And hither are brought divers manuscripts or written books out of Barbary, which are sold for more money than any other merchandise." Arabs, Indians, Indonesians, and, later, Portuguese, Dutch, French, Belgians, Germans, Italians, and British all made an impact on African town life in various parts of the continent.

When the Europeans settled in southern, eastern, and central Africa, they usually imposed some form of segregation. The Europeans generally lived apart in large houses built in the most pleasant and healthful areas. As some Africans began to become professionally trained as doctors, lawyers, teachers, or civil servants, they, too, built big houses in selective districts. In certain regions, particularly in eastern Africa, Asian merchants also lived in their own areas. The rest of the people, the African workers, lived in various forms of shantytowns in primitive shelters built with whatever was at hand—wood, straw, tin cans, or bricks.

At the beginning of the independence era in the late 1950s, the wealthier and more prominent Africans started to move into the former European areas. As many Europeans have remained, these areas are now inhabited by mixed populations of white and black. Many new housing developments have been built since independence. But in a large number of communities, the shanties remain or have actually increased as the urban population has rapidly grown. Today in most African towns and cities, one sees men and women who are poorly dressed, others in smart European suits and dresses, and still others wearing local togalike cloths or the long, flowing robes of the Muslims. The scene in every African town is full of color, noise, and bustle. Street markets abound, selling an infinite variety of wares—newspapers, wood carvings for tourists, fruits, vegetables, hot coffee, and peanuts.

Communal Organizations. In most towns and villages throughout Africa, the rural communal organizations persist among the inhabitants. Thus, age-group associations, family, clan, and larger ethnic groupings continue to influence the social life. This is so even among those who have left their family homes.

As in the rural areas, this way of life provides some form of social security. Shelter and food are always available to the needy members of a community. It also means that once an African has secured a good wage or accumulated some wealth, his dependents increase. For it is expected that he will share his good fortune with the less fortunate members of his group.

A Different Way of Life

There is one region in which town life long differed from that in other parts of Africa. In the southern African country of South Africa (and, until 1990, in the neighboring territory of Namibia, which South Africa administered), it was considered that the cities belonged to people of European descent, and segregation was imposed by law. Until 1986 blacks had to justify their presence in the cities by showing a pass, and separate areas were set aside for different racial groups. The basic laws of this system of segregation (known as apartheid) were repealed in 1991. They included the laws that enforced residential segregation, reserved 87 percent of the land in South Africa for whites, and required all South Africans to register their race with the government.

Mother and child outside their house in the former Coloured area of Durban, South Africa.

Modern apartment and office buildings line the beach in Durban, South Africa.

Even during the years under apartheid, South African gold mines and industry demanded large labor forces, which could be drawn only from the black community. Because of this, and the fact that most white households expected to employ black domestic labor, the black populations of the towns actually increased. Even when blacks found work and homes in a town, however, they were not considered citizens of it. They had voting rights only in the generally poor and overcrowded rural homelands to which all blacks were assigned. Four of the 10 homelands were declared independent by the South African Government, although no other country recognized their independence. As pressure to end the apartheid system mounted, the government announced its intention to reintegrate all of the homelands into South Africa. Late in 1992, however, blacks still had no voice in the national government of South Africa, and negotiations to draw up a new constitution were threatened by black-on-black violence.

THE REGIONS

For the sake of clarity, Africa can be divided into five regions—northern, western, eastern, central, and southern. Of course, this is an arbitrary division. Several countries could well be allocated to other regions, and there are inevitable overlaps in their features.

NORTHERN REGION

The northern area of Africa includes Algeria, Morocco, Tunisia, Libya, Egypt, and Sudan. In all of these countries, the Muslim religion is dominant, or at least accepted by a large number of the inhabitants. Most of the populations are Arab. Arabic and French are the main languages. All the countries have been involved in Mediterranean history, although Sudan's connection was only through Egypt, and Sudan alone of the group has no Mediterranean coastline. The Persians, Greeks, and Romans knew these shores well, trading with, and sometimes fighting, the societies that were established there.

As far back as 5,000 years ago, there were highly developed civilizations along the North African coast. Egypt was one of the first settled communities in the world. Its inhabitants developed a high standard of living. They had stone buildings, carved statues, seaworthy ships, a solar calendar, and a form of writing. They used irrigation, grew large quantities of food, were metalworkers, potters, engineers, and carpenters. One of their most notable surviving buildings, the royal tomb, or pyramid, at Giza, near Cairo, is 480 ft. (146 m.) high. This magnificent structure took 100,000 men 20 years to erect.

Nor was the influence of Egypt confined to North Africa and the Mediterranean. The Nile was one of the earliest channels of man's cultural exchange. Connections with Egypt influenced the formation of African states to the south. One of the best known of these states was Kush, sometimes called Meroë, after its capital city. This state was situated in a region of what is now modern Sudan. On the coast, in Tunisia, stood the now-historic city of Carthage. It was vividly described by Herodotus 500 years before the birth of Christ.

In the 7th century A.D., the Muslim faith, which originated in the Arabian Peninsula, expanded along the whole North African coast, from where it penetrated into southern Europe. Since that time the Muslim

Kasr-el-Nil Bridge joins a suburb on the island of Gezira to Cairo, Egypt.

religion has remained the most important cultural factor throughout North Africa. From this base it has extended widely into the western region of the continent.

Climate and Its Effects

The Mediterranean produces a temperate climate along the coastal belt of Africa. In the interior, especially in the Sahara, the temperature ranges between day and night are very wide. Rainfall is adequate along the coast and on the northern slopes of the Atlas Mountains. But in much of the interior area, including the Sahara, it is negligible.

As a result of these climatic features and their effects on the land, most of the population is concentrated along the coastal belt and on the northern slopes of the mountains. Usually the people live in stone houses, though in the interior, groups of nomads use tents, caves, or even holes dug in the ground for shelter.

North Africa is traditionally a food-producing region. This is what made it valuable to early European empires. Dates, olives, and grapes are grown, along with vegetables and cereals. The grazing lands are used for sheep, goats, and cattle, whose wool and hides are exported, leather being a specialty.

Resources

There is some mining of metals in northern Africa, but it is the discovery and exploitation of oil that has begun to transform the economic importance of the region. Algeria and Libya have already become important oil producers. Consequently, their national revenues have increased tremendously. It is known that considerable quantities of oil, natural gas, phosphates, and metals are to be found in the Sahara. It could well become a source of great wealth.

Algeria, Tunisia, and Morocco

Algeria was the scene of fighting during the period of decolonization. The country was seized by the French in 1830 and later made an integral part of France. A nationalist rebellion broke out in 1954, and was opposed by French and other European settlers, together with large sections of the French Army sympathetic to the settlers. The fighting continued until 1962, when French President Charles de Gaulle initiated negotiations that ended with Algerian independence. The country's population consists mainly of Arabs and Berbers. There are also several thousand Europeans.

Morocco and Tunisia also had to fight for their independence against the French. Tunisia became a French protectorate in 1883, Morocco in 1912. Although waging separate struggles, the two countries gained their independence in the same year—1956. Both countries have narrow Mediterranean coastlines, with desert in the southern hinterland. In Morocco, the Atlas Mountains divide the country in two. In Tunisia, the mountains are well-watered, providing irrigation for agriculture. In both countries, olives, dates, grapes, and other fruits are grown, along with vegetables and grain. Morocco also has considerable deposits of ores, such as iron, coal, manganese, lead, and zinc, as well as phosphates and oil. Like Algeria, Tunisia has a population consisting mainly of Arabs and Berbers.

Libya

For most of the 19th century Libya was under Turkish authority. In 1912, however, it was annexed by Italy. After its defeat in World War II, Italy renounced all claims to the territory. Libya became independent in 1951. The country has three distinct geographical regions, Cyrenaica in the east, Tripolitania in the extreme northwest, and Fezzan in the southwest. From independence through the mid-1960's, the inhabitants of Libya were among the poorest of Africa's peoples. Until 1965, Libya was greatly dependent on American, British, and United Nations aid. Since then, however, the economy has been revolutionized by the discovery of oil. Libya has become one of the world's top producers of oil. Petroleum is the major industry and makes up about 95 percent of the country's exports.

Egypt

Egypt took the name United Arab Republic in 1958, when it formed a union with Syria. However, the union lasted only a few years. In early 1971, the governments of Egypt, Libya, and Syria announced plans to form a federation—the result being a short-lived unified military command. In September of 1971, the United Arab Republic changed its name to the Arab Republic of Egypt.

Two factors have dominated Egyptian history: first, the 3,500-mile-long (5,600 km.) Nile River and its delta have provided land that has been cultivated for 7,000 years; second, the Egyptian population has been able to inhabit slightly less than four percent of the country's area; the rest is uncultivable desert.

Because of its strategic location Egypt has always been coveted by imperialists—Romans, Turks, French, and British among them. It became even more attractive with the opening of the Suez Canal in 1869. Britain

Detail of painted limestone statue of Prince Rahotep and his wife Nofret. The statue, 2610? B.C., is in the Egyptian Museum, Cairo.

first occupied the country in 1882 and, with a gap between 1936 and 1939, its troops remained there until 1956.

In 1952 King Farouk was deposed. The monarchy was abolished in 1953, and Egypt became a republic. The following year, Gamel Abdel Nasser took over control of the government. In 1956 Nasser nationalized the Suez Canal.

Egypt and Israel have fought three wars since 1948—in 1956, 1967, and 1973. As a result of the wars, the Suez Canal was closed for many years, and was not reopened to international shipping until 1975. Egypt and Israel established formal diplomatic relations in 1979, after signing a peace treaty.

The many years of war with the Israelis handicapped Egypt's development. Because most Arabs opposed the Egyptian-Israeli peace treaty, Egypt was banned from the Arab League between 1979 and 1989. However, after Iraq's 1990 invasion of Kuwait and during the resulting 1991 Gulf War, Egypt reasserted its position as a leader of the Arab world.

The mammoth Aswan High Dam, opened in January 1971, was designed to regulate the flow of the Nile, doing away with the periods of flood and drought. It also doubled Egypt's power capacity and increased the country's arable land by providing water for irrigation. Unfortunately, since the mid-1980s, drought and overuse have forced drastic reductions in the use of water behind the dam for irrigation and power generation. Rapid population growth and urban sprawl have placed further stress on the limited amount of farmland, and Egypt now imports much of its food.

Tourism is one of the country's main sources of income. People come from all over the world to see the many ancient monuments and sites such as the Sphinx and the pyramids. The largest city in Egypt, as well as the largest in all Africa, is Cairo, the capital.

Sudan

Sudan is included in the northern region of Africa because of its close association with Egypt. From 1899 until 1951, it was administered jointly by Britain and Egypt. However, because of British power, it was mainly in London that Sudan's governmental policy was determined. In 1956 Sudan became independent. Two-thirds of its people are Arab or Nubian. They are largely Muslim and live mainly in the north. In

This statue, carved in Sudan, captures the pride and grace of the Sudanese people.

the south, most of the population are of Nilotic or Negro descent. They resent the Islamic Arab domination from the north. Drought and a long civil war have devastated the economy of the Sudan, which has the potential to become the breadbasket of Africa.

Much of the Sudan is desert, swamp, or forest. In the 1950s the government developed an irrigation project called the Gezira Scheme. Cotton grown in the Gezira region is a valuable export. Another huge development project, the Jonglei Canal, was begun in 1980 to divert the White Nile and provide irrigation water for northern Sudan and Egypt. Work on this project, however, had to be abandoned because of the civil war. Khartoum is the capital city, and Port Sudan is the leading port.

THE EASTERN REGION

This region includes Ethiopia, Somalia, Djibouti, Rwanda, Burundi, Uganda, Kenya, and Tanzania. It is an area of narrow coastline rising to high plateaus, broken by numerous lakes and lofty mountains. Most of its people come from Bantu-speaking stock, especially in the southern areas. But in the north is a large block of Cushitic-speaking peoples, particularly the Galla. Cushitic- and Nilotic-speaking peoples are also interspersed among the dominant Bantu farther south. There are also a few small communities whose members still live like early man, by hunting and gathering berries.

There are hundreds of different ethnic communities in East Africa, each speaking its own language, though Swahili is becoming a common language in the southern countries. The coastal belt has had a history largely separate from the interior. It was part of the Indian Ocean trading area for many centuries, though it drew many of its commercial goods from the peoples of the interior. This trading interest brought Arabs, Asians, and Portuguese to the coast. Many Arabs and people from the Indian subcontinent settled in East Africa. From the beginning of the 20th century, they were joined by Europeans, who found fertile farming land, especially in Kenya. During the colonial era, the present boundaries of the countries were drawn according to European interests, cutting right across ethnic groupings. The Somali are a case in point. Because their land was cut up, Somali live not only in Somalia, but also in Ethiopia and Kenya. Ethnic Somali in the Ogaden region of Ethiopia have been fighting to secede from Ethiopia. As a result of the fighting, many people from this area are now in refugee camps in Somalia. Somalia may have more refugees than any other nation, which places a severe strain on its resources.

In the three ex-British territories—Uganda, Kenya, and Tanzania—attempts were made to coordinate such services as mail, railways, and civil aviation. But cooperation lapsed during the years that Idi Amin ruled Uganda, and has not yet been completely restored. Both the Germans, when they ruled their East African colony before World War I, and the British built railways that have since been extended.

Ethiopia

Ethiopia has played a special part in African history. It is the oldest continually independent state on the continent, and thus has come to symbolize the African homeland to many blacks in other parts of the world, especially America and the Caribbean. Most people speak Amharic

These huge stained-glass windows are in Africa Hall, Addis Ababa, Ethiopia.

Grain is one of the leading agricultural products of Ethiopia.

Coptic monks celebrate religious services at Aksum, Ethiopia.

or Oromo. Many of the people practice the Coptic form of Christianity, although there are also many Muslims. Ethiopia's Falasha, who practice an ancient form of Judaism, were airlifted to Israel from 1984 to 1991.

Much of the land is very high, and most people live at an elevation of about 5,000 ft. (1,500 m.), where the temperature is moderate. The low coastal strip beside the Red Sea is very hot. Much of the country is still undeveloped. Ethiopia's Communist government, which came to power in 1974 after overthrowing Emperor Haile Selassie, was overthrown in 1991 after a long civil war. The new government gave the country's various ethnic groups a large measure of autonomy, and the region of Eritrea was scheduled to hold a referendum on independence in 1993.

Animal grazing and growing cereal crops and coffee are the chief pursuits of the people. Addis Ababa is the capital and chief city of the country. It serves as headquarters for many inter-African organizations, such as the important Economic Commission for Africa (ECA) and the Organization of African Unity (OAU).

Somalia

The Somali Democratic Republic, or Somalia, as it is also called, was created in 1960. It brought together Somalia, which had been a United Nations trust territory administered by the Italians, and the British Somaliland Protectorate. After Mohammed Siad Barré, Somalia's ruler from 1969, was overthrown in 1991, the country was engulfed in civil war.

Many of the people of Somalia are nomadic herdsmen. These people have very strong ties with other Somali who live in the neighboring countries of Ethiopia, Kenya, and Djibouti. Mogadishu is the capital and chief port of the country.

Djibouti

Djibouti (formerly the French Territory of the Afars and the Issas) is located on the east coast of Africa, just before the continental landmass juts out into the Indian Ocean. Djibouti is a small land about the size of the state of New Hampshire. Nearly all of the people are Muslim. French is the official language, but Arabic is taught in the schools, and Afar and Somali are widely spoken. Djibouti is the capital and the chief city of the country.

Rwanda and Burundi

These two countries formed part of German East Africa until after World War I. They were then placed under the League of Nations as the mandated territory of Ruanda-Urundi and administered by Belgium. In 1962 they became two separate independent states with a customs union between them. This union was ended in 1964. Each country has since gone its own way.

Cattle grazing and subsistence agriculture are the main occupations, with some coffee and cotton grown as cash crops. Tin has been found in large quantities in Rwanda. People of Rwanda and Burundi migrate to Uganda and the Republic of Zaïre to find work. Both Rwanda and Burundi are overpopulated and underdeveloped. The most important issue has been the antagonism between the two main communities in both countries: the Tutsi and the Hutu. The Tutsi are very tall, handsome people and the traditional leaders. But the Hutu are more numerous. In

Tutsi (Watusi) dancers of Burundi.

Rwanda, the Hutu revolted before independence and subsequently gained control of the country. Many Tutsi refugees are living outside their country, particularly in Uganda. In Burundi, the Tutsi-controlled monarchy kept its powers until the country became a republic in 1966.

Uganda

Uganda straddles the equator but since much of the country is a plateau, between 3,000 and 5,000 feet (900–1,500 m.) above sea level, the temperatures are comfortable. Uganda has a number of large lakes. Lake Victoria, which also lies partly in neighboring Zambia and Kenya, has an area of over 26,000 square miles (69,575 sq. km.). In the western part of the country the Ruwenzori range rises to nearly 17,000 feet (5,180 m.). Grassy pastures provide good grazing for cattle in the north if rinderpest and tsetse-carried sleeping sickness can be controlled. There are deposits of several minerals, the most important being copper.

Kampala is the capital and largest city of Uganda. But much of the city was destroyed during the fighting that overthrew Idi Amin in 1979. Uganda was created by the British because of its strategic position at the source of the Nile. During the 19th century, a number of missionaries came into Uganda. In the years that followed, there were bitter battles between Catholics and Protestants and between Christians and Muslims. At this time there were four African kingdoms—Buganda, Toro, Ankole, and Bunyoro—in the area. The King, or Kabaka, of Buganda was made president of the whole country shortly after independence in 1962. In 1966 Dr. Milton Obote overthrew the Kabaka. The constitution was suspended, and Dr. Obote became president of the country. In 1971 Uganda's army ousted President Obote and set up a military government headed by Idi Amin. Idi Amin was overthrown by Ugandan and Tanzanian military forces in 1979. A succession of governments, including one led by Obote, tried, but failed, to restore law and order and rebuild the shattered economy. The regime established by insurgent leader Yoweri Museveni in 1986 seemed to be restoring stability.

Kenya

Kenya's population is mainly African, but also includes a considerable number of Europeans and Asians. Its first interest to the British was as the territory through which the railway had to be laid from Mombasa, on the coast, to Lake Victoria, on the southwestern border.

By the beginning of the 20th century, however, the high plateau was found to contain very fertile land between 5,000 and 9,000 feet (1,520–2,740 m.) above sea level. Here Europeans were encouraged to settle as farmers. The area, called the White Highlands, was restricted by the British for the use of white settlers. It was Jomo Kenyatta, later to become Kenya's president, who most effectively challenged white privilege. During the 1950's he became the accepted leader of the Kikuyu, Kenya's largest ethnic group. But Kenyatta was convicted of participation in the Mau Mau uprising of 1952–59 and went to prison for 7 years.

During this time other leaders, such as Tom Mboya and Oginga Odinga, both Luo, carried on the anti-colonial struggle. When Kenyatta was freed in August, 1961, he became a national leader, fully accepted by people from all groups. He brought his country to independence in 1963. There are still fears, though, that inter-group conflicts might start again,

Students in front of library and sculpture of University College, Nairobi, Kenya.

despite the peaceful transfer of presidential power to Vice-President Daniel Moi following the death of President Jomo Kenyatta in 1978.

Kenya is still mainly an agricultural country, with African farmers now admitted to the highlands. Light industries are rapidly developing. Tourism has greatly expanded. There are many modern hotels in Nairobi. It is but a short drive from these hotels into the game parks where large numbers of wild animals may be seen in their natural surroundings.

Tanzania

This country is a federal state, formed by the association of Tanganyika and Zanzibar in 1964. Tanganyika was a German colony until the end of World War I. It became a League of Nations mandate and was subsequently administered by Britain. The island of Zanzibar, under its Arab sultan, dominated the East African coast during the 19th century. It eventually became a British protectorate. The island is famous for its production of cloves. When its African population revolted against rule by the Arabs in 1964 and expelled the Sultan, Tanganyika offered a union, which was accepted. However, the island still retains much local autonomy.

Much of Tanzania is infested by tsetse. This prevents habitation by human beings or cattle in the affected areas. To add to the difficulties of the country, rainfall is very irregular. Tanzania's main cash crops are cotton, cashew nuts, tea, and coffee. Diamonds are mined just south of Lake Victoria. Most of the people still live on a subsistence basis. This means that they grow their own food, make their own clothing and shelter, and exchange hardly any goods.

Tanzania gained its independence by the most peaceful methods of organized political pressure. One helpful factor was the absence of any large ethnic group, which would ordinarily attempt to dominate the others. There are about 120 different groups in the country. But the major influence was undoubtedly the skillful leadership of Julius Nyerere, who became president in 1962. He introduced a single-party state, with elections between rival members of the same party. In 1967 the Arusha Declaration was proclaimed. This declaration pledged the country to socialist objectives. As the Tanzanian economy deteriorated, Nyerere retired in 1985. The government then began to modify its strict socialist economic policies, and a multiparty system was introduced in 1992.

THE CENTRAL REGION

It was in the center of the continent that the various European empires of Africa met each other. The region was once made up of Belgian, French, and British territories. Today Central Africa consists of the Republic of Zaïre, formerly the Belgian Congo and later the Democratic Republic of the Congo, or Congo (Kinshasa); the ex–French Equatorial territories of Gabon, the People's Republic of the Congo, the Central African Republic, and Chad; and the former British territories of Zambia and Malawi. The People's Republic of the Congo is now the only country that is called Congo.

Much of this central area is part of the main African plateau. The exceptions are the basin of the great Congo River, the coastline of Gabon and Congo, and the mountains of Malawi. This whole area is one of sharply contrasting wealth and poverty. The large mineral deposits of the Republic of Zaïre, Gabon, and Zambia provide these countries with the greatest potential wealth of black-governed Africa. At the other end of the scale, the entire northern half of Chad is in the Saharan zone, where there is virtually no fertile land.

Zaïre

This country has been in the center of events twice in this century. First, it was the scene of appalling atrocities when it was owned by King Leopold II of Belgium. Revelations of the brutalities committed in forcing Africans to produce rubber for Leopold's company shocked the world and led to the Belgian Government's taking control of the African country. The second occasion followed immediately after the grant of independence in 1960. The Congolese Army mutinied. The copper-rich province of Katanga tried to break away from the central government. The great national powers, together with a United Nations force, were involved in the turbulence that followed.

Eventually a United Nations force prevented Katanga from setting up a separate state and thus depriving the central government of its main mineral revenues. But confusion and weak government continued, marked by attempts by other provinces to set up their own governments. In one such incident, rebel soldiers held a number of hostages in Stanleyville (now Kisangani) until Belgian paratroopers helped free them. Exiled rebel forces invaded Shaba (formerly Katanga) province from neighboring Angola in 1977 and 1978, but were quickly defeated.

Zaïre, a very large country, is about one-fourth the size of the United States. It is the third largest (after the Sudan and Algeria) of the

This Gabonese mask is formed out of copper and brass on wood.

African countries. The capital and chief city of Zaïre is Kinshasa. Many Zaïrians are craftsmen in iron working, carving, and pottery making. Half the population is Christian. The rest of the people follow their own traditional religions.

The Former French Territories

Four countries that fall within the Central Region of Africa were once French colonies, constituting what used to be called French Equatorial Africa. The countries are Gabon, Congo, the Central African Republic, and Chad. Chad is the largest in area and population. But all four have relatively small populations and are poor.

Gabon

Gabon is not as poor as the other countries. It has the world's largest manganese deposit. Gabon is now mining uranium and has large deposits of iron ore. Another source of the country's export income is the wood of the okoume tree, which is used in the making of plywood. Libreville is the capital and largest city. It lies on the coast and is the country's chief port. South of Libreville, on the coast also, is Gabon's second largest city, Port-Gentil. A world-famous community is the town of Lambaréné. Third in size of Gabon's cities, it became famous because it was there that Dr. Albert Schweitzer, the noted philosopher, physician, humanist, and winner of a Nobel prize, maintained a hospital for more than half a century.

Congo

The People's Republic of Congo, a long and narrow country, lies astride the equator. The exploitation of offshore oil deposits has provided Congo with a major source of income that is being used to develop the country. Nevertheless, some 60 percent of the inhabitants are still subsistence farmers. Manufacturing is on a relatively small scale. Besides the oil refinery, there are factories producing sugar, flour, beverages, soap, textiles, cement, and glass.

Central African Republic

The southern part of the Central African Republic is forested, and the north is largely savanna. Subsistence food growing is the main occupation, although some cotton is grown for export. The capital and largest city of the country is Bangui. Once the French administrative capital of the territory of Ubangi-Chari, this city is located on the Ubangi River. Over the years it has grown into the country's chief river port, major air terminal, and commercial center. Bouar and Bambari are other important population centers.

Bales of cotton stand ready for shipment in Bangui, Central African Republic.

Chad

Chad is a large, sprawling country that covers an area about the size of Texas and California combined. The southern savanna region allows cattle, sheep, and goats to graze, but much of the rest of the country is arid. The capital city is N'Djamena. Since it gained its independence from France in 1960, Chad has been torn by civil war. Neighboring Libya, which claims the mineral-rich Aozou Strip in Chad, has intervened militarily in support of various factions during the long civil war.

Two Former British Territories

Two other countries within the Central Region are Zambia and Malawi. Zambia, by far the larger of the two, covers an area that is almost six and a half times greater than that of Malawi. Malawi borders Zambia on the east.

Zambia

Zambia's copper wealth provides the government with the revenue to create a prosperous society. Yet this former British territory faces many problems. Although the majority of the people still practice subsistence farming, they are being encouraged by the government to raise chickens and grow cash crops, such as maize, cotton, and tobacco.

Many light industries are developing in the copper belt around Lusaka, the capital. Tourism is also encouraged. There are several fine game parks and a growing number of modern and well-equipped hotels. The awe-inspiring Victoria Falls attracts many visitors each year.

The government participates in industry in a major way. It has nationalized the copper mines and a number of other businesses in order to control revenues and to develop them in the national interest.

Above all, education has been tremendously expanded. Since 1964, the year of Zambia's independence from British rule, the number of children in the country's schools has increased greatly. The University of Zambia was opened in 1966.

In the past, Zambia was dependent upon Rhodesia (now Zimbabwe) for oil. This situation was changed when an oil pipeline was built between Zambia and Tanzania. With the help of the Chinese, a railway system along the same route was completed in 1975. Some African leaders feel that the outcome of all this national planning in Zambia will have great bearing on the future of all Africans.

Malawi

Like Zambia, this nation also was once a British territory, known as Nyasaland. It gained its independence in 1964. Its present name, Malawi, means "land of flames." The "flames" may have originated in the shimmering waters of Lake Malawi. Malawi's capital is Lilongwe.

A small, mountainous country, Malawi has no substantial mineral resources, and its economy is based largely on agriculture. Tobacco, cotton, and tea are among its important exports. Because Malawi has difficulty supporting its population, many Malawian men traditionally have worked in neighboring Zambia or in the mines of South Africa.

Malawi's president, H. Kamuzu Banda, led the country to independence and steered it through the difficult transition away from colonialism. By the early 1990s, he had become Africa's longest-ruling head of state.

THE SOUTHERN REGION

The countries included in the southern region are South Africa, Namibia (formerly South-West Africa), Lesotho, Swaziland, Botswana, Zimbabwe (formerly Rhodesia), Mozambique, Angola, and the island nations of Madagascar, Mauritius, Seychelles, and Comoros. Many of these nations had, until recently, one feature in common: they were dominated by southern Africa's white minority population. These countries formed the southern stronghold of white control. The first crack in this stronghold came when Mozambique and Angola won their independence from Portugal in 1975. The next came when Rhodesia in 1980 became the independent nation of Zimbabwe under black majority rule. On May 31, 1991, the warring factions in Angola signed a U.N.-monitored peace accord, although it appeared that war might resume after the inconclusive elections of October 1992. A tenuous cease-fire accord was also signed in Mozambique on October 4, 1992. The early 1990s were a time of momentous change in South Africa, as Nelson Mandela and other black nationalists were released from prison and negotiations began to determine how South Africa would be governed in a post-apartheid era.

South Africa

South Africa was the first territory of the continent to be settled by Europeans. When the Dutch, in 1652, established their refreshment station at the Cape of Good Hope for ships sailing to Asia, they found only a few Hottentots and Bushmen on the peninsula. In other parts of South Africa, African communities had already made their homes, but these were far from the Cape of Good Hope.

For close to 300 years the Dutch settlement grew, and many French, Germans, and British were added to it. Ties with Holland were eventually broken and lost for good. The Europeans developed their own language, Afrikaans, and their own culture. Today South Africa's Europeans can be divided into two sections. The larger one is known as Afrikaans-speaking, the smaller one as English-speaking. The black African communities have also grown. Because of South Africa's economic development, black African wages, though much lower than those of the Europeans, are generally better than in undeveloped areas of the continent.

From the 18th century on, various forms of contact, often violent, took place between Africans and Europeans. A strong sense of racial exclusiveness long dominated Afrikaner culture. From the late 1940s to the early 1990s, this traditional attitude was solidified by an official policy of apartheid. Apartheid theoretically aimed to set up separate racial communities, each with the right to govern itself. All blacks would be citizens of one of 10 homelands, four of which had been declared "independent" by 1990. But as only 13 percent of the land was allocated to the Africans, who formed the great majority of the population, and as South Africa's industrial growth depended increasingly on African labor, the policy of absolute separation remained theoretical, rather than practical. No country except South Africa recognized the independence of the homelands. Modest reforms to South Africa's apartheid laws were instituted in the 1980s, but the country's black majority still was denied a role in the national government. In 1990, the government said that the homelands would be reintegrated into South Africa as part of an overall settlement. The following year the basic apartheid laws, including those classifying

South Africans by race at birth and those specifying where people of various races might live, were repealed.

The People.   Over 70 percent of the people of South Africa are black Africans. Whites, or Europeans, make up almost 15 percent of the population. The balance are Cape Coloured and Asians. The blacks include many different ethnic groups. Among them are the Zulu, Xhosa, and the Sotho. The Europeans are generally of two groups: Afrikaners, who are descendants of the early settlers, and English-speakers, whose forebears came there later. The Cape Coloured are the products of mixed marriages or extramarital unions. The Asians first came to the Natal Province of South Africa in the 19th century to work on sugar plantations. They came from India or what is now Pakistan.

Economy.   South Africa, in African terms, is a very rich and powerful industrial country. Its wealth was originally based on the discovery of diamonds in 1867 and gold in 1884. Since then many other minerals have been found, such as coal, uranium, iron, and manganese. In addition, the country is richly endowed for agricultural production—citrus fruits, cereals, sugar, and vines are all grown. But the factor mainly responsible for transforming the country from a rural backwater into an industrial power is the use made of the wealth gained from minerals to develop manufacturing. This industrial development led to the employment of more Africans in urban areas and contributed to the weakening of discriminatory practices.

Namibia

This is a dry, drought-ridden country, although it has considerable potential for development. Formerly called South-West Africa, it produces valuable quantities of diamonds and has many other mineral resources. About 85 percent of its inhabitants are black Africans, who were long treated almost the same as black South Africans. In 1920, South-West Africa was established as a mandated territory by the League of Nations. South Africa was made the administrator. Despite constant United Nations pressure, South African governments refused to admit United Nations authority. In 1968 the United Nations changed the name of the country to Namibia and claimed it as a trust territory, but South Africa refused to recognize the action. A liberation movement then became active in the territory. South Africa agreed in principle to let Namibia become independent, but negotiations dragged on until a settlement was reached in late 1988. Namibia became independent in 1990.

Lesotho, Swaziland, and Botswana

These countries were called the British High Commission Territories until they became independent—Swaziland in 1968, the others in 1966.

Lesotho is a small, mountainous country which has had little economic development. Therefore, a good part of the male population has to find work in South Africa.

Swaziland is much richer. It has valuable asbestos and iron mines and is known to possess other minerals.

Botswana's population is mostly engaged in subsistence agriculture and cattle rearing. The country's lack of water is a handicap, but the development of diamonds, copper, and nickel during the 1970s helped transform the economy.

Mauritius, Seychelles, and Comoros

Mauritius and Seychelles, both small island nations, were French and then British possessions. On Mauritius, laborers from India replaced freed African slaves on the sugar plantations. Seychelles' mixed population of European, African, and Asian descent depends on tourism and coconut products for economic survival. Mauritius became independent in 1968, Seychelles in 1976.

The four islands and many islets of Comoros lie in the Indian Ocean between Africa and Madagascar. They became independent of France in 1975, but the island of Mayotte voted to remain a part of France.

Angola and Mozambique

These were once overseas provinces of Portugal. The Portuguese settled in Angola early in the 15th century, and in Mozambique in the 16th century. Portuguese rule of the two territories lasted until independence came in 1975.

Angola was the center of Portuguese slave trading for 300 years. Thousands of Africans were captured and put on ships in Angola, to be transported across the Atlantic, many of them to Brazil. When the slave era ended, Portugal encouraged many of its people to emigrate to Angola. Today there are relatively few Portuguese remaining of the several hundred thousand who once lived there. Most fled the country during the period of civil war at the time of Angola's independence. Most of Angola is given over to agriculture. Coffee, tobacco, maize (corn), and sisal are the chief plantation crops. The country also has great mineral wealth, including oil and iron ore.

Both Angola and Mozambique are large in size, although Mozambique is the smaller of the two. Agriculture is the mainstay of Mozambique's economy. The capital, Maputo, is a major port.

In Angola and Mozambique, years of guerrilla war preceded independence. A political upheaval in Portugal that led to a change of government there finally paved the way for independence. Civil war then broke out in both Angola and Mozambique. There were fears of renewed violence after Angola's inconclusive October 1992 elections; also in 1992, a Mozambique cease-fire was signed.

Zimbabwe

This country was formerly called Southern Rhodesia, and then Rhodesia. It was originally penetrated by Cecil Rhodes's pioneers, who were looking for gold. After successful wars with the two main African communities, the Matabele and the Mashona, the British South Africa Company gained control and ruled the territory until 1923. In that year the company's charter expired. The British Government offered the European settlers the alternatives of incorporation into South Africa or British rule. They accepted the latter, and the territory became a British colony.

But unlike other colonists, the Rhodesians had always elected their own parliament and government and controlled their own civil service, police, and armed forces. There had never been an absolute color bar in politics, but the qualifications for the vote had always been such that few Africans were able to qualify. Political domination had always been held by the tiny minority of Europeans. About 50 percent of the land, including most of the best areas, was reserved for the European settlers.

Britain insisted that Rhodesian independence await the coming of a more democratic system. The Rhodesian Government, led by Ian Smith, defied Britain and unilaterally declared the country independent in 1965. First Britain, and then the United Nations, imposed economic sanctions on Rhodesia. There was increasing pressure from black nationalist guerrilla groups based in neighboring countries and from various governments to grant majority African rule.

In 1979 Smith and black nationalist leaders without ties to the foreign-based guerrillas drafted a new constitution allowing for black majority rule with safeguards for the white minority. Bishop Abel Muzorewa became the country's first black prime minister, but guerrilla warfare continued. Late in 1979, Britain helped to arrange a cease-fire agreement under which Rhodesia reverted to the status of a British colony. New elections were held in which all groups participated, and former guerrilla leader Robert Mugabe became prime minister of the new black-ruled nation of Zimbabwe in 1980.

Madagascar

The country of Madagascar is made up of the island of Madagascar and a number of smaller islands that are located nearby. The country lies in the Indian Ocean about 250 miles (400 km.) from the southeastern coast of Africa. Its inhabitants are mainly farmers. About 90 percent of Madagascar's exports are agricultural products. Because of rich soil and a good climate, many crops are raised. The most important cash crops are coffee, vanilla, sugar, sisal, and tobacco. Madagascar produces about two thirds of the world's vanilla. Antananarivo is the capital and largest city of the country.

WESTERN REGION

The western region of Africa is made up of Mali, Burkina, Niger, the Ivory Coast, Guinea, Senegal, Mauritania, Benin, Togo, Cameroon, Guinea-Bissau, São Tomé and Príncipe, Cape Verde, Equatorial Guinea, Western Sahara, Liberia, Sierra Leone, The Gambia, Ghana, and Nigeria. This entire area can be divided in several ways. First, physically, it consists of a strip of tropical rain forest along the coast. Inland is a region of upland savanna, which at times rises to a higher plateau. The forest area has mangrove swamps and coconut and palm trees.

The second division of the western region is according to colonization. All of the West African countries except Liberia formed part of some European empire. The Germans were there until after World War I, when their colonies were taken from them and mandated under the League of Nations to Britain or France. After that, Portugal, Britain, and France were the dominant colonizers. West Africa can also be divided between the English-speaking and French-speaking states, although in all of them local languages are also spoken.

The western region was the first part of Africa visited by Europeans. The Portuguese led the way in exploration during the 1400's. They found kingdoms and communities that had established trading links with Mediterranean countries. These links were set up by Arab merchants.

For 3 centuries, Europeans conducted their slave trade mainly from the west coast. Millions of Africans were transported under the most brutal conditions across the Atlantic to the plantations of the Americas.

An exciting art work from the Yoruba people of western Nigeria. This fetish statuette has a cowrie shell coat.

Merchants sent their ships to the West African coast to load slaves, take them across the Atlantic, sell them in the Americas and return with sugar, rum, cotton, jewels, and bullion. On the African coast the Europeans had to buy the slaves from African merchants. Most of the slaves were prisoners of war, criminals, or opponents of African regimes. This trade tore large numbers of young men and women from their homelands and dislocated society throughout West Africa.

After the slave trade was abolished early in the 19th century, it was replaced by other trade, principally in the palm oil needed by industrial Europe for lubricants. From the middle of the century on, and especially from 1880 through 1900, Europeans began to colonize West Africa.

Mali, Burkina, and Niger

These countries share the common problem of being landlocked. Mali and Niger are large countries but have relatively small populations for their size. All are poor and all have suffered in recent years from drought. The Senegal and Niger rivers provide Mali with irrigation for cotton and rice. The government has tried to organize co-operatives among the people it has settled in the irrigated areas. Peanuts (groundnuts) provide considerable exports from each country. Live animals are the main export of Burkina (formerly Upper Volta). Most of the people of these three countries are farmers who also raise livestock.

Ivory Coast

Perhaps the most important French-speaking country in the western region is the Ivory Coast. One of the major differences between French

This 19th-century Bobo mask from Burkina is made of wood and fiber. It is now in the collection of the Brooklyn Museum, Brooklyn, New York.

and British colonial rule was that French Africans were encouraged to participate in French politics and after 1945 were able to vote in French elections. Consequently, French-speaking Africa has generally remained closer economically and politically to France since independence than have the English-speaking countries to Britain.

The Ivory Coast's first president, Félix Houphouët-Boigny, was a prominent politician in France as well as in Africa before his country's independence. Houphouët-Boigny was a minister in French governments during the 1950's, and he became one of General Charles de Gaulle's ministers of state when the General returned to power in 1958.

The trading strength of the Ivory Coast is based on its agricultural exports, such as coffee, cacao, bananas, pineapple, cotton, palm oils, and timber. Since independence, French investment has gone up considerably. This is especially so in Abidjan, the nation's largest city. A modern-looking city, it is now becoming an important industrial and com-

Africa has a rich heritage of art. Here a Senufo artist of the Ivory Coast paints a funeral cloth.

mercial center. In addition, cacao and coffee plantations are being developed with foreign capital. The government believes in private enterprise as the basis of development for its people.

Guinea

Guinea was the only territory to reject de Gaulle's 1958 offer of association with France in a French community. The French then pulled out of Guinea immediately and completely, taking all of the country's industrial and agricultural equipment with them. Sékou Touré, president of the country, convinced his people that they could become self-reliant. They secured some help, particularly from the Soviet Union and Eastern Europe. But the country remains poor. The people of Guinea are largely dependent on agriculture. There are, however, considerable deposits of bauxite, and alumina is produced north of Conakry, the capital of the country.

Papa Ibra Tall, noted Senegalese painter, in his studio at Thiès, Senegal.

Fishermen of Benin.

Senegal

France's first African colony, dating from the middle of the 17th century, Senegal gained full independence in 1960. It has an agricultural economy, with peanuts as one of the chief exports. Its capital, Dakar, is a leading African port. Léopold Sédar Senghor, the first president, governed the country from independence until his retirement in 1980.

Mauritania

Mauritania is a large country but thinly populated. Its coastline is sand-duned, and behind it lie salt lagoons and desert. Only the Senegal River basin can be intensively cultivated. Iron ore and copper are present in Mauritania; these minerals have attracted international investment and may considerably improve the economic situation.

Benin

This country was formerly known as Dahomey. Its natural poverty is aggravated by a dense population, particularly in the southern part of the country, and a high birthrate. Although Porto-Novo is the capital of Benin, Cotonou is the largest city and main port. The country's only substantial export crop is palm products.

Togo and Cameroon

France also administered two mandated former German territories in West Africa—Togo and Cameroon. In both cases the countries were divided between Britain and France. In the case of Togo the British section, called British Togoland, voted to be incorporated as part of Ghana. French Togoland became the independent country of Togo. One of the world's richest phosphate mines is located at Kpémé, at the southern tip of the country.

In Cameroon the British southern area decided to join with the French territory to form an independent republic in 1961. But the north voted for incorporation with Nigeria. Most of the people of Cameroon are engaged in agriculture. There is, however, sizable offshore oil production. Bauxite, imported from Guinea, forms the basis of a considerable aluminum production.

Guinea-Bissau, Cape Verde, and São Tomé and Príncipe

These are three of the smaller African countries. All were formerly Portuguese territories and won their independence in the 1970's. Guinea-Bissau is made up of a mainland area plus offshore islands. São Tomé and Príncipe consists of two main islands plus a number of smaller ones. Fifteen islands comprise Cape Verde, ten of which are inhabited.

Equatorial Guinea and Western Sahara

These were once Spanish territories. Equatorial Guinea became independent in 1968. It includes the mainland area of Río Muni, the island of Bioko (formerly Fernando Po), and several smaller islands.

Western Sahara was formerly known as Spanish Sahara. Spain officially gave up the region in 1976, transferring it to Morocco and Mauritania. Mauritania renounced its claim to Western Sahara in 1979. A Saharan liberation group, known as the Polisario, has demanded independence for the territory.

Western Sahara has a small population, most of whom are nomads. The land is largely desert, but it is rich in phosphates.

Liberia

Because it was founded as a settlement for freed American slaves in 1821, Liberia is the African country that most often interests Americans. The descendants of the freed slaves formed a coastal society separate from that of the indigenous Africans of the interior. They controlled the economy and government until young military officers from the interior staged a military coup in 1980. In the early 1990s, the country was engulfed in a bloody civil war.

Liberia is in the rain-forest area, and rubber and iron ore are its leading products. Monrovia is the capital.

Sierra Leone

There are some similarities between Liberia and its neighbor Sierra Leone. The latter was founded by British opponents of slavery in 1787 as a haven for released slaves. Again, the descendants of the slaves, known as Creoles, have remained a separate community. Most of them live near the capital and port, Freetown. Their contact with the people of the interior has been tenuous and often hostile. Although smaller in area than Liberia, Sierra Leone is larger in population. In the interior the Mende and Temne communities predominate. Many tropical agricultural products are grown, but the revenues of the country depend heavily on the mining of diamonds and iron.

The Gambia

The most northerly of the former British territories is The Gambia. This small country is made up of a narrow strip of land that lies on either side of the Gambia River. It was the first British colony in all Africa. Except for the Atlantic Ocean on the west, The Gambia is surrounded by Senegal. From 1981 to 1989, the two countries formed the Confederation of Senegambia to coordinate their foreign and domestic policies. The export of peanuts is The Gambia's main source of income.

Ghana

The two major English-speaking states of West Africa are undoubtedly Ghana and Nigeria. Both countries have been in the news often over the years. In 1957 Ghana was the first British African colony to gain independence.

Ghana can be divided broadly into three regions: the hot, dry, open country of the north; the Ashanti forestland; and the coastal plain of the south. Accra is the capital. There is a new port at Tema, a few miles away from Accra. Kumasi is the center for the Ashanti people, whose kingdom was defeated by the British at the beginning of the 20th century. There are many schools and universities in the country. The largest is the University of Ghana in Accra.

Nigeria

Nigeria is the most populous country in Africa. Its chief city, Lagos, the longtime capital, is the acting capital while a new national capital is being built at Abuja. Ibadan, the second-largest city, is the home

Benin bronze sculpture has become world-famous. This 17th- or 18th-century piece shows a queen and her attendants. Brooklyn Museum, Brooklyn, New York.

An Oshogbo artist painting an expressive mural in western Nigeria.

Students come from a lecture in University of Ibadan, Nigeria.

of the University of Ibadan. Nigeria produces many tropical products, palm oil, cacao, rubber, and timber. There are also quantities of coal, tin, and now, most important of all, large yields of oil. Nigeria suffered greatly from slave trading. It was the center of a trade in palm products with the European merchants of the 19th century.

It is the composition of its people that partly explains the root causes of the civil war that ravaged the country in the late 1960's. Not only is Nigeria a large country, but its people form quite different ethnic communities. Many of these were enemies in the past. It was only for administrative convenience that Britain brought them together in 1914 and created a Nigeria that had never previously existed. It was found necessary to establish a federation of regions with local powers for these different communities. The main groups were the Hausa and Fulani of the north, almost all of whom are Muslim; the Yoruba of the southwest, with mixed religions; and the Ibo of the east, many of whom are Christian, mostly Catholic.

When Nigeria became independent in 1960 the federation was preserved, with Nnamdi Azikiwe, the father of Nigerian nationalism and an Ibo, as governor-general and then president. In 1967 a civil war began when the eastern region seceded and formed the state of Biafra. The war ended in 1970 with the eastern region again becoming an integral part of Nigeria. In the years since, its economy has been Nigeria's main concern. The failure of Nigerian political leaders to solve economic problems has led to a series of military takeovers of the government.

AFRICA TODAY

By the mid-1980's almost all of Africa had gained its independence. But independence has brought is own problems to the continent. These can be broadly divided into two categories—the political, or the idea of national consciousness; and the economic, or the problem of poverty.

National Consciousness

Throughout the continent, separate and different ethnic communities were brought together by the colonial powers and administered as single national units. The African nationalist who aimed to overthrow colonial rule had to accept these units or face chaos throughout Africa. So long as the alien rulers survived it was usually easy for such movements to unite their various followers in a single-minded effort.

But after independence the task of maintaining unity became much more difficult. The new government leaders had to try to create a national consciousness that would rise above all other loyalties. At the same time they were left with the legacy of colonial rule. There were social and political institutions that were based upon the European rather than the African experience.

African leaders had to try to combine what was useful in these institutions with African traditions. They had to create an organization capable of providing the modern standards of life their people needed and demanded. This necessity for organization led in some instances to the creation of the single-party state. Those who favor the single-party state claim that it brings about a unity essential for economic development and true national well-being.

The control room of an iron ore processing plant in Liberia.

But single-party states have their dangers, too, especially when they establish permanent ruling groups who use political office for personal gain. Often these groups cannot be removed without violence.

In the early 1990s, however, Africa experienced a wave of political change greater than any since the early 1960s, when many of its nations gained independence from colonial rule. In country after country, popular protests sparked in part by declining standards of living led to the introduction of democratic reforms. In most cases, countries underwent orderly transitions from one-party to multi-party systems culminating in free elections. In others, the overthrow of dictatorial leaders was followed by bloody civil wars. Some of Africa's long-time leaders still clung stubbornly to power, but the end of the Cold War meant that foreign aid donors often were no longer willing to intervene to prop up their unpopular regimes. While the transition to democracy will be difficult in many countries, the continent has large numbers of well-educated citizens prepared to guide their nations in this new era.

Poverty

The second problem facing independent Africa is that of poverty. In many countries, the standard of living actually declined during the 1980s due to rising debt, recurrent drought, economic mismanagement, and falling world prices for agricultural and mineral exports. The continent's total debt burden increased from $140 billion in 1982 to $272 billion in 1990—the equivalent of 90 percent of the continent's gross domestic product, nearly double that of Latin America. The cost of servicing this debt alone consumed 30 percent of all export earnings. There are growing demands that lenders reduce the debts owed by the poorest African countries to free funds for the economic and social development that will enable them to break out of the cycle of poverty.

The vast majority of Africans still live in villages and other rural communities and make their living from the soil. But agricultural production has not kept pace with population growth. In 1950, subsaharan Africa had 200 million less people than did Europe. By 1991, it had 56 million more, and its population was expected to grow from more than 558 million in 1991 to nearly 1.3 billion by 2020. Tragically, some scientists believe that the impact of the AIDS epidemic will drastically reduce population growth in Africa after the year 2000.

Increasingly, investment is being concentrated in the long-neglected agricultural sector. It has been suggested that intensive industrialization could solve many of Africa's economic problems. There is little likelihood of mass industrialization in the near future because there are hardly any savings to invest in industrial projects. Thus, much of what little industrial investment is taking place in Africa comes from outside the continent. Africans have often resented foreign ownership of economic activities, but today many countries are actively courting foreign investors. They have also formed regional common markets and created an African Development Bank to try to solve some of their economic problems.

Despite its problems, Africa has made great advances in education, health, and social services since the 1960s. Today its people are winning political and economic reforms that they hope will better their lives.

JOHN HATCH, Author, *Africa Today and Tomorrow; Everyman's Africa; A History of Post War Africa; Nigeria: The Seeds of Disaster*

SAHARA

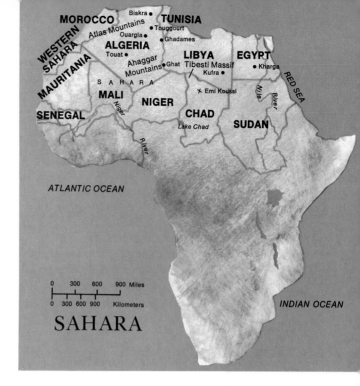

SAHARA

For hundreds of years men have told of the bleakness of the Sahara, the greatest of deserts. They have spoken of the endless shifting sands stretching as far as the eye can see. The Sahara was called El Khela—"the emptiness"—a flat, waterless wasteland known only to a few caravan leaders. The desert, they said, was virtually devoid of life.

Yet the Sahara has not always been a wasteland. Once the desert was a vast fertile region. Its huge area supported lush vegetation, and a variety of animals roamed over the land. Streams rising high in mountain crevices swelled into rivers capable of watering numerous acres. In these rivers many kinds of life existed. Archeological findings of plant and animal fossils and human artifacts, such as fishhooks, prove that the Sahara once bloomed.

Over millions of years the forces of nature worked on the land, crumbling high mountains and pounding rocks into grains of sand. Moisture-laden winds shifted course, and the area grew drier and drier. Flowing rivers disappeared; their dried up courses, called wadis (oueds), can be found throughout the desert today. Still, there has always been life in the desert. Oases, evidence of the Sahara's fertile past, thrive as agricultural and trading centers. And beneath the dry topsoil, underground rivers continue to flow. Some scientists believe that if this resource could be adequately tapped it could enable large numbers of people to live where there is now only enough water for a few.

The Land

The Sahara is the largest desert in the world. It covers 3,500,000 square miles (7,100,000 square kilometers), about one third of Africa, and extends across the northern part of the continent from the Atlantic Ocean to the Red Sea. The Sahara is bounded on the north by the Atlas Mountains of Algeria, Tunisia, and Morocco. The desert extends eastward into Egypt, and includes parts of Mauritania, Mali, Algeria, Morocco, Tunisia, Libya, Niger, Chad, Senegal, Sudan, and Western Sahara.

The most overwhelming feature of the desert is sand. Yet only about 10 to 20 percent of the Sahara is actually sand. The desert has three characteristic landforms: ergs, regs, and hammadas. Great expanses of sand, with magnificent dunes, are called ergs. The whiteness of these sandy reaches merges suddenly with the purple blackness of the regs—gravel-covered plains. Then there are rocky plateaus and platforms called hammadas. Far from being a land of monotony, the Sahara is a constant series of contrasts, and the sudden change of topography from sandy or stony plains to rocky plateaus is awesome. There are also towering volcanic mountain ranges. The major Saharan ranges are the Ahaggar (Hoggar) Mountains of Algeria and the Tibesti Massif in Libya and Chad. The Emi Koussi volcano in the Tibesti range in Chad reaches 11,204 feet (3,415 meters), the highest point in the desert. Adjacent to some of these mountains are great hollowed-out places. Many of these are filled with salt water, creating lakes such as the Chott Melrhir in Algeria. Some lake surfaces are 60 feet (18 m.) below sea level. The only freshwater lake in the region is Lake Chad, which lies on the borderland of the Sahara.

The Nile and Niger rivers water the fringes of the Sahara, but over the vast expanse of desert only the wadis remain as relics of once important rivers. During the unpredictable rainy seasons, the wadis fill up and for a time become active rivers. Many, like the Oued Igharghar, rise as actual rivers in the foothills of the Ahaggar Mountains and sustain several oases before drying up in the desert sands. Some rivers follow underground courses and re-emerge at intervals, where they again evaporate in the hot sunlight, leaving glistening patches of salt.

Moving from north to south in the Sahara, the temperature rises and the humidity decreases. Temperatures can range from well below freezing on a winter night to the extreme of 130 degrees Fahrenheit (54 de-

In the heat of the day, a camel caravan makes its way across the Sahara.

grees Celsius) on a summer afternoon. Rainfall varies greatly from year to year, averaging less than 10 inches (25 centimeters) annually. In some areas virtually no rain falls for years. Then a tremendous downpour will occur, flooding a wadi. Sometimes caravans of traders and animals using the dry riverbed as a path have been drowned in the sudden flooding.

The People

Thousands of years ago, Negroid tribes from the Sudan region moved northward into the Sahara. Berbers soon followed, and after them the Arabs from the north came into the region. These three groups were the ancestors of the present Saharan population.

No precise population figures are available concerning Saharan peoples. It is estimated that about one third are nomads or seminomads, who travel from place to place seeking out fertile ground for water and food. The remaining two thirds are settled in oases scattered across the desert. Major oases include Kharga in Egypt; Kufra, Ghat, and Ghadames in Libya; Biskra, Touggourt, Ouargla, and Touat in Algeria. Generally, oasis towns are built on rocky hillsides in a fortress-like arrangement called a *ksar*, leaving the more arable land at the bottom available for cultivation.

Among the nomadic and seminomadic peoples, the Teda (Tibu), Tuareg, and the Chaamba stand out. The Teda, in the Tibesti mountains, are the only major group in the Sahara today exhibiting predominantly Negroid characteristics. Of the Berber peoples who once dominated the desert, the Tuareg are the most noted. The Tuareg, who are especially numerous in the Ahaggar, are among the tallest people in the world. At one time they held virtual control of the essential caravan routes across the desert. Among the Arab nomads, the Chaamba are probably the most resourceful. They eke out a living in the central desert, the most forbidding region of the Sahara.

Teda, Berber, and Arabic are the three major language groups. Almost the entire desert population is Muslim, although there are settled groups of Jews and Arab Christians.

Economy

Date palms, cereal grains, and some vegetables are the most widely cultivated oasis crops. Water is drawn up through underground channels called *foggaras*. These were introduced into the desert some 2,000 years ago, and some time later, the camel, used widely for transportation, was brought into the Sahara. Romans, Arabs, and later the French, British, and Germans have all explored and traded across the Sahara. Two 19th-century explorers, René Caillié, a Frenchman, and Heinrich Barth, a German, contributed much to the knowledge of the Sahara in recent times. Plans for a trans-Saharan railroad have existed for more than 100 years, but to date only the northern part is completed. However, many parts of the desert can now be reached by airplane.

Although agriculture, local trading, and herding have been the basis of the desert economy, explorations since the late 1950's have unearthed important deposits of oil, gas, iron, copper, and manganese. These resources indicate that an ancient land long considered barren has a future of promise.

Reviewed by HENRY J. WARMAN, School of Geography, Clark University

CANARY ISLANDS

Although they were visited by Egyptian, Phoenician, Greek, and Roman sailors during ancient times, the Canary Islands remained a region of mystery because they were so far from the civilized world. Some accounts said the islands were all that was left of the sunken continent of Atlantis, thought to have been in the same area. The Romans called the Canaries Canariae Insulae, or "islands of the dogs," after the large dogs they found. The islands were also known as Fortunatae Insulae or "islands of the fortunate." Later, the islands gave their name to canaries, the yellow songbirds that were discovered there and are now found all over the world.

The Canary Islands are a group of Spanish islands set in the Atlantic Ocean off the northwest coast of Africa. They are about 70 miles (110 kilometers) west of Morocco, and 680 miles (1,100 km.) southwest of Spain. The islands are divided into two provinces. The province of Santa Cruz de Tenerife consists of the islands of Tenerife, Gomera, La Palma, and Hierro. The province of Las Palmas includes Grand Canary, Fuerteventura, and Lanzarote islands, plus six tiny islets. The largest cities are Santa Cruz de Tenerife and Las Palmas.

The city and busy harbor of Las Palmas, capital of Las Palmas Province.

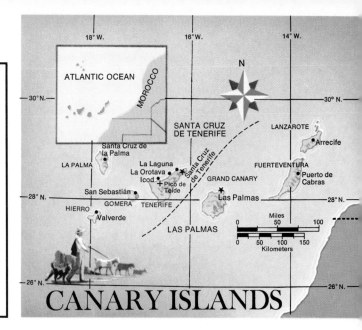

CANARY ISLANDS

FACTS AND FIGURES

THE PEOPLE—are called Canarians.

CAPITAL: Las Palmas, Santa Cruz de Tenerife.

LOCATION: Atlantic Ocean off northwest Africa.

AREA: 2,900 sq. mi. (7,511 sq. km.).

PHYSICAL FEATURES: Highest point—Pico de Teide (12,200 ft.; 3,720 m.). **Lowest point**—sea level.

POPULATION: 1,495,000 (latest estimate).

MAJOR LANGUAGE: Spanish.

MAJOR RELIGION: Roman Catholicism.

GOVERNMENT: Autonomous overseas region of Spain represented in the Spanish legislature.

CHIEF CITIES: Las Palmas, Santa Cruz de Tenerife.

ECONOMY: Chief minerals—pumice, sulfur. **Chief agricultural products**—bananas, sugarcane, citrus fruits, potatoes, tobacco. **Industries and products**—tourism, salted and dried fish. **Chief exports**—fruits, fish, vegetables. **Chief imports**—machinery, consumer goods.

MONETARY UNIT: 1 Spanish peseta = 100 céntimos.

Because they lie north of the tropics and are exposed to warm trade winds, large parts of the Canary Islands have an extremely pleasant climate. But desert conditions prevail in the regions that face the hot, dry African winds. Away from the coast, the land rises sharply to areas of temperate climate and volcanoes. Pico de Teide, on Tenerife, is the highest mountain in Spanish territory and reaches 12,200 feet (3,720 meters) into the sky.

The People

Most of the people of the islands are farmers. Near the sea and wherever else there is enough water, bananas are the most important crop, but other fruits and sugarcane are also grown. In the regions slightly above sea level, citrus fruits and vegetables are raised. High in the mountains, livestock graze. Where water is plentiful, farming in the Canary Islands is not difficult, because the volcanic soil is very fertile. The ocean around the islands is full of fish, which provide food for the islanders. Salted and dried fish is a major export.

A growing number of islanders who used to be farmers or fishermen are now employed in the tourist and shipping industries. The Canaries have been the crossroads of the Atlantic since Columbus stopped there on one of his voyages to the Americas.

Most tourists come to the islands during the winter and spring months. In the spring, during the Corpus Christi celebration, the famous flower festivals are held on Grand Canary and Tenerife. Intricate designs of brightly colored flower petals are created and hung in front of houses and public buildings. In the evenings, most of the people turn out to admire the arrangements and to try to decide which of the various floral arrangements is the best.

History

Egyptian, Phoenician, Greek, and Roman sailors made many voyages to the Canary Islands, but the islands were unknown to most of the people of the ancient world. After the fall of the Roman Empire in A.D. 476, very few ships visited the Canaries. For many centuries after that, contact between the Canary Islands and the outside world was for all practical purposes cut off. Near the end of the 10th century Arab merchants landed on Grand Canary and traded with the inhabitants. During the 13th and 14th centuries Portuguese and French navigators came to the islands. However, they never established permanent settlements there. In the early 15th century Jean de Béthencourt, a Norman in the service of the King of Castile, arrived on the islands. He found them inhabited by a people called Guanches. The Guanches, who originally came from North Africa, resisted the Europeans but were eventually overpowered. Many of the Normans, and the Spaniards who followed, enjoyed the climate and the beauty of the islands so much that they stayed. Today, common family names like Béthencourt and Bétancour show the islanders' heritage.

Spain had firm control of the islands by the end of the 15th century and defeated several attempts by other countries to capture them. In 1797 the famous English admiral, Lord Nelson, lost an arm during an attack on the islands. In 1927 the Spanish Government divided the Canary Islands into two provinces, each of which is represented in Spain's legislature, the Cortes. In 1936 Francisco Franco launched the nationalist rebellion against the Spanish republic from the Canary Islands.

Reviewed by ALBERTO FERNÁNDEZ GALAR, Governor, Las Palmas, Canary Islands

The saltworks on Lanzarote, where seawater is used to make salt.

The Rif mountains tower over surrounding fields.

MOROCCO

Most afternoons at approximately 4 o'clock, in the open square of Marrakesh, a performance takes place—a wonderful performance that excites a large audience of children and adults. While old men sit and children run and laugh, jugglers, snake charmers, and acrobats on various kinds of wheels and balance beams perform great feats. Dancers passing through from Mauritania, or from Black Africa farther south, swing their bodies in graceful rhythm. Trained animals perform for the crowd's approval. Moroccans, true to their Berber and Arab ancestors, carefully appraise a fine horse or camel. The square in this old Moroccan city of Marrakesh never leaves the memory.

Narrow streets lead from the square past stalls where craftsmen pound their metals, making beautiful geometric designs. Wool dyers are on another street, where pots of brewing dyes produce bright colored lengths of wool. Ropes stretched across the street serve as drying lines. The craftsmen and dyers joke as they labor, scarcely noticing the rare beauty of their work.

A few miles from the excitement of Marrakesh, in a meadow of the Atlas Mountains, a boy stands tending his sheep. He is all alone, far

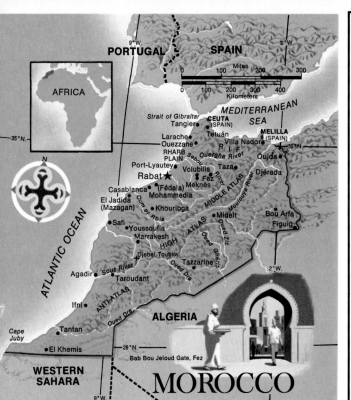

FACTS AND FIGURES

KINGDOM OF MOROCCO—El Mamlaka el Maghribiya —is the official name of the country.

THE PEOPLE—are called Moroccans.

CAPITAL Rabat.

LOCATION: Northwest Africa. **Boundaries**—Spain, Mediterranean Sea, Algeria, Western Sahara, Atlantic Ocean.

AREA: 157,992 sq. mi. (409,200 sq. km.).

PHYSICAL FEATURES: Highest point—Djebel Toubkal (13,665 ft.; 4,165 m.). **Lowest point**—sea level. **Chief rivers**—Moulouya, Sebou, Oum er Rbia.

POPULATION: 22,000,000 (1982 census); 22,889,000 (latest estimate).

MAJOR LANGUAGES: Arabic (official), Berber, French.

MAJOR RELIGIONS: Islam (official), Roman Catholicism, Judaism.

GOVERNMENT: Constitutional monarchy. **Head of state** —king. **Head of government**—prime minister. **Legislature**—one-house parliament (Majlis).

CHIEF CITIES: Casablanca (3,500,000), Rabat (900,000), Marrakesh (436,000).

ECONOMY: Chief minerals—phosphates, coal, iron, copper, lead, zinc, cobalt, manganese. **Chief agricultural products**—barley, wheat, citrus fruits, tomatoes, sugar beets, potatoes, olives, dates, cattle. **Industries and products**—food processing, fishing, chemicals, fertilizers, textiles. **Chief exports**—phosphates, citrus fruits, tomatoes, canned fish, textiles, carpets. **Chief imports**—petroleum, foodstuffs, machinery, consumer goods, iron and steel.

MONETARY UNIT: 1 dirham = 100 Moroccan francs.

from any other person or shelter. This Berber shepherd traces his ancestry back to one of the first known peoples to settle in the land. He, too, is part of the colorful and ancient country of Morocco.

THE LAND

The Kingdom of Morocco lies in the northwestern corner of Africa. Its neighboring countries are Algeria on the east and southeast and Western Sahara on the southwest. Of all the African countries Morocco is closest to Europe. Just across the Strait of Gibraltar, no more than 9 miles (14 kilometers) away, is Spain.

The Kingdom of Morocco, farthest west of all the Arab countries, is known in Arabic as El Mamlaka el Maghribiya, which means "kingdom of the west." With seacoasts on both the Atlantic Ocean and the Mediterranean Sea, Morocco has a wide range of landscapes. There are plains, plateaus, mountains, and desert. The Atlas Mountains run roughly parallel to Morocco's Atlantic coast. Djebel Toubkal, the country's highest peak, reaches over 13,000 feet (4,000 meters). The Rif mountains are located in the north. Morocco's rivers begin in the mountains. They are the Moulouya, Sebou, Oum er Rbia, Dra, Ziz, and Ghéris.

Climate. The climate is as varied as the landscape. Along the Atlantic coast enough rain falls to keep the land fertile. The rain falls more frequently in the middle Atlas and Rif mountain regions. The winters in this area can be very cold. Southern Morocco's Sahara gets less than 4 inches (10 centimeters) of rainfall each year. The desert is extremely hot in the summer but cools off somewhat during the winter months. Morocco's Mediterranean coast has a mild, sunny climate. April through October are generally the dry months in most of Morocco.

Cities. The nation's largest city and chief port is **Casablanca.** This city, with a population of over 3,000,000 is a community of startling contrasts. It has the charm and grace of an old-world Arab community, and the glitter and modernity of the 20th century. The center of the city has white buildings, which rise many stories and are built in the latest architectural styles. Its harbor is one of the largest and best equipped in all Africa. But in sharp contrast to all this are the overcrowded slum quarters where thousands of the poor live.

Rabat, which became the capital of Morocco in 1912, is the nation's second largest city. **Marrakesh,** founded in the 11th century, is the third largest. Other important cities in Morocco include Fez, Meknès, Tangier, Oujda, and Tetuán.

A street in Casablanca shows some of the city's charm and appeal.

The Casbah section of Tangier is famous for its many shops and displays.

Tangier, which lies near the Strait of Gibraltar, is a great tourist center. It has a mild climate and a lovely seacoast. Many writers and artists from many parts of the world make their homes there. Its Casbah, the old section of Tangier and the scene of a number of motion pictures, lies high above the rest of the city. Tourists from all over the world mount the stone steps that lead up into the narrow twisting streets to find themselves in a world of centuries ago.

THE PEOPLE

Historians disagree about the origin of the Berbers. But they do agree that aside from the Stone Age inhabitants of prehistoric times, the Berbers were the first people to settle in Morocco. They stayed on through wars and conquests, rarely giving up their basic beliefs and ways of life. To this day the Berber language does not have any written form.

In the 7th century Arab invaders mixed with the Berbers, but only in the towns. Not until much later, from the 12th to the 15th century, did the Bedouin Arabs bring their language and the Muslim religion to the back country of Morocco. Today Berber children in ever larger numbers attend state schools, where their education tends to make them similar to Arabs in training.

The Berbers are a beautiful people—often tall, sometimes blue-eyed, with a great range of skin coloring due to generations of intermarriage with Mediterraneans, Arabs, and black Africans. The Berbers carry themselves erect. The women easily balance filled baskets on their heads and walk along gracefully, never slowing their pace. Like women throughout the world, they love jewelry. And like women throughout the world, they do their best to make themselves attractive to their men. The Berber women mark their faces with ink or dye, just as Western women use lipstick and face powder.

Most of the people of Morocco are Muslims. Islam is the official religion of the country, but freedom of religion is given to all. The majority of the French and Spanish residents are Roman Catholic. There was at one time a fair-sized Jewish community in Morocco that numbered close to 200,000 inhabitants. Many of them were descendants of Jews who had fled Spain in the 15th century. Others traced their origins back to Berbers who had converted to Judaism. Since 1948, with the establishment of the state of Israel, there has been a steady emigration of Moroccan Jews. Today the remaining Jewish community is a fairly small one.

Berbers take part in the National Folklore Festival held at Marrakesh.

Rabat, the capital city, lies on the Atlantic coast of Morocco.

Move to Cities

The end of World War II in Morocco saw a major movement of people into the cities. They came in search of work and a better life. People left the rural areas with great hopes, little planning, and practically no resources. They came in droves. Casablanca, for example, attracted people for several reasons. The development of the port facilities during the war led to more job openings. New textile and sugar mills, tobacco factories, and food-processing plants; the tourist trade; and an increase in commerce opened up opportunities for newcomers. A huge rural population lived near the city, so the trip was a short one.

But there were not enough jobs for all the people who came. The cities swelled in population and the lack of decent housing became a severe problem. Thousands of jobless and hungry people fought to survive in *bidonvilles,* or shanty towns, where they built shelters of anything they could find. They built huts of wood, heavy cloth, or sheet metal on land they neither owned nor rented. The government tried to meet the crisis. New houses of a simple design were built, and jobs were sought for the unemployed in agriculture and industry. But to this day the problem has by no means been solved.

The range of living conditions in the cities is great, from *bidonvilles* to luxury apartments. Prosperous businessmen and landowners may live in the older sections or in the surrounding areas. The younger middle-class people live in the more modern buildings of the city.

In the countryside and the villages the range of housing is more narrow. Here the houses are usually made of stone or clay. Not all farm workers own their own homes. Many must work for others and find shelter somewhere, often on the land they work. Most herdsmen live in tents, which are generally made of wool or goatskin.

Food

Diet varies according to custom, education, and economic status. Cereals are prepared in a number of ways. A favorite dish is couscous, made of a cereal and served with a hot, tasty sauce that contains meat. Tea with mint is the most popular drink and is usually offered to a visitor as a sign of hospitality. Lamb and chicken make up basic meat dishes for those who can afford it. Fish is cooked in a variety of ways.

Customs

Hospitality is an art practiced in the city and in the small villages scattered along the countryside. In the Muslim world the host feels responsibility for his guest, even to the point of protecting the guest with his own life, if necessary.

Traditionally the Moroccan woman lived a protected and extremely restricted life. She rarely went outdoors, and if she did it was to take care of a family errand or a household chore. Outside she wore a veil and covered herself with a long, flowing cotton robe called a jellaba or with a white sheetlike haik. Today these traditions are changing. The majority of women do go out to stores, mosques, the public baths, and the movies. Young Moroccan women attend school, hold jobs of responsibility, and frequently, in the cities, adopt Western dress. Increasingly, too, the Moroccan woman is protected by law. Polygyny, the institution allowing a man to have more than one wife at the same time, is not encouraged.

Education

No change in Morocco is more striking than that in the field of education. A tremendous growth has taken place in facilities and in the number of students enrolled. On the eve of independence, many of the students in Moroccan schools were Europeans, generally French or Spanish. Today an increasing number of Moroccan boys and girls attend primary and secondary schools. In recent years the enrollment in Moroccan universities has also grown rapidly. The nation's major universities are the University of Rabat and the Islamic Karaouine University, which is located in Fez. Founded in the 9th century, Karaouine University is one of the oldest universities in the world. Moroccans also attend universities in Europe, the Middle East, and the United States.

ECONOMY

Although Morocco's industries are growing rapidly, the country is still primarily agricultural. About three quarters of the population work the land. Some farmers use modern methods and techniques, but many stay with the old habits that once were adequate but today are not very productive. The government is doing its best to teach these farmers better and more effective methods of production. It helps supply them with tools, seed, fertilizers, and credit. But most of all the government is trying to change attitudes—to make the old farmer turn away from the traditional world and step into the modern world of today.

The most fertile regions of the country are the province of Casablanca, the districts surrounding the cities of Meknès and Fez, the Rharb plain area, and the Ouergha Valley. Ninety percent of the cultivated land is planted with cereal crops. Wheat is most widely produced. Barley and corn, too, make up an important fraction of cereal output.

Citrus fruits supply the home market and are exported. Through the years Muslims have kept control of the olive, fig, and almond orchards, while the French have continued to be the major wine producers. Most of the wine and grapes from Morocco's vineyards are sent to France. Sugar beets and truck garden vegetables reach Moroccan tables, but only recently has sugar been refined in the country.

A number of Moroccans are engaged in raising livestock, such as sheep, cattle, donkeys, horses, and mules. For travel and work in the desert, no machine or animal can match the dromedary (a one-humped camel noted for speed). These "desert taxis" are raised and sold for fairly high prices. Wool and hides provide the basic materials for the textile and leather industries of the country.

Industry

Though industry is not as important as agriculture, the mines of Morocco provide jobs for the people, income for the owners, and taxes for the state. Phosphate mines in Kouribga and Youssoufia are known throughout most of Africa. Not much petroleum has yet been found, but a refinery at Mohammedia processes crude oil. Coal, iron, lead, zinc, cobalt, and manganese round out the resources of the growing mineral industry. The government is encouraging the establishment of small industries. Morocco has textile, cement, and paint factories, sugar mills, food-processing plants, and canneries. Tourism has been growing rapidly in the past few years. Morocco's many places of interest, good hotels, and excellent climate attract people from all over the world.

Fishing has become an important industry, giving work to thousands of people. The waters off Morocco's more than 1,000-mile-long (1,600 km.) coast are filled with fish. Large catches of sardine and smaller catches of tuna and mackerel are made every year. Safi, which was once a Portuguese settlement, is one of the world's leading sardine ports. Another important fishing port is Agadir. Fish caught in Safi and Agadir is canned in these communities or shipped to canneries in Casablanca.

HISTORY

There is strong archeological evidence that Morocco was inhabited by cave dwellers of the Stone Age. They left many traces of their presence. Somewhere around 2000 B.C. the Berbers came to the region and settled there. The Phoenicians appeared in the area around the 11th century B.C., when they established a few trading posts on the Mediterranean coast. Later the Carthaginians built trading centers on the Mediterranean and Atlantic coastal areas of Morocco. After a series of historic battles the Carthaginians were finally crushed by the Romans. From the 1st century B.C. until the 5th century A.D. the land was a Roman province. Rome's influence outlived even the Germanic Vandals, who moved through the territory before conquering southern Italy. To

The arches and pillars of Volubilis are relics of a once flourishing city.

this day Roman ruins can still be seen in the north of Morocco. During the 2nd and 3rd centuries A.D. Volubilis, at the foot of the Zerhoun hills, was a flourishing Roman city. But now about all that remains of the former Roman glory are some arches and stone pillars.

In the middle of the 7th century the Muslim Arabs invaded from the east. Few Arabs from this original force stayed in Morocco. But other Arab invasions followed, and in the beginning of the 8th century the Arabs occupied the country. The Berbers kept their identity through all the invasions, but eventually accepted the Muslim religion. However, they did this only after making changes and adaptations that made it fit in with their traditional ways of life. The Berbers then joined forces with the Arabs to conquer parts of Spain, where they first struck in 711. Towards the end of the 8th century Idris I, a descendant of Mohammed, established the first Muslim dynasty of Morocco. His son, Idris II, founded the city of Fez, which became noted as a center of Islamic religion and culture. Today thousands of pilgrims come from all over Morocco to visit the shrine dedicated to the memory of Idris II.

The first great Moroccan empire was founded by the Almoravids in the 11th century. Excellent horsemen and fierce fighters, the Almoravids swept into Morocco from across the desert. They established the capital of their empire at Marrakesh. Almoravid influence reached eastward to Tunisia and north to Spain, binding more tightly the history of Spain and Morocco. But in the centuries that followed Morocco gradually lost its outlying territories. Spain and Portugal invaded the country, built fortified settlements, and occupied several Moroccan ports. In the 16th century the Moroccans were able to gather enough strength to drive out the invaders. From the end of the 17th century until early in the 19th century Morocco kept almost entirely free from foreign influence.

But after the French occupied the city of Algiers in 1830, interest of the imperialist European powers in North Africa quickened. France, Spain, Britain, and later, Germany had ambitions for territory and economic influence. Located just 9 mi. (14 km.) from Gibraltar and controlling the western entry into the Mediterranean, Morocco had great strategic value. The Treaty of Fez in 1912 made the country a protectorate of France. Spain took over the northern part of the country.

During World War II Morocco was very important to the Allied war effort. On November 8, 1942, American soldiers made a historic landing in Morocco. The following year United States President Franklin D. Roosevelt and Britain's Prime Minister Winston Churchill met secretly in Morocco at the Casablanca Conference.

Near the end of the war a strong movement for Moroccan independence came into being. The movement was spearheaded by a group of nationalists who had fervent support from the people of the country. The Istiqlal Party was formed to wage the fight for independence.

In 1953 the French deposed and exiled Sultan Mohammed V for his support of the independence movement. This action brought two years of turbulence and bloodshed to Morocco. Finally in 1955 the French allowed Mohammed V to return. In the following year Morocco gained full independence. In 1957, Mohammed V took the title of king. He ruled until his death in 1961, when he was succeeded by his son Hassan II.

Morocco obtained the international zone of Tangier and most of Spanish Morocco soon after independence. The enclave of Ifni was ceded by Spain in 1969. Spain still maintains two small ports on the Mediterranean coast of Morocco, Ceuta and Melilla.

Recent Events. Spain ceded part of Spanish (now Western) Sahara to Morocco in 1976; Morocco claimed the rest in 1979 when Mauritania gave up its claim to the territory. Western Sahara is also claimed by the Polisario, which seeks independence for the region. (An article on WESTERN SAHARA appears in this volume.) The dispute over Western Sahara led Morocco to withdraw from the Organization of African Unity in 1984. A planned mid-1992 UN-supervised referendum on Western Saharan independence was postponed, and Morocco said it would hold national legislative elections later that year throughout the country, including Western Sahara.

GOVERNMENT

Morocco is a constitutional monarchy. The king is head of state and also exercises great authority over the government, which is headed by a prime minister appointed by the king. The legislature consists of 206 members elected directly by the people and 100 members chosen by an electoral college. The king may dissolve the legislature at will.

RICHARD M. BRACE, Oakland University

Algiers, Algeria's capital, rises above the bay.

ALGERIA

Algeria is filled with monuments of its past and signs of its future. In the village of Djemila the stone arch, temple, and forum of a Roman city still stand, while in Algiers, the capital, huge skyscrapers rise on the hills on which the city is built. In Annaba (formerly Bône) are the remains of the church of the 4th-century Christian leader, Saint Augustine. And deep in the Sahara, oil rigs stand in the sand like candles on a cake.

THE PEOPLE

The earliest known inhabitants of Algeria were Berbers, who had their own language and customs. No one is sure where they came from. Arabs came from the Arabian Peninsula at the end of the 7th century A.D., bringing with them a new language—Arabic—and a new religion—Islam. In 1830 the French began their conquest of Algeria. Today Algeria's population is made up mainly of descendants of Arabs and Berbers. Berbers still live, as they have for centuries, in the mountainous Kabylia region along the coast, in the Aurès mountains farther inland, and in the Mzab oases beyond the mountains. In the Sahara are the Tuareg, a nomadic Berber group. Before Algeria's long war for independence, there were an estimated 1,000,000 Europeans living in Algeria, but the number dropped very sharply after 1962.

Arabic is the official language of the country, and French is widely spoken. About a fifth of the people speak Berber.

Ghardaïa is the chief town of the Mzab oases in the northern Sahara.

Without camels life in the desert would not be possible.

A doorway provides some shade from the fierce noonday sun.

Most Algerians live in the cities and towns along the Mediterranean coast. The rest live inland in villages around oases or in the desert itself. Few have gone far in school although half of the population is under 20. Algeria is a Muslim country. Muslims feel that God's kingdom is here and now. Religion is not just for the mosque or for Friday (the day Muslims gather to pray together), but for every day and every sort of human activity. When a man makes plans, he always adds, "Insha' Lla [If God wills it]." When God does not will it, there is nothing to be done, for after all, everything is in God's hands. The very soul of the country is resigned.

The Family. Among the millions of people in the countryside, and even among some of the millions in the cities, the one social organization that matters is the family. In Algeria the family does not mean just parents and children, but parents' parents and children's children. When the group gets too big for people to keep track of one another and know one another well, it splits into several families. In the countryside, land and work are divided within this large family. Young men marry girls within the group. When parts of the large family move into the cities, they stick together and keep in touch with the family back home. When they travel to France, they send money home to their relatives. Wherever they work, they find jobs for brothers and cousins.

Houses. Along the narrow streets of a traditional Algerian town, whitewashed stone or brick houses open onto shaded inner courtyards. As industry grows and new districts spring up on the outskirts of cities, blocks of small homes built on this same traditional plan appear, along with modern apartment buildings.

In small mountain villages, the simplest kind of one-room dwelling is the *gourbi,* with walls of uncemented stones or of clay mixed with grass. In the Kabylia, houses are built on mountaintops above fig and olive groves. The houses have stone walls and roofs of round, rust-colored tiles. A low wall separates the house into two sections: one section for the family and one for the animals. On the low wall the family stores its supply of wheat in earthenware jars.

Dark-colored tents woven of goat's hair, wool, and grass are the homes of nomads in the Sahara and the High Plateaus of the interior. In oasis villages in the desert each mud-brick home has a courtyard enclosed by a high mud-brick wall. Women do their household tasks in the shelter of the courtyard.

The Role of Women. For Muslim women, the traditional pattern of life meant staying at home and taking care of the household, except for afternoon visits to women relatives. For most women, life still goes on in the old way, but in the cities there are signs of change, particularly among the young. Women go about more freely, shop in department stores, and hold jobs. The change is partly the result of the war for independence, when men were away from home and women took on new responsibilities. The change results also from the spread of education. As more and more young girls receive educations, they think in terms of greater freedom.

Clothing. The traditional dress for women is a long white robe, worn with a short starched veil that hides all but the eyes. Even today in Algiers, less than a third of the women wear Western-style dresses. The traditional garment for men is the *gandoura,* a loose robe of linen or wool. But in the cities most men wear a shirt (usually without a tie), a jacket, and either Western-style or very full trousers. In the Sahara, the Tuareg wear distinctive long blue robes. Their faces are protected from the desert sands by a black veil.

Food. The food of Algeria is highly seasoned with such condiments as pepper, pimiento, cumin, ginger, fennel, anise, coriander, parsley, mint, cinnamon, and cloves. Couscous is the national dish. It is a main course, consisting of large grains of semolina steamed and served with lamb, chicken, or fish, cooked with a variety of vegetables (carrots, onions, green peppers, squash, chick-peas), and seasoned with a hot pimiento sauce.

People enjoy drinking strong black coffee, served in small cups; sweet mint tea from a glass; and *syrop,* a sweet fruit drink.

Education and Culture. Education is free at all levels, with attendance from age 6 to 15 required in principle. After independence great emphasis was placed on teaching and using Arabic in schools that had been French. A major effort is being made to end illiteracy by increasing the number of classrooms and teachers each year.

Algeria has eight institutions of higher learning, two in Algiers, two in Oran, and four in other cities. The leading institution is the University of Algiers, which was founded in 1879.

Among the country's fine libraries are the National Library in Algiers and those of the universities of Algiers, Oran, and Constantine. In Algiers there are museums of prehistory and ethnography, fine arts, and antiquities and Islamic art.

An important literary figure who was born in Algeria and used it

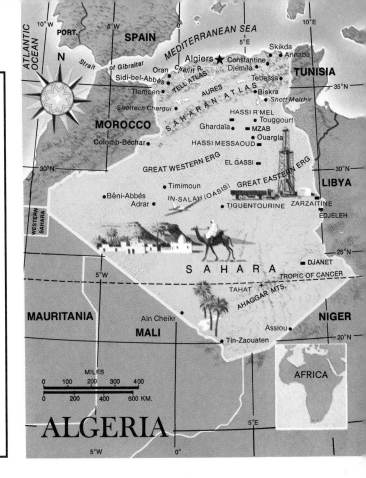

the background for much of his work is the French writer Albert Camus. Camus won the Nobel prize for literature in 1957. Prominent Algerian novelists and playwrights are Kateb Yacine and Mohamed Dib. Frantz Fanon, who lived and wrote in Algeria, is famous as a modern political writer.

THE LAND

Two ranges of the Atlas Mountains—the Tell Atlas and the Saharan Atlas—stretching across Algeria divide the country into three physical regions. Along the coast is a region of fertile farmland, rolling upward to the Tell Atlas. This region is known as the Tell. (*Tell* means "hill" in Arabic.) Grain, vegetables, native cork oak forests, citrus trees first brought by the Phoenicians, olive groves started by the Romans, and vineyards planted by the French all grow there. Between the Tell Atlas and the Saharan Atlas is a region of broad, rather dry, grass-covered plateaus, the High Plateaus. Here wheat and barley are grown, esparto grass is cut, and stock farming, especially sheep farming, is carried on. Throughout the region there are *shotts*, or salt lakes, that dry up in the summer.

South of the High Plateaus is the second line of mountains, the Saharan Atlas, which catches the last moisture in the air. The remaining two thirds of the country is desert, with the Ahaggar Mountains rising in the southeast. Some of the desert is flat, some high, rugged, and rocky. The desert is not all sand dunes and oases. Much of southern Algeria is covered with large rock formations and stony wastelands, rather than fine sand.

The Algerian plateaus, an important grain-growing and stock-raising area.

Minerals. Even in the dry wasteland of the Sahara there are riches for Algeria. It is here that vast deposits of oil and natural gas were found in the 1950's. Hassi Messaoud ("happy spring") is one of the most important oil fields. Others are El Gassi, Edjeleh, Tiguentourine, and Zarzaïtine. Gas is drilled at In Salah and Hassi R'Mel. There are also important deposits of iron ore and phosphates in the Aurès, and iron ore in the western Sahara.

Cities. Most of the big cities are in the heavily populated coastal region. **Algiers,** the largest city as well as the capital, has a population of more than 2,000,000. Whitewashed buildings line the hillsides that rise above the turquoise, semicircular harbor. The city is named for some islands that were once in the harbor. Al-Jezair, the Arabic name of Algiers, means "the islands."

Algiers is a city built on several levels. The waterfront is a bustling, commercial area. Near the waterfront is a famous landmark, the Great Mosque, parts of which may date from the 11th century. Partway up the hillside is an area of arcaded streets, elegant shops, and hotels. Occupying a section of the hillside above it is the Casbah, which was once a fortress. Today the Casbah is filled with people living in crowded quarters, and buying and selling in the hundreds of shops that line the twisting, narrow streets. Algerian handicrafts—brass and copper trays

The city of Constantine is built on a rock high above a plain.

and bright rugs made in Tlemcen—can be found in Casbah shops. Higher still on the hillside is a section of luxurious villas.

Oran, the second largest city, is a seaport and industrial center. **Constantine** is the largest inland city. About 50 miles (80 kilometers) to the northeast is its Mediterranean port, **Skikda** (formerly Philippeville). **Annaba** is also an important port and industrial city.

ECONOMY

Jobs are hard to find in Algeria. That is why over 500,000 Algerians work in France today. Something like a third of the Algerians are without work or hold small, part-time jobs. How can Algerians be so poor while their country looks so rich—with its cities, oil wells, and farms? The answer lies in the recent history of the country.

The Algerians often stated that they did not want to drive out the French settlers, but simply to restore the rights of the Algerian nation. However, the settlers were not sure, and when independence came, they fled on their own. Behind them they left their apartments and office buildings and their vast farms. They also left their industrial plants. (Algeria's main industries are the processing of food products—wine making, flour milling, fish canning; metalworking—assembling cars and trucks; building and construction; manufacturing leather goods;

and making paper from esparto grass.) However, some of the settlers stayed with the oil wells as technicians.

Naturally, the Algerians moved into the vacant properties, and as they continued to move in, the settlers continued to move out, until only about 100,000 of the former 1 million Frenchmen were left. But what were the Algerians to do with the factories and farms? There were few Algerian businessmen and few Algerians trained in running large farms. So the Algerian state, rather than individual Algerians, took over the French property, nationalizing it in the name of the Algerian people.

Management Committees. In the nationalized factories and farms, management committees of the workers were set up to run the businesses. In some cases, the farms and factories were well run. But in others, the workers had no idea of how to keep the business going. Worse yet, the state had no idea of how to sell the products abroad. As a result, the economy slowed down. Corruption became widespread, foreign debt increased, and a country once nearly self-sufficient in agricultural production became increasingly reliant on food imports.

The Modern Economy. Most Algerian farmers still till their own little plots of poor land as they have always done. (The best land is in the self-managed sector.) As it became harder and harder to make a living, many of the farmers moved into the city, but there was no work for them there either. Income from oil, which had financed much of Algeria's post-independence economic growth, declined dramatically in the mid-1980s. So did Algeria's export earnings. There was no money to invest in housing, schools, medical care, or agriculture, or to buy the raw materials needed to keep Algeria's factories running. By 1992 unemployment was estimated to be 30 percent, fueling social tensions.

The country's economic decline is not irreversible. Algeria has valuable mineral deposits and an already developed industrial base, and the government is modifying some of its socialist economic policies in an effort to stimulate economic growth and defuse popular discontent.

Orange groves flourish in the fertile farmland along the coast.

Ruins at Djemila are a reminder of the centuries of Roman rule.

HISTORY

The earliest known inhabitants of Algeria were the Berbers, a nomadic people of North Africa. Late in the 9th century B.C. the Phoenicians founded the state of Carthage in neighboring Tunisia and for centuries spread their rule along the Algerian coast. After the Romans defeated Carthage in 146 B.C., they moved in on the local Berbers and made the region one of the farmlands that fed the Roman Empire. After several centuries of Roman rule, the Vandals came through from Spain (in A.D. 429), and Roman rule was shaken. A century later the Byzantine Empire conquered the Vandals. In the late 7th century, the Arabs began their conquest, converting the Berbers to Islam, and introducing the Arabic language. In the 11th and 12th centuries, Muslim Berber dynasties from neighboring Morocco swept across the country, giving way briefly in the 13th century to an independent Algerian dynasty.

Early in the 16th century the Spanish occupied the most important Algerian ports. Algiers sought the help of the Barbarossa brothers in clearing the Spanish out of its harbor. (The Barbarossas were Barbary pirates who had allied themselves with the Turks.) But once the harbor was cleared, the brothers took control of the area for the Turks. Thus began 3 centuries of Ottoman Turkish rule. In 1830 the French came and, moving inland bit by bit, overcame Berber resistance, conquered the Tuareg of the Sahara, and united the country under one rule. Algeria became part of France.

The Revolution. In the course of the past century, the French, as well as Spaniards and people from other European countries, settled in Algeria. They took over a third of all the arable land and had financial help from Europe. These settlers lived as a country within a country. They governed their own affairs and the Algerians' as well.

For many years, since Algeria was legally part of France and not a colony, the Algerians asked to be treated like Frenchmen, with equal rights and opportunities. But there were 10 Algerians for every settler, so the settlers pressured Paris into keeping the laws as they were.

On November 1, 1954, an organization known as the National Liberation Front (FLN) launched the struggle for independence. French troops were unable to put down the rebellion, but France did not negotiate with the rebels until 1960, after General Charles de Gaulle had come to power as president of the French Fifth Republic. In March 1962, a cease-fire agreement was signed at Evian-les-Bains, France. In April the Secret Army Organization (OAS), made up of French soldiers and settlers opposed to Algerian independence, staged a revolt against de Gaulle's policies and began a campaign of terrorism against Muslims. The OAS campaign lost strength, however, and on July 1, 1962, a referendum in Algeria supported independence. On July 3, de Gaulle proclaimed the country independent.

Since Independence. In 1962 many groups were struggling to take charge of the new state. One leader, Ahmed Ben Bella, was able to bring these groups together. He was elected president of the country in 1963. In that same year, a constitution was approved. It provided for a president to be elected for a five-year term and for a single legislative body, the National Assembly. In 1964 Ben Bella was elected secretary-general of the FLN, the country's one political party.

In 1965 the Army overthrew Ben Bella, and Colonel Houari Boumedienne took over, placing the government in the hands of a 26-member Council of the Revolution. Boumedienne's main goal was to set up solid state institutions to replace the one-man rule of Ben Bella. In 1967 elections with a choice of candidates were held for the first time for local councils. In 1969 the same system was used to elect provincial councils. In 1976 a new constitution was adopted under which the president was designated head of state and the National Assembly was revived. Boumedienne, the only candidate, was elected president. After Boumedienne's death in December 1978, the constitution was amended to require the president to appoint a prime minister. In 1990, in the first multiparty elections since independence, the Islamic Salvation Front (FIS) won a majority of seats on municipal and provincial councils.

In December 1991, the FIS also won a majority in the first round of national parliamentary elections, but many secular Algerians opposed the FIS's goal of creating a fundamentalist regime based on Islamic law. Chadli Bendjedid, Boumedienne's successor, resigned as president in January and the military took control. The second round of legislative elections was cancelled, and a newly-created State Council made up of civilian and military leaders assumed presidential functions. The courts outlawed the FIS in March, but the economic problems that had contributed to its rise in power remained unresolved.

I. WILLIAM ZARTMAN, New York University
Author, *Government and Politics in Northern Africa*

The beach resort of Hammamet, on Tunisia's east coast.

TUNISIA

Tunisia's long ribbon of sunbathed Mediterranean coastline is a tourist's dream. Rocky capes and sandy beaches, deserted for the most part, are sprinkled with hospitable villages and towns.

Tunisia is in North Africa, facing both Europe and the Middle East. (Sicily is just 86 miles—138 kilometers—away.) For over 3,000 years Tunisia's shores have acted as a magnet to Europeans and Middle Easterners, travelers and invaders.

Today Tunis, the capital city, reflects this meeting of Western and Eastern civilization. A visitor who walks from the modern port up the main boulevard, in the shade of ficus trees, may almost think he is in a French town. Dusk is falling, and the whole city is in movement. The sidewalk cafés are crowded with people sipping drinks. Along the avenue strollers stop to greet their friends. The street is jammed with traffic—hand-drawn carts as well as French cars—and it is impossible to find a free taxi.

Yet the setting is not quite France. A young street vendor urges a string of sweet jasmine on the visitor. A woman enveloped in a white robe, her face hidden behind a white veil, walks beside her miniskirted

The Cathedral of Tunis faces a shaded square in the busy center of the city.

daughter. Workmen wearing red chechias (brimless caps) pass by, and now and then the visitor sees a man dressed in a *jebba* (loose robe) rather than Western clothes.

At the end of the boulevard, past shops and the big, brown Cathedral of Tunis, is a small square. The street leads on, but now it is too narrow for cars, and the city changes. This is the medina, or old quarter. The visitor threads his way through a maze of alleys, crowded with people and donkeys, into the covered souks (markets). Here shopkeepers sell everything from radios and Western clothes to Oriental rugs and *babbouches* (Tunisian footwear). Past the souks the way winds up to the Grand Mosque of Zitouna ("olive tree"), first built in the 9th century. Five times each day from the mosque, the muezzin, or crier, calls Muslims to prayer. Now the cry of the muezzin floats on the evening air as it has since the Middle Ages.

THE PEOPLE

Long before the first Asian and European seamen reached the shores of present-day Tunisia, there were people living in the interior of the country. These early inhabitants, who moved with their flocks in search of pasture, were Berbers. Historians know that Berbers lived throughout North Africa, but no one is sure of their origins. The Berbers had their own religious beliefs and their own language, which belongs to the

Hamitic group of languages of northeast Africa. Berber is unwritten, except among the Tuareg of the Sahara.

Arabs invaded North Africa in the 7th and 8th centuries and brought with them the Arabic language and Muslim religion. From 1881 until independence in 1956, the French occupied Tunisia. Their cultural influence on the country is second only to Arab influence in importance. Tunisia's population is made up mostly of descendants of Arabs and Berbers. Almost all Tunisians are Muslims. Arabic is the official language, and French is widely spoken. Today in Tunisia, unlike neighboring Morocco or Algeria, only a tiny fraction of the people speak Berber.

A New Need . . . the Need for Dignity. After Habib Bourguiba became Tunisia's first president in 1957, he directed all his efforts toward bringing the country into the modern world. Political independence, he felt, was not enough. In a speech in 1961, the President said, "A new need must be taught people: the need for dignity. . . . It is necessary that our Tunisian compatriot feel the need to improve his living standards by work, that he aspire to dress better, to eat better, to look after his family decently, to educate his children, to look after his health, in a word to live honorably as advanced people do."

To become a modern nation, the President felt it was necessary to knit together a community of modern people. Yet tremendous problems stand in the way. Tunisia is a poor country and the majority of people live in the most extreme poverty. The government is trying to encourage family planning in order eventually to cut down the enormous birthrate. But right now it is all Tunisia can do to stimulate enough economic growth to keep it up with the annual population increase of approximately 2.5 percent.

Huge amounts are being spent on education to ensure that almost every Tunisian child will soon be in school. Yet about half of the population remains unable to read and write. These people are exposed to many of the elements of modern life—transistor radios, pinball machines, soft drinks, and teeming cities. About half of the population now lives in urban localities. But many people, even though they have an idea of modern life, feel there is nothing they can do to change their own chances in life. They believe their fate is in the hands of Allah.

The Battle Against Underdevelopment. Bourguiba called the attack on these problems the "battle against underdevelopment." In Tunisia there is a small group of Western-educated technicians who are at home in their adopted French culture and in their traditional culture as well. This group is in agreement on the need to modernize the country. As a result, Bourguiba was able to undertake striking reforms in areas that no one ever thought could be changed.

Important steps have been taken to liberate women. Muslim law allows a man to have as many as four wives. But in Tunisia it is now illegal for a man to have more than one wife. Traditional Islamic family law has been greatly changed. A father no longer has absolute power over his daughter, for example, and a woman cannot be married to a man unless she consents. Bourguiba encouraged women to discard the veil, which he called a "dust rag," for Western dress. Women are being educated, and they have the right to work and to vote.

Bourguiba also attacked the practice of fasting during the daylight hours in the Muslim month of Ramadan. The fast is one of the obligations of devout Muslims, but Bourguiba called it economically wasteful. He said that people who fast cannot put in a full day's work. Economic problems and a rising tide of Islamic fundamentalism throughout the Arab world led to antigovernment protests and the retirement of Bourguiba in 1987. Since that time the government has tried to be more responsive to Muslim concerns.

Education and Culture. The goal of the Tunisian Government is to provide free primary schooling for all Tunisians of school age. Primary-school enrollment has increased rapidly since independence. Throughout the country, there is a unified program of instruction for primary, intermediate, and secondary schools. At the primary level, the emphasis is on the Arabic language and on Arab culture, while in more-advanced grades, French is still commonly used as a language of instruction.

Tunisia's first modern institution of higher learning, the University of Tunis, was recreated in 1960. It has over 20,000 students. The Pasteur Institute, established in Tunis in 1893, is a major center of scientific research. Outstanding museums are Le Bardo Museum in Tunis, which is world-famous for its collection of Roman mosaics, and the museum in Sousse, which has treasures dating from the 6th century B.C.

In present-day Tunisia, painting is one of the most highly developed of all art forms. The painters, who belong to a group called the School of Tunis, show their works all over the world. Zoubeir Turki and Abdelaziz Gorgi are two well-known Tunisian painters.

Houses. Throughout the country, one-story houses of whitewashed stone, with blue or green doors and window frames, are a cool shelter from the dazzling sun. Houses have either flat roofs, which can serve as outdoor sitting rooms in the evening, or vaulted roofs. These are often covered with rust-colored tiles. The art of mosaic has flourished in Tunisia since the 1st century, and the interiors of many homes are decorated with blue-and-yellow mosaic tiles.

In the countryside the simplest home is a one-room dwelling, usually made of stones plastered with mud and whitewashed. Inside the house, large pottery urns hold oil and wheat.

Food. In Tunisia, as in Algeria and Morocco, couscous is the most popular main dish. It is made from grains of semolina cooked in the steam of a flavorful vegetable stew. The grains are heaped on a platter and surrounded by pieces of cooked meat, usually lamb or beef.

Sweetened couscous, called *mesfouf,* mixed with raisins and pomegranates or dates, is served as a dessert. Tunisia is famous for its fruits—pomegranates, dates, apricots, peaches, plums, pears, apples, grapes, and oranges. The dates known as *deglet en nour* ("date of the light") are especially prized. The date palm also yields a liquid that is made into a distilled drink called *legmi.* With meals, *Iban* (skim milk) is popular.

THE LAND

Tunisia is the smallest of the three countries—Tunisia, Algeria, and Morocco—that make up a region called the Maghreb. In Arabic the word means "west." The region is the western part of the Arab world.

From Algeria the Atlas Mountains extend eastward into Tunisia. The chain, called the Dorsale, runs southwest to northeast across the northern part of the country. North of the mountains is the Tell, a fertile region with plentiful rainfall. This is a wheat- and barley-growing area.

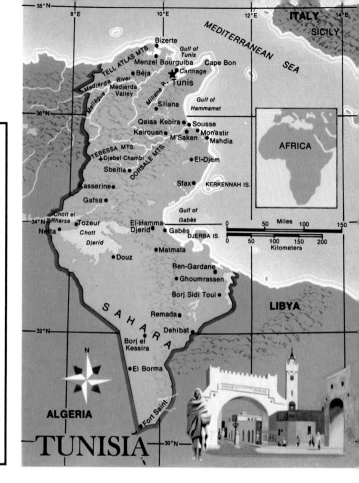

The steppes, a zone of grassy highlands, lie south of the mountains. Here seminomadic herders pasture their sheep and goats.

The Sahara occupies the country south of the Chott Djerid, a large salt lake. In the oases of the desert there are large groves of date palms. Fruits and vegetables grow in the shade of the palms. In the 1st century Pliny the Elder, the Roman historian, described Tunisia's oasis gardens: "There under a tall palm tree the olive tree hides, under the olive tree the fig tree, under the fig tree the pomegranate, and under the pomegranate, the vine; under the vine, wheat is sown, then vegetables and at last pot-herbs, all in the same year; and all these varieties grow in the shade of the other."

Along the eastern coast is a region of plains called the Sahel. Olive trees, grape vines, citrus trees, and almond trees are all cultivated here.

Resources. Tunisia has been developing its natural resources. Oil is found in the south at El Borma (near the Libyan-Algerian border), in the Gulf of Gabès, and at other sites. Phosphates are another important source of mineral wealth, and there are also deposits of iron ore, zinc, and lead. In the north, in the Cape Bon area, there is a small deposit of natural gas. The main forest resource is cork, from the cork oak forests of the northwest.

Cities. The port of **Tunis** is both the capital of Tunisia and the largest city. **Sfax** and **Sousse,** in the olive-growing region on the east coast, are major ports for the shipment of olive oil. **Bizerte,** for many years a naval base for the French, is an iron-ore port and fishing center.

Kairouan, the fourth holy city of Islam, after Mecca, Medina, and Jerusalem.

A number of towns in Tunisia tell the story of the country's great past. Just 9 miles (14 km.) out of Tunis by rickety commuter train is the fashionable suburb of **Carthage**. Under the superb villas of high-ranking Tunisian officials and foreign diplomats, there is little left of the city destroyed by the Romans in 146 B.C. The visitor can see Punic (Carthaginian) graves and the ruins of Roman baths. By the sea there is an amphitheater where plays are staged on warm summer nights.

Kairouan is a holy city founded in the central steppes about 670. A major attraction in Kairouan is the Great Mosque completed in the 9th century. The city is also a center for the weaving of carpets. In El-Djem are the remains of a 3rd-century Roman amphitheater that seated 30,000 people.

A number of oases, including Gabès, Tozeur, Nefta, and Djerba, offer tourists a unique combination of calm and beauty. Djerba is an island, said to be Homer's Isle of the Lotus-Eaters.

ECONOMY

An important industry is the mining of phosphates in the south. There is also some mining of iron ore, zinc, and lead. Phosphates are processed into high-grade fertilizer, mostly for export, and chemical industries are developing. There is some light manufacturing, mainly in textiles and foods. The foods produced include olive oil, wine, flour, canned vegetables and fruits, and sugar (refined from imported raw sugar and from sugar beets).

There is little heavy industry apart from a small steel mill. In Bizerte there is an oil refinery. The fishing industry is expanding through the use of modern methods and equipment. Mahdia on the east coast is a fishing center, and there are tuna and sardine canneries along the coast.

Since independence, hotels have been built and great efforts have gone into developing the tourist industry. The National Handicrafts Office controls the quality and promotion of traditional handicrafts. These include carpets, handwoven materials, and pottery.

Oil production, though modest, is an important source of income. However, Tunisia, as in Roman times, is mainly an agricultural country. Thus the economy is subject to the uncertainties of the weather. Much of the country lies in dry or semidry regions where crops are good only in years that are especially rainy. And even in those years the rains must come at the right time. Rainfall in North Africa is very irregular, and 2 years of drought out of 5 are not uncommon in the dry regions in central and southern Tunisia. There the government must provide food and jobs so that people do not starve when the rains fail to come.

Even in the north where there is more rain, agricultural production varies greatly from year to year. A vast irrigation project in the Medjerda Valley has been under way for years. But irrigation is expensive, and increases in agricultural production take time and skill. On rare occasions floods, like the heavy floods of 1969, occur, setting back the economy cruelly.

In 1964 the government began a system of land reforms to establish agricultural co-operatives. Individual landowners were forced to group their lands. Each landowner was paid out of profits, and farm workers received a daily wage. Along the eastern coast, especially, the government tried to encourage agricultural co-operatives to service the olive tree orchards. Many of the trees are old and unproductive.

The land reforms were generally unpopular, and production fell sharply. In 1969 the co-operative system was reversed, and much of the land was returned to individual owners.

HISTORY

Seafaring Phoenician merchants from western Asia established trading ports in northern Africa perhaps as early as the 12th century B.C. By the 5th century B.C. Carthage was the seat of a powerful trading empire. It took the Romans more than a century (264–146 B.C.) to subdue Carthage and capture its home settlements along the Tunisian shores. To a greater extent than the Carthaginians, the Romans occupied the Tunisian countryside. They created a united province more or less covering Tunisia's present area. During the 2nd, 3rd, and 4th centuries the province flourished as Rome's granary. Olive trees were cultivated, and Tunisia became a major producer of olive oil for the Roman Empire. Olive oil was needed for food, light, and soap.

Under Roman rule, Carthage became the scene of the most intense Christian activity. The list of early Christian figures who were active in Carthage includes Tertullian, Saint Cyprian, Saint Monica, and her son,

Saint Augustine. Yet, like the Carthaginians, the Romans failed to mark Tunisia with either a lasting language or religion. In the interior of the country the Berbers kept their own language and animistic beliefs.

By the 5th century the Roman Empire had weakened, and Vandals invaded the country. Of far greater importance were the 7th- and 8th-century invasions by the Arabs. They had little trouble wiping out the last traces of the Roman occupation. The Arabs destroyed Carthage in 698 and built the town of Tunis, until then a tiny village sheltered from the sea by a lagoon. The Berbers, who were fiercely independent, were more difficult to overcome. Until the French occupation centuries later, the history of Tunisia was one of constant struggle between the settled populations of the coast and the nomads and seminomads of the interior.

The Arabs succeeded, however, in unifying the country in a cultural sense. Arab invasions of the 11th and 12th centuries extended the Muslim religion and Arabic language to almost all the people of the interior.

A succession of dynasties ruled the country. Under the Hafsid dynasty (1228–1574) Tunis became one of the most brilliant cultural centers of the Muslim world. It was during this period that ibn-Khaldun wrote some of the world's first sociology.

In 1574 Tunisia became part of the Ottoman (Turkish) Empire but gradually gained the right to govern itself. The Husseinite dynasty was founded in 1705 and ruled the country until it became a republic. In 1881 France, which already occupied Algeria, occupied Tunisia. In 1883 the country became a French protectorate.

The French extended settled farming, built new cities around the old Arab cities, and built a network of roads and railways. The biggest French contribution, although it affected only a minority of Tunisians, was modern education. Under the French just a fourth of the Muslim children received schooling. But a new Tunisian middle class grew up. It was one that had absorbed French cultural currents without giving up its Arab-Islamic heritage. The Tunisian struggle against foreign occupation was waged and won by that group.

In the early 1930s, Habib Bourguiba and his Neo-Destour Party (renamed the Destour Socialist Party in 1964) assumed the leadership. The Neo-Destour welcomed the modern Western civilization introduced by France but opposed colonial rule and fought for self-government. Finally, in 1956 after a long and sometimes bloody struggle, Tunisia became independent, with Bourguiba as its president. He was named president for life in 1975. Bourguiba's rule became increasingly repressive in its last years. In late 1987, he was overthrown by Premier Zine el-Abidine Ben Ali, who said Bourguiba was not fit to rule. Ben Ali, who assumed the presidency, was elected to the office without opposition in 1989.

Government.   Tunisia had a single-party system until 1981, when the first multiparty legislative elections were held. Members of the unitary legislature, the National Assembly, are elected to 5-year terms. All citizens age 20 or over may vote.

In every village and city neighborhood, as well as in larger enterprises, the Destour Socialist Party has a cell of loyal and active workers. Although there is no major opposition party, there is some democratic participation in Tunisia's political life.

CLEMENT HENRY MOORE, University of California at Berkeley
Reviewed by M. L. FAYACHE, Permanent Mission of Tunisia to the United Nations

LIBYA

For a long time historians thought that Libya offered nothing more ancient than relics left by the Berber people and the remnants of Phoenician, Greek, and Roman towns and settlements. But during the past few decades archeologists, historians, and travelers have uncovered beautiful paintings drawn on the walls of the caves of southern Libya— far into the desert lands. The earliest of these paintings go back about 10,000 years in time.

Some of the drawings show elephants, rhinoceroses, giraffes, and other animals that have not inhabited North Africa for many thousands of years. Often, the very earliest drawings were covered by the work of several later artists. Little is yet known about the people who painted these pictures. But the paintings are a valuable guide for the researchers seeking knowledge about Libya's early history.

The ruins of an ancient Roman marketplace in Leptis Magna.

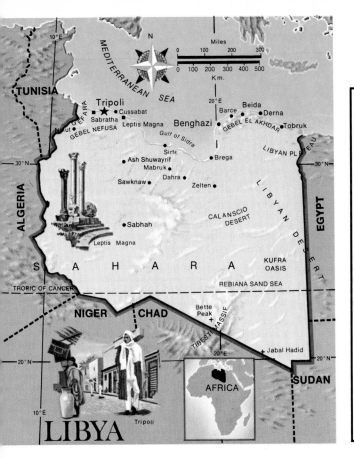

LIBYA

FACTS AND FIGURES

OFFICIAL NAME: Socialist People's Libyan Arab Jamahiriya.

NATIONALITY: Libyan(s).

CAPITAL: Tripoli.

LOCATION: North Africa. **Boundaries**—Mediterranean Sea, Egypt, Sudan, Chad, Niger, Algeria, Tunisia.

AREA: 679,362 sq. mi. (1,759,540 sq. km.).

PHYSICAL FEATURES: Highest point—Bette Peak (7,500 ft.; 2,286 m.). **Lowest point**—80 ft. (24 m.) below sea level.

POPULATION: 4,351,000 (1991; annual growth 3.0%).

MAJOR LANGUAGES: Arabic (official), English, Italian, Berber.

MAJOR RELIGION: Islam (official).

GOVERNMENT: Islamic socialist republic. **Head of state** —no formal head of state; Revolutionary Leader (de facto). **Legislature**—General People's Congress.

CHIEF CITIES: Tripoli, Benghazi.

ECONOMY: Chief minerals—oil, natural gas, iron. **Chief agricultural products**—tomatoes, melons, olives, wheat, potatoes, dates, barley, onions, citrus fruits. **Industries and products**—petroleum refining, food processing (olive oil, canned fruits and vegetables, flour), textiles, handicrafts. **Chief exports**—crude oil, petroleum products. **Chief imports**—machinery, transport equipment, foodstuffs, consumer goods.

MONETARY UNIT: 1 Libyan dinar = 1,000 dirhams.

THE LAND

Libya, once aptly called the Desert Kingdom of Africa, has a coastal frontage of over 1,000 mi. (1,600 km.), stretching between Tunisia and Egypt in northern Africa. The shores of the three countries are washed by the waters of the Mediterranean Sea. From the coast, Libya extends from 500 to 800 mi. (800 to 1,300 km.) south, making most of the country part of the great Sahara, the sea of sand that separates North Africa from Equatorial Africa. Libya, covering an area of 679,362 sq. mi. (1,759,540 sq. km.), is traditionally considered as three separate and diverse regions: Cyrenaica in the east, Tripolitania in the extreme northwest, and Fezzan in the southwest.

Cyrenaica. The shore of Cyrenaica resembles an arch protruding into the Mediterranean. Apart from one fairly large bay located near Tobruk, the coast is smooth and unbroken. The Green Mountain (Gebel el Akhdar), a plateau reaching to almost 2,900 ft. (880 m.), runs parallel to the coast from Benghazi to Derna. The plateau rises abruptly from the narrow coastal plain, but descends gradually southward toward the Libyan Desert, part of the Sahara. This fertile plateau captures almost all the heavy rain that falls in the country. The northern slopes are covered with vineyards and fruit trees, while woodlands are found on the southern slopes. To the south of the plateau, there is an almost immediate disappearance of woods, and small bushes and grasses appear. But the scorching winds and semi-arid areas gradually present themselves until the land loses itself in the very heart of the desert.

Tripolitania. The coastal plains of the Tripolitania region contain many oases. This is one of the most productive agricultural areas of the country. Between the coastal stretches and the mountainous region lies the sandy plain of Gefara. Gebel Nefusa, which is a plateau reaching from Nalut to Cussabat, with an elevation of between 1,500 and 3,000 feet (460–910 m.), has numerous wide valleys. The fertile soils of these valleys enable the people to grow cereals and plant trees on the slopes.

The southern desert of both Cyrenaica and Tripolitania has a number of oases that have always been important trading centers between central and northern Africa. The largest of these oases is Kufra, with an inhabited area of about 430 sq. mi. (1,110 sq. km.) and a population of about 5,000 people.

Fezzan. Most of Fezzan is a vast region of desert and oases in southwest Libya. Much of the land is barren, with great areas of plateaus and sand dunes. The Tibesti Massif is located along the southern border with Chad. Date palms flourish in the oases of Fezzan, providing a major source of food for the people.

There are no large, permanent rivers or lakes in Libya. Small streams may form during the rainy season, but even these disappear during the dry months.

Cities

Tripoli and Benghazi are the most important cities of Libya. Tripoli, probably founded over 2,500 years ago, is the capital and largest city and port. The old part of the city contains many remnants of its past. Perhaps the most impressive is the great white marble triumphal arch built in honor of Marcus Aurelius by the Romans around A.D. 163.

Bazaars in Tripoli attract tourists from many parts of the world.

Tripoli is Libya's capital and largest city as well as its chief port.

Here, too, are the bazaars that attract Libyans from all over the country. The narrow, winding streets and coffee shops of the old quarter of Tripoli are crowded with people who have come to the city to sell and exchange their goods. Traditional Arab handicrafts are displayed in shops alongside radios, modern appliances, and auto accessories. Nearby, bakers toil in front of primitive ovens much as their ancestors did centuries ago. At the large market on the outskirts of Tripoli, farmers buy and sell sheep, camels, and other livestock.

The modern section of the city contains many new, air-conditioned office buildings, apartments, and hotels. Automobile agencies can be found on many streets in the downtown area, and there are large shopping arcades in the center of town. A wide boulevard and a picturesque seafront promenade shaded by palm trees run along the coast of the Mediterranean.

Benghazi, the second largest city, is located on the Gulf of Sidra. Benghazi is the principal urban center and seaport of eastern Libya. This ancient city was founded by the Greeks in the 6th century B.C. Some of the ruins from this period still lie covered by the sands of the desert.

Like Tripoli, this city has grown remarkably since the discovery of Libya's vast oil deposits. Modern office buildings, mosques, and apartment houses dominate the skyline.

Beida is located near the Mediterranean coast about 120 miles (190 kilometers) east of Benghazi. In the past the small town of Beida served as the summer capital of Libya. In recent years the government has expanded and modernized the city.

Derna, a coastal town located east of Beida, lies at the foot of the Green Mountain. It is a quaint town, surrounded by palm trees and made more beautiful by the jasmines whose fragrance fills the air. After 1915 Derna was the site of a large Italian community. However, by 1970 most of the Italian population had left Libya.

Tobruk is a Mediterranean port in northeastern Libya. During the early stages of World War II, Tobruk was the scene of intense fighting between the Germans and the British.

Climate

The climate of Libya varies according to the altitude of the area and its closeness to the sea. Most of the country has a desert climate. The summers are hot and rainless; the winters are generally mild with some cold spells. Rain falls only during the short winter months and the rainy season generally does not exceed a few weeks; sometimes it lasts only a few days, when the rain falls in torrents.

During the spring and fall the *ghibli,* a hot, dry, sand-laden wind, blows in from the Sahara. It usually lasts for a period of 1 to 4 days, causing a rapid rise in temperature and destroying most of the crops.

THE PEOPLE

The people of Libya are mainly Arabs and Berbers. The family ties are very strong and the head of each large family group is obeyed and respected by all the members. There are small groups of Italians, Greeks, and Maltese. The official language of the country is Arabic, but English, Italian, and some Berber are also spoken.

Before the Arabs settled in Libya, Berbers inhabited the country. The Arab population, whether settled, nomadic, or seminomadic, is the result of great invasions that began after A.D. 600. Through the centuries, most of the Berbers have been assimilated into the Arab culture and way of life.

Those Arabs not living in the cities of the Cyrenaica region of Libya are mostly seminomadic. These people, who raise goats and sheep, spend part of the year traveling about in search of food and water for their animals. There are also farmers who live in the fertile Green Mountain region of Cyrenaica, where barley, grapes, dates, fruits, and wheat are grown.

The Arabs of the Tripolitania region depend primarily on agriculture for their livelihood. The majority of the people in this region are settled on farms along the coast. The climate here is more agreeable for the growing of the major crops: barley, wheat, olives, and dates.

Life is very difficult for the people living in the scattered oases of southern Libya. The oases are small, compact villages with narrow streets, and the houses are usually rectangular in shape with closed courtyards. Agriculture is limited to the areas where water is found on or near the

A farmer draws water from a well on an oasis in the Tripolitania region.

surface. Many people are engaged in basket weaving, leather tanning, and pottery making. Some of the inhabitants tend herds of camel. Camel breeding is considered a noble profession by the people of this region.

Nomads roam the desert searching for grazing land for their sheep and camels.

Life in the Cities

Many of the farmers living in rural areas and the oasis dwellers of the south are leaving their homes and moving to the major cities of northern Libya. Employment opportunities are becoming greater, particularly since the discovery of oil. The petroleum industry has made available many jobs that did not exist before. Libyans now also fill many administrative positions in offices, banks, and stores that were once held by foreigners.

In recent years there has been a change in dress. Most of the older women still prefer to wear the *barracano,* a long, loose robe that covers them from head to foot, leaving only one eye exposed. But the younger people seem to prefer Western styles of dress.

Education

The government of Libya has been directing a great portion of its oil royalties to education. Prior to 1960 only a small percentage of the children went to the few schools that existed in the urban centers of northern Libya. However, beginning in the 1960's, schools were opened throughout the country. Education is free and compulsory for all children between the ages of 6 and 12.

Libya has several universities. They include Alfatah University in Tripoli, the capital; the University of Garyounis, with campuses in Benghazi and Beida (the two were formerly known as the University of Libya); and Bright Star Technological University, founded in 1981.

Religion

Approximately 97 percent of the people are Muslims, and Islam is the state religion. In the 1840's Sayyid Muhammad ibn-Ali al-Senusi began to preach to the Libyans and then to Muslims far and wide. He emphasized the need to return to the true and genuine teachings of Islam. His was a reform movement based on thorough understanding of the Koran (the holy book) and traditions of the prophet Mohammed.

The Grand Senusi, as Sayyid Muhammad came to be known, sent teachers to live among the different groups scattered throughout Libya. *Zawiya* ("lodges") were built by the people. Each *zawiya* was headed by a sheikh, or teacher, appointed by the Grand Senusi. It was the duty of the sheikh to educate the people and to act as administrator, judge, arbitrator, and spiritual leader.

ECONOMY

With the discovery of its first major oil field in 1959, Libya's economic position in the world changed drastically. Oil has become the principal product and the main source of Libya's revenue. Petroleum

An oil refinery located in the desert just outside of Benghazi.

now forms about 95 percent of Libya's total exports and has made the country one of the world's leading oil producers.

However, Libya is still largely an agricultural country. About three fourths of the population is engaged in growing crops and raising animals. Cereals, vegetables, dates, citrus fruits, and olives are the main products grown. The oases in the southern region produce a variety of vegetables and fruits, but dates are the mainstay. These foods are usually grown as subsistence crops, although some are exported or traded.

The country is rich in livestock—sheep, goats, cattle, and camels. Horses and donkeys are much less numerous.

HISTORY AND GOVERNMENT

Although the cave paintings found in the Sahara go back some 10,000 years, little is known of the country until the arrival of the Berbers about 4,000 years ago. The Berbers probably came from the eastern Mediterranean area sometime before 2000 B.C. About the 7th century B.C. the Phoenicians came to northeast Africa, pushing the Berbers deep into the desert regions. At this same period Greece was ruling the Cyrenaica region. Later, the Romans conquered present-day northern Libya and added the territory to the Roman Empire. During the 5th century A.D. the Vandals, a Germanic people, crossed the Mediterranean from Spain and pushed the Romans out of Libya. Beginning in A.D. 643 the Arabs came, displacing all previous invaders.

In the mid-16th century Libya fell to the Ottoman Turks and remained a Turkish province until 1911, when Italy attacked the country. When the Turks withdrew the following year, Italy annexed the country.

British and French troops occupied Libya during World War II. Under the terms of the peace treaty, Italy renounced its claims to the territory. Libya was governed for a time by Britain and France before gaining its independence in 1951. Mohammed Idris el-Senusi, emir of Cyrenaica, was proclaimed king as Idris I. Libya remained a constitutional monarchy under Idris I until 1969, when the King was overthrown in a military coup led by Colonel Muammar el-Qaddafi.

Libya Today. Libya now has a government based on socialism combined with Islamic principles. According to the constitution, power is exercised by the people through political organizations at various levels. In theory, the chief organ of government is the General People's Congress. But this body meets only occasionally and its authority is delegated to the General Secretariat. The day-to-day activities of the government are handled by the General People's Committee, which acts as a kind of cabinet. Qaddafi, however, remains the country's real leader.

Under Qaddafi's leadership, Libya has played an aggressive role in the Arab world. Qaddafi has encouraged revolutionary movements in the Middle East, Africa, and other parts of the world. Libyan troops have intervened in civil wars in Uganda and Chad. Qaddafi himself has been accused by Western governments of encouraging terrorism. In 1986, U.S. warplanes bombed targets in Libya in retaliation for what the United States called Libya's part in attacks on U.S. servicemen in Europe.

Qaddafi several times has tried to form unions with other Arab nations. His most recent attempt came in 1984, when Libya signed a treaty of union with Morocco. But Morocco cancelled the treaty in 1986.

NICOLA A. ZIADEH, The American University of Beirut

EGYPT

The Arab Republic of Egypt is a new name for the very ancient land of Egypt. Over 5,000 years have passed since the first pharaoh ruled, but the same kind of oxen pictured on the walls of early tombs can still be seen drawing plows in Egyptian fields. Centuries ago Egyptians worshiped the Nile, and each year when the river flooded they sacrificed a beautiful young maiden to the river god. Today when the Nile flood reaches its height, a public holiday is declared and elaborately decorated dolls are thrown into the river. Near the bustling Cairo railway terminal stands an enormous statue of the pharaoh Ramses II, a constant reminder to 20th-century travelers of the long history of Egypt.

King Tutankhamen and his wife are pictured in gold and ceramic on the back of his throne (about 1350 B.C.). Egyptian Museum, Cairo.

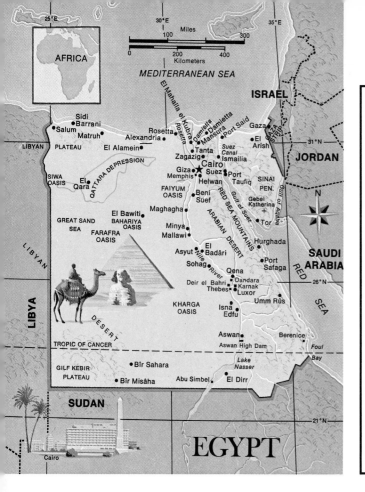

FACTS AND FIGURES

OFFICIAL NAME: Arab Republic of Egypt (Jumhuriat Misr el Arabiya).

NATIONALITY: Egyptian(s).

CAPITAL: Cairo.

LOCATION: Northeast Africa. **Boundaries**—Mediterranean Sea, Israel, Red Sea, Sudan, Libya.

AREA: 386,660 sq. mi. (1,001,449 sq. km.).

PHYSICAL FEATURES: Highest point—Gebel Katherina (8,651 ft.; 2,637 m.). **Lowest point**—440 ft. (134 m.) below sea level. **Chief river**—Nile.

POPULATION: 54,777,615 (1989).

MAJOR LANGUAGES: Arabic (official), English, French.

MAJOR RELIGIONS: Islam (official), Coptic Christianity.

GOVERNMENT: Republic. **Head of state**—president. **Head of government**—prime minister. **Legislature**—one-house People's Assembly.

CHIEF CITIES: Cairo (5,881,000), Alexandria (2,708,000), Giza (1,509,000).

ECONOMY: Chief minerals—petroleum, phosphates, iron, salt, coal. **Chief agricultural products**—cotton, corn, rice, wheat, sugarcane, citrus fruits, potatoes. **Industries and products**—iron and steel, textiles, chemicals, cement, food processing, petroleum refining, tourism. **Chief exports**—crude petroleum, cotton, yarns and fabrics. **Chief imports**—capital goods, industrial raw materials, grains and grain products.

MONETARY UNIT: 1 Egyptian pound = 100 piasters.

Egypt lies at the northeastern corner of Africa. The country is bounded on the west by Libya, on the south by Sudan, on the north by the Mediterranean Sea, and on the east by the Gaza Strip, Israel, and the Red Sea.

THE PEOPLE

Egypt is the second most populous country of Africa. Peasant farmers called fellahin (singular: fellah) make up over 40 percent of the population. But less than 4 percent of Egypt's land is suitable for farming. Before the leaders of the 1952 revolution introduced land reform, less than 2 percent of the landowners owned half of the land available for farming. Most of the fellahin were tenants or owned very tiny farms. A man who owned 3 to 5 acres (1–2 hectares) was considered well-off. Now no one is permitted to own more than 50 acres, and the average Egyptian farm is generally much smaller than that.

The Farmer's Life

An Egyptian farmer's main tools are the hoe, a simple plow, and the *sakia*, or waterwheel. The fellah, his wife, and their children all work together in the fields. The dreary routine of their lives is relieved only on a few occasions—the group prayer in the mosques on Fridays, religious feasts, and family events such as weddings or the circumcisions of young boys.

A farmer's most valuable possession is the water buffalo, cow, or ox that helps him with the heavy farm work. The water buffalo or ox draws the plow, turns the waterwheel, and pulls the *nowraj*. The *nowraj* is a wooden platform mounted on four or five iron disks. The sharpened edges of the disks crush the stalks of wheat so that the grain can be separated from the chaff. The water buffalo or the cow also supplies the fellah's family with milk and with calves that can be sold. Very often the fellah shares his house with his animals. This is unsanitary, but it is the farmer's preferred way of protecting them. The theft of an animal could mean economic catastrophe for the poor fellah.

The Fellahin's Clothing

The fellah wears a loose, long cotton robe called a *gallabiyea,* loose cotton pants, and a wool cap, which he makes himself. For special events he makes a turban by folding a white sash around the cap. Flat, yellow slippers complete the fellah's outfit.

The fellaha, the wife of the fellah, wears dresses with long sleeves and trailing flounces and a black veil, which she sometimes uses to cover her face. On market days and other special occasions the women wear earrings, necklaces, bracelets, and anklets. These ornaments are usually made of beads, silver, glass, copper, or gold. They make a pleasant musical sound as the fellaha walks along the dusty lanes of the village.

THE VILLAGE

Most of Egypt's fellahin live in villages along the Nile. The villages invariably look gray because the houses are whitewashed only for important events such as weddings. The houses are usually small and huddled together without planning.

An account of the owner's journey to Mecca is painted on this house in Dandara.

The typical house is made of sunbaked bricks, which keep the indoors cool during the summer. There are only one or two bedrooms, an animal shed, and a small courtyard. In the courtyard there is a primitive oven that is heated by burning stalks of cotton or corn, which are stored on the roof. The oven is used to bake the big, round, thin bread that makes up 80 percent of the fellahin's diet. The bedroom might contain a bed made of wood or iron, but the fellah's family usually sleep on mats made of reeds.

The house of a wealthier fellah has a living room and an upper story with extra bedrooms and storage space. The living room is furnished with long wooden seats, a few chairs, and reed mats.

In many villages the women still draw water from one of the Nile canals and carry it home in water jars balanced gracefully on their heads. But many other villages now have a clean water supply. In these villages there is a pump in the village square. Water from the pumps is carried home in the traditional jars or tin containers. Water pipes have been extended into a few homes. The houses are usually lit by kerosene lamps. However, since the opening of the Aswan Dam, electrical service is being extended throughout Egypt.

The most important places in any Egyptian village are the mosque or the Coptic Church, the house of the headman, the rural social center, the police station, and the market. The mosque and the church are often used as schools as well as houses of worship.

The Market.   Weekly or biweekly, the fellahin flock to the village market, or souk. In the souk the farmers buy and sell cows, water buffalos, donkeys, camels, sheep, and goats, as well as agricultural and dairy products. In the larger markets, food, clothing, jewelry, and farm tools are bought and sold. Water and soft drinks are sold by vendors who sing or shout their wares. The market is a noisy place as the fellahin continually haggle and bargain at the top of their lungs. No transaction is concluded without bargaining, or *fissal*. Prices are decided by a series of compromises. Religious vows are invoked and the words "by Allah," "by

Merchants on their way to market unload produce and livestock from ferry at Luxor.

Mohammed," or "by Al-Masseh" ("by Christ") are heard everywhere as the bargaining reaches its climax and the price is about to be fixed. The market is not just an opportunity to buy and sell, it is an important social event. Friends and relatives meet and exchange news and gossip. People dress in their finest, and the monotonous lives of the fellahin become lively for a while.

The Umdah. The *umdah,* or village headman, is usually a native of the village, over 25 years old, the owner of 10 or more acres, and in good standing with the community. He is nominated by the villagers and appointed by the Ministry of the Interior. The *umdah* is the liaison between the local community and the central and provincial governments. He settles disputes, helps maintain law and order, and assists in the collection of taxes.

The Rural Social Centers. The first rural social centers were established in the 1940's, and they were so successful that there are now centers all over Egypt. The primary task of these centers is to improve the living conditions of the fellahin. Traditionally the only government workers commonly seen in rural Egypt were the tax collector and the engineer who directed the control of the irrigation system. The staff of a social center usually includes a doctor, nurses, a veterinarian, an agricultural adviser, and the teacher of the local elementary school. The advice and help that these specialists provide have had a definite impact on the life of the fellahin. The government is attacking problems that were previously the burden of family and neighbors. The task of changing tradition-bound rural Egypt is tremendous, but progress is being made.

LIFE IN THE CITY

Life in Egyptian cities has been strongly influenced by modern European culture. Urban planning is reflected in the broad, paved streets and the well-tended parks. A city is usually linked to the national network of highways and railroads. Many government offices and the courts of justice are located in urban centers. There are more elementary schools in the cities than in the rural villages. Most of the secondary schools and all of the universities are in cities.

Large, modern apartment buildings line many streets in Egyptian cities. These buildings are not distinctively Egyptian. If you set one down on a similar street in Tokyo or New York, it would not look out of place. But in the older areas of the cities, homes are often built in the traditional Islamic style of architecture, which is also seen in the mosques and public buildings. Electricity and running water are more common in city houses than they are in village homes. The new buildings are often air-conditioned.

The city-dweller dresses mostly in Western-style clothing. If he still wears the *gallabiyea,* it is usually of a better quality than the one worn by the fellah. The city-dweller often speaks Arabic with an intonation and accent different from those of the fellah. His places of entertainment are not necessarily centered around the family. He frequents the city's cafés, goes to the movies, or attends public concerts.

The urban workers are more receptive to change and innovation than are the tradition-oriented fellahin. Family ties in the city are weaker than in the village. But the city-dweller often keeps up his ties to the village, especially if he is a recent migrant.

RELIGION

Over 90 percent of Egyptians are Muslims. The skylines of Egypt's cities are filled with minarets, the towers of mosques. Five times a day the voice of the muezzin ("prayer-caller") calls the faithful to prayer. Traditionally he called the faithful from the top of the minaret, but now the call is often amplified by a public-address system or broadcast by radio. When Muslims pray they face Mecca, the city in Saudi Arabia where Mohammed was born. The Muslim prays to Allah (God), declaring in his prayers that "there is no God but the one God and Mohammed is His prophet." During the holy month of Ramadan, one of the 12 months of the Islamic lunar calendar, Muslims fast from sunrise to sunset. Muslims are also obliged to give alms to the poor. At least once in a lifetime, when it is financially and physically possible, a Muslim is called upon to make a pilgrimage to Mecca.

Islam is closely related to Judaism and Christianity. Muslims revere Abraham, Moses, and Jesus as prophets of God. Mohammed is seen as their successor and the last of God's prophets. Islam stresses equality regardless of ethnic or social origins. There is no clergy because the religion establishes a direct relationship between the Muslim and his Creator. Islam calls for both submission to the will of God and jihad, the use of armed force for the defense of Islam.

Among the most important Muslim feasts are Eid Al-Sagheer, Eid Al-Kabeer, and Mawlid Al-Nabi. Eid Al-Sagheer (or Id Al-Fitr) marks the end of Ramadan, and Mawlid Al-Nabi is the Prophet's birthday. Eid Al-Kabeer (or Id Al-Adha), the feast of sacrifice, commemorates God's substitution of a sacrificial ram for Abraham's son. It also celebrates the end of the season during which pilgrimages to Mecca are made.

About 8 percent of the Egyptians are Christians, most of whom belong to the Coptic Church. Copts believe in the single nature of Jesus Christ. Egypt was the birthplace of monasticism, and even today the monasteries play an important role in the Coptic Church. The patriarch who heads the church is usually a member of one of the monastic communities.

There are also small groups of Roman Catholics, Greek Orthodox, Armenians, and Protestants in Egypt. Although the Jewish population was once large, there is now only a small number of Jews in the country.

EDUCATION

Elementary education is free and compulsory for children aged 6 to 12. The law decreeing compulsory education was passed in 1933 but was not carried out effectively until 1950. In that year the Minister of Education, Taha Hussein, declared that education is as essential to the citizen "as air and water." Free, hot midday meals are provided at the elementary and secondary levels. Over 75 percent of school-age children attend classes, and girls make up 40 percent of the total school population. Arabic is the main language of instruction in state schools. English and French are taught to students above the primary level.

Egyptian secondary schools and universities are also tuition free. Secondary schools are academic or technical. The academic schools prepare students for the universities, while the technical schools provide vocational education in agriculture, industry, and commerce.

Four of Egypt's universities are located in Cairo—Al-Azhar, Cairo

Children participate in physical education class at elementary school in Cairo.

University, Helwan University, and Ain Shams University. The American University is also located in Cairo. Al-Azhar was established in the 10th century by Jawhar Al-Siqilli, the founder of modern Cairo. The rector of Al-Azhar traditionally wields great influence throughout the Muslim world. Cairo University was established in 1908 as a private institution. It was taken over by the state in 1925 and renamed Fuad I University after the king who was then on the throne. With the revolution in 1952, it once more became Cairo University. There are also universities at Alexandria and Asyut, and plans are being implemented to open more universities in other parts of Egypt.

Language

The language of Egypt is Arabic. Classical Arabic is both written and spoken. It is used on the radio, in the press, in business transactions, court decisions, government decrees, and in the schools. Colloquial

For centuries the Sphinx at Giza has withstood the ravages of violent sandstorms. To many it symbolizes the glory of ancient Egypt.

Arabic, the language of the street, is seldom written. There are two types of Arabic script. Naskh is the ordinary cursive form used in books. The Kufi form is not just a script, it is an art form. It is found in elaborate copies of the Koran. These books are similar to the richly ornamented Bibles and prayer books produced in medieval Europe.

In addition to Arabic, four other languages are used in Egypt. Coptic, which developed from ancient Egyptian, was spoken until the 12th century. It is now used only in the liturgy of the Coptic Church. Nubian is spoken by the Egyptians who live south of Aswan. Beja is the language of the nomads who live along the Egyptian-Sudanese border east of the Nile, and Berber is spoken by the people of Siwa, an oasis of the Libyan Desert. Nubian and Beja are not written languages.

TOMBS AND TEMPLES

Most of our knowledge about ancient Egyptian civilization comes from the ruins of the tombs built for the pharaohs. The Egyptians believed in life after death, and therefore the tombs were filled with all the things it was assumed a man would need in the next world. The walls of the tombs were decorated with scenes of daily life, which were described by hieroglyphics. Many of these tombs can still be seen along the Nile.

The Great Pyramids and Sphinx at Giza are probably the most famous sights in Egypt. The largest of the pyramids was built for Cheops, or Khufu, in the 27th century B.C. It took over 20 years to build the pyramid, and more than 2,000,000 limestone blocks were used. Nearby are the smaller pyramids built by Cheops' successors. The approach to the pyramids is guarded by the Sphinx. The Sphinx is actually the head

The three great pyramids of Cheops, Khafre, and Menkure, dating from the 27th century B.C., tower above the surrounding irrigated fields at Giza.

The ruins at Luxor are all that remain of the temple of the sun god, Amon-Re.

Avenue of Sphinxes lines the approach to the great temple of Amon-Re at Karnak.

of a man attached to the body of a lion. The oldest pyramid is that of Zoser at Sakkara, located 15 miles (24 km.) south of Cairo. It was designed as a series of steps by Imhotep, the Pharaoh's vizier.

At Deir el-Bahri near Thebes stands the temple of Queen Hatshepsut. Ramps and terraces lead up to the temple, which is carved into the cliffs. The terraces before the temple were once filled with exotic plants brought to Egypt from the Land of Punt (Somaliland). Across the river from Hatshepsut's temple is Medinet Habu, built by Ramses III. Medinet Habu is a series of temples and palaces, and it is one of the best-preserved sites in Egypt. Farther south along the Nile stands Abu Simbel. Early in the 1960's Abu Simbel was endangered by the rising waters of Lake Nasser, but an international effort saved the entire temple,

Hatshepsut's dramatic mortuary temple matches the semicircular formation of cliffs that rises behind it.

including the enormous statues of Ramses II that adorn the entrance. The structure was disassembled, moved to higher ground, and reconstructed in its original form.

Other important relics of ancient Egyptian civilization that can still be seen include the Colossi of Memnon at Thebes, the Valley of the Kings at Luxor, and the temples of Amon-Re at Karnak and Luxor. At Edfu and Dandara are the great temples built by the Ptolemies. In Cairo the centuries of Islamic rule in Egypt are reflected in the mosques and palaces built by the Muslim rulers.

THE LAND

The Arab Republic of Egypt occupies a strategic position at the meeting point of Africa and Asia. With long coasts on both the Mediterranean and Red seas, Egypt has been for centuries an important center of trade and communication between Asia, Africa, and Europe. Egypt's position became even more important when the Suez Canal was opened in 1869. The canal made the long voyage around the southern tip of Africa unnecessary.

The Deserts. Without the Nile, Egypt would have remained just another stretch of the desert that extends across North Africa from the Atlantic Ocean to the Red Sea. To the west of the Nile is the Libyan, or Western, Desert, part of the much larger Sahara. Most of this region is a barren plateau that rises to over 6,000 feet (1,800 meters) in the southwest. To the northeast the Qattara Depression drops to about 440 feet (134 m.) below sea level. The oases of the Libyan Desert are the only areas in Egypt outside the Nile Valley that are suitable for farming. Among the most important of these oases are the Siwa, the Farafra, and the Kharga. The Faiyum oasis, which lies to the west of the Nile, is connected to the river by an irrigation canal.

The Arabian, or Eastern, Desert lies between the Nile and the Red Sea. Most of the Arabian Desert is an arid plateau broken up by numerous dried-up riverbeds called wadis. Along the eastern coast a narrow mountain range, the Red Sea Mountains, rises to heights of over 7,000 feet (2,100 m.).

The Sinai Peninsula, the only part of the Arab Republic of Egypt that is on the Asian continent, is bordered on the east by the Gaza Strip, Israel, and the Gulf of Aqaba and on the west by the Suez Canal and the Gulf of Suez. Following the 1967 Arab-Israeli War, the Sinai Peninsula came under Israeli occupation. But under the terms of the Egyptian-Israeli peace treaty of March, 1979, the Sinai was returned to Egypt in three stages—the first two thirds of the area on January 25, 1980, and the final third on April 25, 1982. Sinai is mostly barren mountains and desert. With a height of over 8,600 feet (2,620 m.), Gebel Katherina in the southern Sinai is the highest point in Egypt.

The Suez Canal, which lies west of the Sinai Peninsula, divides "Asian" Egypt from "African" Egypt. The canal stretches from Port Said on the Mediterranean to Suez on the Gulf of Suez, a distance of about 100 miles (160 kilometers).

The Nile. Over 2,000 years ago the Greek historian Herodotus called Egypt "the gift of the Nile." He was referring of course to the life-giving water and rich silt that the river carries from equatorial Africa to the desert of Egypt. Traditionally Egyptian farmers had to await the ar-

Animals graze on fertile land along the Nile. In the background is a felucca.

rival of the annual flood to plant their crops. During the 20th century, however, an extensive system of dams, reservoirs, and canals has been built to harness the waters of the Nile more effectively.

The Nile travels over 3,000 miles (4,800 km.) through Africa before it enters Egypt. In southern, or Upper, Egypt the river flows between high sandstone cliffs. The construction of the Aswan High Dam gradually created a large lake in this region. Lake Nasser stretches from Aswan into the Sudan. The Aswan High Dam will eventually provide enough power

Camel stable at Giza is the starting point for trips to the ancient pyramids.

and water to irrigate an additional 2 million acres (800,000 hectares) of Egyptian farmland.

From Aswan the Nile flows north to Cairo. Just below Cairo the river splits into two major branches, the Rosetta and the Damietta. The branches are named after the cities where the river enters the Mediterranean. This area of the country is known as the Delta, or Lower Egypt. The entire region is crisscrossed by canals that provide year-round irrigation. (An article on the NILE RIVER appears in this volume.)

Climate.   Egypt's climate is warm and sunny throughout the year. The summer months are very hot and dry. Winter is cooler, and most of the rain the country receives falls during this season. But the wettest part of the country, the Mediterranean coast, gets only about 8 in. (20 cm.) of rain per year. From April to May the khamsin blows across Egypt from the Sahara. The khamsin, a hot, dry wind, may carry with it so much sand and dust that it makes a sunny day appear cloudy.

Cities

Cairo and Alexandria are the most important cities in Egypt. Cairo, the national capital, has a population of more than 5 million and is the largest city in Africa. Alexandria has nearly 3 million inhabitants. Other important cities include Giza (a suburb of Cairo) and the Suez Canal ports of Ismailia, Suez, and Port Said. Aswan is growing rapidly as a result of the construction of the High Dam.

Cairo.   Cairo lies on the east bank of the Nile, just south of the Delta. The city is a religious and cultural center for the Arab and Muslim worlds, and its influence is felt far beyond the boundaries of Egypt. This influence is probably as old as Egypt itself. The site on which Cairo is built has been an administrative center since the time of the pharaohs. Cairo in Arabic is Al-Qahira, meaning "the victorious." The modern city

Cairo, the largest city in Africa, is situated on the Nile River.

Afternoon crowds browse and shop in Khan Al-Khalili,
the famous bazaar located in the old section of Cairo.

Alexandria, Egypt's main port, lies on the Mediterranean coast.

was founded in the 10th century by the Fatimids, a Muslim dynasty from North Africa that conquered Egypt.

Cairo houses the three branches of the national government as well as several universities and many mosques and churches. The city is the main railway and highway junction of Egypt, and flights from all over the world land at Cairo International Airport.

Many treasures of ancient Egypt, including the fabulous relics found in the tomb of Pharaoh Tutankhamen, are preserved in Cairo's Egyptian Museum. Not far from the city, the pyramids and Sphinx at Giza attract thousands of visitors each year.

Old Cairo reflects the successive centuries of Islamic rule in Egypt. The Khan Al-Khalili, or bazaar, is located in the Old City. The artisans of the Khan still practice arts and crafts that reflect ancient Egyptian and Muslim motifs. Islamic architecture is well represented in Cairo. The Al-Azhar Mosque, built by the Fatimid general Jawhar Al-Siqilli in the 10th century, later became one of the great centers of Islamic learning. The Blue Mosque took its name from the tiles that decorate some of its walls. The Citadel, begun by Saladin, also contains the Alabaster Mosque built during the 19th century. Other famous mosques include those of Mehemet Ali, Sultan Hassan, and Al Rifai.

Alexandria. Alexandria, Egypt's second largest city, lies on the Mediterranean coast. It was founded by Alexander the Great in 332 B.C. His successors in Egypt, the Ptolemies, built the famous Pharos of Alexandria, a lighthouse that became one of the seven wonders of the world. The Ptolemies also supported the great library at Alexandria, which attracted scholars such as the mathematician Euclid.

Today, Alexandria is Egypt's chief port. Most of Egypt's imports and exports pass through the harbor at Alexandria.

ECONOMY

Egypt's main hopes for accelerated development in industry and agriculture are dependent on the Aswan High Dam. The dam's turbines generate enormous amounts of hydroelectricity for industrial use. The water stored by the dam is being used to convert once dry desert land into fertile farm acreage.

Agriculture. The majority of Egyptians earn their living from farming. Cotton is the country's most important crop. It is grown throughout the Nile Valley and the Delta. Cotton and cotton products make up over 10 percent of Egypt's exports. Corn and wheat are the staple food crops. Sorghum, sugarcane, vegetables, and fruits are other important agricultural products. A mild climate and irrigation make it possible to grow more than one crop a year. In some areas, particularly the Delta, three crops a year can be produced.

Industry. Egypt is attempting to break its dependency on agriculture through rapid industrialization. Textile manufacturing and food processing are traditionally the most important industries. But newer industries such as the manufacture of steel, chemicals, and automobiles are expanding rapidly. Most of Egypt's industries are located in Cairo, Alexandria, and the cities of the Delta, but the High Dam is attracting manufacturers south to Aswan and to other cities in Upper Egypt.

Mining. Egypt's natural resources include oil, iron, lead, phosphates, manganese, gold, asbestos, chromium, titanium, and sulfur. Exploration

Harvesting of cotton, Egypt's most important agricultural crop.

is continuing for nuclear raw materials. The Arabian Desert is rich in phosphates and iron deposits, and manganese is found in the Sinai Peninsula. The chief mineral is petroleum, however, mostly extracted from Arabian Desert wells or offshore wells in the Gulf of Suez. Crude oil now accounts for more than half of Egypt's exports in value.

HISTORY

Thousands of years ago the Sahara was a fertile region, not a desert. It was an area of lush vegetation and had many streams and rivers. Over the centuries rainfall in the area decreased, and the plain dried up. But the Nile continued to flow through the eastern section of the desert, creating a fertile island in the midst of barrenness. The wild game that once roamed across northern Africa migrated to the Nile Valley. The hunters who wandered across the Sahara in search of game followed the animals to the green oasis along the Nile. Eventually the hunters learned how to raise crops and domesticate animals. These early farmers in the Nile Valley were among the first peoples in the world to practice settled agriculture. Whether they or the inhabitants of Mesopotamia, who began farming around the same time, were actually the first farmers in the world no one can say for sure.

By 5000 B.C. villages were established by clans or family groups. In later centuries these villages formed states, or nomes, led by chiefs. Eventually the nomes formed two powerful kingdoms, Upper Egypt in the south and Lower Egypt in the north. Tradition says that around 3200 B.C. Menes, the King of Upper Egypt, conquered Lower Egypt, united the two states, and founded the first dynasty.

The Old Kingdom.   With the beginning of the fourth dynasty around 2600 B.C., Egyptian civilization entered a golden age. The Egyptians had already devised a lunar calendar and invented a form of writing known as hieroglyphics. It was the pharaohs of the Old Kingdom who built the great pyramids that became one of the seven wonders of the world. The pyramids reveal the ancient Egyptians' mastery of mathematics and engineering. They also indicate the enormous power and prestige of the pharaoh. He was not just the ruler, he was the state. Cheops, whose body was entombed in the largest of the pyramids at Giza, was one of the early rulers of the period. But this great age did not last long. The power of the pharaohs declined, and after 2200 B.C. the powerful centralized state of the Old Kingdom was replaced by a loose federation.

The Middle Kingdom.   It was not until 2050 B.C. that the kings of Thebes in Upper Egypt reunited the country under one powerful ruler. Although the Middle Kingdom endured until 1786 B.C., the pharaohs never regained the absolute power held by earlier rulers.

The years of the Middle Kingdom were prosperous ones for Egypt. During the reign of Amenemhet III an extensive series of irrigation and land reclamation projects was undertaken. Egyptians extended their rule over Nubia, in what is now northern Sudan.

The Hyksos.   Under the rulers of the 13th dynasty, the power of the pharaohs once again declined, and civil war raged in Egypt. The country was in an extremely weak position, and a group of Asian warriors known as the Hyksos easily conquered Egypt around 1675 B.C. The Hyksos ruled until the middle of the 16th century B.C. Very little is known about them, but they were responsible for introducing the horse-drawn chariot and the use of body armor to the Egyptians.

The Empire or New Kingdom.   Ahmose I succeeded in driving the Hyksos back into Palestine. Ahmose was the founder of the 18th dynasty, which ruled from 1570 to 1304 B.C. Ahmose's successors Amenhotep I and Thutmose I extended Egyptian power and boundaries south into the Sudan and east to the Euphrates in Mesopotamia.

Among the more outstanding rulers of the 18th dynasty was Queen Hatshepsut, who ruled for 20 years. During her reign trade expeditions were sent to the East African coast, and extensive construction projects were begun in Egypt. Her stepson and successor, Thutmose III, consolidated the territorial gains of earlier pharaohs with the aid of an efficient professional army and bureaucracy. During this period large numbers of conquered peoples were brought to Egypt as slaves. Many of them served in the army or in the enormous building projects undertaken by the pharaohs. The enslavement of the Jews in Egypt during this period is described in the Old Testament. Modern Jews still commemorate the Exodus from Egypt at the Passover feast.

In the 14th century B.C. Amenhotep IV, another member of the 18th dynasty, ascended the throne. As a monotheist, or believer in one god, Amenhotep rejected the many traditional gods of Egypt and focused his religion on Aten, who was represented by the sun. Amenhotep changed his name to Akhenaten and moved the capital of Egypt from Thebes to a new city, which he called Akhetaton. But Akhenaten ignored the foreign threats to the Egyptian Empire, and during his reign large portions of the empire were lost.

After Akhenaten's death, the new religion was destroyed, and

The solid gold mask of King Tutankhamen (about 1350 B.C.). Egyptian Museum, Cairo.

attempts were made to restore Egyptian power and influence. Both Ramses II and Ramses III fought valiantly to maintain the empire in the face of continued threats from the east. But domestic problems had begun to destroy Egypt, and the empire gradually disappeared. Egypt once again divided into two states. In the succeeding centuries Libyan and Ethiopian conquerors adopted the title of pharaoh and ruled Egypt. They were followed in the 7th century B.C. by the Assyrians, who occupied Egypt for a short period before being expelled by the 26th, or Saite, dynasty.

Egypt Under Foreign Rule

In 525 B.C. Cambyses, the son of the Persian ruler Cyrus the Great, invaded and conquered Egypt. For all but 60 of the next 200 years Egypt remained a province of the Persian Empire.

In 332 B.C. Alexander the Great drove the Persians out of Egypt. During this campaign he established the city of Alexandria. After Alexander's death one of his Greek generals, Ptolemy, gained control of Egypt. Under the Ptolemies, Alexandria became an important cultural and commercial center. The library they established attracted scholars from all over the Mediterranean world. Ptolemaic rule in Egypt ended with the death of Cleopatra VII in 30 B.C. Octavian, later the Emperor Augustus, made Egypt part of the growing Roman Empire.

The Christian Era

Christianity was probably introduced into Egypt in the 1st century, and Egypt rapidly became Christian. At the end of the 3rd century Emperor Diocletian divided the Roman Empire into two regions. Egypt became part of the Eastern, or Byzantine, Empire, which had its capital at Constantinople in what is now Turkey. In the 4th century the Emperor Constantine made Christianity the official religion of the empire. But a split soon developed between the Egyptian and Byzantine Christians. The Egyptians believed in the single nature of God, the Byzantines in the Trinity. Since the Byzantine belief had become the official religion of the empire, the Egyptians were persecuted as heretics.

The Muslim Conquest

The religious quarrels between the Egyptians and the Byzantines paved the way for the Arab Muslim conquerors who invaded Egypt in 640 during the reign of Caliph Omar. Many Egyptians eagerly adopted the new religion of Islam introduced by the conquerors. The caliph was the religious leader of all Islam. The first four caliphs were all based in Mecca. In the 8th century Egypt became a province of the Abbasid caliphs, whose capital was Baghdad. But in the 9th century the power of the Abbasid caliphs entered a period of decline. The Turkish Abbasid general, Ahmed ibn-Tulun, ruled Egypt as an independent state although the caliph still nominally controlled the area. Over the next century control of Egypt passed from the Tulunids back to the Abbasids, and finally to the Ikhshidis, another Turkish dynasty. In 969 Egypt was once again occupied by Arabs—this time the Fatimids—who came from northwest Africa. The Fatimids established Cairo as the capital, built the Mosque of Al-Azhar, and made Cairo the cultural center of the Muslim world. At the height of their power the Fatimids ruled all of North Africa, Sicily, Syria, and parts of Arabia. In the 12th century the last Fatimid ruler was overthrown by Saladin, a Kurd, who set up an independent state in Egypt. He was the best-known of the Muslim leaders who went into battle against the Crusaders. Saladin's descendants ruled Egypt until 1250, when they were overthrown by the Mamelukes. The Mamelukes were former slaves who served in the royal bodyguard. In 1517 the Ottoman Turks defeated the Mamelukes and made Egypt part of the Ottoman Empire. The Mamelukes continued to rule Egypt as local governors under the Turkish sultans until the 19th century.

Napoleon in Egypt

In 1798 Napoleon Bonaparte invaded Egypt in an attempt to block British access to their possessions in India. The French were defeated by an Anglo-Turkish force, and French troops withdrew from Egypt in

The Alabaster Mosque is one of the famous landmarks in old Cairo.

1801. Scientists and scholars who accompanied Napoleon's expedition explored the country and uncovered many of the relics and monuments of ancient Egypt. The Rosetta Stone, discovered at this time, enabled scholars to decipher the ancient Egyptian hieroglyphics.

Mehemet Ali

Mehemet Ali, a general who led the Turkish Sultan's Albanian troops against the French, remained in Egypt. By 1805 he had become pasha under the Sultan, and by 1811 he had managed to destroy the power of the Mamelukes. Mehemet Ali began a program of modernization and development in Egypt in order to support his policy of enhancing Egyptian power and prestige. His armies gained control of the Sudan, the Arabian Peninsula, and Greece. After conquering Syria, he marched on Turkey. However, Mehemet Ali was forced to withdraw under pressure from the French and British. In return the Turkish sultan recognized Mehemet Ali's family as the hereditary governors of Egypt.

During Mehemet Ali's reign cotton was introduced and soon became the major cash crop. For the first time in thousands of years, Egyptian peasants were taken into the army to replace foreign slaves and mercenaries. Mehemet Ali also instituted extensive irrigation projects.

Ismail and the Suez Canal

Mehemet Ali's son, Said Pasha, granted Ferdinand de Lesseps, a Frenchman, a concession to build the Suez Canal. But the project was not completed until the reign of Said's son Ismail I. For the opening of the canal in 1869 Ismail commissioned Giuseppe Verdi to compose the opera *Aïda*. Ismail built a new opera house in Cairo, and the first performance of *Aïda* was given on December 24, 1871. By 1875 Ismail's reckless financial policies had brought Egypt to the brink of bankruptcy, and he was forced to sell his shares in the Suez Canal Company to the

British. The British and the French assumed responsibility for the finances of the Egyptian Government. In 1879 Ismail abdicated in favor of his son, Tewfik. (An article on the SUEZ CANAL appears in this volume.)

Dissatisfaction with foreign control led to an uprising by Egyptian nationalists in 1882. The rebels were led by Ahmed Orabi, a colonel in the Egyptian Army. The British sent troops to Egypt to end the rebellion. They defeated the army of Orabi at the battle of Tell el Kebir and occupied Egypt. From that time the British controlled Egypt, although the country technically remained part of the Ottoman Empire. In the 1880's the Egyptians lost control of the Sudan to the forces of the Mahdi, Mohammed Ahmed, a Muslim religious leader. Led by the British, the Egyptian Army retook the Sudan in 1898. An Anglo-Egyptian condominium (joint rule) was set up in the Sudan, but the British actually controlled the country as they did Egypt.

World War I and Independence

Turkey allied itself with Germany against the British when World War I broke out. In order to punish Turkey and protect the Suez Canal the British declared a protectorate over Egypt. After the war the Egyptian nationalists put increasing pressure on the British for independence. Saad Zaghlul Pasha, the founder of the Wafd party, led the movement to oust the British. A 1922 declaration by the British granted Egypt conditional independence. A constitutional monarchy was established with Fuad I, a descendant of Mehemet Ali, as king. However, the privileges of foreigners in Egypt were protected, and British troops were still stationed in the country. The declaration also provided for continued British control of the Anglo-Egyptian Sudan.

In 1936 a treaty was concluded with the British. British troops were withdrawn to the Canal Zone, the special privileges of foreigners in Egypt were withdrawn, and Egypt was given more of a voice in the administration of the Sudan.

World War II and the Arab-Israeli War

Egypt was invaded by the Germans and Italians during World War II. Allied troops stationed in Egypt, repelled the German and Italian advance. The Axis troops were defeated at El Alamein, near Alexandria, in 1942, but Egypt did not officially declare war on Germany until 1945. In the same year Cairo was the scene of the founding meeting of the Arab League. Egypt also became a founding member of the United Nations.

Along with the other Arab nations Egypt strongly objected to the creation of the Jewish state of Israel in the former British mandate of Palestine. War broke out between the Israelis and Arabs in 1948. Egypt and other Arab countries were defeated. Under United Nations auspices, an armistice was signed in 1949.

The 1952 Revolt and the Sinai War

The Israeli defeat of the Egyptian Army and the widespread corruption in the government of King Farouk contributed to the rise of revolutionary ferment in Egypt. On July 23, 1952, a group of young army officers led by Colonel Gamal Abdel Nasser overthrew the monarchy. For the first time since the Persian conquest, native Egyptians took over the government of Egypt. The king abdicated in favor of his infant son, and General Mohammad Naguib became head of the Revolutionary Command Council. In June 1953, the monarchy was abolished, and Egypt became a republic, with Naguib as the first president. In 1954 Nasser ousted Naguib and took over control of the government.

In July 1956, Nasser announced the nationalization of the Suez Canal Company, whose assets were controlled by the British and the French. Three months later Britain and France invaded Egypt. Israel, which was in a veritable state of war with Egypt despite the 1949 armistice agreements, and whose ships were barred from the canal, joined in the attack. The three countries occupied the Sinai Peninsula and a part of the Canal Zone. The United Nations intervened, and the British, French, and Israeli troops were withdrawn. A United Nations peacekeeping force was stationed along the Egyptian-Israeli demarcation lines in the Sinai.

From War to Peace with Israel

The Suez campaign of 1956 bolstered Nasser's position in the Arab world and paved the way for the political union of Egypt and Syria in 1958. The new state adopted the name of the United Arab Republic, and Gamal Abdel Nasser was elected its president. But in 1961 Syria withdrew from the union and organized its own independent government.

In May 1967, the United Nations peacekeeping force in the Sinai was withdrawn at Egypt's request. In June, war broke out again between the Egyptians and the Israelis. Israel defeated the Egyptian armies and occupied the Gaza Strip, the Sinai Peninsula, and the east bank of the Suez Canal. When Nasser died in 1970, he was succeeded by Anwar el-Sadat.

The fourth conflict between Egypt and Israel broke out in October 1973. It was a hard-fought war that raged on both sides of the canal until a cease-fire brought it to a halt. United Nations peacekeeping forces were once again stationed in the Sinai. In November 1977, Sadat made a historic trip to Israel, becoming the first Arab leader to visit the Jewish state. This contact led to negotiations between the two countries that produced the Camp David agreements of 1978. These agreements led in turn to the Egyptian-Israeli peace treaty of 1979. Under the treaty, Egypt recognized Israel's right to exist. Israel withdrew from the Sinai and agreed to discuss Palestinian self-rule in Gaza and the West Bank.

The assassination of Sadat on October 6, 1981, capped a period of increasing domestic tension and isolation from the rest of the Arab world. Sadat's successor, Hosni Mubarak, while pledged to continue Sadat's policies, moved to restore harmony at home and with Egypt's Arab neighbors. Egypt was readmitted to the Arab League in 1989. Mubarak was a leader in convincing many Arab nations to join the multinational coalition that expelled Iraq from Kuwait during the 1991 Gulf War.

GOVERNMENT

Under the Constitution of 1971, Egypt's president is elected by universal suffrage for a six-year term. Members of the one-house People's Assembly are also elected by universal suffrage and serve five-year terms. Constitutional changes in 1980 allow the president to serve an indefinite number of terms, and make the Islamic code the principal source of law. A prime minister and council of ministers assist the president.

YASSIN EL-AYOUTY, St. John's University

SUEZ CANAL

About 4,000 years ago an Egyptian pharaoh ordered the digging of a canal connecting the Nile River with the Red Sea. In the centuries that followed, the canal, frequently falling into disuse, was rebuilt and its course changed several times. Eventually it fell into disrepair and was finally abandoned during the 8th century A.D.

Thereafter, travelers going by boat from Europe to Asia had to sail a long, hazardous, uncharted course around the African continent. However, interest in a canal that would shorten the distance between Asia and Europe never ceased. In 1854, Ferdinand de Lesseps, a French diplomat and engineer, was granted permission by Said Pasha, the Viceroy of Egypt, to form a company that would handle the construction and operation of a canal to be built through the Isthmus of Suez. De Lesseps founded the Suez Canal Company, which sold shares of stock to provide the financial backing needed for the waterway.

Construction of the canal began on April 25, 1859. After 10 long, arduous years, De Lesseps finished the waterway, and it was formally opened on November 17, 1869.

The approximately 107-mile-long (172 kilometers) Suez Canal stretches across the Isthmus of Suez and separates the continents of Africa and Asia. The canal runs from Port Said on the Mediterranean Sea through lakes Timsah, Great Bitter, and Little Bitter and emerges at the Gulf of Suez. Many improvements have been made since its completion, and today the canal has a width of over 500 feet (150 meters) and a maximum depth of 46 feet (14 m.).

According to an international agreement, the 1888 Constantinople Convention, the canal is open for passage by ships of all nations at all times. Under the terms of the convention, Egypt was permitted to take measures deemed necessary for national defense in time of war.

Following the first Arab-Israeli conflict (1948–49), the Egyptian Government refused to allow shipping to or from Israel through the waterway on the grounds that a state of war existed between the two nations.

In 1956, the Egyptian Government under President Gamal Abdel Nasser nationalized the Universal Company of the Suez Canal, the operating agency for the waterway. All of the shareholders in the Suez Canal Company were eventually reimbursed by the Egyptian Government.

War broke out once again between Egypt and Israel. France and Britain claimed that this military action was a threat to the security of the canal. Both countries landed troops in Egypt and occupied the Port Said area until a ceasefire was declared shortly after. During the fighting in 1956, many ships were sunk in the waterway, rendering it unusable. A salvage operation was undertaken after the war, and the canal was reopened in March, 1957. However, the ban on Israeli ships was still in effect. The Suez Canal was the scene of further conflicts between Egypt and Israel in 1967 and 1973. After the 1967 war the canal was closed because of sunken vessels clogging the waterway and because Israel occupied the east bank of the canal. After the end of the 1973 war, work began on clearing the canal and it was reopened to shipping in 1975.

Reviewed by YASSIN EL-AYOUTY, St. John's University

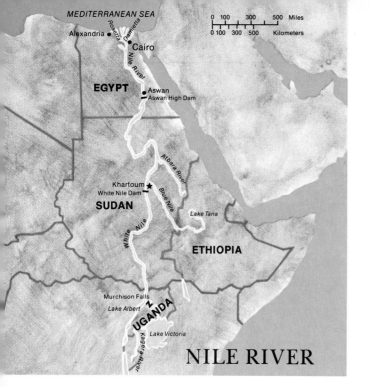

NILE RIVER

NILE RIVER

It is a great river, one of the great rivers of the world, flowing on endlessly from a dim and ancient past into the turbulent present. And yet it is more than a river; to the people lining its banks it has been a god, a source and a way of life. For thousands of years the Nile has been the main source of water, food, and transportation for millions of Africans.

The ancient Egyptians worshiped the Nile and dedicated songs to its power and beauty. Each year they appealed to the god of the Nile to bring forth the flood, which made the land fertile. As part of their appeal, the Egyptians threw a young maiden, the Nile bride, into the waters of the river. After the flood the Egyptians gave thanks to the god who filled the barns and granaries and provided for the poor. In a famous hymn to the Nile, they praised the river that issued forth from the earth to nourish the people of Egypt. But the ancient Hebrews came to dread the Nile. One Pharaoh, who feared an uprising, decreed that the Hebrews' firstborn sons must be cast into the river. A thrilling episode of the Old Testament tells of the Pharaoh's daughter, who found the Hebrew child Moses in the bullrushes of the Nile.

The great river is history, colorful and significant. Cleopatra, Queen of Egypt, sailed the Nile. Julius Caesar and Mark Antony stood by its then already ancient waters. Empires sprang up on the banks of this huge river: Nubia, Meroë, and Egypt.

The empires have disappeared, but the mighty river still flows on. Today some of the world's most modern dams span its waters, turning millions of acres of desert into fertile farmland. The Father of the Rivers, as the Egyptians reverently called the Nile, still gives sustenance to millions of people, as it did in the distant past.

Two Rivers

The Nile system is composed of two branches, the White Nile and the Blue Nile. The two branches join at Khartoum, the capital of Sudan.

It is at Khartoum in Sudan that the Blue and the White Nile come together.

The White Nile begins high in the mountains of Uganda at Lake Victoria.

For the 1,900 miles (3,000 kilometers) of its journey to the sea from Khartoum, the merged river is called the Nile.

The Nile is the longest river in Africa and one of the longest in the world. Some leading geographers say it is the longest. On its journey to the Mediterranean, the Nile passes through rugged mountains, tropical forests, and deserts.

White Nile

The beginning of the White Nile is usually placed at Lake Victoria, 3,720 feet (1,134 meters) high in the mountains of Uganda. Here the river is some 3,500 miles (5,600 km.) from the sea. Some geographers, however, pinpoint the White Nile's source at the headwaters of the Kagera River, 500 miles (800 km.) farther from the sea.

The White Nile is known by several different names. When it leaves the lake, it is called the Victoria Nile. After pouring over Murchison Falls and flowing through Lake Albert, it is called the Albert Nile. The people along this part of the river raise grain, vegetables, and fruits.

Below Lake Albert, the river's valley widens, and the White Nile wanders through lush parkland full of elephants, lions, giraffes, and other African game animals. The river, now called the Bahr el Jebel, drifts for more than 350 miles (560 km.) in narrow, marshy channels through an area in the Sudan known as the Sudd. Here, because the river moves so slowly under the hot sun, it loses almost half of its volume through evaporation and dispersal. Until the 19th century the marshes of the Sudd prevented explorers from tracing the White Nile to its source.

Once the White Nile leaves the Sudd, it moves on to Khartoum, where it is joined by the Blue Nile.

Blue Nile

The headwaters of the Blue Nile are 6,000 feet (1,800 m.) above sea level at Lake Tana, in Ethiopia. During its early stages, the river passes

A felucca works its way up the long river and passes the city of Tanta.

At Aswan the Nile begins its uninterrupted flow to the sea.

through rugged country. But before reaching Khartoum, the Blue Nile's valley broadens, and the river is used to irrigate the Gezira. The Gezira in Sudan is a vast plain of nearly 2,000,000 acres (800,000 hectares), whose main crop is cotton.

The brief summer flood of the Blue Nile carries about 60 percent of the waters of the Nile, and its flow is so strong that it blocks the much slower waters of the White Nile. During the flood, rich silt from the Ethiopian mountains is deposited in the Nile Valley.

From Khartoum to Aswan the Nile is broken by six cataracts, which alternate with smoothly flowing stretches. From Aswan, the Nile flows without interruption to the sea. Seen from the air the Nile Valley looks like a thin green ribbon winding through the desert. Except for the delta region below Cairo, the green ribbon averages only 10 to 15 miles (16–24 km.) in width.

As they have for thousands of years, farmers along the Nile still wait for the late summer flood, which leaves rich deposits of silt that help crops grow. In the past the river in some years flooded too much, and in other years too little. Today, however, large dams, especially the Aswan High Dam, help control the flow of the Nile.

After the Nile leaves Cairo, it enters the delta and splits into two main channels called the Damietta and Rosetta. The river runs through these channels for 150 miles (240 km.) and then empties into the Mediterranean.

So the historic river ends its long, long journey, a journey that took it through mountains, jungles, and arid deserts, a journey that took it past the ageless pyramids and the ancient temples of Ramses II at Abu Simbel, past Medinet Habu, and Deir el Bahari, past a farmer getting water from a waterwheel called a *sakia,* and past farmers using diesel pumps to irrigate their land. Past the inscrutable Sphinx at Giza and past the shining skyscrapers of Cairo, the river flows on, ancient and ever new.

Reviewed by YASSIN EL-AYOUTY, Fellow, African Studies Association

124

The Blue and White Nile rivers meet at Khartoum.

SUDAN

Fierce sandstorms, called haboobs, roll in over the broad expanse of yellow sand and gravel to envelop Khartoum, the capital of Sudan. The tree-lined boulevards, gardens, and flower beds, an amazing contrast to the desert a few miles from the Nile River, are soon covered with sand. The people walking on the streets are accustomed to these summer storms. They quickly gather up their belongings and take refuge in nearby buildings. Soon the storm passes, and the people return to their business.

THE LAND
The Republic of the Sudan is the largest country on the African continent and has a coastline of 450 miles (725 km) on the strategic Red Sea. Located in northeast Africa, it is bounded by Libya on the extreme northwest; the Arab Republic of Egypt on the north; the Red Sea and the Republic of Ethiopia on the east; the republics of Kenya, Uganda, and Zaïre on the south; and the Central African Republic and the Republic of

Chad on the west. In central Sudan are the Nuba Mountains; and in the west are the Jabal Marra. The Imatong Mountains in the south include Sudan's highest peak, the 10,456-foot-high (3,187 meters) Mount Kinyeti.

The Nile is the chief river. Its two chief headwaters—the Blue Nile and the White Nile—come together to form the Nile River at Khartoum. Each carries into Sudan's northern deserts life-giving waters from more rainy areas far to the south and southeast. The White Nile, which enters Sudan from Uganda, has the more regular flow. Much of its waters are lost, however, in the vast swampy area between Juba and Malakal known as the Sudd. The Jonglei Diversion, when completed, is designed to canalize the White Nile in this area and lessen water losses due to evaporation. The Blue Nile has a highly seasonal flow. It rises rapidly in the summer months, carrying rains from the Ethiopian Highlands where it originates. Dams at Sennar and Roseires hold back some of the summer flood waters for later use in irrigating cotton and other crops in the land between the two Niles known as the Gezira.

Climate. The climate is tropical with daytime highs of 100 degrees Fahrenheit (38 degrees Celsius) from February to November and 94 degrees F. (34 degrees C.) in December and January. The northern one third of the country is arid desert. The central one third has a tropical wet-and-dry type of climate with a dry season lasting from 6 to 9 months and a wooded grassland vegetation cover. Tropical rainy conditions, with high humidity and dense forests, prevail in the southern one third.

Cities

Khartoum, near the confluence of the Blue and White Nile, is the capital city. This modern city is the business and banking center of Sudan. Other important metropolitan areas are **Omdurman,** which serves as one of the great trading markets of northeastern Africa, and **Khartoum North,** which is the chief industrial center of the country. **Port Sudan** is a major commercial and shipping center.

THE PEOPLE

The Sudan is sparsely populated. Nomads make up about 10 percent of the total population, urban dwellers only about 25 percent. Traditionally, the north has been dominated by Arabic-speaking Muslims and the south by black Africans following local and Christian beliefs. Language, religion, traditional ethnic hostilities, and varying lifestyles further divide the people. This great cultural mix poses special problems for the central government of Sudan as it strives to create a national identity and still satisfy the sometimes conflicting regional needs of the people.

Peoples of the North. Arabic-speaking Muslims make up more than half of the total population. Most Arabic speakers identify themselves as Arabs (46 percent of all Sudanese), but many are of mixed ancestry. Arabs predominate in the north. Most live in cities, towns, and villages. A few, identified as part of the supertribal group known as the Guhayna, lived as nomads, raising large herds of camels and sheep in the dry lands away from the Nile River and its tributaries. During the dry season, they wander southward in search of grazing lands. In summer, as sporadic rains refresh the northern pastures, they move northward again. Baqqara Arabs living in the plains southwest of Khartoum follow a similar nomadic lifestyle but raise cattle instead of sheep and camels.

The leading non-Arab Muslim group consists of the Nubians, who are descendants of the Negroid people of the ancient empire of Kush. These people are Muslims who still speak Nubian dialects, which are giving way slowly to the Arabic language. Most Nubians occupy permanent hamlets or small villages.

The Red Sea Mountains are the home of the Beja, camel-owning Muslims who wander in small bands, following the rains for pasture for their flocks and herds. The Beja camp in rectangular tents made of a framework of poles covered with grass or palm-leaf mats.

Peoples of the South. For many years the black African peoples of southern Sudan have been under pressure to adopt lifestyles of the Muslim Sudanese to the north. Many have refused and have exerted pressures of their own on the national government to provide some form of regional autonomy for the south. It is this continuing opposition to northern control that unites the otherwise very diverse peoples of the south—the Nilotes, who live along the Nile River, and the non-Nilotic peoples. The Nilotes are dominated by three large and powerful groups: the Dinka, the Nuer, and the Shilluk. The Dinka, including more than 10 percent of all Sudanese, are the south's single largest group. Their great concern for cattle dominates their economic and religious life. The Dinka are seminomadic people, living in scattered homesteads. The houses, each surrounded by a fence or a thorn hedge, are cone-shaped. They consist of a frame of bent poles fastened together at the top and covered with interlaced branches, grass, or skins. During the dry season, when the Dinka are on the move hunting pastureland for their cattle, they live in temporary camps. While they travel, home is usually a temporary shelter made of brush and grass.

Cattle raising is the chief occupation of the Dinka, who live in southern Sudan.

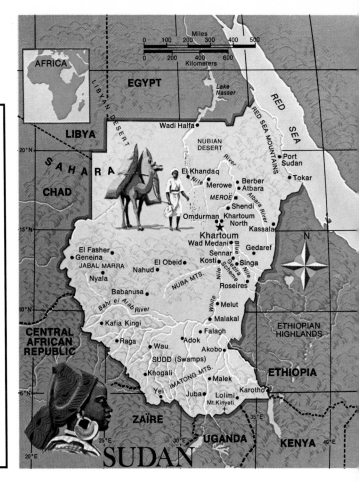

The Nuer live in the most inaccessible areas of the great swamps of the Nile, interested mainly in their large herds of cattle. They live in permanent settlements during the rainy season, and their houses are usually round with conical thatched roofs. Like the neighboring Dinka, the Nuer move their cattle to more favorable pastureland during the dry season.

The Shilluk occupy a comparatively small area on the west bank of the Nile near the settlement of Fashoda. Unlike the Nuer and Dinka, they keep only a few cattle, preferring to cultivate the land. The local community consists of either a single compact village or a cluster of hamlets. The houses are cone-shaped, made of wood or grass thatch.

The largest of the non-Nilotic groups is the Azande, who live in the region between the Zaïre and Nile basins. The Azande are primarily hunters and farmers. Their subsistence crops include peas, maize, sweet potatoes, and peanuts. The Azande are renowned as fine craftsmen and musicians.

Religion. More than 50 percent of all Sudanese and a majority of peoples in the north are Muslims. They succeeded in pressuring the national government to declare Islam the official state religion in 1983. Continuing Islamization campaigns also resulted in incorporation of traditional Islamic punishments of the Shari'a (Islamic law) into Sudan's civil penal code. Many non-Muslims, including most of the peoples of the south, oppose the new laws. Most of Sudan's non-Muslims follow local

A Sudanese classroom. Free education is available from the primary to the university level.

animist religions. A small minority, products largely of missionary schools, are Christian.

Language.   More than 100 separate languages and many more local dialects are spoken in Sudan. Arabic, the language of the northern majority, is the official language. English is widely spoken in the linguistically diverse southern region.

Food.   *Kisra,* made from sorghum, is a staple food in Sudan. It is made into thin pancakes and is often served with meat or vegetables.

Cattle herders depend on their livestock for their main source of food in the forms of milk and meat. The milk is drunk fresh, mixed with millet as a porridge, or churned into cheese and butter.

Millet is also an important food. It is made into porridge and can be brewed into a weak alcoholic beer. Fish is a staple food for those people living along the Nile River and the Red Sea coast.

Education.   Education is compulsory for ages 7 to 13 and available free from the primary to the university level. In the mid-1980s only about one-third of school-age children were enrolled in public or private elementary, intermediate, and secondary schools. However, both the number of schools and the number of pupils is on the increase. Most of the schools are operated or subsidized by the government. Sudan has two important schools of higher education, the University of Khartoum and the Khartoum Polytechnic Institute. A branch of Egypt's Cairo University is also located in Khartoum. Other important educational facilities are the Islamic University of Omdurman and universities at Wad Medani and Juba.

ECONOMY

Sudan is one of the world's poorest and least-developed countries. About 60 to 65 percent of the labor force is engaged in subsistence agriculture or livestock production. Cotton and cottonseed, grown on irrigated fields, are the chief cash crops and exports. Other export crops include sugar, gum arabic (Sudan is the world's leading supplier), sesame seeds, and peanuts. Wheat, sorghum, millet, peanuts, and beans are leading subsistence crops. Livestock herding is common in semiarid regions but is associated more with traditional nomadic lifestyles than with production for sale or export.

The economy of the dry northern half of Sudan depends largely on the Nile River and irrigation systems. One such project, the Gezira Scheme, has opened the land between the White and Blue Niles to crop raising. An agricultural development program planned for the southern region is linked to the completion of the Jonglei Canal on the White Nile. The Jonglei Canal is also expected to deliver more White Nile waters to the arid north. Other irrigation water comes from Lake Nasser, an artificial lake created by Aswan High Dam in Egypt. Wadi Halfa and many other former Sudanese settlements now lie beneath its waters.

Agricultural production in southern Sudan is limited because much of the land will not support crops and the distance is too great to the

Cotton, Sudan's major cash crop, is weighed at a station prior to export.

major markets and ports in the north to make crop production in the south economically feasible. Tobacco, sugar, rice, coffee, and oil palm have all been cultivated, but primarily on an experimental basis.

Manufacturing is on a small scale and provides less than 7 percent of the country's wealth. Textiles as well as sugar refining and other food-processing activities are the leading industries. Internal unrest postponed development of a large oil field discovered in the south in 1979.

Although Sudan does not have a good network of all-weather roads, there is an extensive railroad system in northern Sudan and limited river steamboat service between northern Sudan and Egypt. Transportation systems have not been fully developed in southern Sudan, and most long-distance travel is restricted to steamboat service along the Nile River and domestic airline service. An international airport is located at Khartoum, and there is a modern air terminal at Port Sudan.

HISTORY AND GOVERNMENT
The earliest known inhabitants of Sudan were ancient African peoples who lived there in the Stone Age. At the end of the 4th millennium B.C. the kings of the first Egyptian dynasty conquered Nubia (Northern Sudan), and thereafter Egyptian cultural influence spread upriver, culminating in the founding of the kingdom of Kush, in Nubia. Kush continued to rule over the middle Nile for about 1,000 years. In the middle of the 4th century the King of Aksum marched down from the Ethiopian Highlands, captured Meroë, the capital of Kush, and destroyed the surrounding towns.

After the fall of Kush two kingdoms emerged—Maqurra, located in Nubia, and Alwa, with its capital at Soba near modern Khartoum.

In the 14th century Maqurra fell to the Arabs. They intermarried with the Nubians and migrated southward, introducing Arabic and Muslim culture to the inhabitants. Pressing up the Nile, the Arabs allied with the Funj, a people of mysterious origins, to destroy Alwa. Thereafter the Funj dynasty, with its capital established at Sennar, ruled Sudan until 1821, when the army of the Turkish viceroy of Egypt, Mehemet Ali, invaded Sudan and destroyed the last traces of the Funj Empire.

Mehemet Ali conquered the territory that is present-day Sudan and opened it to technical and cultural innovations from the outside world. He sought to develop and control the country by introducing modern means of communication, transport, and administration. The Sudanese, under the leadership of Mohammed Ahmed, known as the Mahdi, rebelled against Egyptian control. They defeated the Egyptian armies, and destroyed Egyptian administration in Sudan. In 1898 an Anglo-Egyptian army under General Sir H. H. Kitchener reconquered Sudan. Western education and medicine were introduced, and communications—road, rail, and river transport—were expanded. In February, 1953, Britain and Egypt concluded an agreement providing for Sudanese self-government and self-determination. On January 1, 1956, Sudan achieved independence, and it was admitted to membership in the United Nations on November 12, 1956.

Following independence, a parliamentary coalition government held power in Sudan. A military coup in 1958 deposed the government, and all political parties were banned. A Supreme Council of the Armed Forces was then formed to rule the country. This government also was over-

The king whose portrait is etched on these 2,000-year-old stones ordered the construction of the Lion Temple seen in the background.

thrown, and, from 1965 to 1969, the Sudan was ruled by a five-member Supreme Council of State, a prime minister, a cabinet, and a parliament.

In 1969, after a military coup, a 10-man Revolutionary Council was set up. The council leader, Jaafar Mohammed al Nemery, won election as president under a new constitution in 1971. Running each time without opposition, Nemery was reelected in 1977 and 1983. In 1982 he negotiated an agreement with a southern Sudanese group whose rebellion had troubled the nation since independence. The agreement granted regional autonomy within a federal framework. But old tensions between the Muslim north and non-Muslim south led to civil war after 1983, when Nemery imposed Islamic law on civil courts. Sudan's economic difficulties were aggravated by Africa's great drought and an influx of refugees from Chad and Ethiopia. In 1985 Nemery was ousted from office by a military coup.

A civilian government, formed after elections in 1986, was unable to end the war in the south, and was overthrown by a military junta in 1989. In the early 1990s, the government strengthened its ties with Iran and intensified the war effort, forcibly moving hundreds of thousands of southern refugees from Khartoum to desolate refugee camps. In 1992 a transitional parliament was created to pave the way for new elections.

ROBERT O. COLLINS, University of California at Santa Barbara

WESTERN SAHARA

There is a sense of immensity, of nothingness, of a land without end. The sand stretches out to the glittering horizon. Here and there are clumps of dry grass. Overhead, the sky is blue and blazing. The heat rises in wave after wave and makes the distant sand dunes shimmer. All about is silence, complete silence. Gradually one becomes aware of a tiny, almost threadlike, moving line deep in the well of distance, near the horizon. The line begins to form moving shapes that get larger and begin to become recognizable. Now they are closer—from almost a full mile away the sound of human voices drifts across the sand. A dusty caravan of camels and riders passes by, ever moving on their journey from horizon to horizon—nomads of the desert, nomads of the Western Sahara.

THE LAND

Western Sahara is located in northwest Africa along the Atlantic coast. Morocco lies to its north. Algeria is to the northeast, and Mauritania forms the boundary on the east and the south. It was for-

The city of Al Aiún lies in the afternoon sun of a waning day.

FACTS AND FIGURES

OFFICIAL NAME: Western Sahara.

NATIONALITY: Sahrawi(s).

CAPITAL: Al Aiún.

LOCATION: Northwest Africa. **Boundaries:** Morocco, Algeria, Mauritania, Atlantic Ocean.

AREA: 102,703 sq. mi. (266,000 sq. km.).

PHYSICAL FEATURES: Highest point—2,700 ft. (820 m.). **Lowest point**—sea level.

POPULATION: 196,700 (1991; annual growth 2.6%).

MAJOR LANGUAGES: Hassaniya Arabic, Moroccan Arabic.

MAJOR RELIGION: Islam.

GOVERNMENT: Administered by Morocco. The Sahrawi Arab Democratic Republic government-in-exile became a member of the Organization of African Unity in 1984.

CHIEF CITY: Al Aiún.

ECONOMY: Chief minerals—phosphates. **Chief agricultural products**—barley, livestock. **Chief exports**—phosphates. **Chief imports**—fuel, foodstuffs.

MONETARY UNIT: Moroccan dirham.

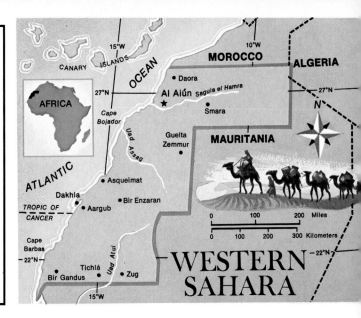

merly known as Spanish Sahara and was an overseas province of Spain. The territory was divided between Morocco and Mauritania in 1976, and has been administered by Morocco since 1979. **Al Aiún,** the capital of this low-lying, mostly arid land, is the center of Moroccan administration.

THE PEOPLE AND ECONOMY

The population of Western Sahara is extremely small. Traditionally, most Sahrawis were nomadic Arabs or Berbers raising cattle, camels, sheep, and goats. During the annual rainy season, thousands of nomads from neighboring countries that were having their dry season came to Western Sahara. When the rainy season ended, they would drift back across the borders.

Western Sahara has no agriculture and little developed industry. It does have rich coastal fisheries, and its valuable phosphate deposits have been developed by Morocco. Since 1979 Morocco has built a fortified defense wall enclosing most of Western Sahara, including almost all of its people, its fisheries, and its mineral resources. The Europeans living in the cities have been joined by Moroccans and by formerly nomadic Sahrawis forced by drought to abandon their traditional way of life.

HISTORY

During the 15th century, the country was discovered by Portuguese navigators. Spain's early attempts to colonize the area were unsuccessful. In the late 19th century, however, a protectorate was established, and in 1958 the region became an overseas province of Spain. In 1976 Spain transferred sovereignty to Morocco and Mauritania. An Algerian-backed Saharan guerrilla group, the Polisario Front, fought for independence. In 1979 Mauritania renounced its claim and made peace with the Polisario. Morocco then annexed the entire Western Sahara, but the Polisario continued to demand independence. A cease-fire supervised by U.N. observers finally went into effect in 1991. A referendum on independence was scheduled for 1992, but there was controversy over who should be eligible to vote.

Reviewed by HUGH C. BROOKS
Director, Center for African Studies, St. John's University

Mauritania's capital, Nouakchott, is a new city.

MAURITANIA

Mauritania, in northwestern Africa, is a little-known country just beginning to enter the modern world. In the north, center, and east of the country lie vast stretches of the Sahara desert, where the camel caravan is still seen much more often than the jeep or truck. The people of this region, who live by herding camels, sheep, and goats, wear turbans and long, flowing garments just as their ancestors did to protect themselves from the heat and sun.

In the south of Mauritania, the desert gradually gives way to scrub and then to humid grasslands and some areas of forest. The people of the humid lands live mainly in villages and have little in common with the desert herdsmen to the north.

THE LAND

Mauritania is sometimes called the Atlantic Sahara because here the desert and the Atlantic Ocean meet. The country has three geographic zones—the Saharan, the sahelian (semidesert), and the tropical. The Sahara desert covers about 60 percent of Mauritania—in the country's northern, central, and eastern sections.

At least half the Mauritanian Sahara fits exactly the classic picture of a cruel desert. In all directions, as far as the eye can see, are immense stretches of sand broken only by dunes (hills or ridges of sand formed by the wind), isolated rocky peaks, and plateaus. There are tremendous differences between daytime and nighttime temperatures. From November to March temperatures vary from freezing at sunrise to over 100 degrees Fahrenheit (38 degrees Celsius) by afternoon. Between April and

October the daily range is from 60 degrees F. (16 degrees C.) to more than 120 degrees F. (49 degrees C.).

The sahel lies south of the Sahara. It is a dry and scrubby steppe region only slightly less dry than the desert.

Farther south still, toward the Senegal River, lies 10 percent of Mauritania where heat, humidity, and seasonal floods have made for the growth of bushy savanna (grassland) and traces of tropical forest.

Mauritania acquired the southern part of the territory of Spanish Sahara (now Western Sahara) when Spain gave up its claims in 1976. In 1979, however, Mauritania renounced its sovereignty, and Morocco, which had acquired the northern part, laid claim to the entire area.

THE PEOPLE

Mauritania's small but varied population lives in a country 397,956 square miles (1,030,700 square kilometers) in area. The Moors ("Maures" in French) are the people for whom Mauritania was named. They are a people chiefly of mixed Arab and Berber descent who are herders of the desert and semidesert regions. They form about 60 percent of the population. The black Africans of the south make up about 40 percent of the population, and are seeking a greater voice in their nation's affairs. The main black groups are the Fulani (or Fulbe), the Tukulor (or Toucouleur, also called the Halphoolaren), and the Sarakole (or Soninke).

Moorish woman, snug within her tent, serves the traditional green tea.

The Moors speak different dialects of Hassaniyya, which is a form of Arabic. The Fulani and Tukulor speak Fulfulde (or Phoolor), a West African language, though the Tukulor speak a considerably altered dialect. The Sarakoles belong to the Mandingo language group. Mauritania's government officials usually use French. Both French and Hassaniyya Arabic are official languages of the country.

Each of the different peoples of Mauritania has its own traditions and customs. The only common bond is Islam, their religion.

Moorish Way of Life. The character of the Moor has been molded by the desert, by Islam, and by influences from black Africa. The Moor is a herdsman, of camels or of sheep and goats, depending on the region. He drives his herds from water point to water point in well established patterns. At the main stopping points he sets up camel's hair tents.

To survive in the desert, the Moor has to be resourceful and to develop his senses to a remarkable degree. He has an acute sense of direction and incredibly sharp eyes. In what looks to an outsider like a monotonous desert, the Moor sees variety—different shapes to the sand dunes and rocky crags, different shades to the sand. He can spot any moving thing at a vast distance and can make out nearly invisible paths that tell him where he is. He can also tell his location just by sniffing the air.

The Moor has an amazing memory. He is a storehouse of information about all the Moorish tribes and can recite all their family histories.

Hospitality is a strong tradition with the Moors because they all live on the move and know the needs of the wayfarer. Also, the life of the Moorish herdsman is so lonely that meetings with other people are precious. Often an invitation to a meal follows a desert encounter. The main dish served is *meshwi* (barbecued lamb, goat, or antelope). The meal begins and ends with the ritual drinking of three short glasses of *at'tay,* or tea.

Town Life. Town life is strange to the Moors, who usually prefer living in the desert. Some who now live and work in the cities of Nouakchott, Nouadhibou, and Atar shun the modern housing and set up their tents right in the town. Others, who work in offices and live in modern houses, take their lunches and tea breaks under the tents of their friends.

Black African Ways of Life. The Fulani, or Fulbe, are Mauritania's chief cowherds. They drive their herds from place to place in Mauritania's band of humid savanna. They live in temporary beehive huts (*ruga*). Their cows, which are precious to them, are kept in stockades and rarely slaughtered. The Fulani thus live mainly on milk, milk products, and millet, eating little meat.

The Tukulor (Halphoolaren), Mauritania's most numerous black group, are an offshoot of the Fulani. They gain their livelihood mainly from farming and fishing. Among the Tukulor the large extended family is important. Each such family lives in a *galle,* or large family compound. Within the compound each household has its own separate dwelling, or *poyre.* The household can look to the *galle* for help with special expenses.

The Sarakole were very likely among the first inhabitants of Mauritania. It is almost certain they were the ruling class of the old Ghana empire. Their social organization is rather like the Tukulor's.

FACTS AND FIGURES

OFFICIAL NAME: Mauritanian Islamic Republic (République Islamique de Mauritanie, or El Jumhuriya el Islamiya el Muritaniya).

NATIONALITY: Mauritanian(s).

CAPITAL: Nouakchott.

LOCATION: Northwest Africa. **Boundaries**—Algeria, Mali, Senegal, Atlantic Ocean, Western Sahara.

AREA: 397,956 sq. mi. (1,030,700 sq. km.).

PHYSICAL FEATURES: Highest point—Kédia d'Idjil (3,009 ft.; 917 m.). **Lowest point**—sea level. **Chief river**—Senegal.

POPULATION: 1,996,000 (1991; annual growth 3.1%).

MAJOR LANGUAGES: Arabic (official), French.

MAJOR RELIGION: Islam.

GOVERNMENT: Republic. **Head of state**—president. **Legislature**—National Assembly, Senate.

CHIEF CITIES: Nouakchott, Nouadhibou, Atar.

ECONOMY: Chief mineral—iron. **Chief agricultural products**—animal products (milk and meat), millet, sorghum, rice, dates, corn, cowpeas. **Industries and products**—fish and fish products, traditional handicrafts. **Chief exports**—fish products, iron ore. **Chief imports**—foodstuffs, petroleum products, machinery and equipment, consumer goods.

MONETARY UNIT: 1 ouguiya = 5 khoums.

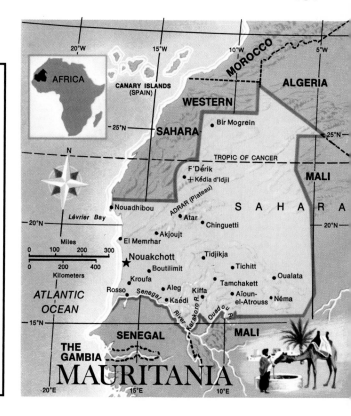

Cities. Mauritania's cities are very small. The capital, **Nouakchott,** has the largest population. It is located about 4 mi. (6 km.) inland from the coast. The city, built almost entirely since 1958, has grown rapidly in recent years. Most of the newcomers are animal herders who lost their livestock due to recurrent droughts. Many live in tent camps and survive on food aid. More than 80 percent of the population in the early 1960s were nomads; today only about 25 percent follow this life-style.

Mauritania's second largest city, **Nouadhibou,** lying at the northern end of the country's Atlantic coast, is a port of call for fishing ships from many lands. On the Senegal River are the river ports of Rosso and Kaédi. **Atar,** in the west-central region, is one of Mauritania's oldest trading towns, having been a stop on a caravan route for centuries.

Education. Although education is compulsory in principle between the ages of 6 and 12, only a minority of school-age children actually go to school. The literacy rate is below 20 percent. The country has a shortage of classrooms, well-trained teachers, and money for expansion. But the government has been innovative in its use of traveling schools. Since so many children live on the move, classrooms have been devised that can be packed up to follow the larger groups of herders.

Economy. Mauritania is one of the world's poorest countries, but its situation is no longer as hopeless as it once seemed to be. Until the 1960s Mauritania had few exploited resources and few exports. This picture changed when large deposits of high-grade iron ore in the northwest near F'Dérik began to be worked. Copper deposits were also mined in the 1970s.

Animal raising is Mauritania's chief agricultural pursuit. Sheep and goats are the most numerous, cattle next, and camels third. In the Senegal

Nouakchott's Moors and blacks, Muslims all, gather before the Grand Mosque.

River Valley, millet and other grains are grown. Dates from the date palm are raised in the highlands and in most of the oases. Mauritania's dates, grains, and animal products are mostly consumed in Mauritania.

Mauritania's offshore fishing grounds are among the richest in the world. Only foreign fleets have the technology to exploit these waters, but they are required to take the catch to Mauritanian ports for processing. Fish products are now Mauritania's chief export.

Plans to develop the iron deposits near F'Dérik began in 1952, when Miferma, an international mining company, was set up. Formerly, Miferma was controlled by French interests, but in 1974 it was taken over by the government of Mauritania. Miferma built a railroad between F'Dérik and Nouadhibou to bring out the ore. Iron ore exports total as much as 12 million tons a year.

HISTORY AND GOVERNMENT

Apparently there was no desert in Mauritania in Stone Age times. Tools, weapons, and rock drawings found in Saharan caves indicate that a Negroid people once tilled well-watered fields where there are only desert wastes today. The people, known as the Bafour, seem to have left the region when the climate changed.

Sometime before the Christian Era, the Sanhadja Berbers, a group of tribes, pushed deep into the Atlantic Sahara (Mauritania) from the north. In the 4th and 5th centuries A.D., the Sanhadjas drove southward, blazing one of the first desert trails to the Senegal River and Ghana.

When the Arabs stormed out of Arabia and across North Africa in the 7th century, the Sanhadja tribes stemmed their advance. For several hundred years, the Atlantic Sahara remained a haven for all the Berbers who opposed Arab influences and Islam.

By the 11th century, a form of Islam had filtered into the Sanhadja lands. Toward mid-century, Abdallah ibn-Yasin, a Muslim fanatic, turned the Sanhadja Berbers into religious zealots. Called *al-murabitun* (Arabic for "monks"), they overcame the wealthy Ghana empire to the south, converting its Sarakole (Soninke) leaders to Islam. Under the name Al-moravids (a corruption of *al-murabitun*), the Sanhadjas carried their strict brand of Islam into Morocco, Algeria, and Spain in the north.

The Almoravid empire collapsed about 1150, but the Sanhadjas had firmly converted northwestern Africa to their form of Islam. And on their southern flank, the conversion of Ghana's aristocracy sparked the growth of Islam throughout the West African Sudan (the northern regions of black West Africa).

About the year 1270, fierce Bedouin Arabs from southern Arabia reached Mauritania. The Beni Hassan, as these people were called, terrorized the Sanhadjas, but later merged with them. Out of this blending of adversaries came the Arab-Berber, or Moorish, people.

European Period. The Portuguese set up trading bases in Mauritania in the 15th century. The Spanish followed in the late 16th century, to be succeeded in the 17th and 18th centuries by the Dutch, the French, and the English. The Treaty of Paris of 1814 gave France rights over the coasts of the western Sahara (Mauritania) and Senegal.

The Moorish emirs of Mauritania resented French rule and fought back fiercely. By 1899 the French grew tired of Moorish raids and rebellions, and the French colonial minister announced his intention "to bring together . . . the different regions inhabited by Moors . . . under the name of Western Mauritania." The "pacification" of Mauritania covered the years 1901 to 1934, and after 1905 was marked by constant bloodshed. In 1920 Mauritania was made a part of French West Africa, which was administered from Senegal.

In 1946 Mauritania was made a separate overseas territory with its own assembly and representative in the French parliament. But it was still governed from Senegal. Finally, in 1958, Mauritania became self-governing and began to build its own capital, Nouakchott.

Independence. Mauritania became an independent republic on November 28, 1960. Moktar Ould Daddah, the nation's president since independence, was overthrown in a military coup in 1978. The following year, Mauritania renounced its claim to neighboring Western Sahara. Demands for political reform led to the adoption of a new constitution in 1991 providing for a directly elected president and a two-house legislature. Multiparty elections to return the country to civilian rule were held in 1992.

ALFRED G. GERTEINY, University of Bridgeport; author, *Mauritania*
Reviewed by ABDOU O. HACHEME
The Permanent Mission of Mauritania to the United Nations

A mosque of striking design in Djenné, a town in central Mali.

MALI

The name Mali reaches back into West Africa's past. Within the bounds of what is now the Republic of Mali lie the centers of three of the earliest and most powerful of the vanished kingdoms of Black Africa. The name of Mali is taken from one of these former empires, that of the Mandingo people.

The three kingdoms were Ghana (which should not be confused with the modern country of the same name), Mali, and Songhai. All of these kingdoms engaged in trans-Saharan trade. The earliest of the kingdoms was Ghana, which developed a flourishing gold trade. Ghana lay far from the centers of culture of the Mediterranean and the Middle East. Few people from beyond the Sahara visited it. But those rare bold merchants who did venture there came back to speak of greatness and wealth. Just as Marco Polo did a few centuries later, after his return from the Orient, these merchants spun tales that grew into legends. The commodity of trade most sought after by the people of the Ghana empire was salt. It was transported in great blocks on the backs of camels across the desert from the salt mines of Taoudéni and other salt centers in the north.

Mali also was an empire of wealth and power. Controlling territory along the Niger Valley, Mali had strong political influence in the surrounding regions. Through extensive trade its fame spread to Europe and the Middle East. The kingdom reached its peak during the 13th and 14th centuries. After that, a period of decline began and the empire slowly fell apart. By the 17th century the former kingdom of Mali had become almost a legend.

Another historic name was that of Timbuktu (Tombouctou), a town in Songhai territory. It was situated on the edge of the southern Sahara at the big bend of the Niger River. Timbuktu was founded around the beginning of the 12th century by Tuareg nomads who came down from the desert to the river during the dry season. The site had well water that was sweet and good.

From the 13th century on, Timbuktu was a trade center of the Muslim world, as well as an important spiritual, educational, and cultural center. Late in the 16th century, the city was captured by invaders from Morocco. From then on Timbuktu gradually lost its importance. But strangely enough, the glamour and mystery of the city remained. In 1827 a Frenchman, René Auguste Caillié, started a long and arduous journey to the city. He found that historic Timbuktu had dwindled to a small, sunbaked town of dried mud houses. To this day the town exists, and camel caravans still carry salt from Taoudéni to Timbuktu.

THE LAND

The Republic of Mali is a vast landlocked country in western Africa. It has an area of 465,000 square miles (1,204,350 square kilometers) and

Malians ride their bicycles past a modern bank in Bamako.

a steadily growing population. It has seven countries on its borders: Algeria, Mauritania, Senegal, Guinea, Ivory Coast, Burkina, and Niger. All of these countries, like Mali, are former French territories.

Mali covers an area that extends from desert to a semidesert region and then to partly arid tropical savannas of grassland and brush, rich with wild game. It is generally hot the year round. In the desert, which includes the northern third of the country, there is almost continuous drought and no predictable rainfall. Farther south the climate changes to one of alternate wet and dry spells.

The Niger River. The Niger, Africa's third longest river, is of great importance to the life and future development of Mali. It sweeps in a huge arc across the central part of the country. Large riverboats are able to navigate most of the river from mid-June to mid-December. At this time of the year the water level of the river is quite high. Smaller boats manage to sail the river throughout the year. In the center of the country is the fertile Niger Valley, which is one of Mali's important agricultural areas. (A separate article on the NIGER RIVER appears in this volume.)

Cities. Mali has few large cities. **Bamako,** the capital, lies in the southwest, along the Niger River. This city of palm-shaded streets and white buildings is the largest in Mali. Another important urban center is **Kayes,** situated northwest of the capital. These two cities are the leading markets in Mali for animals, hides, and skins. Kayes is also an important river and rail center. It is located in the far west of the country on the Senegal River and is a gateway to neighboring Senegal. Ségou, Sikasso, Mopti, Gao, Timbuktu, and Taoudéni are other communities in Mali.

THE PEOPLE

Mali lies in the area where white and black peoples meet. The people of the country are made up of several ethnic groups. About five sixths of the Malians are black, and of these the Mandingo are the most numerous. Among the white ethnic groups are Moors and Tuaregs, who are mostly nomadic and inhabit the desert west of the Adrar des Iforas. In the main, the black peoples tend to inhabit the wetter areas of the south, while those belonging to white ethnic groups are likely to be pastoral and to occupy the semi-arid and arid two thirds of the country.

To those who live in the dry savannas and near-desert areas, a nomadic way of life is essential to their very existence. These people follow their herds of sheep, goats, camels, and donkeys as the seasons and pasturage change. During the rainy season the nomads move toward the desert. They turn southward during the dry season.

Fishing is important to people living along the Niger. Mali is one of the few countries of Black Africa that has developed river fishing commercially.

ECONOMY

Mali has no large industries. There are small factories that produce food, beverages, soap, cigarettes, matches, and textiles. The economy of the country is based mainly upon agriculture, livestock raising, and fishing. Some Malians are irrigation farmers whose leading crops are rice, cotton, and peanuts. Other farmers cultivate lands along the Niger that are not irrigated. After the floods or during the rainy season, they plant

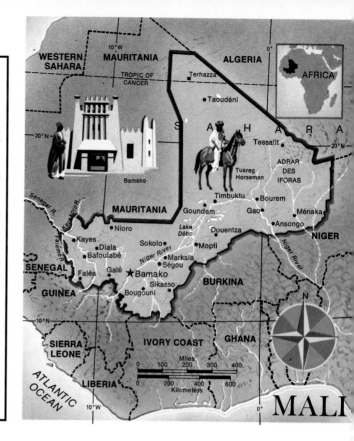

MALI

their fields of millet and rice. Still other farmers plant the uplands with cotton, millet, and peanuts during the rainy season.

Mali has, as far as is known, little mineral wealth. Some gold is being produced, but in small quantities. Salt is still mined, as in the old days.

HISTORY AND GOVERNMENT

The early history of Mali is the history of the empires of Ghana, Mali, and Songhai. Songhai was the last of these empires. It was finally destroyed by a Moroccan invasion around 1600.

Late in the 19th century, the French began to explore and then to occupy the western Sudan region. France established the territories of French West Africa in 1904. Much of the area that makes up Mali today was then called French Sudan.

In 1958, Mali, then known as the Sudanese Republic, became a self-governing member of the French Community, a group of former French colonies in Africa. In 1959 it joined with Senegal to form the Mali Federation. The federation was dissolved in 1960, and the Sudanese Republic declared its independence as the Republic of Mali.

Mali's first president, Modibo Keita, governed until 1968, when he was overthrown by the military. A 1979 constitution created a one-party state headed by an elected president. Coup leader Moussa Traoré was elected president. He held that office despite mounting pressure for democratic reform until he was overthrown in March 1991. A new constitution was adopted in January 1992. After Mali's first multiparty legislative and presidential elections, held later that same year, the military head of state Amadou Toumani Touré turned power over to an elected civilian president.

LUCILE CARLSON, Case Western Reserve University

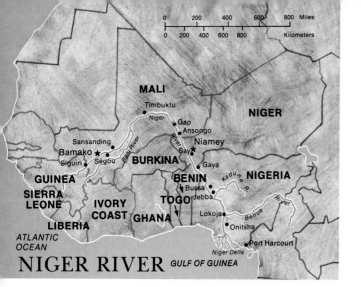

NIGER RIVER GULF OF GUINEA

NIGER RIVER

On the banks of the Niger River, a weaver sits working his strands of thread into a brilliant design. As he weaves he remembers a proverb: "As the river is eternal so will my work be eternal."

At his feet the river sweeps endlessly past, alternately raging and flowing, now twisting, now straight. From its source to its mouth, the Niger is a river of contrasts, marking great changes in the land along its course. For thousands of years the course of the river was a mystery. Since the days of the ancient Greeks, explorers dreamed of tracing its path. But it was not until the 19th century that this dream became a reality.

Life-Giver of Mali and Niger

The Niger is the third largest river in Africa—only the Nile and the Congo are longer. The impact of the Niger on the people of West Africa, however, has been as great as the influence of its sister rivers on the people of their regions. In fact, the Niger has been called "the life-giver of Mali and Niger."

For some 2,600 miles (4,180 kilometers) the Niger cuts a wide path through four West African countries—Guinea, Mali, Niger, and Nigeria—before emptying into the Gulf of Guinea. At one point the river flows along the northern border of Benin. The headwaters of the Niger are in the Fouta Djallon plateau region of Guinea, near the Sierra Leone frontier. At this point, the Niger is about 175 miles (280 km.) from the Atlantic Ocean.

The Niger River flows first northeast through the countries of Guinea and Mali until it reaches the edge of the Sahara. In its upper course, until it nears Timbuktu, in Mali, the Niger is locally called the Joliba River. The Joliba is vital to the development of two important cities in Mali, the capital, Bamako, the country's market and export center, and Ségou, for years famous for its rugs and now the headquarters of a large irrigation project.

Beyond Timbuktu the Niger flows southeast past Gao, site of the 11th-century empires of the Songhai and Mali peoples. It crosses the extreme western end of the Republic of Niger, where it is alternately navigable and made perilous by rapids until the town of Say. The dangerous Bussa rapids impede navigation as the river rushes on to Jebba, Nigeria, where one of the three bridges that span the Niger is located. The town of Jebba marks the end of the Niger's middle course. The river is navigable from Jebba to the sea between July and October, when the water level of the Niger is highest.

At its lower reaches, the Niger is joined by its most important tributaries, the Kaduna and the Benue. Below the confluence of the Benue and the Niger, in southern Nigeria, the river delta begins. It covers an area of about 14,000 square miles (36,260 square kilometers). Port Harcourt, Nigeria's second largest port city, stands near the end of the delta.

The Niger drains an area of some 580,000 sq. mi. (1,500,000 sq. km.), and throughout its long course the river affects the life of millions. For some this life continues as it has done for thousands of years. The Hausa and Djerma-Songhai peoples farm rice, peanuts (groundnuts), and millet in the fertile Niger Valley. Fishing in the Niger is extremely important to the economy of Mali. Mali is one of the few countries in black Africa that has developed river fishing commercially. The desert Tuareg and the Fulani nomads pasture their flocks on the riverbanks as they have for ages past. Near Port Harcourt, the Ibibio and Efik peoples still make their livelihood from the oil palms growing on both sides of the great river.

History

Although the existence of the Niger River was known to the ancient Greeks, its course was not explored by Europeans until the late 18th and early 19th centuries. The Scottish explorer Mungo Park is credited with the discovery of the Niger. He came upon the river during his explorations of 1795–96. But it was not until 1830 that two Englishmen, Richard and John Lander, reached the mouth of the Niger River.

In the 20th century, efforts were made to harness the power of the Niger for industrial development. One of the largest development projects is the Sansanding Dam in Mali, which has reclaimed thousands of acres of swampland since its completion in the mid-1940's.

Reviewed by SOUMANA OUSSEINI
Permanent Mission of the Republic of Niger to the United Nations

The Niger River gently flows past the small port of Kabara, located near Timbuktu, in Mali. Salt slabs, awaiting ferry transport, line the shore.

Canoes are used for transport on the Niger River.

NIGER

The town of Dosso in southwest Niger is alive with music. An air of gaiety prevails, and the sound of laughter is everywhere. Families have come from all the nearby villages to witness the colorful festivities. For the children this is a special time.

A parade is about to begin. Everyone is in readiness as the drummer in his white gown summons the warriors to assemble. He keeps beating the drum until the men of the Dosso cavalry mount their horses. Soldiers and horses alike are dressed in decorative quilted coverings. In the past the coverings worn by the horses concealed metal armor. The headpieces worn by the men are topped with a cluster of feathers. At last the warriors are in parade formation, armed with sabers, spears, and shields. Traditionally the Dosso cavalry were daring warriors, and their costumes and weapons are part of their past.

The roll of the drum stops, and the parade to celebrate Republic Day in Niger begins.

THE LAND

A glance at a map of Africa will show why Niger is sometimes called the heart of Africa or the crossroads of the continent. Covering an area of 489,000 square miles (1,266,500 square kilometers), the country is bounded on the north by Algeria and Libya, on the east by Chad, on the west by Mali and Burkina, and on the south by the nations of Benin and Nigeria.

The country can be described as a vast semi-arid to arid plateau. The greater part of Niger has an average elevation of 1,200 feet (360 meters) above sea level, with higher elevations in the central and northeastern areas. The Aïr Massif, a large mountain mass, extends from north to south across north central Niger. It includes a number of peaks above 3,000 feet (900 m.), with the highest reaching almost 6,000 feet (1,800 m.).

In the north lies the large area of desert and semidesert land, which forms part of the Sahara. Very few people live in this region because of the intense heat and lack of rainfall. Niger's most productive zone is the steppe and savanna country in the south, which extends from the Niger River in the west to Lake Chad in the east. This is the only fertile region in the country. It supports trees and shrubs, interspersed with cultivated land. Most of the people of Niger live in this area.

The most important river is the Niger, from which the country takes its name. Yet this 2,600-mile-long (4,180 kilometers) river flows through only 185 miles (298 km.) of Niger's southwestern corner.

Climate

The climate in Niger is hot and dry. Nowhere in this tropical steppe and desert land is the amount of rainfall very great, and the northern half of the country receives less than 4 inches (10 centimeters) a year. At times the heat is so intense that the rain evaporates before it hits the ground. The rainy season runs from June through September. Total rainfall decreases from south to north, and the climate becomes hotter

A nomad rests in the shade and watches as workers prepare a new roadbed.

and drier. Daytime temperatures of over 90 degrees Fahrenheit (32 degrees Celsius), and frequently over 100 degrees F. (38 degrees C.), are not exceptional.

Cities

The few and relatively small cities in Niger are located in the southern half of the country. **Niamey,** the capital and largest city, is a port on the Niger River. It serves as the principal focus of trade routes in the southwest. **Zinder, Maradi,** and **Tahoua** are the other towns of significant size. These towns are the administrative and trade centers in south central Niger. The only sizable community in the northern half of the country is Agades. This was the main stopping place for caravans en route from Libya to Nigeria. Today, the market square in Agades is the trading center for livestock and agricultural products raised in southern Niger. It is from the markets of Agades that many goods are shipped to other parts of western Africa.

THE PEOPLE

The population of Niger is extremely diverse. It consists of numerous ethnic groups, some of whose traditional lands extend across existing political boundaries. The Hausa are the largest group, making up more than 50 percent of the country's total population. They are farmers living in southern Niger and are separated only by a boundary from their kinsmen in northern Nigeria. The second principal group is the Djerma-Songhai. They, too, are primarily farming people, living in the southwest along the Niger River. The area, watered by the Niger River and its tributaries, affords an opportunity for the people to cultivate rice, millet, and peanuts. There is also a belt across southern Niger where underground water tapped by wells is used by the farmers in raising peanuts, millet, sorghum, peas, and beans. Lesser concentrations of population are found in the area around Lake Chad in the southeast. Outside these areas there are small, scattered groups of nomadic herders who raise cattle, sheep, and

Friends greet each other on a street in Niamey, the capital of Niger.

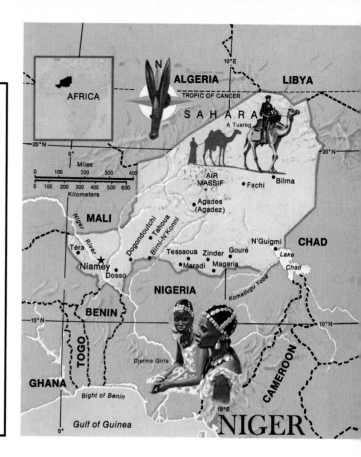

FACTS AND FIGURES

OFFICIAL NAME: Republic of the Niger (République du Niger).

NATIONALITY: Nigerian(s).

CAPITAL: Niamey.

LOCATION: Northwest Africa. **Boundaries**—Libya, Chad, Nigeria, Benin, Burkina, Mali, Algeria.

AREA: 489,000 sq. mi. (1,266,500 sq. km.).

PHYSICAL FEATURES: Highest point—5,900 ft. (1,798 m.). **Lowest point**—300 ft. (91 m.). **Chief river**—Niger.

POPULATION: 7,448,048 (1989).

MAJOR LANGUAGES: French (official), Hausa, Djerma.

MAJOR RELIGIONS: Islam, traditional African religions, Christianity.

GOVERNMENT: Republic. **Head of state and government**—president. **Lesiglature**—National Assembly.

CHIEF CITIES: Niamey, Zinder, Maradi, Tahoua, Agades.

ECONOMY: Chief minerals—uranium, tin, tungsten. **Chief agricultural products**—millet, sorghum, cowpeas, cassava, peanuts, sugarcane, onions, sweet potatoes, cotton. **Industries and products**—food processing, livestock, hides and skins, soap, textiles. **Chief exports**—uranium, live animals, vegetables, cigarettes, hides and skins, peanuts and peanut oil. **Chief imports**—petroleum products, machinery and transport equipment, foodstuffs.

MONETARY UNIT: Franc CFA (African Financial Community).

goats. The Tuareg, the most notable of these groups, live in the highlands of north central Niger.

Way of Life

The people of Niger, particularly those in the rural communities, have kept alive the rich artistic traditions of their forefathers. On market day in Niamey, women tend the stalls. They wear fine gold and silver jewelry made by native artisans. Displays of decorated gourds, bowls, and chiseled pieces of pottery can be seen, along with musical instruments made from roughly tanned and treated leather. There are delicately sculptured animals and figurines made of beaten gold. The work of Niger's artisans has been seen and admired far beyond the country's borders. Their talent has enabled these craftsmen to win gold and silver medals at exhibitions in Paris.

Most of the population of Niger are of the Islamic (Mulsim) faith. There are some Christians and animists, but they are in the minority.

Education

Because of the sparseness of population and the nomadic ways of the people, educational facilities did not develop. There are few schools in the towns, and classes for children in the villages are often held in straw huts. France, however, has helped its former colony to expand the system, and by 1980 some 200,000 pupils attended elementary and secondary schools. The University of Niamey accommodates about 1,000 students, and some receive scholarships to study in other countries.

French is the official language of the country, although there are virtually as many languages as there are ethnic groups.

ECONOMY

About 95 percent of the people are dependent on agriculture or herding for their livelihood. Peanuts have been the leading cash crop and in some years bring 60 to 75 percent of the export earnings. For many years income from this crop was assured because the French guaranteed to purchase the peanuts at a price above general world market prices, but in recent years this support has been discontinued. Niger must compete with other West African producers on the open world market. Other exports include livestock, hides and skins, and gum arabic. Until the late 1960's mineral production was virtually unknown, with the exception of salt quarries at Bilma and small quantities of tin mined in the Aïr Massif region. But the mineral picture has changed markedly with the discovery of high-grade uranium deposits in the remote Arlit district, north of Agades. The governments of France and Niger financed a project for the mining and processing of uranium, and by 1981 Niger had become the world's fourth-leading producer.

A number of smaller projects are under way or completed. Construction has begun on a textile plant, a cement plant, a flour mill, and a meat cold-storage plant. In agriculture, cotton production is being encouraged with some success, and there are programs for digging more wells and introducing methods of improving the quality of livestock.

Transportation

With about 5,000 miles (8,000 km.) of roads, some of which are paved, and no railroads, vast stretches of the country cannot be easily reached and are visited only rarely by those willing to undergo the hardships of a difficult overland journey. Aircraft can overcome time and distance in reaching remote areas, and though there is no need for regular air service to such areas, the government has built a number of landing fields, recognizing that air service can be indispensable in emergency situations. There is a large international airport located in Niamey as well as smaller fields in outlying towns.

In this arid country there are practically no water routes except for some seasonal navigation on the Niger. Since rapids form a natural barrier both at the Mali border and at Bussa in Nigeria, river travel from Niger to neighboring countries is almost impossible. However, the construction of a dam and other river improvements at Kainji, in Nigeria, offers the prospect of a water route from Niamey to the Gulf of Guinea.

HISTORY AND GOVERNMENT

The first historical references to Niger date back to Roman times. Despite its inaccessibility—it lies almost 1,000 miles (1,600 km.) from the Mediterranean coast—Roman expeditions penetrated the region.

The beginnings of the Songhai Empire, which was based at Gao on the Niger River in Mali, have been traced back as far as the 7th century. The 1,000 years that followed were a time of warfare, as tribes migrated into the territory and the different groups vied for domination of the area. In the 10th century immigrants from eastern and northern Africa took control of much of the land along the trade routes in what is now southern Niger and northern Nigeria, and established small kingdoms known as the Hausa city-states. These people eventually set up prosperous farming and trading communities. The Fulani, rebelling against the

Hausa rulers, conquered the territory and set up their own kingdom at the beginning of the 19th century.

During this same period, the first Europeans appeared in the area. Mungo Park, a Scotsman, was the first to explore the southwestern part of the territory. He was followed by a succession of European explorers, who passed through the territory in the middle of the 19th century.

French occupation of the area of present-day Niger took place in the late 1890s. The Colony of the Niger, the forerunner of the modern state, was established in 1922. It became the largest and probably the poorest of the eight colonies that made up French West Africa. In 1958 President de Gaulle of France presented the Constitution of the Fifth French Republic to the French dependencies, giving the people of each of those territories more control over their internal affairs. Niger achieved full independence on August 3, 1960.

GOVERNMENT

Under the Constitution of 1960, Niger was a republic with an elected president. Legislative power was vested in an elected National Assembly. In 1974 the government was overthrown, and all executive and legislative powers were assumed by a military council. A "Second Republic" was declared in 1989, following unopposed elections for the presidency and the restored legislature. In 1991 demands for reform led to the convening of a national conference that stripped President Ali Saibou of his powers. A prime minister, aided by a high council (transitional parliament), was to run the government pending multiparty elections scheduled for 1993.

EUGENE C. KIRCHHERR, Western Michigan University
Reviewed by SOUMANA OUSSEINI
Permanent Mission of the Republic of Niger to the United Nations

A traffic policeman in front of the National Assembly Building in Niamey.

CAPE VERDE

Cape Verde is a crescent-shaped archipelago of 15 islands lying in the Atlantic Ocean about 300 miles (480 kilometers) west of Senegal. This former territory of Portugal consists of 10 large islands and five smaller, uninhabited ones. The total land area is 1,557 square miles (4,033 square kilometers). Cape Verde has been an independent nation since 1975.

The islands are largely volcanic in origin and, for the most part, mountainous and rugged. The only active crater, Pico do Fogo, which last erupted in 1951, is located on Fogo Island. This rather imposing half-moon-shaped volcano reaches a height of 9,281 feet (2,829 meters).

The Cape Verde islands have strange and strong contrasts. The higher regions and the coasts have little plant life and are, in fact, almost barren. However, there are some large areas of luxuriant tropical vegetation found in the interior valleys. Animal life is limited to what one might find on a farm: goats, pigs, sheep, and cattle. There are several varieties of birds. Perhaps the greatest attraction of the province is the exceptional clearness of the waters, abounding in fish of all species, which provides great opportunities for underwater fishing. Whales are seen quite often and were the object of great whaling activity in the 1800's.

The climate of the islands is generally warm with temperatures averaging about 75 degrees Fahrenheit (24 degrees Celsius) throughout the year. The rainy season for the province is from July to November. But there have been years when no rain has fallen at all.

Towns.   **Mindêlo,** on São Vicente Island, is the largest town in the archipelago and serves as an international fueling station for the sea trade. Its harbor, Pôrto Grande, is one of the finest ports along the Atlantic coast. **Praia,** located on São Tiago Island, is the capital of Cape Verde.

THE PEOPLE

Cape Verde has a mixed Portuguese-African population. The archipelago was uninhabited when the Portuguese first arrived in the 1460's. They set up plantations and brought in workers from the nearby African mainland to cultivate the land. Through the centuries, the Portuguese and the Africans intermarried. Today their descendants make up about 70 percent of the population. There are a few thousand Europeans living on the islands, and the rest of the people are Africans.

The people on each island have developed their own customs and traditions, including differing dialects made up of Portuguese and various African tongues. However, the dominant language of the province is Verdean creole, which is basically a simplification of Portuguese. Roman Catholicism is the official religion.

The Cape Verdeans have the highest rate of literacy of all the people of the former Portuguese territories. The schools on the islands are run by the government.

ECONOMY

Although arable land is at a premium, the economy is based primarily on agriculture. Most of the people are subsistence farmers raising

FACTS AND FIGURES

OFFICIAL NAME: Republic of Cape Verde (República do Cabo Verde).

NATIONALITY: Cape Verdean(s).

CAPITAL: Praia.

LOCATION: Atlantic Ocean west of Senegal.

AREA: 1,557 sq. mi. (4,033 sq. km.).

PHYSICAL FEATURES: Highest point—Pico do Fogo (9,281 ft.; 2,829 m.). **Lowest point**—sea level.

POPULATION: 386,500 (1991; annual growth 3.0%).

MAJOR LANGUAGES: Portuguese (official), Crioulo or Verdean creole.

MAJOR RELIGION: Roman Catholicism.

GOVERNMENT: Republic. **Head of state**—president. **Head of government**—prime minister. **Legislature**—one-house National People's Assembly.

ECONOMY: Chief mineral—salt. **Chief agricultural products**—sugarcane, bananas, cassava, sweet potatoes, corn, potatoes. **Chief industries**—fish processing, salt refining. **Chief exports**—fish, bananas, salt. **Chief imports**—foodstuffs, machinery and transport equipment, petroleum products.

MONETARY UNIT: 1 escudo = 100 centavos.

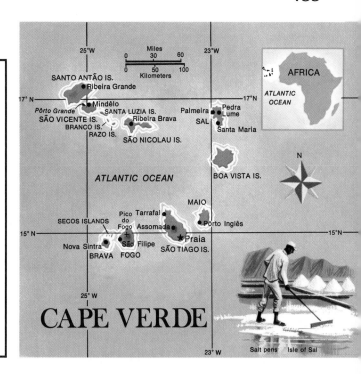

CAPE VERDE

Salt pens   Isle of Sal

such crops as beans, corn, sweet potatoes, and sugarcane. Bananas are the only important cash crop. An aggressive reforestation program has been under way since independence to combat severe soil erosion. Salt abounds on many of the islands and is a major export.

Fishing is the leading industry. The government is also encouraging tourism and light industry. Because the islands offer so little employment, as many as 700,000 Cape Verdeans have emigrated to the United States, Europe, Brazil, and other parts of Africa. Remittances from overseas workers and foreign aid are economic mainstays.

HISTORY AND GOVERNMENT

The archipelago was discovered and claimed between 1460 and 1462 by the Portuguese. For the next three centuries, the islands had a period of peace and prosperity. Recurrent drought, famine, and crop failure have plagued the islands since the late 1800s. In the 20th century, the archipelago regained some importance as a refueling stop on transatlantic trade routes.

The Cape Verde islands remained a part of Portugal for more than 500 years. In 1974 the government of Portugal was overthrown, and the new Portuguese leaders promised independence to the African territories. Cape Verde officially became independent on July 5, 1975. It has a republican form of government. The president is the head of state. The prime minister serves as the head of government. The legislature is the National People's Assembly. Plans to unite Cape Verde with Guinea-Bissau were abandoned in 1981. Cape Verde was a one-party state until 1990. In the nation's first multiparty elections, which were held in 1991, the ruling African Party for the Independence of Cape Verde was defeated.

Reviewed by HUGH C. BROOKS
Director, Center for African Studies, St. John's University

SENEGAL

Léopold Sédar Senghor, the first president of Senegal, is a world renowned author and poet, who expresses his feelings and hopes for his homeland through his writings. In one poem he sings of his dry, sandy homeland, a landscape dotted with scrub trees and the gnarled, twisted branches of the baobab.

Throughout Senghor's works there is a love for his people and their way of life. He has long pressed the claims of African culture under the banner of *negritude,* and he sponsored the first World Festival of Negro Arts in 1966 in Dakar.

THE LAND

Senegal is on the Atlantic coast of West Africa, bounded on the north by Mauritania, on the east by Mali, and on the south by the Republic of Guinea and Guinea-Bissau (formerly Portuguese Guinea). It has an area of nearly 76,000 square miles (196,800 square kilometers). Except for a short coastline, Senegal completely surrounds The Gambia, a country that stretches inland for about 200 miles (320 kilometers) on either side of the Gambia River.

Most of Senegal is a rolling plain less than 500 feet (150 meters) above sea level, sloping gently downward from foothills in the southeast toward the Atlantic and the Sahara. Around the Casamance River in the south, there are swamps and woodlands. Oil palms are predominant in

Children play in front of their village near the Casamance River.

this area. In the semi-arid and sandy soils of the central and northern regions, the vegetation consists mainly of the squat acacia and baobab trees. This vegetation gradually thins out toward the desert until only clumps of scrub are found.

The Senegal River, the longest in the country, flows along the northern border. It is navigable all year round from Saint-Louis to Podor, and during the rainy season as far as Mali. Two other important rivers, each having a port for oceangoing ships, are the Saloum and Casamance.

Climate

The climate throughout most of Senegal is generally warm with little temperature variation. There are only two seasons in Senegal—wet and dry. During the rainy season, from June to October, the southern part of the country has quite a bit of rainfall, but little or no rain falls in the dry season, November to May. The northern section of the country receives less than 20 inches (50 centimeters) during a somewhat shorter rainy season.

Cities

Dakar, Senegal's capital, has a population of about 1,000,000. It is situated on the Cape Verde peninsula, the westernmost extension of the African continent. This strategic position has led to Dakar's development as a major ocean port and air center. The Yoff International Airport handles jet planes and is a principal stop between Europe and South America and between North America and southern Africa. Dakar is the administrative and industrial center of Senegal. Its busy streets, planned

A newly built office building stands on Place de la Independence, Dakar.

to catch both sea and land breezes, are dotted with vast stone administration buildings, new high-rise apartment houses, and modern hotels.

Saint-Louis, with a population of about 50,000, was the capital of Senegal until 1958. It is the center of the coastal fishing industry, and its shady streets recall provincial towns of southern France. **Kaolack**, a major rail center, is in the heart of the peanut-producing area. Other important cities are Thiès, Ziguinchor, Rufisque, Tambacounda, and Diourbel.

THE PEOPLE

Most Senegalese are dark-skinned and slender. Wolof is the most widely used language, although French is Senegal's official language. Some 80 percent of the Senegalese are Muslim, 5 percent are Christian, and the rest hold animistic beliefs.

In the country, long flowing robes and light caps are worn by Muslim men. Women wear long dresses or multicolored robes with overblouses and head scarves to match. They often adorn themselves with gold or silver bracelets, rings, and earrings.

The fish market on the beach of Dakar is often a busy place.

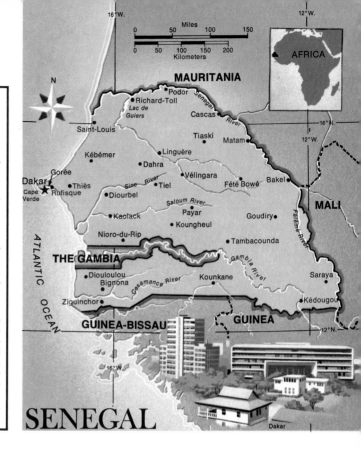

SENEGAL

FACTS AND FIGURES

OFFICIAL NAME: Republic of Senegal.

NATIONALITY: Senegalese.

CAPITAL: Dakar.

LOCATION: West Africa. **Boundaries:** Mauritania, Mali, Guinea, Guinea-Bissau, Atlantic Ocean.

AREA: 75,750 sq. mi. (196,192 sq. km.).

PHYSICAL FEATURES: Highest point—1,906 ft. (581 m.). **Lowest point**—sea level. **Chief river**—Senegal.

POPULATION: 7,953,000 (1991; annual growth 3.1%).

MAJOR LANGUAGES: French (official), Wolof.

MAJOR RELIGIONS: Islam, animistic beliefs, Christianity.

GOVERNMENT: Republic. **Head of state**—president. **Head of government**—prime minister. **Legislature**—National Assembly.

CHIEF CITIES: Dakar, Thiès, Kaolack.

ECONOMY: Chief minerals—calcium and aluminum phosphates. **Chief agricultural products**—peanuts, cotton, millet, sorghum, rice, sweet potatoes, beans. **Industries and products**—food processing, peanuts and peanut products, fishing. **Chief exports**—manufactures, fish products, peanuts, petroleum products, phosphates. **Chief imports**—textiles, motor vehicles, petroleum products, rice, sugar, machinery.

MONETARY UNIT: Franc CFA (African Financial Community).

The Wolof account for 44 percent of the population, which numbers 7,953,000. They live mainly in the area between Saint-Louis and Dakar and are primarily farmers who raise millet and peanuts. Although the majority of the Wolof are Muslims, they still practice the ancient custom of honoring and making offerings to household deities. A group of people closely related to the Wolof are the Lebu. They are primarily fishermen who live in the Dakar area. The Serer resemble the Wolof, but are smaller in stature. They live in the area between Dakar and The Gambia. Like the Wolof, the Serer cultivate peanuts. They are efficient farmers who also keep cattle, sheep, and goats to help fertilize their lands.

The Tukulor and Fulani live in the Senegal River valley. The black Tukulor are farmers, while the light-skinned Fulani are nomadic herdsmen. During the dry season, the Fulani graze their cattle in the farmlands of the Tukulor people. When the Tukulor farmers begin cultivation of their crops in the wet season, the Fulani move on to other parts of the river valley. There are Fulani in the Casamance region who, unlike their nomadic brothers in the north, are settled and semiagricultural.

South of The Gambia are the Diola, industrious farmers who are related to the Serer. The Mandinka-Bambara live mainly in the foothills of the southeast, where they cultivate millet. Many of these people often find work in Dakar and neighboring towns.

Europeans, Syrians, and Lebanese account for the approximately 1 percent of the population that is non-African. These people are concentrated chiefly in the large cities, and hold teaching, technical, and administrative positions. A number of the Lebanese and Syrians are merchants, and the majority of the large commercial houses and most of the industries are under the control of non-Senegalese.

From fortified Gorée island many slaves were shipped to America.

Way of Life

Most Senegalese, except the nomadic Fulani, are traditionally divided into distinct social classes. The highest classes are the nobles and freeborn peasants. Below them are the artisans (blacksmiths and leatherworkers) and minstrels. At the bottom are the descendants of slaves. The nobles and freeborn peasants freely intermarry. The artisans and minstrels, however, are traditionally bound to their inherited status and rarely marry out of it. The minstrels are musician storytellers attached to noble families, and their occupation is to sing the praises of those who performed great deeds in the past. Although these class distinctions are still observed among the Wolof, Serer, and Diola, they are gradually disappearing. The government, through education and by providing better economic opportunities, is making all of the people of its country truly Senegalese.

In the countryside, farmers, who work small plots of land, live together in villages with communal granaries and ovens. Their houses are made of sun-dried mud bricks, with conelike thatched roofs. In the interior of Senegal it is usual for an extended family of at least three generations to live together, acknowledging the authority of a family head. The head of such a family group must ensure that the proper respect is shown to the spirits of the family's ancestors, who are expected to guard the welfare of the living. Heads of families usually make up a village council. Except among the Christians, polygyny is practiced by men who can afford separate households for each wife. A woman's daily chores include pounding millet into flour, washing clothes, spinning cotton, tending a small vegetable garden, and attending the daily market. Most children work in the fields alongside the men.

About 25 percent of Senegalese children attend elementary and secondary schools. The University of Dakar, established in 1957 from

Workers collect harvested peanuts on the outskirts of Dakar.

already existing colleges of medicine, law, science, and liberal arts, has about 10,000 students.

ECONOMY

Senegal is primarily an agricultural country. Peanuts are the main crop, with millet, sorghum, and rice important secondary crops. Millet is grown in rotation with peanuts, sweet potatoes, beans, and corn. The cultivation of rice in the Casamance swamps has met with less than satisfactory results. Experiments in mechanized agriculture and irrigation are being made to increase rice production. Farmers still prefer to plant the income-producing peanut. The peanut and its by-products form about 80 percent of Senegal's exports. Commercial fishing is rapidly becoming an important industry, and of the new cash crops being developed, cotton has proved the most successful.

Of the few minerals found in Senegal, phosphates are the most important. They are among the leading exports of the country.

HISTORY AND GOVERNMENT

The ancient Tukulor kingdom of Tekrur developed in the Senegal River valley in the 9th century as a southern terminus to the trans-Saharan caravan trade route of the Moors. The Tukulor people adopted Islam in the 11th century and were largely instrumental in spreading the new faith in western Africa. Tekrur resisted outright conquest by the empires of Ghana and Mali, but at various times it was brought under the sway of Wolof and Fulani rulers. The Wolof established a considerable coastal empire by the 15th century, but it gradually broke up into component states.

The first Europeans to arrive were Portuguese mariners, who reached the Cape Verde peninsula by 1445 and set up trading posts along the

In colorful costume, Senegalese women dance at a backyard party.

Atlantic coast. By the 17th century, the French had replaced the Portuguese at several of these posts. During this time and into the 18th century, the French concentrated mainly on the slave trade.

In the mid-19th century, the French began moving inland from the coast. Though they met with resistance from the people, by the end of the century, they had conquered all challenges to French rule.

Senegal was administered as an overseas province of France, though it remained culturally African and predominantly Muslim in religion. During the 19th century, the Senegalese inhabitants of Saint-Louis, Gorée, Rufisque, and Dakar became full citizens of France with voting privileges. From 1900 on, however, the Senegalese began to demand more control over their own affairs.

After World War II, Senegal sought independence. It became self-governing within the French Community in 1958, and joined with the Sudanese Republic (now Mali) in the Mali Federation in 1959. When the federation broke up in 1960, Senegal became independent. The poet Léopold Sédar Senghor, who had led Senegal's drive to independence, served as president from independence until his retirement in 1980. His successor, Abdou Diouf, won presidential elections in 1983 and 1988.

Senegal has been a multiparty democracy since independence. The president, who is limited to two seven-year terms, is the head of state. The post of prime minister, abolished in 1983, was restored in 1991. Members of the National Assembly are elected for five-year terms.

From 1982 to 1989, Senegal and The Gambia were joined in a confederation called Senegambia. Border conflicts with Mauritania in 1989 led to violent riots and mass deportations from both countries. Senegal joined the military alliance against Iraq in the 1991 Gulf War.

DOROTHY O. HELLY, Hunter College of the City University of New York

THE GAMBIA

On February 18, 1965, the nation of The Gambia was born. The British flag, after flying for almost 200 years, was slowly lowered. With great joy the people unfurled the red, green, and blue Gambian flag. The band played the stirring music of the new national anthem, whose first stanza expresses the hope of The Gambia's diverse people:

For The Gambia, our homeland
We strive and work and pray,
That all may live in unity,
Freedom and peace each day.

This anthem is a wedding of the old and the new, for the melody is an old African one and the words are new English ones. And so The Gambia became the 115th member of the United Nations and a member of the Commonwealth of Nations.

THE LAND

The Gambia is located directly on the bulge of the west coast of Africa. Three of its sides are completely surrounded by Senegal, while the fourth side fronts on the Atlantic Ocean. The country is a tiny one, both in area and in population; its area is 4,361 square miles (11,295 square

Peanuts, The Gambia's major crop, are loaded on boats at the port of Banjul.

kilometers), and its population is among the smallest on the African mainland. The one large city is Banjul (formerly called Bathurst), which is also the nation's capital.

Banjul lies at the mouth of the Gambia River and is the country's only seaport. It is the center of the peanut trade and also plays a major role in fish processing. It has an excellent natural harbor and can dock large oceangoing ships. Smaller towns include Brikama, Bakau, Kuntaur, Georgetown, and Basse.

The major river is the Gambia, which flows through the heart of the country. Steamers travel up and down the river frequently and are the principal means of communication between the people in the capital city and those up-country.

Climate

The Gambia is a low-lying country covered by coarse grass and clumps of small trees. Along the riverbank, however, there are thick mangrove swamps containing trees up to 100 feet (30 meters) high. The climate is subtropical. From November to May the country is generally dry and cool with low humidity. It is during these months that a dusty wind often blows down from the Sahara. From June to October rainfall is heavy, averaging about 40 inches (100 centimeters) on the coast. The temperature ranges annually from 60 degrees Fahrenheit (16 degrees Celsius) to 110 degrees F. (43 degrees C.).

THE PEOPLE

Except for the inhabitants of Banjul and the few small population centers, most of the people of The Gambia are settled in rural areas. They usually live in a compound that consists of a group of huts arranged in a circle and surrounded by a wall or a fence. The huts are round and made of mud walls with thatched roofs. People a little better off than their fellows might use bricks, stone, or plaited bamboo, with corrugated iron sheets for the roof. The people who live in a compound form a group that sociologists call an extended family. This type of family consists of a husband with his wife, or in some cases several wives, their children, plus the husband's brothers and their families. The relationship between all these people is as brother and sister, uncle and aunt. Several of these compounds grouped together form a village. Usually, all of the people within one such village trace their descent from a common ancestor, generally on the father's side.

The major peoples of The Gambia form five distinct groups: the Mandingo, the Fula, the Wolof, the Jola, and the Serahuli. They may all appear to live in much the same manner, but their histories are quite different, as are their social systems. For example, in some groups the oldest citizen is considered the chief, and he exercises traditional authority. In others there is only a village council of elders that makes decisions.

On a national level there are two major political parties. The head of government is the president. The legislature, the House of Representatives, is a unicameral body (having a single house).

The Mandingo and the Serahuli

The Mandingo are by far the largest group of people in The Gambia. Together with the Serahuli they account for about half the population.

FACTS AND FIGURES

THE GAMBIA is the official name of the country.
THE PEOPLE—are called Gambians.
CAPITAL: Banjul.
LOCATION: West Africa. **Boundaries**—Senegal, Atlantic Ocean.
AREA: 4,361 sq. mi. (11,295 sq. km.).
PHYSICAL FEATURES: Highest point—240 ft. (73 m.) above sea level. **Lowest point**—sea level. **Chief river**—Gambia.
POPULATION: 700,000 (latest estimate).
MAJOR LANGUAGES: English (official), Mandingo, Wolof, Fula.
MAJOR RELIGIONS: Islam, Roman Catholicism, traditional African religions.
GOVERNMENT: Republic. **Head of state**—president. **Legislature**—one-chamber House of Representatives.
CHIEF CITY: Banjul (44,500).
ECONOMY: Chief agricultural products—peanuts, rice, millet, corn. **Industries and products**—peanut processing, fishing, handicrafts. **Chief exports**—peanuts and peanut products, fish and fish products. **Chief imports**—foodstuffs, machinery and transport equipment.
MONETARY UNIT: 1 dalasi = 100 butut.

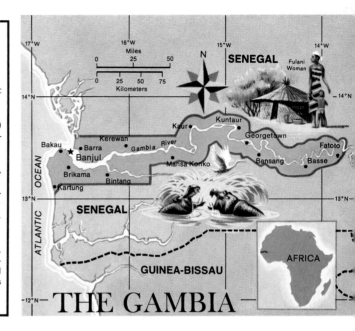

THE GAMBIA

Most Mandingo are farmers, raising peanuts for export. The Mandingo trace their origins to the great kingdom of Mali in the Sudan. They are also traders and shopkeepers. During the height of the slave trade, the Mandingo bought slaves in the interior and then sold them to Europeans on the coast. Today the Mandingo language is the most widely spoken in business, although English is the official language of the government. The Serahuli, who are culturally related to the Mandingo, live in the eastern part of the country and are mainly traders or farmers.

The Fula

The Fula, who are called Fulani in Nigeria, are the second largest group, and are in many ways different from the others. They are a pastoral people whose culture revolves around the raising of cattle. Some Fula have left the land and settled in the towns, but most of them have remained with their flocks. These Fula are always moving, looking for better pasture when the old is exhausted.

The Wolof

At one time the Wolof were ruled by hereditary kings, to whom certain divine characteristics were attributed. They maintained elaborate courts in capital villages, and taxes were paid to them to support their court and servants.

In addition to the aristocracy in the Wolof state, there were a hereditary military class, a class of commoners, a class of servants to the king, hereditary house servants who were descendants of slaves, and some true slaves.

Today the Wolof are mostly farmers, living in rural communities consisting of thatched huts grouped around a village square. Drumming, wrestling, and dancing are forms of entertainment. Wolof women are among the most beautiful in Africa today. They dress in bright-colored garments, use heavy gold earrings and other jewelry, and have a regal bearing.

Household utensils as well as food are sold in the market at Banjul.

In Banjul, the Wolof are among the best educated of the Gambians and provide many leaders of the country. They play an important part as traders, teachers, craftsmen, and civil servants.

The Jola

The Jola are found mostly along the Gambia River. Traditionally, they had no kings and lived in small, tight-knit communities that ruled themselves without formal governments. Each man's wealth was measured by the number of cattle and goats he owned. Each head of a family lived with his relatives, dependents, and servants in an enclosed village. The Jola are hardworking people, and their way of life is little changed from that of their forefathers centuries ago.

Economy

The Gambia is primarily an agricultural country. Peanuts are the main crop, accounting for some 80 percent of the exports, and they are often planted instead of needed food crops. Because of this practice much of The Gambia's food has to be imported. In the past only a small quantity of rice was grown, mostly by women. However, since 1965 the nation has greatly increased the cultivation of this staple food.

The Gambia has no known minerals of any value and practically no large industries. There are some fairly small local industries devoted to weaving, garment making, rice milling, peanut oil refining, soft drink bottling, and fishing. Along with peanuts, other exports are palm kernels, hides, dried mollusks, beeswax, and dried and smoked fish. Leading imports are cotton cloth, foodstuffs, petroleum products, and machinery. The country has no railroads, but it does have good all-weather roads.

EDUCATION

Nearly two-thirds of the nation's children attend primary schools, but only about 16 percent go on to secondary schools; only about 27 percent of the adult population is literate. Gambia College offers post-secondary school courses in teacher-training, health, and agriculture, and there are several post-secondary technical training schools. Students seeking a university education must study abroad.

HISTORY AND GOVERNMENT

This region of West Africa was one of the first discovered by the Europeans in the 15th century, when Portuguese explorers arrived at the mouth of the Gambia River. But long before that The Gambia was part of a large territory that was controlled by the medieval kingdoms of the Sudan. One of these kingdoms was Mali, and the descendants of its people, the Mandingo, live in The Gambia today. Since Mali and its successor, the Songhai Kingdom, had strong connections with the peoples of the Sahara and North Africa, the influence of these areas eventually reached The Gambia. The northern traders brought the Muslim religion with them, and almost everyone in The Gambia became a follower of Mohammed. Today Islam is the principal religion of the country.

The Portuguese explorers were followed by traders from their own country. In later years the Dutch, the British, the French, and the American colonists sent traders to the area. All sought the riches of this part of Africa. First they came looking for gold, then they took slaves, ivory, hides, and beeswax. The brig *Revenge* sailed to The Gambia from New York in 1748 with a cargo of rum, muskets, and brass pans and basins and returned with slaves, gold, and dyewood. Thirty to 40 ships from the American colonies called there each year.

But it was eventually the British and the French who contested for permanent occupation of what is now The Gambia. The Treaty of Versailles (1783) confirmed British claims to the area. Until 1888 the area was governed by British merchant groups. In that year, the British Government made The Gambia a crown colony and protectorate. In 1965 full independence was granted to the country.

The Gambia became a republic under a new constitution in 1970. A president, who has been directly elected by universal adult suffrage since 1982, is head of state. Most members of the legislature, the single-chamber House of Representatives, are elected. Sir Dawda Jawara, The Gambia's president since 1970, remained in office following elections in 1972, 1977, 1982, 1987, and 1992. From 1982 to 1989 The Gambia and neighboring Senegal were joined in the Confederation of Senegambia and cooperated on matters of defense and economic development. The president of The Gambia served as vice-president of Senegambia.

EDWARD H. SCHILLER, Nassau Community College
Reviewed by HUGH C. BROOKS, Director, African Studies Program, St. John's University

GUINEA-BISSAU

Guinea-Bissau is a small country lying on the west coast of Africa. Until recently it was governed as an overseas province of Portugal and was known as Portuguese Guinea. In 1974 it became one of the newest of the world's independent nations. Guinea-Bissau includes both an area on the African mainland and a group of offshore islands. The total land area is 13,943 square miles (36,125 square kilometers).

THE LAND AND PEOPLE

The coastline is heavily indented by inlets and gulfs. Almost the entire country is flat lowland, with many swamps and pools in the southwest. The only high ground is located in the southeast and rises to about 800 feet (240 meters). The coastal region and the islands are covered with forests and palm trees. The rest of the country is less forested. The major rivers are the Cacheu Mansôa, Corubal, and Geba. The rivers, lagoons, and canals provide the most important means of transportation within Guinea-Bissau. The capital and chief port of the country is **Bissau,** situated on the Geba River estuary. It is a modern city with a radio station, museum, cathedral, hospital, and well-equipped airport. It also has regular steamship connections with Portugal. Other cities are Cacheu, Bolama, Bafata, and Farim.

The population of Guinea-Bissau numbers over 800,000. Most of the people are Africans from many distinct ethnic groups. The principal groups are the Balante, Fulani, and Mandingo. These peoples present great differences in language and customs. The Balante are scattered

A rope footbridge crosses one of Guinea-Bissau's many streams.

FACTS AND FIGURES

OFFICIAL NAME: Republic of Guinea-Bissau.

NATIONALITY: Guinea-Bissauan(s).

CAPITAL: Bissau.

LOCATION: West Africa. **Boundaries:** Senegal, Guinea, Atlantic Ocean.

AREA: 13,948 sq. mi. (36,125 sq. km.).

PHYSICAL FEATURES: Most of the country is flat. **Chief rivers**—Cacheu, Mansôa, Geba, Corubal.

POPULATION: 1,023,544 (1991; annual growth 2.4%).

MAJOR LANGUAGES: Portuguese (official), Cape Verde-Guinea creole, Fulah, Mandingo, Balante.

MAJOR RELIGIONS: Islam, animistic beliefs, Christianity.

GOVERNMENT: Republic. **Head of state**—president. **Head of government**—prime minister. **Legislature**—National People's Assembly.

CHIEF CITY: Bissau.

ECONOMY: Chief agricultural products—peanuts, rice, palm kernels. **Industries and products**—oil refining, soap, processing of agricultural products. **Chief exports**—peanuts, coconuts, timber. **Chief Imports**—foodstuffs, machinery.

MONETARY UNIT: Peso.

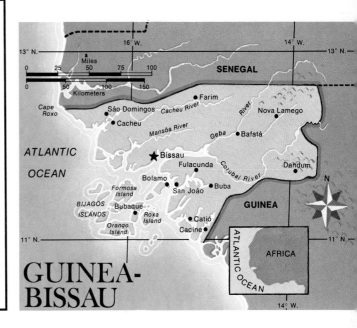

GUINEA-BISSAU

over a wide area in the coastal lowlands. The Mandingo and Fulani live mostly in the interior of the country in small communities. Important crops include peanuts (the largest export item), rice, and palm kernels.

Many people speak Portuguese. Other languages include Cape Verde-Guinea creole, Fulah, Mandingo, and Balante.

HISTORY AND GOVERNMENT

Portuguese Guinea was discovered by Europeans in 1446 by Nuno Tristão, a Portuguese explorer. Few trading posts were set up in the territory before the 1600s. From then until the 19th century the territory was used mainly as a source of slaves.

Because Portugal did not explore and settle the interior, its territorial claim in Guinea was disputed by both the British and the French. In 1879 the territory formally became a colony of Portugal. Most claims were settled in 1886, and final boundaries were achieved in 1905.

In the 1950s Dr. Amílcar Cabral formed the African Party for the Independence of Guinea and Cape Verde (PAIGC). By the early 1960s guerrilla attacks had begun against the Portuguese. In 1973 the PAIGC declared the territory's independence as the Republic of Guinea-Bissau. Portugal recognized Guinea-Bissau's independence in 1974.

Guinea-Bissau and Cape Verde had planned eventual unification into a single nation. Guinea-Bissau's pro-union government, however, was overthrown in a military coup in 1980. The constitution of 1984 vested legislative power in the indirectly elected National People's Assembly. The president of the Council of State, chosen by the Assembly from among its members, served as head of state and government. In 1991, faced with popular pressure for political reform, the ruling PAIGC ended 17 years of one-party rule. The post of prime minister, abolished in 1984, was reestablished later that year. Multiparty presidential and legislative elections were scheduled for late in 1992, and a presidential form of government was to be instituted in 1993, after the elections.

Reviewed by HUGH C. BROOKS, Director, Center for African Studies, St. John's University

City and harbor of Conakry.

GUINEA

The children of Guinea are growing up in two different worlds, the world of the old and the world of the new. Many still have parents engaged in traditional activities: growing crops by hand or raising cattle. At the same time that their parents earn their livings in this old, traditional way, the children go to modern schools where they learn French, English, and Arabic. Each child also speaks his traditional language, which is the language of his family, his mother tongue. So in the very languages he learns to speak, the child expresses the old and the new in Guinea.

THE LAND AND THE PEOPLE

The Republic of Guinea lies on the west coast of Africa. It is bounded by Guinea-Bissau (formerly Portuguese Guinea), Senegal, and Mali on the north, the Ivory Coast on the east, and Sierra Leone and Liberia on the south. Guinea has a total land area of almost 95,000 square miles (246,000 square kilometers).

The sources of a number of important rivers are in Guinea. Two of West Africa's major rivers, the Niger and the Senegal (called the Bafing in Guinea), begin in the plateau region of the country. The waters of these rivers and those of the Konkouré River are very helpful to Guinea's agriculture. The Niger, which rises 175 miles (280 kilometers) from the Atlantic Ocean, flows through a number of countries before sweeping into the Gulf of Guinea, 2,600 miles (4,200 km.) from its source.

Guinea consists of four geographical regions, each with different characteristics and different peoples. The first region is the coastal plain, a low-lying area close to the Atlantic Ocean. It has a typically tropical

Students parade in Conakry to celebrate Guinea's Independence Day.

climate with rainfall of usually over 100 inches (250 centimeters) annually and high temperatures throughout the year. This area is inhabited by a number of ethnic groups of which the most important are the Susu and the Landuman. The second region is the Fouta Djallon, also known as Middle Guinea. This, the country's most spectacular area, is a land of cliffs and plateaus. It is cut through by many rivers and valleys and is inhabited largely by the Fulani peoples. The third region, which lies lower than the Fouta Djallon, is Upper Guinea. Through it a series of small rivers drain into the mighty Niger. This is drier country than the coastal plain or the Fouta Djallon and is the home of the Fulani and the Malinke peoples. The fourth region is the Guinea highlands, a forest area in the southern part of the country. It is Guinea's most remote area and is inhabited by a variety of smaller ethnic groups, including the Kissi, Guerzi, Toma, Malinke, and Kouranke.

The government has made great efforts to bring about change in the country's educational system. It plans to have every child in a classroom and encourages adults to attend special classes to learn reading and other skills. Education is free and compulsory in principle for all children between the ages of 7 and 13. The educational system was nationalized in 1961, and new emphasis was placed upon technical, commercial, and political training The structure of Guinea's educational system still resembles the French model, but the major Guinean languages are now used in the schools along with French. Both the number of schools and the number of students enrolled in them have risen rapidly since independence. Despite this progress, however, it is estimated that only 20 percent of adult Guineans are able to read and write.

Cities. Conakry, a modern community, is the national capital and major port and the hub of Guinea's transport network. Rising on the island of Tombo, it is linked by bridge to the mainland. Conakry has a natural deepwater harbor. Guinea's second city, **Kankan,** is much smaller in size but is a major inland trading center. Other important towns are Kindia, Labé, and Siguiri.

ECONOMY

Guinea is primarily an agricultural country. Most of the people make their living through the traditional pursuits of agriculture and cattle raising. Livestock is raised throughout much of the country except on the coastal plain, and there are an estimated 1,800,000 cattle and 400,000 goats.

The farmers raise crops to be exported or to be sold locally. These crops vary in the different regions of Guinea. In the coastal plain, for example, bananas are grown on plantations, largely for export. Many of the plantations are located close to railway lines or to the port of Conakry. The port has special equipment for the loading of bananas. Rice is cultivated in two varieties, the wet type, which is raised underwater, and hill rice, which is grown dry. Yams and cassava are also cultivated, primarily for family consumption.

In the Fouta Djallon, bananas, citrus fruits, and pineapples are grown. The hill country is also suitable for coffee cultivation. Inhabited by the Fulani, who have been herders for centuries, this is also an area for cattle raising. The Fulani and their cattle herds are also found in the region of Upper Guinea. The farmers there grow groundnuts (peanuts), tobacco, cotton, and seeds for commercial sale, while they cultivate cassava and millet for family use. There is little farming in the remote Guinea highlands. Kola nuts are grown on a small scale, and some coffee and tobacco are also cultivated.

A Guinean choral group. The photograph is of Sékou Touré, the country's first president.

FACTS AND FIGURES

OFFICIAL NAME: Republic of Guinea.

NATIONALITY: Guinean(s).

CAPITAL: Conakry.

LOCATION: West Africa. **Boundaries**—Senegal, Mali, Ivory Coast, Liberia, Sierra Leone, Atlantic Ocean, Guinea-Bissau.

AREA: 95,000 sq. mi. (246,000 sq. km.).

PHYSICAL FEATURES: Highest point—5,748 ft. (1,752 m.), in the Nimba Mountains. **Lowest point**—sea level. **Chief rivers**—Senegal, Niger, Konkouré.

POPULATION: 7,455,850 (1991; annual growth 2.5%).

MAJOR LANGUAGES: French (official), numerous local languages.

MAJOR RELIGIONS: Islam, traditional African religions, Christianity.

GOVERNMENT: Republic. **Head of state**—president. **Legislature**—National Assembly.

CHIEF CITIES: Conakry, Kankan.

ECONOMY: Chief minerals—bauxite, diamonds, iron. **Chief agricultural products**—cassava, rice, plantains, sugarcane, citrus fruits, bananas, peanuts, corn, palm kernels, coconuts, coffee, pineapples. **Industries and products**—alumina, food processing, palm oil, textiles. **Chief exports**—bauxite and alumina, pineapples, bananas, palm kernels, coffee. **Chief imports**—petroleum products, metals, machinery and transport equipment, foodstuffs.

MONETARY UNIT: 1 syli = 100 cauris.

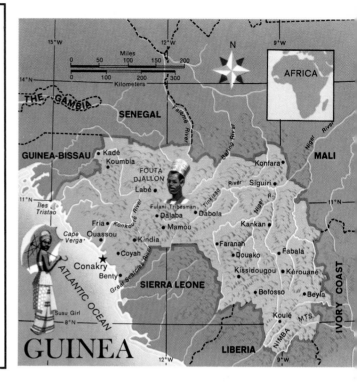

GUINEA

Guinea's most important minerals are bauxite, diamonds, and iron ore. The diamonds are mainly of an industrial variety—very few of them are gemstones. Bauxite ore, used to make aluminum, is found in rich deposits, the most important of which is at the town of Fria, about 90 mi. (140 km.) from Conakry. Here the ore is used to make alumina that is exported to aluminum refineries elsewhere in the world. Large deposits of iron ore are being worked at quarries in the Kaloum Peninsula, around Beyla and Kérouané, and in the Nimba Mountains.

Transportation in Guinea is not well developed, although a network of roads now covers much of the country. The main railroad, originating in Conakry, runs to the Niger River at Kankan, a distance of about 400 mi. (640 km.). Other lines connect the main mining areas with Conakry. International airports are located at Conakry and Kankan.

HISTORY AND GOVERNMENT

The Upper Niger Basin, which includes Upper Guinea, is part of the landmass that lies south of the Sahara. In this region a number of African kingdoms began and flowered.

In the 11th century A.D. the Arabs moved from northern Africa into the regions of the Sudan. From then on, it is believed, a number of kingdoms existed in the area. Some of them have become well-known, such as the kingdoms of Ghana, Mali, and Gao. At various times the Fouta Djallon was part of these kingdoms.

The Portuguese came into the area sometime during the 14th century. However, they did not establish any lasting settlements in what is now Guinea. The French established trading posts along the Atlantic coast inland from Senegal. They developed commercial interests in Guinea in the 1850s. As they moved inland, they came into conflict with a kingdom created by Samory Touré. Samory Touré, the son of a trader, had built his kingdom through military genius and political wisdom. By 1875, he had established his authority over many of the small chieftainships in the Upper Niger Basin. By 1886 he had extended his kingdom to include all of the Guinea highlands area and portions of present-day Mali and the Ivory Coast.

When the French came into his territory, Samory Touré led a brilliant campaign, but his forces were outnumbered and had to retreat. As his nation retreated, they conquered new peoples to the east. By 1896 Touré had lost much of his kingdom within Guinea. However, he maintained an almost completely new domain covering the entire northern portion of the Ivory Coast, northwestern Ghana, and the southern segment of present-day Burkina.

In 1898 he was captured by the French and deported to an island off the coast of Gabon, where he died two years later. Samory Touré remains an important historic figure of modern Guinea. His memory is revered. After Samory Touré's death, Guinea's history followed that of the other French West African colonies.

Until the end of World War II, French policy emphasized the differences between the ethnic groups in Guinea and those in other parts of French Africa. In the years following the war, a new sense of unity began to emerge among the educated Africans—the sense of being African. A political party arose in Guinea that emphasized the similarities between Africans rather than the differences between ethnic groups. A leader of this party was Sékou Touré. He pointed out again and again that all men are brothers and all men are equal. He said to his people, "I am a man like you, and I am an African." Using this kind of aproach, the Guinea Democratic Party (Parti Démocratique de Guinée, or PDG) soon emerged and began to move the country toward independence. This was achieved on October 2, 1958, after the Guinean people, following the leadership of the PDG, voted against association with France. Sékou Touré became the first president of the new Republic of Guinea.

During the next 25 years, Sékou Touré transformed the nation into the People's Revolutionary Republic of Guinea. Officially the country had a republican form of government, with a popularly elected president and a one-chamber legislature, the National Assembly. In practice, however, Guinea became what political scientists call a one-party mobilizational state. There was only one legal political party, the Guinea Democratic Party, which operated by mobilizing as much of the population as possible to participate in political life. The government took a very active role in the economy through state agencies and long-term planning.

Touré was elected to a fourth term as president in May 1982. A new constitution was adopted during the same month. On March 27, 1984, Touré died of a heart ailment. Only a week later, the armed forces staged a coup. The constitution was suspended, and the country was administered by the Military Committee for National Regeneration (CMRN); its chairman served as head of state. A new constitution approved late in 1990 led to the replacement of the CMRN in January 1991 by a military-civilian National Transition Council that would oversee a transition to multiparty democracy. After parliamentary elections planned for late 1992 and presidential elections in 1993, Guinea was to return to civilian rule.

WILLIAM FRIEDLAND, University of California at Santa Cruz

A view of Freetown and its excellent harbor.

SIERRA LEONE

Sierra Leone is a small country on the west coast of Africa, situated just at the bulge of the continent. Its name, a curious one for a land and its people, means "mountains of the lion." Some say the name comes from the sound of the thunder rolling through the mountains during a storm, a fearsome sound like the roar of a huge lion. Others say that during the 15th century Portuguese sailors, far from their homeland, suddenly sighted wooded peaks rising abruptly from the swampy coast of West Africa. They saw in the outlines of the rugged and majestic mountains the shape of a lion. Their imaginations were fired and they called the area Serra Lyoa. The name gradually changed over the centuries to the present one of Sierra Leone.

THE LAND

Sierra Leone has a land area of 27,900 square miles (72,261 square kilometers). It is bordered on the north and west by Guinea and on the southeast by Liberia. Sierra Leone's 210-mile (338-kilometer) coastline features one of the world's largest natural harbors, at Freetown. **Freetown,** located on the north shore of the Sierra Leone Peninsula, is the nation's capital, largest city, and principal port. The other main towns, including Bo, Makeni, and Kenema, are much smaller There is a minor port at Pepel, the mining depot for iron ore exports. Sierra Leone has an international airport at Lungi, which is linked to Freetown by ferry.

Father and son, dressed in caftans, stroll along a street of Bo.

The land lying behind the rugged Sierra Leone Peninsula ranges from mangrove swamps by the ocean, to broad, flat plains farther inland, to the mountains in the southeast corner of Sierra Leone. The interior of the country is well-watered by a network of rivers and streams, some of which flow rapidly through deep and narrow valleys. Others meander, losing themselves in swamps, letting their waters seep slowly through rice fields and marshes to the sea. The chief rivers of the country are the Great Scarcies and Little Scarcies, located in the north, and the Sewa and Moa in the south.

Climate. The climate is hot and quite humid. There are two distinct seasons—wet and dry. The rainy season lasts from May to November. Its arrival is heralded by fierce thunderstorms. These storms are most violent along the Sierra Leone Peninsula, where churning black clouds, pierced by thrusts of lightning, race along the coast. The storms are followed by 5 months of steady monsoon rains before another, shorter, storm period precedes the dry season.

The harmattan, the hot, dry wind blowing south from the Sahara, which is responsible for the dry season, is felt most strongly in the interior and northern regions of Sierra Leone. As the harmattan pushes southward during December and January, the humidity falls and the air fills with dust particles. When the harmattan retreats during March and April, the air gradually clears again and it rains more frequently.

ECONOMY

Sierra Leone's economy is basically agricultural, with more than 80 percent of the population working on the land. The country's main crop is rice. It also produces coffee, cacao, fruits, cassava, groundnuts (peanuts), palm products, and lumber. Sierra Leone's main industries include

FACTS AND FIGURES

OFFICIAL NAME: Republic of Sierra Leone.

NATIONALITY: Sierra Leonean(s).

CAPITAL: Freetown.

LOCATION: West Africa. **Boundaries**—Guinea, Liberia, Atlantic Ocean.

AREA: 27,900 sq. mi. (72,261 sq. km.).

PHYSICAL FEATURES: Highest point—6,390 ft. (1,948 m.). **Lowest point**—sea level. **Chief rivers**—Great Scarcies, Little Scarcies, Sewa, Moa.

POPULATION: 4,274,543 (1991; annual growth 2.6%).

MAJOR LANGUAGES: English (official), Krio, Mende, Temne.

MAJOR RELIGIONS: traditional African religions, Islam, Christianity.

GOVERNMENT: Republic under military rule. National Provisional Defense Council wields executive and legislative power.

CHIEF CITIES: Freetown, Bo, Kenema, Makeni.

ECONOMY: Chief minerals—diamonds, iron, bauxite, rutile, gold. **Chief agricultural products**—rice, coffee, cacao, fruits, cassava, palm products. **Industries and products**—palm processing, clothing, footwear, cigarettes, furniture, handicrafts. **Chief exports**—rutile, bauxite, diamonds, coffee, cacao, palm kernels. **Chief imports**—vehicles and machinery, manufactured goods, foodstuffs, petroleum products.

MONETARY UNIT: 1 leone = 50 cents.

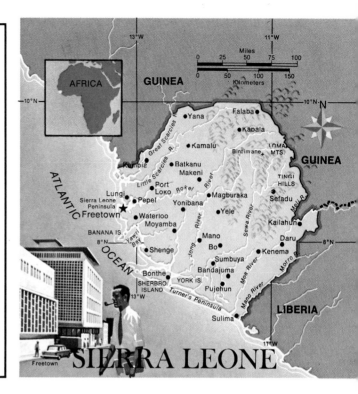

SIERRA LEONE

processing rice and palm kernels; manufacturing cigarettes, shoes, clothing, furniture, and cement; brewing beer; and canning fish. The country's mineral wealth, considering its small size, is large. Iron and rutile, a form of titanium oxide used in making paints, are valuable exports. Diamonds are an important source of foreign currency. Bauxite, from which aluminum is made, is another major export. Sierra Leone also produces small quantities of gold and platinum.

THE PEOPLE

There are many ethnic groups in Sierra Leone, but the way of life for most of them is basically similar. The two major groups in the interior are the Temne, predominant in the north and west, and the Mende, in the south and southeast. There are also significant numbers of people who identify themselves as Fulani, Limba, Loko, Kono, Yalunka, Koranko, Susu, and Sherbro. A group known as the Creoles live mainly in the Freetown area. There are also small communities of Lebanese and Syrians.

Religion. Most Sierra Leoneans follow animistic beliefs. There are, however, many Muslims and Christians in the country. A large proportion of the Temne and neighboring groups like the Koranko, Susu, and Yalunka are Muslims. Most of these people were converted to Islam during the 19th century. At that time, Fulani peoples from an area in present-day Guinea brought Islam into Sierra Leone and across West Africa during a jihad, or holy war, against nonbelievers.

Some people in the country believe in a single god who created the earth, but then chose to withdraw and not interfere in the day-to-day life of the people. The control over life crises, such as birth and death, good or bad harvests, or illness and health, was left to lesser spirits and the influence of one's ancestors. The sacred law of the ancestors, combined with a belief in the power of the ancestors to reward and punish, is the most powerful force maintaining law and order in the everyday life of many Sierra Leoneans.

The south and southeastern parts of the interior are largely Christian, as a result of European missionary efforts in the 19th and 20th centuries. But in every village, as in the Freetown metropolis, people of all three religions live side by side.

Way of Life

Most of the people of the interior are farmers. They live in houses that are made by building a frame of sticks, filling in the open spaces with mud, and covering the roof with savanna grass, palm thatch, bamboo tiles, or sheets of corrugated iron. The houses may be round, square, or rectangular, depending upon the ethnic group and the region of the country. Mende people tend to build square or rectangular houses, while Temne people favor circular styles. The houses are clustered into villages along wide central streets. Often one's nearest neighbor is also a relative, such as an uncle or cousin.

Each household consists of a man, his wife, his children, and perhaps grandparents and unmarried sisters or brothers. If a man is well-to-do he may have more than one wife. He usually builds a separate hut for each wife and her children. A Sierra Leone household, therefore, may actually have many buildings and consist of a large number of related people. The sense of family unity is very strong in Sierra Leone, as it is throughout Africa. Many evenings are spent with the entire family gathered around the last coals of the cooking fires, sipping palm wine and listening to stories of famous warriors and great hunters of the past. The people also listen to simple tales such as those of Cunnie Rabbit, the clever folk hero of the animal kingdom.

The farmer in the provinces grows rice, his basic food. Cassava is a popular substitute when the rice harvest is poor. In the form known as *fufu*, cassava is eaten with *palaver* sauce. Peanuts, fruits, such as oranges, bananas, plantains, and pineapples, and vegetables like okra, tomatoes, and beans are grown. Usually the farms are small, about 4 acres (2 hectares), and only produce enough food for a man and his family. Sometimes a man has extra rice or fruits to sell in the market. He may then acquire enough money to buy better agricultural equipment, or to send his son to the government school with a supply of books, or to buy a brightly colored *lappa* for a new dress to please his wife.

There are three groups in Sierra Leone who do little or no farming. They are the Fulani in the north, the Sherbro on the coast, and the Creoles in Freetown and in the mountain villages of the peninsula.

The Fulani live in a thinly populated region around Kabala, a town in the northeastern part of the country. They move frequently so their herds of small fat Ndama cattle can graze in the sparse bush country. Here they must be very careful not to damage the rice fields planted by the Limba, Yalunka, or Koranko farmers. Because the Fulani live in temporary huts much of the year, they keep their personal possessions simple—a few cooking pots, hammocks, and a little clothing. When they come into the villages they exchange meat, milk, and butter for rice and vegetables with the farmers. Some Fulani families have moved farther south where they have become herdsmen in Temne or Mende villages. They often tend large herds for the chiefs. Travelers often meet Fulani herders, clad in colorful flowing robes, driving their cattle to the markets of the major provincial towns or to those of Freetown.

The Sherbro live in small, crowded villages along the southern coast, and they spend a great deal of their time fishing. They paddle their long canoes a distance from the shore, trailing baited lines and simultaneously casting nets into schools of fish. These huge schools of fish can generally be seen swimming just below the surface of the crystal-clear water. Fishermen also use tremendous nets that have a funnel or pocket in the center. One end of the net is anchored on the beach while the other is carried by a boat through the churning surf. The fishermen usually spread

King Jimmy's Wharf, Freetown, is a meeting place for the city's people.

their nets twice, once in the early dawn and again with the approach of evening. As their boats return to shore at sunset after a long, hard day of fishing, they chant in rhythm to the even motion of the wet paddles.

The fishermen keep some of the day's catch for their own use, but most of the fish is immediately sold. Women of the markets gather on the beaches to meet the boats. They load big enamel pans with fresh fish and then return to Freetown to sell their purchases.

The Creoles are descendants of freed slaves from England and America who settled in Freetown and the surrounding area. A great number of Creoles are also descended from slaves liberated after 1807 from slave ships destined for the New World. The Creoles wear Western-style clothing, speak English, and generally live in two-story wood or concrete houses, similar in style to those in Europe and America.

Life in Freetown Today. Traditional life in Sierra Leone is changing rapidly, especially in the towns and cities. A good example is the capital city of Freetown. Students from every ethnic group attend the University of Sierra Leone. On the main streets of the city are modern office buildings. On other avenues are clusters of small houses of the newly arrived up-country peoples. The many markets are crowded with shoppers. Hawkers thread their way through the bustling streets selling hammocks, colorful straw baskets, and *garra* cloth, beautifully dyed from locally grown indigo. European, Lebanese, and Creole traders fill every alcove with hardware, shoes, tinned groceries, records, and curios for the tourists.

Life in this city seems to vibrate far into the night. People walk in the evenings, listening to music from radios in open windows, chatting with friends, and buying shish kebabs or slices of fresh coconut from lantern-lit stalls. The quiet of a village in the interior and the divisions of language and culture are forgotten in the excitement of the development of a new and modern Sierra Leone.

Education

For many years the government and the leading educators of Sierra Leone have struggled with the problem of wide-ranging illiteracy. Even today only about 15 percent of all adults in Sierra Leone know how to read and write. Nevertheless, the nation has made a great deal of progress in education. Many primary schools have been built, and hundreds of thousands of students have received basic education. The government is also building more secondary schools and granting scholarships to needy and deserving students. The most important advanced institution is the University of Sierra Leone, which consists of Fourah Bay College and Njala University College. Fourah Bay College, founded in 1827, is the oldest institution of higher learning in West Africa.

HISTORY AND GOVERNMENT

Portuguese sailors were the first Europeans to venture into the area. During the 15th century, traders sailed past the mountains rising on the coast, landed, but did not settle. For 3 centuries the people of the area were plagued by the slave trade. Neither the Portuguese traders nor the British, who followed them, established any truly permanent settlements. In 1787 Granville Sharp, a noted and energetic British abolitionist, established a colony as a home for freed slaves. Appropriately, the col-

The busy fish market in Freetown attracts many buyers.

ony originally was called the Province of Freedom. Sierra Leone was under British control during the years from 1787 until 1961, when it gained its independence.

Milton Margai, who had led the country to independence, became its first prime minister. At his death in 1964, he was succeeded by his half brother, Albert Margai. Following disputed elections in 1967, the army took over the control of the government. A civilian government was re-established in 1968 under Siaka Stevens. In 1971 Sierra Leone became a republic headed by a president. In 1978 a new constitution made Sierra Leone a one-party state. General Joseph Momoh succeeded Stevens as president in 1985, but Stevens remained head of the ruling All People's Congress until his death in 1988. In the 1990s economic problems sparked demands for political reform. A new multiparty constitution was adopted in 1991, but elections were delayed after the civil war in neighboring Liberia spilled over into Sierra Leone. In 1992 Momoh was ousted by military officers who established the National Provisional Defense Council to rule the nation. They said they favored a return to democracy.

LEO SPITZER, Dartmouth College, and MANON L. SPITZER

This small village lies in a rain forest in central Liberia.

LIBERIA

Pepper birds twitter overhead in the banana trees as two young boys, Como and Juju, and their mother walk silently through the forest. They carry baskets of purple-red kola nuts and slowly make their way to the village clearing. A group of mud huts, quiet in the hot tropical sun, comes into view.

It is market day. Men in striped robes gather with friends, while their wives, in flashing copper jewelry and bright head scarves, lay out their food and wares on bamboo mats. The village marketplace abounds with color—heaps of white rice, green okra, purple-blue eggplants, and kola nuts against the rich browns of baskets and mats. Como and Juju dash off to greet and play games with other children before the chief officially opens the market. In Liberia market day is more than a time for selling goods. It is the time for seeing old friends, exchanging news and good stories, and feeling pride in the community—all important parts of the African way of life.

THE LAND

The Republic of Liberia is located on the western bulge of Africa, a few degrees north of the equator. Its Atlantic coastline stretches about 350 miles (560 kilometers) between Sierra Leone on the northwest and the Ivory Coast on the southeast. Guinea is the bordering country to the north. At Cape Palmas, Liberia's southernmost point, the shoreline of West Africa turns eastward and fronts the Gulf of Guinea. Liberia has an area of about 43,000 square miles (111,370 square kilometers). Its coast was once known as the Grain Coast, after the "grains of paradise," or malagueta peppers, which attracted European traders long before Liberia became a republic.

Liberia is a well-watered land. Its chief rivers are the Mano, St. Paul, St. John, Cestos, and Cavally. All except the Cavally flow southwestward across the country to the Atlantic Ocean.

Much of the country is covered by thick forests. There is grassland only in the extreme northwest. The coastal region is rather flat, but the interior rises to heights of 5,000 feet (1,525 meters) in the Nimba Mountains. In the interior are elephants, pygmy hippopotamuses, buffalo ("bush cows"), duikers, and leopards and other members of the cat family. There are monkeys of all kinds, which do much damage to crops.

Climate.   Liberia has a tropical monsoon climate. It is warm all year, with alternating wet and dry seasons. The coast has the heaviest annual rainfall, averaging 150 inches (380 centimeters). But toward the interior this drops to an average of 75 inches (190 cm.). Most of the rain falls during the wet season, lasting from April through November.

Cities

Most of the people in Liberia live in a wide band extending from the coast near Monrovia northward to southern Guinea. By far the nation's largest city is **Monrovia,** the modern capital of Liberia as well as the main seaport. Monrovia was named after U.S. President James Monroe. Lying near the mouth of the St. Paul River, the city is a major marketing center. Most of Liberia's export products pass through Monrovia's harbor. The city is also important educationally and culturally.

Other important but smaller coastal cities are Buchanan, Harper, and Greenville. Vonjama, Gbarnga, Sanoquelli, and Kolahun are the chief communities in the interior.

The Supreme Court Building stands near the center of Monrovia.

HISTORY

In the early 1800s there were large numbers of freed black slaves and their freeborn children and grandchildren living in the United States. The American Colonization Society was organized in 1816 to resettle these freed blacks on the west coast of Africa. Members of the Society had many different reasons for wanting to do this. Some detested slavery and felt that even freed blacks would find it hard to live in a slave-holding culture. Others, who were slave owners, feared that the presence of freed blacks would make their slaves more discontented. Still others hoped that black Americans might help spread Christianity in Africa.

In 1821 the first black American colonists arrived in what was later to become Liberia. They bought land from the native chiefs and settled on the coast, displacing native residents. Tensions and rivalry between local peoples and the new settlers, as well as among themselves, became a central fact of life in Liberia. These divisions culminated in tribal massacres during the revolution of 1990.

The black American colonists, later called Americo-Liberians, brought with them the way of life they had known in the southeastern United States. Few had ever been to Africa or knew very much about the people who lived there. As a result they looked down upon the natives, treated them harshly, and sometimes even enslaved them. In 1847, after enjoying many years of virtually full internal self-government, the settlers proclaimed their independence. One of their group, Joseph Jenkins Roberts, was elected the first president of Liberia. From that time until a group of young military officers from the interior seized control of the government in 1980, the Americo-Liberians controlled the government and the economy of the country, and the original inhabitants had little power.

THE PEOPLE

The Americo-Liberians make up less than one-quarter of the population. For the most part they live in Monrovia and cities on the coast. They are Christians, mainly Protestants, who speak English, the official language of the country. Their dress and way of life are Western, although they are influenced more and more by African customs.

The rest of Liberia's population are members of more than 20 groups who live in the interior of the country. Some of the important ones are the Bassa, Kru, Kpelle, Gio, Loma, Gola, Gbande, Mandingo, and Vai. They speak variations of many languages, including Kwa and Mande. Many of the children, however, are learning English at schools run by the Liberian government and Christian missions.

Some of these peoples have followed the Muslim faith for centuries, while others still hold to ancient African beliefs. There is also a steady stream of Christian converts. Secret societies, which control religious activities, are found throughout the country. These are the Poro (for men) and Sande (for women). Poro and Sande societies also help with the education of the young.

Women usually wear the *lappa*. This is a piece of cotton cloth, called country cloth, about 1 yd. (1 m.) wide, which may be worn in many ways. Generally it is wrapped around the body at the waist, often over a blouse. Men wear baggy trousers. Muslim men wear hats called fezzes. Women are seen in brightly colored head scarves. As in most

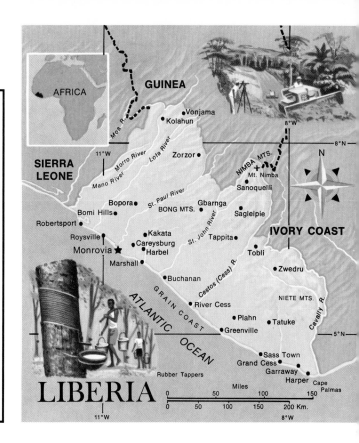

tropical countries, children are lightly clad except on special occasions and wear sandals rather than shoes, or go barefoot.

Family Life and Education

Traditionally, a typical well-to-do Americo-Liberian family lived in a modern-looking house, perhaps of corrugated iron, with two stories and a red roof. The children of these families were often sent to the United States, England, or Germany for their education. Many, however, attended government or mission-run schools, until the civil war that began in 1989 forced foreign missionaries to leave the country. There are universities and colleges in Monrovia, Suakoko, and Harper. From the mid-1940s, the government financed an extensive scholarship program under which Liberians of all backgrounds were sent overseas (most of them to the United States) for post-secondary training.

The traditional way of life for both wealthy urbanites and the majority of Liberia's people, who lived in farming villages on land usually owned by a family group or tribe, was disrupted in recent years by the civil war. Thousands of people were slaughtered, homes and businesses were destroyed, and the planting and harvesting of crops was disrupted. Threatened by famine and war, an estimated 50 percent of Liberia's people had become refugees within or outside the country by the early 1990s.

Before the civil war, rural Liberians generally lived in round or rectangular homes with conical thatched roofs. Groups of such homes within a fenced compound were occupied by extended families—that is, a husband, his wife or wives, their young children, older sons and their wives, and grandchildren. Before the civil war, increasing numbers of rural children were being educated by the government or missions. Many children attended the "bush schools" conducted by the Poro and Sande societies. As the children near adulthood they are taught the customs, beliefs, and ceremonies of their people. Books are not used for instruction. There is a rich oral literature of history, legends, and folktales, which are passed on by word of mouth to the children. To prove they are ready to live in the grown-up world, the young people are given difficult tests to pass. These tests may involve some physical or mental ordeal.

Music and Art

The Liberians, like other Africans, have a great love of music and dancing. Drums, clappers, and rattles are the chief instruments. These instruments accompany the singing and dancing that highlight all important occasions, such as the end of the bush training period for the young.

Liberians decorate tools, clothing, and their wooden household articles. But they are better-known for their gold, silver, brass, and copper jewelry and their sculpture. Leatherworking and the making of masks are also important. Masks representing the spirits of dead ancestors and the gods are used by the secret Poro and Sande societies for religious ceremonies.

ECONOMY

The land provides the livelihood for most of the people. Rice is the most important food and is grown on small farms that have been hacked

This mine in the Nimba Mountains produces iron ore, Liberia's chief mineral.

Women harvest rice in a field not too far from the Bong Mountains.

out of the forest. The men cut down all but the largest trees and burn the brush in January and February. Women and children plant the rice on the hillsides and tend the crop until harvest. Another food crop is cassava, from which tapioca is made. Coffee, palm nuts (from which palm oil is extracted), and cacao are grown and gathered for export. Fish from the ocean and rivers is an important source of protein.

In 1925 rubber cultivation in Liberia began. Rubber soon became the chief export. In 1951 a railroad was built from Monrovia to the rich iron ore deposits in the Bomi Hills. Even richer deposits in the Nimba Mountains were later linked by another railway to the port of Buchanan. Iron ore eventually surpassed rubber as Liberia's most important export. By the early 1990s, however, the economy was in a state of virtual collapse.

GOVERNMENT

Liberia was governed under a constitution much like that of the United States, with an elected president, a vice-president, and a legislature consisting of a Senate and House of Representatives. William V. S. Tubman, who held the presidency for more than 25 years, died in office in 1971. He was succeeded by his vice-president, William R. Tolbert, Jr., who was killed during the 1980 coup. Samuel K. Doe, the coup leader, was himself killed in 1990. Rival factions claimed power, and many civilians were massacred in tribal retributions. A multinational force from neighboring countries intervened to try to impose order. An interim president was named in 1991, but fighting continued in rural areas and it was unclear whether elections scheduled for 1992 could be held.

WILLIAM R. STANLEY, University of South Carolina
KAREN E. FRENCH, Bryn Mawr College

Place de la République in Abidjan overlooking Ebrié Lagoon.

IVORY COAST

In the 15th century, when daring Portuguese explorers sailed around the western bulge of Africa, they found a part of the Atlantic Ocean now known as the Gulf of Guinea. In the years that followed, the region about the Gulf of Guinea became a rich source of products for a number of European countries. Sections of the Guinea coast became identified with the goods and people that left their shores. Such names as Grain Coast, Ivory Coast, Gold Coast, and Slave Coast appeared on the maps of the time. Centuries have passed, and today a modern, independent country on the Gulf of Guinea has the name of Ivory Coast.

The Ivory Coast is changing. Today the Ivory Coast is more famous for the export of coffee and cacao than for the ivory that gave it its name. New ways of life are slowly but steadily replacing the old. Towns blossom where tiny villages used to sprawl. Thick and sturdy concrete dams harness rivers, while modern roads and gleaming railroad tracks reach inland from the sea. The hustle and bustle of modern life has made time a valuable commodity. In other words, the Ivory Coast is well on its way into the 20th century and beyond.

THE LAND

The Republic of Ivory Coast occupies a square body of land lying about 300 miles (480 kilometers) north of the equator. The country has an area of 124,503 square miles (322,463 square kilometers). It is bordered on the west by Liberia and Guinea, on the north by Mali and Burkina, and on the east by Ghana. Its southern border lies completely on the Gulf of Guinea.

Yamoussoukro was named as the new national capital in 1983. While the new capital is being constructed, **Abidjan,** the longtime capital, largest city, and chief port of the Ivory Coast, remains the acting capital. **Bouaké** is the second largest city. Other towns include Daloa, Gagnoa, Korhogo, Agboville, Abengourou, Man, and Bondoukou.

The Ivory Coast has huge, dense rain forests with trees rising to great heights, spreading dark green canopies over the earth below. There are wide and rolling savannas, or tropical grasslands, with grass and scattered, twisted trees. It is a land alive with animals, insects, and birds. There are hyenas, jackals, leopards, and chimpanzees. In the streams and rivers are hippopotamuses and crocodiles. There are numerous snakes, among which are the dreaded mamba and the enormous python. Elephants once roamed the savanna country in great numbers, but now they are mostly seen in game reserves. The country has well-stocked game parks, such as the Sassandra Reserve.

Climate

The climate of the country is tropical, but there are some regional differences. The south, with its rain forests, is hot and humid. There is a total annual rainfall of more than 90 inches (230 centimeters); temperatures range from 72 to 90 degrees Fahrenheit (22–32 degrees Celsius). There are two rainy seasons. The north, where most of the grassy plains are, has only one rainy season. Temperatures reach greater extremes there than in the south. In the main, the north is drier than the south and has an annual rainfall of about 60 inches (150 cm.).

Rivers

The major rivers of the Ivory Coast—none over 500 miles (800 km.) long—are the Cavally, Sassandra, Bandama, and Comoé. They all flow from north to south and empty into the Gulf of Guinea. Because of many shallows and rapids, none of the rivers are navigable for more than 80 miles (130 km.); but together with their tributaries, the rivers are used for floating lumber to sawmills and factories. The waters of these rivers supply a large number of fish to the people who live in the surrounding areas. Dams have been constructed for flood control and as sources of hydroelectricity.

THE PEOPLE

French is the official language of the country and is used in government offices and educational institutions. But the Ivory Coast is made up of different peoples speaking many different languages. The linguistic groups include both the forest and the savanna peoples. In the forest are the Kru of the southwest, the Dan-Guro of the western region near the Man highlands, and numerous groups along the lagoons of the southeast coast. The Anyi-Baoulé live in both the forest and savanna in

A cluster of homes on the outskirts of the nation's capital.

the southeast and central parts of the country. The savanna is also the home of the Malinke of the northwest, the Senufo of the central north, and the Lobi-Kulango of the northeast.

The Baoulé

The Baoulé are in many ways typical of the people of the country. They are the most numerous ethnic group in the Ivory Coast and speak one of the Anyi-Baoulé dialects. They have had a significant impact upon the political and cultural development of the Ivory Coast.

The Baoulé are mainly farmers who grow yams, manioc, sweet potatoes, rice, corn, and other grains for home use. Life is not always easy; it can be demanding and difficult. Some Baoulé farmers specialize in the cultivation of coffee and cacao for commercial purposes. The boys of the village help their fathers hunt and fish and prepare the land for cultivation. Girls learn housekeeping skills very early, for at the age of 12 or 13 they may be given by the family for betrothal.

City Life

The majority of the people of the Ivory Coast still lead a traditional village life. But with each passing year, as the country becomes more and more industrialized, the cities and towns grow larger in size. Life in a city such as Abidjan is not much different from life in other cities throughout the world. For example, Abidjan has tall modern buildings, well-paved streets, and modern means of transportation. The sidewalks are crowded with people who work in stores and offices and who wear both Western-style and traditional clothes. Manufactured goods and farm produce are brought into the city from outlying areas by rail or truck, and from all over the world by boat and plane. Abidjan has a fine airport equipped to handle the jumbo jet.

FACTS AND FIGURES

OFFICIAL NAME: Republic of Côte d'Ivoire (République de Côte d'Ivoire).

NATIONALITY: Ivorian(s).

CAPITAL: Yamoussoukro (official), Abidjan (acting).

LOCATION: West coast of Africa. **Boundaries**—Mali, Burkina, Ghana, Gulf of Guinea, Liberia, Guinea.

AREA: 124,503 sq. mi. (322,463 sq. km.).

PHYSICAL FEATURES: Highest point—about 5,000 ft. (1,524 m.). **Lowest point**—sea level. **Chief rivers**—Cavally, Sassandra, Bandama, Comoé.

POPULATION: 12,978,000 (1991; annual growth 3.9%).

MAJOR LANGUAGES: French (official), Dioula, and other local languages.

MAJOR RELIGIONS: traditional African religions, Islam, Christianity.

GOVERNMENT: Republic. **Head of state**—president. **Head of government**—prime minister. **Legislature**—one-house National Assembly.

CHIEF CITIES: Abidjan, Bouaké, Daloa, Yamoussoukro.

ECONOMY: Chief minerals—petroleum, diamonds, gold. **Chief agricultural products**—coffee, cacao, bananas, pineapples, palm products, cotton, plantains, cassava, rice, corn. **Industries and products**—timber, textiles, food processing, fishing, oil refining, assembled motor vehicles. **Chief exports**—cacao, coffee, timber, petroleum products, cotton and cotton fabrics, pineapples, palm products, canned fish. **Chief imports**—foodstuffs, machinery, iron and steel.

MONETARY UNIT: Franc CFA (African Financial Community).

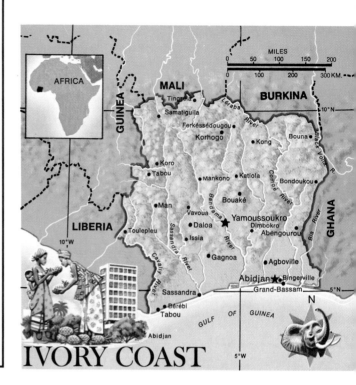

IVORY COAST

Education

The educational system of the Ivory Coast follows closely that of France. The government has made great efforts to see that the people of the nation learn how to read and write, and today the Ivory Coast has one of the highest adult literacy rates in West Africa. The number of children attending school has risen dramatically since independence. The most important institution of higher education is the National University of Ivory Coast, located in Abidjan.

ECONOMY

Agriculture is the mainstay of the Ivory Coast's economy. Most of the people are farmers, and agricultural and forestry products make up the great bulk of the country's exports. The Ivory Coast is the world's leading producer of cacao (from which chocolate and cocoa are made), and ranks among the major producers of coffee, palm oil and palm kernels, and pineapples. Cotton and rubber are other important exports. The main food crops include rice, cassava, plantains, corn, and bananas. Processed foods, textiles, refined petroleum, and assembled motor vehicles are the chief industrial products.

Petroleum is the Ivory Coast's most important mineral. Oil deposits were first discovered in offshore waters in the 1970s. Diamonds and some gold also are mined. The Ivory Coast is believed to have deposits of copper, titanium, iron ore, and bauxite (aluminum ore), but they have not yet been exploited commercially.

The Vridi Canal, completed in 1950, has had a great effect upon the economy of the country. After the canal was built, oceangoing vessels were able to dock at the port of Abidjan. As a result, Abidjan became one of the finest and busiest seaports in western Africa.

An open-air marketplace near the Treichville quarter of Abidjan.

HISTORY

Long before the first European explorers even knew about the Ivory Coast, there were kingdoms in the north and in the east. In the 11th century, the city of Kong was established by the Senufo people, whose descendants now live in the northern region of the Ivory Coast. Kong became a market center where salt and cattle from the north were bartered for kola nuts (now used in making cola drinks) from the south. Later, in the 16th century, traveling traders called the Dioula penetrated from the north.

The Portuguese were the first Europeans to come to the region, and they eventually made the land known to other trading nations. They did not attempt to settle the territory, but concentrated first upon the ivory and then the slave trade. The Portuguese were followed by the Spanish, the Dutch, the English, and finally the French.

The French eventually consolidated their power over the Ivory Coast in 1887. In that year, Louis Binger, a French officer, made several protectorate agreements with various African chiefs. Binger became the first governor of the territory in 1893.

The Ivory Coast became a self-governing republic within the French Community in 1958. In 1960 the country achieved full independence. Félix Houphouët-Boigny, a leader in the movement toward independence, became the first president. Although parliamentary elections had been contested since 1980, the Ivory Coast was a de facto one-party state until 1990. That year, after Houphouët-Boigny was elected to a seventh term, the post of prime minister was created.

ROSS EDGAR BIGELOW, Michigan State University
Reviewed by EMBASSY OF THE IVORY COAST, Washington, D.C.

Graceful dried-mud mosque in Bobo-Dioulasso.

BURKINA (UPPER VOLTA)

About 900 years ago, according to tradition, proud Dagomba horsemen from the south came riding into the Volta River's grassy headstream region. They liked this low plateau, lying south of the Sahara desert but north of the tropical rain forests, and settled down to stay. They married local women, and their children were called the Mossi. For hundreds of years—till the beginning of the present century—the Mossi ruled in the northern, central, and eastern parts of what is now officially called Burkina Faso ("Land of Upright Men").

When the French colonized the area in 1896 and 1897, they brought the Mossi and the other peoples under one administration for the first time. All were included later on in what the French called Upper Volta Colony, which formed the basis of the present country.

THE LAND

Burkina is an inland country of West Africa, about the size of the state of Colorado. Mali lies to the north and west of Burkina, and Niger lies to the northeast. To the south are Ivory Coast, Ghana, Togo, and Benin. Most of Burkina is low plateau country lying astride three headstreams of the Volta River—the White Volta, the Black Volta, and the Red Volta. Most of the country's rivers drain south into the Volta River in Ghana.

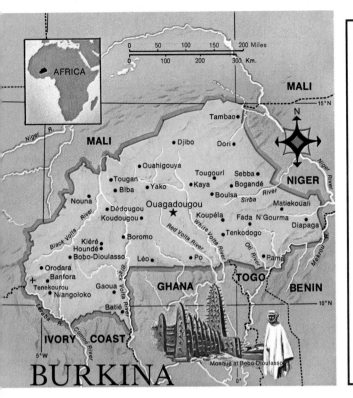

Mosque at Bobo-Dioulasso

BURKINA

FACTS AND FIGURES

OFFICIAL NAME: Burkina Faso.

NATIONALITY: Burkinabe(s).

CAPITAL: Ouagadougou.

LOCATION: West Africa. **Boundaries**—Mali, Niger, Benin, Togo, Ghana, Ivory Coast.

AREA: 105,869 sq. mi. (274,200 sq. km.).

PHYSICAL FEATURES: Highest point—Tenekourou (2,458 ft.; 749 m.). **Lowest point**—650 ft. (198 m.) above sea level. **Chief rivers**—Black Volta, Red Volta, White Volta.

POPULATION: 9,360,000 (1991; annual growth 3.1%).

MAJOR LANGUAGES: French (official), Sudanic languages.

MAJOR RELIGIONS: traditional African religions, Islam, Christianity.

GOVERNMENT: Republic. **Head of government**—prime minister. **Head of state**—president. **Legislature**—National Assembly.

CHIEF CITIES: Ouagadougou , Bobo-Dioulasso.

ECONOMY: Chief minerals—manganese, limestone, marble, gold, antimony, copper, nickel, bauxite, lead. **Chief agricultural products**—peanuts, shea nuts, sesame, cotton, sorghum, millet, corn, rice, livestock. **Industries and products**—food processing, brewing, bricks. **Chief exports**—livestock, cotton, shea nuts, sesame. **Chief imports**—food products, machinery, fuels.

MONETARY UNIT: Franc CFA (African Financial Community).

Burkina is almost entirely savanna (grassland). The grasslands range from a dry and scrubby kind, called sahel, in the north to a wet and wooded kind (sudan) in the south. In the sudan there are many softly rounded hills covered with tall grass and clumps of trees. Low mountain ranges rise in the east and southwest of the country. In the southwest is Tenekourou, Burkina's highest peak. The wide variety of animal life includes elephants, giraffes, monkeys, and crocodiles.

Climate. Warm the year round, Burkina has seasons based mainly on rain and drought. From about late May to October, heavy rains fall. During this season the grass and grain crops grow tall and lush. The season of drought is from about November to May. In this season a parching wind called the *harmattan* blows out of the Sahara, adding to the drought and further drying up the rivers, crops, and vegetation.

THE PEOPLE

The Mossi. The Mossi are the most numerous people in Burkina, making up about 55 percent of the nation's total population. Their kings ruled the region from the 11th century until about 1900—and their kingship still exists, although without power. The word "disciplined' is used of the Mossi, for they live under a strict behavior code.

The Mossi religion is based chiefly on ancestor-worship and the worship of Tenga, an earth deity. Muslims in Burkina constitute a large minority, and there are also a considerable number of Christians. The Mossi always held their kings and chiefs in awe because the rulers made the sacrifices to the ancestors.

The typical Mossi dwelling is a small round hut. Its walls are made of clay or mud, and the cone-shaped roof is made of dried grass. Each

Modern buildings line a thoroughfare in Ouagadougou, Burkina's capital.

family lives in a walled compound containing several such huts and a small clay building used for storing grain. A Mossi family consists of a husband, his several wives, and their children. The husband lives alone in the hut nearest the entrance to the compound. Each wife lives in a separate hut with her children.

A family compound is set apart from its neighbors by encircling fields—of millet, sorghum, or cotton—crisscrossed by narrow paths. The neighbors are likely to be grandparents, aunts and uncles, or cousins.

Non-Mossi Peoples. The Mossi live in central Burkina. The Bobo, the Lobi, and the Gourounsi, peoples related to the Mossi, live in the west and southwest.

The Bobo, another major ethnic group, are an ancient people having their own religion. Besides their ancestors, they worship a supreme god known as Wuro and many lesser gods. The Bobo, like the Mossi, are family-centered. Bobo dwellings are larger than those of the Mossi and are built close together in compact-looking villages or towns.

Other important peoples of Burkina are the Fulani (Fulbe) and several Mande groups. The Fulani are cattle herders living in the north. The Mande groups live in scattered districts in the west and south.

Cities. **Ouagadougou,** the ancient Mossi capital, is the capital of Burkina. "Ouaga," as the city is nearly always called, is located in the center of the country and boasts modern government buildings and apartment houses. Many mud-brick buildings remain from an earlier day, as does a large and colorful outdoor market. Since 1954 Ouagadougou has been the last stop on the railway from the Ivory Coast.

Bobo-Dioulasso, Burkina's second-largest city and the nation's main commercial center, is in the southwest, or Bobo country. Bobo-Dioulasso's houses are usually made of mud-brick.

Education. Although all children in Burkina between the ages of 7 and 14 are required to go to school, only about 15 percent of school-age children actually do attend school. Probably less than 15 percent of the adult population can read and write. Hundreds of elementary schools have been built. However, there are far fewer secondary and vocational schools, and enrollment is quite limited. French is the language of instruction throughout the educational system.

The leading institution of higher education is the University of Ouagadougou. There are several teacher training colleges. Grants are given for advanced study in France or Senegal.

ECONOMY

Burkina is a very poor country. Most of the people are farmers or animal keepers. The farmers grow mainly millet and sorghum. Maize (corn) is important, too, as are peanuts, cowpeas, beans, rice, cassava (manioc), sweet potatoes, and cotton. Shea nuts from the shea tree are a source of vegetable fat for export. Herdsmen keep horses, cattle, sheep, goats, and some camels. Live animals are a major export.

Much of the population is clustered in the center of the country, and crops do not grow there in sufficient amounts to support all the people. So many thousands of men must migrate seasonally to work on coffee and cacao plantations in Ghana and Ivory Coast.

Minerals. Burkina has valuable mineral resources, but these cannot be profitably worked without improvements in the nation's transportation system. Large deposits of limestone and high-grade manganese have been found in the northeast. There is gold southwest of Ouagadougou, and bauxite has also been found. Rich deposits of silver and zinc in the central region may be developed with the help of the World Bank.

Corn, peanuts, and red peppers are dried on a rooftop in a Bobo village.

HISTORY AND GOVERNMENT

The history of the Mossi begins with the coming of strangers to the Voltaic plateau, probably in the 11th century A.D. According to tradition, the intruders were Dagomba horsemen from Gambaga (in present-day Ghana) to the south. They moved into Busansi country (southern Burkina Faso) and married Busansi women. Their offspring, the Mossi, founded Tenkodogo, the first of several great Mossi kingdoms.

Oubri, the grandson of Tenkodogo's founder, took the title Mogho Naba ("ruler of the world"). He set up the kingdom of Ouagadougou in the central plateau. Relatives of Oubri founded the two other major Mossi kingdoms: Yatenga, north of Ouagadougou, and Fada N'Gourma, to the east.

French Rule. The first European to visit Ouagadougou, a German, entered Mossi country in 1886 from German Togoland. Other Europeans followed—German, British, and French. By 1893 the French had taken the region north of Yatenga, and by 1895 they controlled Yatenga, too.

The French pressed south to Ouagadougou, seizing it in 1896. The Mossi king, Mogho Naba Wobogo, retreated, and when he tried to return to his capital, the French burned it to the ground. A little later the Mogho Naba of the Mossi was stripped of nearly all his powers.

In 1919 the French created the colony of Upper Volta. In this colony the Mossi were the main ethnic group, and Ouagadougou was the administrative capital. The new governor, Edouard Hesling, tried to develop the colony's economy. He started cotton plantations and built roads. He also supplied Mossi forced labor to other parts of French West Africa. When Upper Volta Colony was divided up among neighboring colonies in 1932, the chief reason was to supply the Ivory Coast with Mossi labor.

Many Mossi fought for France in World War II. In 1947, in answer to a personal appeal by Mogho Naba Sagha II, France made Upper Volta a separate territory once again. But the Mogho Naba and the chiefs were ignored by most of the young nationalists as Upper Volta moved toward independence in the 1950s. A democratic constitution drafted in 1958 did not even mention them.

Since Independence. The Republic of Upper Volta gained independence on August 5, 1960. The Army seized control in 1966. A new constitution introduced in 1970 was suspended in 1974, when the military again seized power. A constitution providing for an elected president and National Assembly was approved by the voters in 1977, but the Army again took over in 1980. After a series of military coups, Captain Thomas Sankara seized power in August 1983. As a sign that the country had broken with the French colonial past, he changed its name, flag, and national anthem. He told his people they could lift themselves out of poverty by self-sacrifice, cooperation, and hard work. But in 1987 he was overthrown and killed by his chief adviser, Captain Blaise Compaore.

A constitution approved by the voters in June 1991 reduced presidential powers and provided for direct elections for the presidency and legislature. Compaore was elected president in a December 1991 election boycotted by the opposition. His party unexpectedly captured a majority of seats in multiparty legislative elections held in May 1992.

LUCILE CARLSON, Case Western Reserve University
Reviewed by LOUIS-DOMINIQUE QUEDRAOGO, First Counsellor
Permanent Mission of Burkina Faso to the United Nations

Dam at Akosombo controls the waters of the Volta River.

GHANA

Ghana might well be called a country of festivals. In the most remote hamlets and in the largest cities, Ghanaians gather to celebrate major historical events, outstanding feats of war, the beginning of harvest, and the abundance of food. The highlight of each festival is the drumming and dancing. Huge drums, carved from the hollow trunks of large trees and covered with skins of black antelope, are usually accompanied by horns and trumpets. People dance, using traditional steps of their ethnic group as a basis. Slowly, these steps have been developed into popular and catchy dance forms. Originating at a small village festival in Ghana, one such dance, the high life, became a favorite of all Ghanaians, and its popularity spread to many parts of Africa and countries of the Western world.

THE LAND

The Republic of Ghana is made up of the former British colony called the Gold Coast, the inland protectorates of Ashanti and Northern Territories, and the trusteeship territory of British Togoland. The country has an area of 92,099 square miles (238,537 square kilometers). Situated on the Gulf of Guinea in western Africa, Ghana is bordered by Burkina on the north, Togo on the east, and the Ivory Coast on the west.

Sandy beaches with palm trees and mangrove swamps run along the coast. Behind the sandy shoreline, the coastal plain stretches for about 60 miles (97 kilometers) inland. This is rolling country, covered with scrub and grass.

Farther inland the foliage becomes denser, turning into wooded hills and eventually into rain forest. The belt of tropical rain forest stretches across the south central region of the country. It is broken occasionally by wooded hills and rivers. The region, called Ashanti, is a valuable timber area and is the major source of Ghana's agricultural and mineral wealth. North of the rain forest the foliage thins out, and the land gradually becomes rolling plains.

Ghana has no great mountain ranges. The highest point in the country is located along the eastern boundary where the altitude reaches 2,905 feet (885 meters) at Mount Afadjato. Much of the country is less than 500 feet (150 m.) above sea level.

Rivers.   There are many rivers and streams in Ghana. During the rainy season some rivers are raging torrents, while in the dry months they become small streams. The most important river is the Volta, which has two main branches: the White Volta and the Black Volta. Among the smaller rivers of importance are the Tano, Ankobra, and Pra.

In 1965 the completion of a great dam across the Volta River created a huge reservoir just north of Akosombo. Known as Lake Volta, this reservoir is one of the largest man-made bodies of water in the world. It extends 250 miles (400 km.) in length and covers an area of 3,500 square miles (9,065 square kilometers). Electricity from the Lake Volta hydroelectric project supplies almost all the nation's power needs. Lake Bosumtwi, a large natural lake probably of volcanic origin, is southeast of Kumasi.

Climate.   The climate of Ghana is generally tropical. Rainfall varies from about 30 inches (80 centimeters) along the coastal belt of southeast Ghana to 80 inches (200 cm.) in the southwest coastal region. From December to January the *harmattan*, a dry northeasterly wind, blows in from the Sahara, and a fine red dust settles over the land. In northern Ghana, the wind lasts for a longer period of time and is more severe than in the south. The harmattan causes a noticeable drop in humidity, and the days are usually chilly and the nights even cooler.

Cities

Accra, the capital and largest city of Ghana, is situated on the coast of the Gulf of Guinea. During the past 30 years, Accra has changed from a small provincial town to a bustling metropolis and commercial center. The wide streets and boulevards of Accra are crowded with buses, trucks, automobiles, and taxis. There are many modern buildings, governmental as well as commercial, apartment houses, museums, and hotels. The large department stores of the city are well stocked with goods made and manufactured in Ghana as well as in many other parts of the world. The public gardens of Accra give the city a tropical and verdant appearance. Fruit trees such as coconut, papaw, mango, and guava can be seen throughout the city.

The University of Ghana at Legon, a suburb of Accra, is one of the country's leading universities.

Ghanaians attend the horse races, a popular spectator sport, at the Accra Turf Club.

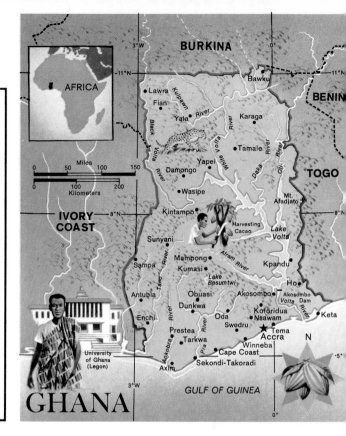

FACTS AND FIGURES

OFFICIAL NAME: Republic of Ghana.

NATIONALITY: Ghanaian(s).

CAPITAL: Accra.

LOCATION: West Africa. **Boundaries**—Burkina, Togo, Gulf of Guinea, Ivory Coast.

AREA: 92,099 sq. mi. (238,537 sq. km.).

PHYSICAL FEATURES: Highest point—Mount Afadjato (2,900 ft.; 884 m.). **Lowest point**—sea level. **Chief river**—Volta. **Major lakes**—Volta, Bosumtwi.

POPULATION: 15,616,934 (1991; annual growth 3.2%).

MAJOR LANGUAGES: English (official), Fanti, Twi, other local languages.

MAJOR RELIGIONS: Traditional African religions, Christianity, Islam.

GOVERNMENT: Republic. **Head of state**—president. **Legislature**—National Assembly.

CHIEF CITIES: Accra, Kumasi, Sekondi-Takoradi.

ECONOMY: Chief minerals—gold, manganese, diamonds, bauxite. **Chief agricultural products**—cacao, coffee, palm products, maize, cassava, plantains, sugarcane. **Industries and products**—food processing, aluminum refining, fishing, timber, oil refining. **Chief exports**—cacao, gold, timber, bauxite, diamonds. **Chief imports**—textiles, foodstuffs, fuels, vehicles.

MONETARY UNIT: 1 cedi = 100 pesewas.

Christiansborg Castle, the official seat of government of Ghana, is one of the major attractions of Accra. The castle, a magnificent white rambling structure, was built in 1657 on the site of a trading post first established by the Portuguese in 1578.

Accra has an international airport and is the terminus of an extensive railway system.

Kumasi is the second largest city in Ghana. Located deep in the forests of the south central region, Kumasi was once the capital of the ancient Ashanti kingdom. At one time a town of thatched mud dwellings, Kumasi has over the years been transformed into a major commercial and transportation center. In recent years the government has concentrated its efforts on the construction of modern housing facilities, hospitals, and factories.

One of the busiest places in Kumasi is the outdoor market, thought to be the largest in West Africa. Every day, hundreds of women, known as market women because of their ability as retail traders, gather in the market to do their shopping. With baskets of produce balanced on their heads, the women rush from vendor to vendor seeking the best buys.

Sekondi-Takoradi, formerly two separate towns, is situated along the coast of Ghana on the Gulf of Guinea. The towns were merged into a municipality in 1946. Sekondi was founded by the Dutch in the 16th century. Today it is basically a residential and commercial area. Takoradi is a modern community with new government buildings, a modern hospital, and department stores. Ghana's first artificial harbor was built at Takoradi in 1928. Now a city, Sekondi-Takoradi has become an important trade and industry center of Ghana.

Up until the 1960s, **Tema,** located about 18 mi. (30 km.) east of

A Ghanaian works on the assembly line at a truck plant in Tema.

Accra, was just a small fishing village. However, in 1961, a huge artificial harbor was completed at Tema. The government, realizing the importance of this harbor, built up a new city around the old one. Residential facilities were constructed to accommodate the influx of workers. Industries, such as an oil refinery, a soap factory, a flour mill, and an aluminum smelter, moved into the area, and Tema soon became the major industrial center of Ghana. However, many of the residents of Tema still depend on fishing for their livelihood, and a large fishing harbor has been completed.

Two other important cities are Cape Coast located on the Gulf of Guinea, and Tamale, the administrative center of the northern region.

THE PEOPLE

There are more than a dozen ethnic groups in Ghana. The majority of the people belong to six major groups: the Ashanti and Brong-Ahafo in the central rain forest region, the Fanti on the coast and in the south central region, the Ga and Ewe in the south and southeast, and the Dagomba and Mamprusi, who live in the north. Culturally, each group maintains a strong sense of identity, speaking separate languages and practicing different customs and traditions.

Way of Life

In recent years there has been a movement of young people from the villages and towns in the north to the major urban centers. Here they work in offices and industries and attend school. However, most Ghanaians are subsistence farmers. Usually the men hunt, clear the land, and fish, and the women keep house and do the marketing. Both men and women take part in the farming of their land. Some groups of people keep sheep, chickens, goats, guinea fowl, pigs, and a few cattle.

Most Ghanaians live in small villages and towns in the interior of the country. Their houses are usually rectangular in shape with mud walls and flat roofs often made of straw or corrugated iron. The small towns are generally divided into business quarters and family compounds.

The Ashanti are famous for their production of bronze and gold works of art. In the past the Ashanti made small brass objects against which gold dust could be weighed in payment for merchandise. In the Ashanti towns there are shops for wood-carvers, leatherworkers, and musical-instrument makers, as well as for a variety of other craftsmen, many of whom specialize in making beautiful textiles. Frequently fathers pass down these traditions to sons so that the skill will remain in the family. An Ashanti proverb says, "When you follow in the path of your father, you learn to walk like him."

Clothing. In the towns of Ghana, most of the men and women wear Western-style clothing. However, for evening wear, formal occasions, and festivals, Ghanaians dress in the graceful and picturesque Kente, which is considered the national dress. These beautifully patterned cloths are handwoven from silk and cotton yarn. The strips of cloth are then sewn together to make yards of material that men drape over themselves in a togalike style. Women usually fashion the cloth into a full-length skirt and blouse with a matching stole.

Education and Language

The school system in Ghana is very extensive, and almost every child attends primary school free. The number of secondary schools and technical schools is growing, and they are free also. Since 1948 Ghana has

The campus and grounds of the University of Ghana at Legon, a suburb of Accra.

developed three institutions of higher learning: the University of Ghana at Legon, a suburb of Accra, the Kumasi University of Science and Technology, and the University College of Cape Coast. Ghana also has a considerable number of technical institutes. Scholarships are made available for Ghanaian students to study abroad. The government is trying very hard to reduce illiteracy by holding classes for adults in towns throughout the country.

English is the official language of the country, although the many different groups speak their own languages as well. Among the most important are: Fanti, Twi, Ga, Dagbani, Ewe, and Hausa.

Religion

Christianity was introduced many centuries ago by European missionaries. Today approximately 43 percent of the people of Ghana are Christians. A substantial part of the population (38 percent), those living in small rural towns, hold traditional animistic beliefs. The role of ancestors in religion is critical and important in almost every aspect of life. About 12 percent of the people practice Islam, which was originally brought to this part of Africa by travelers from North Africa. Seven percent of the population has no religious affiliation.

ECONOMY

Since its independence in 1957, Ghana has made great strides in modernizing its agriculture and in developing industry. However, despite this progress, the people of Ghana are for the most part subsistence farmers. Yams, cassava, rice, sorghum, millet, and nuts are grown for local use. Many of the people are also engaged in the production of cacao, which is Ghana's primary cash crop. More than half of the country's export income is derived from this crop. The world's leading producer of cacao, Ghana also cultivates many other export products, such as rubber, palm oil, and kola nuts. The rain forest belt in central Ghana

Cocoa (processed cacao) is bagged and ready for shipment to foreign ports.

Early in the morning, fishermen arrange their net on a beach near Cape Coast.

provides the timber for a large lumber industry. Because of the ocean, lakes, and many rivers of Ghana, fishing is another major occupation of the people. In recent years the fishing industry has made great progress. Small motorized vessels and large trawlers are now being used, and inland fisheries have been developed.

Because of Ghana's rich deposits of bauxite, the production of aluminum has become one of the country's newest and largest industries. Gold and manganese are still mined, and Ghana is the world's second largest producer of industrial diamonds.

The most significant economic development has been the Volta River Project. Completed in 1965, the dam and power station at Akosombo on the Volta River provide the country with cheap and plentiful hydroelectricity. Previously Ghana had to depend on imported diesel oil for supplies of electricity. Perhaps the greatest beneficiary of the Volta River Project has been the bauxite-aluminum industry—in particular, the huge aluminum smelter at the port of Tema.

HISTORY

Very little is known about the prehistoric period of the region now called Ghana. Many tools, farming instruments, weapons, pottery, and pottery fragments have been found, but not enough to tell historians much about the people who lived in this area of Africa during these early times.

Beginning in the early 13th century and continuing until the mid-1600's, several migratory groups set up small kingdoms in the territory that is present-day Ghana. Most of these groups originally came from the western Sudan region of Africa. They spoke the same language, Akan, and settled in the rain forest of Ghana. In 1695 the Ashanti unified most of the groups into a powerful nation.

The king of the Ashanti was called the *asantehene,* and his palace was in the city of Kumasi. In 1817 British merchants visited the city. On their return home they wrote about the wealth of Kumasi's court royalty, who were attired in fabrics decorated with gold and silver; the cleanliness of the houses; and the hospitality of the citizens.

The first chief of the Ashanti nation was Osei Tutu, who ruled in the city of Kumasi in the late 17th century. Tradition says that one day, during a great windstorm, a golden stool descended from heaven into Osei Tutu's lap. Because of this miracle it was assumed that he would become the *asantehene,* or chief of all the Ashanti. The golden stool has become the symbol of the unity and strength of the Ashanti nation.

King Osei Tutu devised a constitution, built a large standing army, set up a system of courts, and organized the whole empire in a most efficient manner. Ashanti power stretched all the way from central Ghana to the coast, and Kumasi was considered the capital city. The government was a form of divine kingship, but the power of the chief was always controlled and limited by the council of elders. A son did not inherit the throne from his father; instead a new candidate was nominated from one of the royal families. The man on the throne was not considered divine, only his position; and the golden stool was the symbol of the spiritual unity of the Ashanti nation. Its loss would have been a catastrophe. This system of rule still exists in the Ashanti nation today. And every Ashanti owns a stool as part of his household furniture.

European Exploration

Portuguese explorers landed on the coast of present-day Ghana in 1471 and began trading with the people living along the coast. At first, the trade was mainly in ivory, pepper, and gold dust. Because of the large amounts of gold available, the Portuguese named the territory the Gold Coast. The profits from this trade became so immense that they soon attracted other Europeans. British, Dutch, and Swedish traders followed the Portuguese, and by the 18th century a long chain of European forts had been established along the Gold Coast.

The gold trade soon became secondary to traffic in human beings. As plantation life in the Americas demanded more cheap labor, slavery grew in importance. In 1631 England erected Kormantin Fort on the coast of Ghana, and in 1672 the Royal African Company was chartered to take over the slave trade from the Dutch and to ship slaves to the West Indies sugar plantations. The Europeans quarreled among themselves for their share of the slave market. Eventually, the Dutch drove the Portuguese from the Gold Coast, and in time the Dutch sold their interests to the British.

England outlawed the slave trade in 1807. It took many years for the trade to stop entirely, and the damage done to African society was incalculable. Kingdoms disintegrated, wars were encouraged, and insecurity and fear replaced an orderly and generally peaceful existence.

Throughout the 19th century, the British, who were well established along the Ghana coast, were involved in a series of wars with the powerful Ashanti nation in the interior. On February 4, 1874, the British sacked

Kumasi, the capital of the Ashanti kingdom, taking all the gold, silver, and other wealth from the city. British troops entered Kumasi again in 1896, this time conquering the Ashanti and exiling the *asantehene*, Prempeh I, to the Seychelles, an island group in the Indian Ocean.

Colonial Period

In 1901, the Ashanti kingdom became a British colony, and the area just to the north became a protectorate. The coastal region had been made a colony in 1850.

After the Ashanti Wars, the British established themselves as masters of the Gold Coast, although occasionally there was an outbreak of resistance by the Ashanti. Great Britain realized that it would be to its best interests to work with the Africans, use their political systems to maintain order, and eventually bring trained Africans into the government.

Great Britain tried to govern by the principle now known as indirect rule, whereby its decisions were supposed to be made through the traditional rulers. In 1924, Prempeh I was brought back from exile, and in 1935, the British restored the Ashanti state.

Ghana Moves Toward Independence

Slowly, the Africans were given a larger voice in the government, and a variety of organizations, such as the Ashanti Youth Association, were formed to exert political pressure. In 1947 a dynamic political movement was founded, the United Gold Coast Convention. The movement called upon Kwame Nkrumah, then studying law in London, to return to the Gold Coast to become its organizing secretary. While studying in London, Nkrumah had become a leader in the pan-African movement; and when the opportunity came for him to return to his country and take an important political position, he readily accepted. The United Gold Coast Convention was made up mostly of businessmen and intellectuals who were not very radical. Nkrumah saw the need for involving the whole country in the fight for independence.

During March of 1948 there were riots by ex-servicemen who had fought in World War II, and "Self-government now" became the slogan of Nkrumah and his nationalist supporters. This group split off and formed their own, more radical political party, the Convention People's Party, in 1949. Nkrumah started a "positive action" civil disobedience movement and was arrested by the British as a result.

In February, 1951, in the first general election, the Convention People's Party won a majority of the seats in the Assembly. It was only a matter of time before Great Britain would agree to self-government. Nkrumah was released from prison to become leader of government business, and in March, 1952, he was made prime minister.

Great Britain insisted upon new elections to make sure that Nkrumah really had the support of the people. In 1954 and again in 1956, the Convention People's Party won overwhelmingly.

Independence

On March 6, 1957, the Gold Coast (renamed Ghana after the great empire of Africa that flourished in the Sudan during the 11th century) was granted independence. It was an exciting day for Africa, and nationalist movements in many other countries grew stronger. In a few short years, there would be many more independent African nations. But independence was not going to bring solutions to all of the problems that confronted Africa. The poverty of subsistence agriculture, one-crop economies, lack of industry, lack of health facilities, poor transportation, and many more inadequacies were challenges for the new governments.

In Ghana, the situation was not too bad. Over $500,000,000 had been accumulated, mostly from the sale of cacao on the world market. Nkrumah wanted to make Ghana a model African state. He built roads, schools, hospitals, factories, and homes, and through his political party he attempted to stimulate loyalty to the new nation. The great Volta River Project was started; an airline was established; railways were improved; and foreign investments were encouraged. All this progress seemed to indicate that Ghana was on the right road to development. But the power of government increasingly centered in the hands of Nkrumah and his associates.

In internal affairs, certain centers of opposition were developing. Nkrumah had attempted to take away the power of traditional rulers such as the king of the Ashanti. People who lived in the far north felt neglected by the strong central government in Accra. Instead of taking steps to ease these grievances, the government enacted harsh new measures to suppress the opposition. In 1960 a new constitution was passed that made Ghana a republic and Nkrumah its first president.

On February 24, 1966, while President Nkrumah was visiting Communist China, there was a revolt led by the Army and police against Nkrumah's regime. A National Liberation Council was established, and Lieutenant General Joseph A. Ankrah was made chairman and thus the new head of state. Nkrumah was forbidden to return to Ghana. He found asylum in Guinea, where he died in 1972.

General Ankrah was accused of financial irregularities and resigned in 1969. The new head of state was Brigadier A. A. Afrifa, a member of the National Liberation Council. Brigadier Afrifa announced that the government would be returned to civilian rule. Elections were held in 1969 with the Progress Party, headed by Dr. Kofi A. Busia, winning the majority of seats in the National Assembly. In 1972 the government of Prime Minister Busia was overthrown in a bloodless military coup led by Colonel Ignatius Acheampong.

GOVERNMENT

Following the 1972 coup, military officers formed the National Redemption Council to govern Ghana. The constitution and the National Assembly were suspended. In 1975 the government was reorganized. The Supreme Military Council was created as the chief executive and legislative authority. In 1979 the military government was overthrown and free elections were held for a new civilian government. A new constitution provided for a president as head of state and for a one-house parliament. At the end of 1981, however, a young military officer, Flight Lt. Jerry Rawlings, took over the government, ruling as chief of the Provisional National Defense Council. A new constitution approved in April 1992 provided for a president as head of state and an elected National Assembly. Presidential elections were to be held in November and parliamentary elections in December, with a return to civilian rule on Jan. 7, 1993.

EDWARD H. SCHILLER, Nassau Community College

TOGO

Togo is a narrow strip of land wedged in by three other countries and the sea. It is one of the smallest nations in the entire continent of Africa. Yet in this small land, which at no point is more than 100 miles (160 kilometers) wide, more than 40 dialects and languages are spoken.

The Republic of Togo is bordered on the west by Ghana, on the north by Upper Volta, and on the east by Benin. In the south it has a seacoast on the Gulf of Guinea.

THE LAND

The geography of the country varies from the low, flat plains and lagoons of the coastal area to a chain of hills that cross the country from Ghana to Benin. A number of rivers have their sources in these hills. The most important of these rivers is the Mono, which at one point in its course forms part of the border with Benin. Although the larger rivers, such as the Mono, the Ogou, and the Oti, flow all year round, many of the smaller streams dry up during the rainless season.

Climate

The vegetation and the crops of Togo are to a large degree controlled by the succession of rainy and dry seasons. In the north there is a single wet season from April to October. This is followed by months of very little rain. Toward the south there are two wet seasons. The main one is from April to the beginning of July; the second and shorter rainy season runs from October to November. During the dry season from November to March the major crops of the country are harvested.

A busy ferry carries passengers across the broad and calm Mono River.

The white building of the Chamber of Deputies stands in the center of Lomé.

CITIES

Lomé, the capital and chief city of Togo, is situated on the western border of the country, only a few miles from Ghana. It lies on a flat, sandy coastal strip between the ocean and a saltwater lagoon. Many of the streets of this pleasant and airy city are lined with graceful palm trees. White government and office buildings sparkle in the sun. Lomé is a bustling seaport, but until a few years ago its waters were too shallow for large seagoing ships. Small boats had to be used to unload freight and passengers. This condition was changed when a new deepwater harbor was completed in 1968. Lomé, with a population of about 100,000, is Togo's only large city. Other communities, of much smaller size, are Aného, Sokodé, and Atakpamé.

THE PEOPLE

The people of Togo have many languages and religions. In part this is because the mountainous areas to the north have kept groups separate from one another, so that they have been able to develop and maintain their own languages and cultures.

The most important group is the Ewe, who live in the southern third of the country. In relation to other groups, they are the best educated and the most prosperous. The Ewe people, who also live across the border in Ghana, are still for the most part farmers, but a number of them are now in business and trade. Because they were the first to come in contact with the European settlers, the Ewe came under Western influence early. In recent years many have migrated to other countries of West Africa to become clerks in government and business.

Other fair-sized groups, not as large or as influential as the Ewe, are the Akposo and the Ana, who live in the mountainous area of the center of the country. Among the people in the north are the Bassari, the Konkomba, the Kabrai, and the Kotokoli.

Soaps and perfumes are made from the oil of the coconut palm.

Language

French is the official language of the country, but many other languages and dialects are used in daily affairs. In the south, the Ewe language is generally spoken. In other sections of the land, Kotokoli, Kabrai, Hausa, Ana, and Bassari are spoken. All in all, there are more than 40 dialects and languages heard in the tiny country of Togo.

Religion

The people of southern Togo have long been exposed to the influence of Christian missionaries, so that today there are probably some 200,000 Christians in this area of the country. In the north there are about 30,000 Muslims. The remaining population of Togo follow animistic beliefs. Traditional beliefs and practices remain strong in many parts of the land. All groups have their gods, which are represented in different forms, and belief in witchcraft and sorcery is often part of the religious structure.

Most groups are divided into age sections, with elaborate rites of initiation into the adult community at puberty. Group histories are often tied closely to the migration of the group to the area it now occupies. In several groups specific animals such as snakes or lizards are honored as the original guides of the people to their present home. In addition to a supreme being, many groups honor other gods, such as the god of thunder or the gods who derive their powers from the earth itself.

Education

The government has tried to provide adequate education for its people, but there have been many difficulties and disappointments. There is a great shortage of schools and of qualified teachers, particularly at the secondary level. Though primary and secondary education is free, only about one fifth of the students who graduate go on to secondary school. Togo has a university in common with the sister republic of Benin. Established in 1965, L'Institute du Benin has branches in Lomé and in Cotonou.

ECONOMY

As is the case with other West African countries, the Togolese economy rests basically upon its agriculture. Much of the agriculture of the country is taken up with the growing of basic foods for the people. In the south the foundation of the popular diet is corn and manioc. For the people of the central region it is millet, yams, and rice, with the addition of some corn. In the north it is millet, sorghum, and yams. Peanuts are cultivated everywhere for their oil. Major products for export are cacao, cotton, coffee, and palm oil. Togo does not yet raise enough cattle for its own needs, and meat must be imported from the surrounding countries.

Togo's most important mineral product is phosphate, which is used in making chemical fertilizers. One of the world's richest phosphate mines is located at Kpémé, about 20 miles (32 km.) from Lomé. Other minerals found in the country in small quantities are bauxite, hematite, chromite, and iron ore.

The phosphate mine at Kpémé.

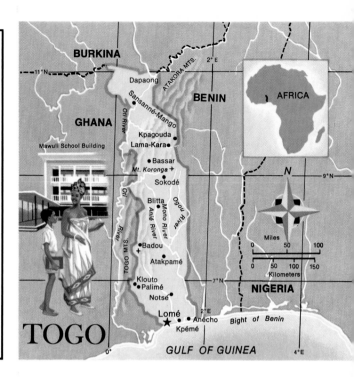

FACTS AND FIGURES

OFFICIAL NAME: Republic of Togo.

NATIONALITY: Togolese.

CAPITAL AND CHIEF CITY: Lomé.

LOCATION: West Africa. **Boundaries**—Ghana, Burkina, Benin, Gulf of Guinea.

AREA: 21,925 sq. mi. (56, 785 sq. km.)

PHYSICAL FEATURES: Highest point—3,346 ft. (1,020 m.). **Lowest point**—sea level. **Chief rivers**—Mono, Oti.

POPULATION: 3,800,000 (1992; annual growth 3.7%).

MAJOR LANGUAGES: French (official), Ewe, Hausa, and other African languages.

MAJOR RELIGIONS: Traditional African religions, Christianity, Islam.

GOVERNMENT: Republic. **Head of state**—president. **Head of government**—prime minister. **Legislature**—High Council of the Republic.

ECONOMY: Chief minerals—phosphates. **Chief agricultural products**—corn, rice, manioc, yams, millet, peanuts. **Industries and produts**—phosphate, soap, perfume, concrete pipes. **Chief exports**—phosphates, cacao, coffee, palm products, cotton. **Chief imports**—machinery and transportation equipment, foodstuffs, yarn and cloth, chemicals, petroleum products.

MONETARY UNIT: Franc CFA (African Financial Community), 1 CFA = 100 centimes.

HISTORY AND GOVERNMENT

Modern Togolese history began with the treaty signed in 1884 between a representative of the German emperor and a Togolese chief. Before this time German missionaries had penetrated north from the coast. Formal German control began after the Conference of Berlin (1884–85) and the agreements (1897 and 1899) between Britain, France, and Germany that established the present borders of Togo.

French and British troops occupied Lomé during the early days of World War I. At the end of the war, the German territory of Togo was divided in two. The western portion was made a British mandate, and the eastern part became a French mandate.

In 1946 the two mandates became trust territories of the United Nations. In 1956, after a plebiscite supervised by the United Nations, the British territory known as British Togoland, became part of the Gold Coast, which later became the nation of Ghana. French Togoland won its independence in 1960 as the Republic of Togo.

Recent Events. Togo's first president, Sylvanus Olympio, was overthrown and killed in 1963 in a military revolt. His successor, Nicolas Grunitzky, was deposed in 1967 in a coup led by Colonel (later General) Etienne Eyadéma, who assumed the presidency and later Africanized his name to Gnassingbe Eyadéma. Eyadéma, who made Togo a one-party state in 1969, was confirmed as president in elections under a new constitution in 1979. He was reelected in 1986, again the only candidate.

A national congress held in 1991 stripped Eyadéma of most of his powers and appointed an interim legislature (High Council of the Republic) and prime minister to oversee a transition to multiparty government under a new constitution. In September 1992 voters overwhelmingly approved the new constitution, paving the way for Togo's first free elections since independence.

L. GRAY COWAN, Director, Institute of African Studies, Columbia University

Craftsmen at work outside of the museum at Abomey.

BENIN

There is a building in Abomey, formerly the capital of one of the ancient kingdoms of Benin, that attracts both people from Benin and visitors from other countries. Once a grand palace of the ancient kingdom, the building is today a museum. Its many treasures—elaborately carved thrones, intricate metal sculpture devoted to gods, and murals in clay relief—depict the traditions, early culture, and history of the people of Benin.

The history of the three early kingdoms of Benin can also be seen in the colorful cloths woven mostly by men on the museum grounds. The cloths are illustrated with symbols and scenes from the lives of former kings as well as with patterns and designs depicting life in the country today.

THE LAND

Benin (formerly called Dahomey) has a total land area of 43,484 square miles (112,622 square kilometers). It is a narrow strip of land about 415 miles (670 kilometers) long but only 78 miles (125 km.) wide at its coastline. Benin lies on the Gulf of Guinea and is bounded on the east by Nigeria, on the west by Togo, and on the north by the nations of Niger and Burkina.

The country has four geographical zones. A narrow, flat, sandy strip of land, varying between 1 and 3 miles (1.6–4.8 km.) in width, runs along the gulf coast. Just beyond lies a network of lagoons and swamps.

Farther north, the country is flat and generally covered with fairly dense vegetation. The land gradually rises to a broad plateau that is broken occasionally by small groups of hills.

In the northwestern part of Benin are the Atakora Mountains, which range between 1,100 and 3,000 feet (335–914 meters) in height. In the northeast are the broad, fertile plains of Borgou and Kandi.

Rivers.   The chief rivers of Benin are found in the southern half of the country. The Ouémé is the longest river in Benin. Rising in the Atakora Mountains, the river travels a 280-mile (450 km.) course before emptying into Lake Nokoué near Porto-Novo. The Mono River, which empties into the Gulf of Guinea, forms part of Benin's southwestern boundary with Togo. Another important river in the south is the Couffo, which forms Lake Ahémé. For the most part, northern Benin is drained by tributaries of the Niger River.

Climate.   The southern part of the country has a very hot and humid climate with two dry and two rainy seasons. Northern Benin has only two seasons, a dry season from October to April and a rainy period from May to September. The latter is shorter in the extreme northern reaches of the country.

Cities.   Porto-Novo is the capital and an important marketing center of Benin. It is a city of narrow, winding, tree-shaded streets and picturesque markets in which artisans, potters, smiths, and tanners sell their wares. Parts of Porto-Novo are taking on a modern appearance with the construction of large buildings, such as the Cultural Center.

Cotonou is the largest city and the main port of Benin. This com-

Midday shoppers gather at Monoprix, the five-and-dime store, in Cotonou.

mercial center is also the terminus of the main railway lines of the country. A new deepwater port was completed here in 1965. Plans were made in 1960 for the government to move the capital from Porto-Novo to Cotonou. However, because of many political difficulties the transfer was never realized.

Abomey was originally established as the capital of the old kingdom of Dahomey in the 17th century. Today, because of its museum, the city is a major tourist attraction. Abomey is also a trading center and has a few small industries. **Ouidah**, a commercial and agricultural town, is located just west of Cotonou on a lagoon. Ouidah has a cathedral, a seminary, many mosques, and the remains of garrisons constructed by the Portuguese, French, Dutch, and British in the 18th century. **Parakou**, in central Benin, is an important agricultural center.

THE PEOPLE

Like the people of most African nations south of the Sahara, the people of Benin are varied in language and culture. The Fon, Adja, Aizo, Pedah, Mina, and Pla peoples account for almost one half of the population. Most of these people live in the southern part of the country and engage in subsistence agriculture and fishing. The farmers keep sheep, goats, chickens, pigs, guinea fowl, and ducks, and some own a few cattle. The men do the hunting and fishing and clearing of the land while the women engage in trading at the markets that are located in the towns and in most villages.

Another group, the Yoruba, came from Nigeria and settled along the southeastern boundary of Benin. They are characteristically town-dwellers who have become particularly adept in marketing and trading. Benin's Yoruba have close linguistic and cultural ties with their millions of kinsmen living across the border in Nigeria.

The Bariba, Somba, and Pilapila, who live in the central and northern regions of Benin, are largely agricultural peoples. They are bound to the land through religious ceremonies devoted to the earth god. The village headman is responsible for keeping harmonious relations with the earth in order to assure a good and fruitful life for his people. The earth god is especially offended when human blood is spilled on the ground through feuding or warfare. It is the sacred duty of the headman to settle disputes before violence occurs. Because of their beliefs, these northerners live an unusually peaceful life.

Also living in the north are the Peul (Peuhl), or Fulani, as they are also known. They are, for the most part, nomads who move their flocks of goats and sheep and herds of cattle from one place to another. The Peul usually occupy temporary camps consisting of a cluster of portable huts. The typical dwelling is built in the shape of a beehive, with a framework of poles covered with mats, grass, or leaves.

Education. Most educational facilities are located in the urban centers of the southern part of Benin. For this reason, the children in this area have a much better opportunity to attend school than those living in the north. About 65 percent of school-age children in or near the urban centers of southern Benin attend primary school, while only 15 percent of the children in the north attend any schools. This rate has been increasing through decentralization and construction of more schools all over the country.

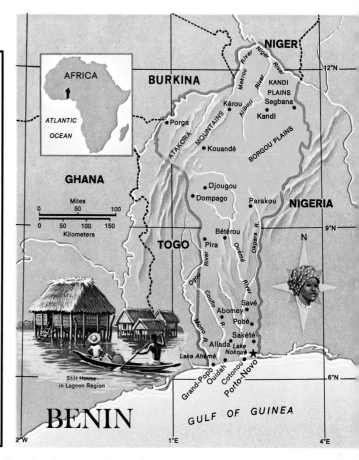

Stilt House
in Lagoon Region

BENIN

FACTS AND FIGURES

OFFICIAL NAME: People's Republic of Benin.

NATIONALITY: Beninese.

CAPITAL: Porto-Novo.

LOCATION: Western Africa. **Boundaries**—Niger, Nigeria, Gulf of Guinea, Togo, Burkina Faso.

AREA: 43,484 sq. mi. (112,622 sq. km.).

PHYSICAL FEATURES: Highest point—Atakora Mountains (2,103 ft.; 641 m.). **Lowest point**—sea level. **Chief rivers**—Mono, Ouémé, Couffo. **Major lakes**—Nokoué, Ahémé.

POPULATION: 4,663,832 (1989).

MAJOR LANGUAGES: French (official), Fon, Yoruba, Bariba, Dendi.

MAJOR RELIGIONS: Animistic and traditional beliefs, Chistianity, Islam.

GOVERNMENT: Emergent democracy. **Head of state and government**—president. **Legislature**—National Revolutionary Assembly. **International cooperation**—United Nations, Organization of African Unity (OAU), Afro-Malagasy Organization of Cooperation.

CHIEF CITIES: Cotonous, Porto-Novo, Ouidah, Abomey, Parakou.

ECONOMY: Chief agricultural products—palm kernels, palm oil, kapok, corn, cotton, coffee, peanuts, tobacco. **Industries and products**—food processing, manufacturing of cotton goods and soap, handicrafts, fishing, bicycles. **Chief exports**—palm kernels, palm oil, cotton, coffee, fuels. **Chief imports**—clothing, food, petroleum products, iron and steel.

MONETARY UNIT: Franc CFA (African Financial Community).

In recent years the government has built a number of secondary and technical schools. There are also two teacher training colleges, one for men and one for women.

Language.   French, the official language of Benin, is used in schools and offices. Fon and Yoruba are widely spoken in southern Benin. Bariba and Dendi are the most important languages spoken by those living in the north.

Religion.   The majority of the people of Benin are animists who worship a central, all-powerful god who mainfests himself through a multitude of divinities and spirits such as *voudouns. Voudouns* are the gods that play an important part in many ceremonies. Of less importance than these great gods are local good and evil spirits as well as ancestral spirits that must be given their due in goods and ceremony.

Many people have been converted to Islam and Christianity. However, some Catholics, particularly in southern Benin, continue to participate in the *voudoun* ceremonies.

ECONOMY

Benin has a predominantly agricultural economy. Palm products, both oil and kernels, provide three-fourths of the country's exports. Kapok, cotton, peanuts, corn, and tobacco are other important crops. More land is devoted to the growing of corn than to any other food crop. Coconut palm plantations along the coast of Benin are owned by the people or by the state. Some of the output is consumed locally in the form of coconut meat or oil, and some of it is exported in the form of copra (dried coconut meat).

Fishing plays a major role in the lives of some of the people of southern Benin. In this region the many small rivers and lagoons abound in fish, and some of the people make their living solely from this occupation. Since the introduction of trawlers, a number of the people have taken up deep-sea fishing.

In recent years, important deposits of marble and limestone have been found. However, evidence indicates that the country has very little in the way of other mineral resources. Some oil reserves have been found off the coast, but as yet they have not been exploited.

Benin has only begun to develop its industries. In the south a few factories exist for the processing of palm oil and cotton and the manufacturing of soap. There is also a meat-packing plant, a brewery, and a textile factory in Cotonou; a cotton-ginning plant in Parakou; and a bicycle plant in Porto-Novo.

HISTORY AND GOVERNMENT

The early history of northern Benin has not yet been documented. It is known, however, that during the 16th and 17th centuries, three kingdoms flourished in the south. These were the kingdoms of Ardra, Jakin (also called Porto-Novo), and Dahomey. The first European contact with what is now Benin occurred around 1500, near present-day Ouidah. In the early days of European exploration of Africa, contact was made with the kingdom of Dahomey. Ouegbadja, one of its first great kings, saw the advantage of trade with the Europeans. He sought to expand his kingdom to the coast, a task that was accomplished by his descendant Agadja in 1727. The goods that flowed in were cloth, liquor, pots, plates, tools, and guns. These products were paid for in human flesh—captives taken from weaker peoples to the west and north.

By the middle of the 18th century, a Yoruba kingdom to the east, Oyo, seized the kingdom of Dahomey and forced it to pay tribute for more than a century. In the mid-19th century, the Yoruba were overthrown, internal order was restored in Dahomey, and formal trade relations were established with France.

There followed a series of bitter wars with the kingdoms in the south, the most important of which were the battles (1890 and 1892–1894) waged against King Béhanzin. As a result of these wars, the French secured all of the territory of present-day Benin, thereby linking this colony to their own West African possessions.

In 1958 Dahomey was made an autonomous state within the French Community, and independence was proclaimed on August 1, 1960.

Recent Events. During the 1960s and early 1970s, Dahomey had numerous changes of government, mainly by military coups. In 1972 political power was assumed by Major (now General) Mathieu Kérékou, who in 1975 changed the country's name from Dahomey to Benin. Kérékou was elected president in 1980 and reelected in 1984.

Benin's regime renounced Marxism-Leninism in 1989, and a transitional government was sworn in in 1990 to oversee a transition to multiparty democracy. Kérékou was defeated in multiparty elections held under a new constitution in March 1991.

J. W. FERNANDEZ, Dartmouth College

Lagos, the capital and chief seaport of Nigeria.

NIGERIA

Nigeria is one of the most interesting countries in Africa. There are great cities with all the luxuries of modern life and remote villages with no electricity or running water. It is a place of sandy countryside, swampy coastlands, grassy plains with trees and bushes, and hot, humid rain forests.

More Africans live in Nigeria than in any other country on the continent. There are 250 tribal groups, but the Hausa, Fulani, Yoruba, and Ibo comprise about 60 percent of the population. The discoveries of beautifully decorated pottery, coins, delicately wrought jewelry, and terra-cotta statuettes show that in some areas of Nigeria a developed culture goes back over 2,000 years.

THE LAND

The Federal Republic of Nigeria extends inland from the eastern end of the Gulf of Guinea to the Republic of Niger in the north. Cameroon

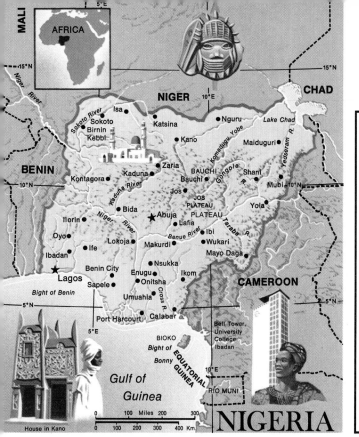

lies on the eastern boundary of Nigeria, with Benin on the west and Chad on the northeast.

The topography of the country, which is more than twice the size of California, is diverse. It has a long coastline on the Gulf of Guinea, which stretches some 500 mi. (800 km.) from Benin to Cameroon. The two great bays of Nigeria, the Bight of Benin and Bight of Bonny, are part of the Gulf of Guinea. Along the coast and inland for up to 60 mi. (100 km.), the land is covered with mangrove swamps and dotted with innumerable rivers and creeks. Stretching northward the land becomes a continuous tropical rain forest, broken only by scattered clearings with small farms. Cattle cannot be raised easily because of the tsetse fly, which brings sleeping sickness to the animals. Many years ago elephants roamed this area, but they have been wiped out, probably because of the introduction of firearms. There is some reptile life in the swampy areas of the country.

The forests gradually merge into woodland and savanna in central Nigeria, and level, treeless plains prevail in the extreme north of the country. Although Nigeria is generally a country of lowlands, some areas in the Jos Plateau in the central part of the country reach an altitude of about 6,000 ft. (1,800 m.).

Rivers. The most important river in Nigeria is the Niger, from which the country takes its name. With a length of 2,600 mi. (4,180 km.), it is one of the longest rivers in the world. The Niger flows in a northeasterly direction from the Fouta Djallon Plateau on the border between Sierra Leone and the Republic of Guinea. As it reaches eastern Mali, the Niger turns sharply to the south and moves down through Nigeria. (An article on the NIGER RIVER appears in this volume.)

The Benue River is the main tributary of the Niger. Rising in Cameroon, it flows west into Nigeria, joining the Niger River at Lokoja, a town in the south-central part of the country. The confluence of the Benue and Niger splits into many smaller rivers in the delta region of southern Nigeria.

Climate

Nigeria is a tropical country with high average temperatures prevalent almost everywhere throughout the year. In the rain-forest region of the south, the summers are hot and humid, with over 100 in. (250 cm.) of rain falling between the months of April and October. The savanna regions to the north are much drier. In the winter months from November to March, a dry, parching wind called the harmattan blows southward from the Sahara Desert, bringing with it deposits of fine sand and dust.

Cities

Nigeria has about 50 cities with populations of more than 100,000, which makes urban life more commonplace than in most other African nations. The oil boom of the mid-1960s to early 1980s led large numbers of Nigerians to abandon the countryside for the cities. This process has continued despite the government's recent efforts to promote farming.

Lagos, in the west near Benin, is the chief port and largest city of Nigeria. (The capital of the country was formally shifted from Lagos to Abuja, a new city located in central Nigeria, in late 1991.) Lagos was originally situated on an island, but the city soon spread to the mainland and other adjoining islands. All are connected by bridges and causeways. High-rise buildings, modern department stores, schools, churches, and hospitals have recently appeared on the streets of Lagos. Still evident are the roofs of the single-story buildings that once were

Noon-hour traffic on a busy street in downtown Lagos.

The British Deputy High Commissioner has offices in the modern Co-operative Bank Building in Ibadan.

prevalent throughout the city. Lagos is an important industrial and commercial center and the western terminus of the Nigerian railway system. The city boasts an international airport.

Ibadan, the second largest city, was formerly the capital of the old Western Region. It was established by the Yoruba people sometime during the late 18th or early 19th century. The city is a major trading and industrial center and has one of the largest open-air markets in Africa. High-rise buildings have been erected in recent years, but one-story and two-story buildings are still seen everywhere. The University of Ibadan is here.

Ogbomosho, an important city about 50 miles northeast of Ibadan, was founded in the 17th century and was a longtime Yoruba stronghold. Today, it is an agricultural center and a textile manufacturing hub.

Kano is the most important city in northern Nigeria. This ancient walled city was built in the 16th century on the site of a settlement dating from the 10th century. During the 1800's, Kano served as a major trading market on the trans-Saharan caravan route. The older part of the walled city contains thousands of homes built of mud bricks. The architecture

The mosque in Kano is one of the major attractions of the old walled city.

of the houses is related to the Moorish style found in North Africa. Most of the houses are square with flat roofs and have either one story or two stories. There is a magnificent mosque in Kano, where believers come to prostrate themselves and pray while facing Mecca. In recent years, modern government buildings, mosques, and hospitals have been built.

Kaduna has been the capital of northern Nigeria from the time of British administration in the early 1900's. In recent years, the city has become an important industrial and commercial center. Because of its large population increase, new housing developments have been built in its outskirts.

A disc jockey in Ibadan plays records in one of Nigeria's radio stations.

The refineries at Port Harcourt process Nigeria's vast amounts of crude oil.

Port Harcourt, the second largest seaport in the country, is the center of the nation's petroleum industry. Ships from all over the world dock here with their cargoes and to take on Nigerian oil and coal. (The city is the terminus of the railway that comes from the Enugu coal mines.) In recent years, large petroleum refineries have been built in the Port Harcourt area.

Other important cities are **Zaria,** the center of the nation's major cotton-growing area; **Benin City,** famous as the center of an ancient civilization; **Ife,** the spiritual capital of the Yoruba people; **Jos,** the center of the tin-mining industry; **Enugu,** the capital of the old Eastern Region and the center of the coal-mining region; and **Calabar,** the oldest settlement and river port in the east.

THE PEOPLE

Nigeria, with its many distinct tribes, is the most heavily populated nation in Africa. The people are divided into many groups, some with as little as 1,000 people and others numbering into the millions. A few of the groups are nomadic, some live in self-contained villages, and others are part of great historical states. Today, each of the areas of Nigeria is dominated by one large group of people: in the north, a combination of Hausa-Fulani; in the southwest, the Yoruba; and in the southeast, the Ibo. Other important groups are the Tiv, Ijaw, Ibibio,

Nupe, Kanuri, Efik, and Edo (Bini). All of these groups are distinctive in their cultural practices and have their own languages.

The Ibo

The Ibo share with their southeastern neighbors an area that stretches roughly south from the Benue River to the Atlantic Ocean and east from the Niger River to Cameroon. From 1967 until 1970 part of this Eastern Region, especially the Ibo-speaking sector, was declared the Republic of Biafra.

This part of Nigeria is one of the most heavily populated areas in all of Africa. It is filled with innumerable villages and farms. The people are primarily farmers, and the principal food crops are yams and cassava. Vegetables, citrus fruits, and bananas are also grown.

An Ibo village, usually enclosed by a wall, contains many houses. Numerous members of one family live together in these villages. The extended family consists of a father, his wife (occasionally several wives, each in her own small house), his brothers, their wives, their children, and grandchildren. To a number of rural Africans, polygyny (having more than one wife at a time) is an essential part of life. Wives are needed to farm, market, raise the children, and conduct the business of the household. Frequently the first wife will encourage her husband to take another so that she can have help in running the household. All of the children are raised co-operatively, and authority over them can be exercised by aunts and uncles as well as by mothers and fathers. The extended family, therefore, is the cornerstone of Ibo village life.

The shortage of land affects the Ibo; consequently, throughout the years many of them have moved into other parts of Nigeria. Wherever the Ibo go, however, they maintain close ties with their family, their village, and their people. When there is sickness or death, the Ibo turn to other members of their clan for help. They are a particularly industrious people, eager for education and for the good things of life. There are many Ibo engineers, government employees, railway workers, clerks, and businessmen in the country. Many Ibo work in the large oil refineries located at Port Harcourt. The Ibo have adapted easily to urbanization and have built many towns and cities in their land.

The Ibo wear either clothing similar to that worn in Europe or America or their traditional dress, which consists of a tunic and a loincloth. Women usually wear brightly colored turbans, blouses, and long, printed wraparound skirts.

The Yoruba

The Yoruba people live primarily in the southwestern part of Nigeria. This is a rich agricultural area and has vast quantities of cacao, kola nuts, palm oil, rubber, and timber for export.

The Yoruba have a history that can be traced back hundreds of years. Sometime before A.D. 1200 they settled in what is now Nigeria and founded many kingdoms, the most important of which were Oyo and Ife. The Yoruba were the first to come into contact with the European traders and missionaries. This gave them an advantage in industrial and technological development.

Yoruba farmers tend to live in villages and travel daily to their farms, which lie outside of town. Some families whose farms are a great distance from their town have built small houses on their land so that they can live there during the height of farming activity.

Only a few of the Yoruba work in factories, and some specialize in crafts such as weaving, carving, leatherwork, and brasswork.

Although Western-style clothing can be seen in some of the major cities of southwest Nigeria, most Yoruba still wear the *agbada*. This is a large robe worn over a tunic and loose-fitting, lightweight pants. The *agbada* is frequently made of brightly colored cloth embroidered about the neck and sleeves.

The Hausa and Fulani

The Hausa and Fulani live in the northern part of Nigeria. This region is a great plain stretching from the borders of Dahomey across to Lake Chad and as far south as Ilorin. The richness of northern Nigeria lies in the production of peanuts and cotton as well as in the cattle raised by the nomadic Fulani. The major crops grown by the Hausa and Fulani are millet, peas, beans, corn, tomatoes, wheat, and sweet potatoes. One of the most important products of this area is a leather made from goat hides. It is shipped to the markets of North Africa, where it is known as Moroccan leather.

The Hausa are excellent farmers, skilled potters, weavers, metalworkers, and embroiderers. Perhaps they are best-known as traders. Trading is a profession that has been handed down within families for hundreds of years. The itinerant traders usually travel from town to town on bicycles, setting up their displays of wooden statues, jewelry, and woven materials at rest houses, lodges, and hotels in the larger cities.

Many Hausa women still dress in the Muslim tradition. Except for the eyes their faces are completely veiled and they are covered from head to foot in long flowing robes. The men usually wear long robes with loose-fitting trousers underneath.

Fulani from northern Nigeria bring their herds to the cattle market in Ibadan.

The Fulani were originally cattle herders and nomadic shepherds who migrated from present-day Senegal into northern Nigeria about 4 centuries ago.

Although some Fulani are still nomadic, most of the people reside in villages and towns. The houses of the Fulani are made of sun-dried brick, with flat terraced roofs and interior courtyards. The men do very little hunting and fishing, preferring to spend their time in agricultural pursuits. The nomadic Fulani wander in groups, occupying temporary camps composed of huts that can be carried on pack animals when camp is shifted.

The family of the nomadic Fulani usually consists of the herder, his wife or wives, and dependent children. They move from place to place living on dairy products and exchanging surpluses for grain in the markets of the farmers in the area. The cattle belong to the father. He gradually turns some of the herd over to his older sons so that they may start their own cattle herd when they marry.

Languages

English was introduced into Nigeria by traders and missionaries in the 18th and 19th centuries. It has become the universal language, and virtually all schoolchildren learn English today. There are as many as 250 distinct languages spoken by the people of Nigeria. Many of these languages have one or more dialects, which makes communication difficult even between people of the same group. Although all Ibo speak the Ibo language, people of this group who live far apart have difficulty in understanding one another.

Hausa is the major language of the people living in the north, and Yoruba is spoken by those residing in western Nigeria.

Education

Christian missionaries brought schooling to Nigeria in the early 1800's. During the next 100 years they set up mission schools throughout the country. However, they were not completely successful. Before the mid-20th century less than one third of the school-age children of Nigeria attended these schools. In 1954 all educational facilities came under the control of the regional governments. Shortages of teachers, classrooms, and supplies, however, have hampered efforts to improve education. The government supports a program that will eventually make primary education free and compulsory for all children. In the mid-1980's, literacy was estimated at 40 percent.

Nigeria has a number of universities and colleges.

Religion

Since the late 14th century the Northern Region of Nigeria has been under the influence of Islam. Today, approximately 75 percent of the Hausa-Fulani are Muslims. The remainder of the population of the north are either Christians or follow animistic traditions.

Missionaries brought Catholicism to the people of southeastern Nigeria. However, many inhabitants of this region still practice their own African religions.

Although most Yoruba are Christians, there are those who still follow their traditional beliefs. Ancestor-worship is an important element of these beliefs. Dead ancestors are supposed always to be with one in spirit, and it is this vital force that sustains the people forever. There is a very high moral and ethical tradition in this religion. The ideas of kindness, goodness, truth, hospitality, and concern for old people are considered most important in Yoruba life.

ECONOMY

Since oil was discovered in the Port Harcourt area in the 1950's, petroleum has come to dominate Nigeria's economy. Today, Nigeria is among the largest petroleum producers in the world and a member of the Organization of Petroleum Exporting Countries (OPEC). Its high-quality crude oil is the greatest single source of income for the nation, and its export has made Nigeria the richest country in black Africa. It is also one of the few countries of Africa that has coal in commercial quantities. Other minerals include tin and columbite, which are mined in the Jos Plateau region.

Despite the nation's oil riches, about 70 percent of the people are still involved in agriculture. In the sandy regions of the north, peanuts and cotton are the important crops. In the south, particularly in the rain forest area, there are many plantations of palm trees that produce a palm oil used for soap-making, cooking, and lubrication. The palm trees are also tapped for what is called palm wine, a favorite drink. Nigeria is one of the largest cacao producers in the world. Other cash crops include kola nuts, rubber, and lumber.

Income from petroleum exports has made it possible for Nigeria to embark on industrialization. Oil refineries predominate in the Port Harcourt region. In the north, textile mills have been built. Handicrafts, building materials, and metal products are other major industries.

The harbor at Lagos is a port of call for ships from many nations.

Workers hang goat skins to dry. Some of the skins are later
sent to Morocco for use in the production of leather goods.

Nigerian women prepare pineapples for canning at a factory in Ibadan.

HISTORY

The origins of the first people to inhabit the region now called Nigeria are uncertain. Many probably migrated from the dry desert area in northern Africa in search of fertile soil for farming and animals for hunting.

The first known culture of Nigeria is that of the Nok, who lived in the Jos Plateau region of central Nigeria. Recent archeological excavations have uncovered terra-cotta statues in the village of Nok. These findings have led historians to believe that a great civilization existed in this area as long ago as 500 B.C.

The Ancient Empires

The written history of Nigeria, taken from Arab chronicles, began with the establishment of Kanem-Bornu in the early part of the 9th century. This was the first known large, powerful state in northern Nigeria. Kanem-Bornu was probably founded by a group of nomads from the Sahara region of North Africa. These people moved southward to the more fertile regions of central and western Sudan (Senegal, Mali, and Niger). For the next 5 centuries, Kanem-Bornu was an important stopover for travelers on the trans-Saharan trade route.

To the west of Kanem-Bornu were the seven Hausa city-states. They were probably established between A.D. 100 and 1200. The Hausa people developed these states into important trading centers. Throughout the centuries, they often fought one another for supremacy but would band together for defense when invasion from outside forces was imminent.

The spread of Islam by merchants who traveled across the desert from Egypt, sometime during the 14th century, brought great changes to these states. The development of sophisticated administration systems, the Muslim system of law and taxation, and the building of armies were just a few of the advances made under Muslim influence.

In the beginning of the 19th century, Usman dan Fodio, a Fulani holy leader, conquered the Hausa city-states. He had been waging war throughout Hausaland in an effort to purify the Muslim religion. Usman dan Fodio made himself sultan and appointed Fulani emirs as rulers over the Hausa states.

During the 14th century three powerful kingdoms flourished in the forests of southern Nigeria. These were Ife, Benin, and Oyo. Ife, one of the oldest Yoruba towns, was probably established as a small kingdom in the 1st millennium A.D. It was here, according to Yoruba legend, that God created men. Oyo and Benin are considered offshoots of Ife, and all three cities were known for the magnificence of their art.

Unlike the northern kingdom of Kanem-Bornu and the Hausa city-states, the growth of Ife, Benin, and Oyo was not influenced by Islam.

European Interests

In the late 1400's Portuguese navigators explored the coastal waters off present-day Nigeria. They were soon followed by the Spanish, Dutch, and English.

Soon after the arrival of the Europeans, the Atlantic slave trade began. It lasted for more than 350 years, and the total number of slaves traded reached over 20,000,000. The British Empire became deeply involved in Nigerian affairs in the 19th century. Their first major accom-

A busy street in a small town near Zaria.

plishment was to abolish the slave trade in 1807. While exploring the interior of Nigeria to set up markets for the products of the Industrial Revolution, the British met with much resistance, and it was not until the early 20th century that all of Nigeria fell under British control.

In 1861 Lagos became a British colony and a governor was installed. In 1885 Britain declared a protectorate over the Niger districts along the coast of the Gulf of Guinea.

Eventually, Britain re-organized Nigeria into two major protectorates, Northern Nigeria and Southern Nigeria, plus the Colony and Protectorate of Lagos. It was the merging of the northern and southern regions in 1914 that created the modern state of Nigeria.

After World War I, a sense of nationalism started to rise, especially among the educated and wealthy Nigerians. They began to consider themselves Nigerians rather than Ibo, Hausa, or Yoruba. Africans at this point began to demand more participation in the affairs of government.

Independence

In 1954 a constitution was agreed upon, confirming the power of the regions—north, west, and east—as opposed to a strong central government. This Constitution eventually established self-government for Nigeria and was in effect when independence came in October, 1960.

The Federation of Nigeria was held together by a very delicate balance. Immediately upon independence the three regional political parties began contesting for power. Since the Northern Region had the greatest population, it had the majority of seats in the legislature. The first prime minister, Sir Abubakar Tafawa Balewa, was a northerner. On January 15, 1966, a military coup took place, apparently planned by junior Ibo officers of the Eastern Region. Prime Minister Balewa was assassinated and power shifted to an Ibo senior officer, Major General Johnson Aguiyi-

The Emir of Katsina and his attendants participate in a traditional ceremony.

Ironsi. At first he supported the concept of a federal Nigeria and appointed military rulers for each region. In the east he selected Lieutenant Colonel C. Odemegwu Ojukwu, an Ibo. There was growing concern that the new government would favor the Ibo and the power of the north would be gone forever. Later, General Ironsi tried to make a unitary state out of Nigeria so that regional rivalries would be ended. This move further intensified tensions in the country, particularly in the north.

In the spring of 1966, uprisings broke out against the Ibo residing in the north, and on July 29, 1966, General Ironsi was killed by Hausa soldiers. During September and October as many as 30,000 Ibo were killed and countless others fled south to their ancestral homelands, although many of them were born in the north and had lived there all their lives.

Power was taken by Lieutenant Colonel Yakubu Gowon, a northerner who attempted to effect a reconciliation. He re-established the federal system of government and made plans for a new constitution. At this time Colonel Ojukwu, military leader of the Eastern Region, demanded restitution to the Ibo for their lost lives and property and punishment of those responsible. Bitterness was growing between the leaders; conferences were held but all to no avail. When the federal government broke the country up into 12 states in an effort to reduce the power of any one of the regions, the Ibo considered this a move directed against them. The division separated them from the tremendous oil deposits at Port Harcourt and also cut them off from the sea. Since Nigerian military strength was no more than 10,000 troops and since the oil reserves from the Eastern Region could provide the necessary financial support, Colonel Ojukwu decided to take his region out of the Federation of Nigeria. On

May 30, 1967, he proclaimed the Eastern Region the independent Republic of Biafra.

Civil War

Troops were mobilized on both sides, and fighting began on July 6, 1967. In the early stages of the war, Biafra made great progress and invaded the Mid-Western State, where many Ibo lived. However, the Nigerian Army soon advanced into Biafra. Enugu, the capital of the secessionist region, was overrun. Densely populated Biafra, swollen with millions of refugees, did not have the food to support its people.

The bloody civil war raged on. In 1969 Umuahia, the provisional capital of Biafra, fell to the Nigerians. The area held by the Biafrans was reduced to about 3,000 sq. mi. (7,770 sq. km.), one-tenth of its original size. All efforts at negotiation failed because Biafra insisted that it would not rejoin Nigeria except in some totally autonomous status. Nigeria, at this point winning the war, would not compromise.

On January 15, 1970, Biafra formally surrendered to Nigeria. The Biafran leader, General Ojukwu, fled the secessionist Eastern Region, and his successor, General Philip Effiong, signed the surrender document that ended the state of Biafra and proclaimed loyalty to the Government of Nigeria. The conflict had lasted 30 months and had caused widespread destruction. The government began the task of healing the scars of war, rebuilding Nigeria, and uniting its people again. This was accomplished quickly—more quickly, in fact, than in any other nation that has fought a civil war in modern times.

Recent Events

During the 1970s its oil resources provided Nigeria with a period of economic prosperity. Political problems, however, continued to plague the country. Since 1966, Nigeria had been governed by the military under Yakubu Gowon, now a general and head of the armed forces. Opposition to Gowon intensified when he repeatedly postponed a return to democratic government, and in 1975 he was overthrown by a group of young Army officers. A new constitution went into effect in 1979, when Alhaji Shehu Shagari was elected president of a civilian government.

Falling world oil prices in the early 1980s badly hurt Nigeria's economy. Although Shagari won reelection in 1983, his failure to solve the economic problems amid charges of governmental corruption led to his downfall and a resumption of military rule, under General Mohammed Buhari. In 1985, Buhari himself was overthrown by General Ibrahim Babangida. In 1991, in an effort to reduce continuing ethnic and religious tensions, nine new states were created, raising the total to 30.

Government. In 1989, the military introduced a new constitution creating a two-party system that would, it was hoped, force ethnic groups to build coalitions. State elections were held in December 1991 and elections for a new two-house legislature in July 1992, but political activities were suspended in October amid charges of election fraud. Babangida served as president and head of the Armed Forces Ruling Council pending a promised return to civilian rule, which had been proposed for 1993.

EDWARD H. SCHILLER, Nassau Community College
Reviewed by EDOHO BASSEY EDOHO, Professor of African History,
State University of New York at Albany

A view of the city of Douala.

CAMEROON

The place is the downtown area of Yaoundé, the capital of the Republic of Cameroon. The time is the early evening hour, when all of the city's cars seem to come together in one spot. Blaring horns blend with the hum of voices, and a blur of figures moves hurriedly along the sidewalks. Many people wear Western-style clothes and drive cars manufactured thousands of miles away on other continents.

Far away in the highlands of western Cameroon another scene is taking place. Here in the Mbem area, some men of the Kaka people have gathered to practice the art of spider divination. No one knows how or where this practice started, for its origins are lost in the dim reaches of time. The men, citizens of the Republic of Cameroon, wait patiently, their eyes focused upon the sorcerers. By reading leaves that have been touched by trap-door spiders, the sorcerers will foretell the future for the Kaka people.

Much farther to the northeast the scene changes. Here one of

Cameroon's noted chiefs, the Lamido of Rei-Bouba, has called the annual gathering of his people. Mounted warriors come in turbans and flowing robes, carrying swords and rifles. The warriors rear their horses and brandish their swords, the steel blades flashing in the sun. A scene that could almost be out of *The Arabian Nights* swirls into colorful life.

If there is one word that describes Cameroon, it is "diversity." This is a land made up of villages with thatched huts and thriving, modern cities with concrete high-rise buildings. Cameroon is an energetic country that is combining the old and the new African ways. It is bringing together modern industry and ancient ways of tilling the soil. It is trying to make Cameroonians of a people speaking over 100 different dialects and belonging to many different ethnic groups. Today the official languages of the country are French and English.

THE LAND

Cameroon is situated on the west coast of central Africa. It has an area of 183,569 square miles (475,442 square kilometers) and is made up of several distinct geographical regions. The country is bounded on the west by Nigeria; on the north and northeast by Lake Chad and the Republic of Chad; on the east by the Central African Republic; and on the south by the People's Republic of Congo, Gabon, and Equatorial Guinea.

Because its southern border is just 2 degrees above the equator, much of Cameroon has a tropical climate. Rainfall is heavy in the southern part of the country. The village of Debundscha, with an annual rainfall of nearly 400 inches (1,000 centimeters), is one of the wettest places in the world.

Workers build a bridge not far from a village in southwestern Cameroon.

Plant and Animal Life

This colorful and diverse country has an amazing variety of vegetation and wildlife. In the north are thorn trees and swamps covered with papyrus and tall grass. Wooded valleys, fern-covered slopes, and wide plateau pastures are found in the mountains. In the south are the rain forests, damp and hot and always green.

In the valleys and forests and on the plateaus live many different animals, ranging from tiny cane rats to huge elephants. In the mountain forests the shrill cries of chimpanzees and monkeys can be heard. Families of gorillas roam silently under high, green canopies. The northern grasslands are dotted with herds of giraffes, antelope, elephants, and other animals.

THE PEOPLE AND THEIR WAY OF LIFE

Douala, the principal port of Cameroon, is a modern city of over 460,000 people. The largest city of the country, it is a railway center and has an excellent international airport. From Douala, on a clear day, one can see the majestic peak of Cameroon Mountain, the highest mountain in West Africa (13,350 feet; 4,069 meters). Cameroon Mountain, an occasionally active volcano, is one of a long chain of volcanic mountains that ages ago extended down the western side of the continent. Today, some of these mountains are the islands of Fernando Po, Annobón, Príncipe, and São Tomé.

At the coastal base of Cameroon Mountain lie Victoria and Tiko, where German colonists once established plantations of rubber, bananas, and oil palms that still provide the basis of West Cameroon's economy. High up on the mountain, facing the sea, the Germans founded the

A cloth market is located on a colorful street in Yaoundé, capital of Cameroon.

FACTS AND FIGURES

OFFICIAL NAME: United Republic of Cameroon.

NATIONALITY: Cameroonian(s).

CAPITAL: Yaoundé.

LOCATION: West Equatorial Africa. **Boundaries:** Chad, Central African Republic, Congo, Gabon, Equatorial Guinea, Gulf of Guinea, Nigeria.

AREA: 183,569 sq. mi. (475,442 sq. km.).

PHYSICAL FEATURES: Highest point—Cameroon Mountain 13,350 ft. (4,069 m.). **Lowest point**—sea level. **Chief rivers**—Sanaga, Nyong, Dja.

POPULATION: 11,390,000 (1991; annual growth 2.7%).

MAJOR LANGUAGES: French and English (official), local languages.

MAJOR RELIGIONS: Christianity, Islam, animistic beliefs.

GOVERNMENT: Republic. **Head of state**—president. **Head of government**—prime minister. **Legislature**—National Assembly.

CHIEF CITIES: Douala, Yaoundé, N'Kongsamba.

ECONOMY: Chief minerals—petroleum, natural gas, bauxite, iron ore. **Chief agricultural products**—cacao, coffee, bananas, cotton, palm oil, rubber, timber. **Industries and products**—processed foods and agricultural products, oil refining, aluminum smelting, lumber. **Chief exports**—petroleum products, cacao, coffee, timber. **Chief imports**—machinery, vehicles, textiles, chemicals, metals, foodstuffs, various consumer goods.

MONETARY UNIT: Franc CFA (African Financial Community).

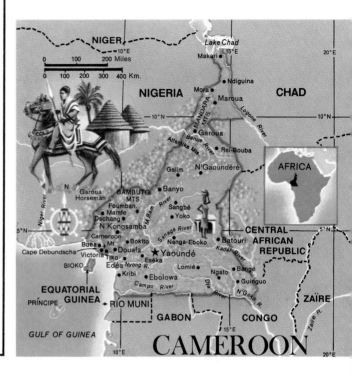

town of **Buea,** which they made the capital of the German Cameroons colony. One colonial governor, in a homesick mood, built a small version of a Rhine River castle in Buea. The *Schloss* (German for "castle") can still be seen in the town.

In the western Cameroon highland area, on hilly, grassy plateaus, live one of Cameroon's most energetic and resourceful peoples, the Tikar. In eastern Cameroon live the Bamiléké. Hardworking and thrifty, the Bamiléké have long been among Cameroon's most successful traders. The people of the highlands grow coffee for export, as well as bananas, pineapples, and other tropical crops.

Also inhabiting the highlands are the Bamoun people. The Bamoun, most of whom are Muslims, are related to the Tikar and the Bamiléké, who practice both Christianity and animism. At the town of **Foumban,** the sons and grandsons of the artisans who once decorated the palace of the Bamoun sultans still work at their ancient craft. They carve wooden panels and cast small brass figures that are greatly prized by collectors of African art.

Along the Mambilla Plateau and close to the Atlantika and Kapsiki ranges are the Kirdi. The Kirdi are a people who still follow ancient animistic beliefs. They live very simply in stone or clay huts and raise sheep, goats, and poultry.

The Kirdi share the dry savanna plains of northern Cameroon with the pastoral Fulani. The Fulani raise vast herds of cattle. The Fulani are Muslims, and their chiefs, called *lamidos,* make their headquarters in the growing towns of Garoua, Maroua, and N'Gaoundéré.

Although it lies on the Benue, a branch of the Niger River, **Garoua** is a seaport. For six weeks during the year, the Benue rises about 20 ft.

(6 m.). It is then that ships come some 700 mi. (1,100 km.) from the sea to take cotton, cattle, and millet to foreign markets.

Yaoundé, the national capital of Cameroon, is located in the central plateau region of the country. A city of more than 300,000 people, it sprawls among low hills near the heart of Cameroon's cacao-growing areas. Cameroon is one of the world's leading producers of cacao, which is used to make chocolate and cocoa.

Yaoundé is a modern city. It has wide, paved streets, concrete-and-steel office and apartment buildings, and heavy automobile traffic. Industry is concentrated around the outer edges of the city. Yaoundé is the site of the University of Yaoundé, founded in 1962.

Aside from French and English, the people of the city speak Ewondo and Bulu. Most of them are Christians. Catholic and Protestant missions have been active here since early in the 19th century. Today Yaoundé is the center of one of Africa's largest Catholic archdioceses.

ECONOMY

Cameroon is one of the most prosperous African nations south of the Sahara. Most of the labor force is engaged in agriculture, with cacao, coffee, bananas, cotton, palm oil, and sugar as the leading cash crops. Petroleum and petroleum products provided 56 percent of exports in 1990, but the nation's petroleum reserves, first discovered in the 1970s, are expected to be exhausted in the early 1990s. Bauxite (aluminum ore) and iron ore are other important minerals. Industries include the processing of agricultural products, oil refining, and aluminum smelting.

HISTORY AND GOVERNMENT

Cameroon is the English version of the name given to the region in the 15th century by Portuguese who explored the northern part of the Wouri River. Dropping anchor near what is now Douala, the Portuguese pulled in nets full of large shrimps. They called the river Rio dos Camarões, or "river of shrimps." The name stuck, and it came to be used by the Germans, who established a protectorate, called Kamerun, in the region in 1884. After its defeat in World War I, Germany was forced to give up its colony, which was divided between France and Britain, first as mandates under the League of Nations and then as trust territories of the United Nations. The French-governed territory gained independence in 1960 as the Republic of Cameroon. When part of the British-governed area joined the republic in 1961 (the rest of British Cameroons merged with Nigeria), the new nation was called the Federal Republic of Cameroon. Following the adoption of a new constitution in 1972, the country became the United Republic of Cameroon. The original name, Republic of Cameroon, was restored in 1984.

An elected president serves as Cameroon's chief of state. Cameroon was long governed by President Ahmadou Ahidjo, who retired in 1982 after 22 years in office. His successor, Paul Biya, won election in his own right in 1984 and was reelected in 1988. The post of prime minister was restored in 1991 following a wave of public protests and demands for democratic reform. That same year, the constitution was revised to create a multiparty system. In 1992, Biya and his party won the nation's first multiparty elections, although there were charges of voting fraud.

VICTOR T. LE VINE, Washington University

EQUATORIAL GUINEA

Equatorial Guinea is made up of two provinces, Río Muni and Bioko (formerly Fernando Po). Río Muni includes the continental area on the African mainland between Cameroon and Gabon, and the offshore islands of Corisco, Elobey Grande, and Elobey Chico. The province of Bioko includes the island of the same name, which lies in the Bight of Bonny about 100 mi. (160 km.) from the Río Muni coast, and the smaller island of Pagalu (formerly Annobón).

The Land and People

Most of Río Muni is a tropical rain forest. It is generally lowland, although several plateaus rise to 4,000 ft. (1,200 m.) in the Crystal Mountains. This mountain system is the source of many short, torrential rivers, which flow over rapids and waterfalls into the Atlantic Ocean. The most important river is the 200-mi. (320-km.)-long Mbini River. Bata is the chief city of Río Muni.

The majority of the inhabitants of Río Muni are the Fang, a branch of the large Bantu family. They occupy most of the province except along the coastal regions. The Fang make their living by hunting and by cultivating such crops as yams, manioc, and bananas. The chief exports of Río Muni are wood and coffee.

Bioko is a volcanic island with two large extinct volcanoes and beautiful crater lakes. The island has densely forested mountains rising to 9,449 ft. (2,880 m.). The capital of Equatorial Guinea, **Malabo**, is located on the northern tip of the island. The city has an excellent harbor, a modern jetport, a new highway system, and a television transmitter at the top of a volcanic peak.

The original inhabitants of Bioko are the Bubi. They are primarily farmers who own small plots of land. The crops grown on these small farms are used not only to feed the family group, but also to supply the local markets with a variety of products. Some of the Bubi are employed in administrative positions, commerce, the public services, and the professions. For about 50 years, large numbers of migrant farm workers from nearby Nigeria worked on the island. After independence, many of these workers returned home. Bioko's principal export is cacao. Fishing, agriculture, and livestock raising are the chief occupations. Before independence, the province had one of the highest per-capita incomes in Africa.

Until the late 1960s Equatorial Guinea had a fairly large Spanish population. However, the coming of independence and a series of mutual misunderstandings brought a wave of hostility against the Spanish. Most of them left the country.

Language and Religion.   Spanish is the official language, but African dialects are also spoken. The literacy rate on Bioko was once one of the highest in Africa. But many teachers left the country after independence, and little schooling was available. The majority of the people of Equatorial Guinea are Roman Catholics. There are some Protestants and Muslims, as well as those who follow animistic beliefs.

Climate.   The climate of Equatorial Guinea is dominated by the

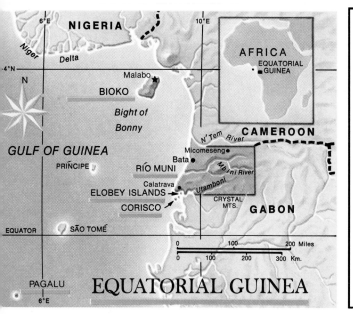

NIGERIA
Niger
Delta
Malabo
BIOKO
Bight of
Bonny
GULF OF GUINEA
PRÍNCIPE
N'Tem River
Micomeseng
Bata
RÍO MUNI
Mbini River
Calatrava
Utamboni
ELOBEY ISLANDS
CORISCO
CRYSTAL MTS.
SÃO TOMÉ
EQUATOR
CAMEROON
GABON
AFRICA
EQUATORIAL GUINEA
PAGALU
EQUATORIAL GUINEA
0   100   200 Miles
0 100 200 300 Km.

FACTS AND FIGURES

OFFICIAL NAME: Republic of Equatorial Guinea.

NATIONALITY: Equatorial Guinean(s).

CAPITAL: Malabo.

LOCATION: West central coast of Africa. **Boundaries:** Cameroon, Gabon, Gulf of Guinea.

AREA: 10,831 sq. mi (28,051 sq. km.).

PHYSICAL FEATURES: Highest point—9,449 ft. (2,880 m.). **Lowest point**—sea level. **Chief river**—Mbini.

POPULATION: 378,729 (1991; annual growth 2.6%).

MAJOR LANGUAGES: Spanish (official), Fang, Bubi.

MAJOR RELIGION: Roman Catholicism.

GOVERNMENT: Republic. **Head of state and government**—president. **Legislature**—House of Representatives of the People.

CHIEF CITIES: Malabo, Bata.

ECONOMY: Chief agricultural products—cacao, coffee, bananas. **Industries and products**—timber, fishing. **Chief exports**—timber, re-exports (alcohol, tobacco, clothing), cacao. **Chief imports**—petroleum, foodstuffs, beverages, clothing.

MONETARY UNIT: CFA franc (African Financial Community).

monsoons and warm gulf currents. High temperatures and great humidity are prevalent throughout most of the year. Rainfall is heavy (approximately 400 in.; 1,000 cm.) from April through October; even during the dry season, showers are not uncommon.

HISTORY

The island of Bioko was discovered in the 15th century by the Portuguese explorer Fernão do Po. Portugal retained it until 1778, when it was ceded to Spain. Yellow fever killed many Spanish settlers and the survivors fled. The island was left unoccupied from 1781 until 1827, when Spain leased bases to the British Royal Navy at Malabo. In British hands, the island became a refuge for freed slaves.

The Spanish made a second attempt to occupy the island in 1843 and some years later expelled the British. In the early 20th century Spain began to concentrate on the economic development of the island.

Little is known of the pre-colonial history of Río Muni. In 1843 Spain made a treaty with Río Munian peoples and Spaniards settled on the mainland. During the first half of the 20th century, the territories were governed by Spain under the name of Spanish Guinea. They were renamed Equatorial Guinea in 1963 and granted independence in 1968.

Government. Under Equatorial Guinea's first elected president, Francisco Macías Nguema, thousands of people were killed or fled the country. Macías was overthrown in 1979, tried, and executed. The leader of the coup, Colonel Teodoro Obiang Nguema Mbasogo, was named president by the military government in 1982. Legislative elections were held in 1983 under a new constitution. In 1991, under pressure from international aid donors, a multiparty constitution was adopted, but control remained in the hands of Obiang Nguema and his supporters.

Reviewed by GUSTAVO ENVELA-MAKONGO
Former Ambassador of Equatorial Guinea to the United Nations

SÃO TOMÉ AND PRÍNCIPE

Lying near the equator, off the African coast in the Gulf of Guinea, is the island nation of São Tomé and Príncipe. These islands were formerly an overseas province of Portugal. Both São Tomé and Príncipe are rich in scenic beauty. There are high mountains covered with dense, luxuriant tropical vegetation and deep gullies that run down to the sea. Inland there is water everywhere. The water leaps from falls in the dense rain forest and runs down to the sea in cascading rivers and streams. These waterways are spanned by natural bridges called "the bridges which God made."

The Land and People

São Tomé, with an area of 330 square miles (855 square kilometers), is the larger and the more populous of the two main islands. Many of the island's inhabitants are descendants of the original Portuguese colonists and Africans from Gabon, Angola, Cape Verde, and Mozambique. The people are principally farmers who cultivate bananas, yams, and cassava for food. Fishing is also an important occupation. The population includes laborers who come from Mozambique and Angola to work and live on the cacao plantations scattered throughout the islands. These plantations and most of the land are owned by large European agricultural companies or absentee landlords. The production of cacao dominates the economy. Other cash crops are coffee, copra, palm oil, palm kernels, and bananas.

People walk along a street in São Tomé, the capital of São Tomé and Príncipe.

Vendors from many parts of the islands sell their produce at the market in São Tomé.

SÃO TOMÉ
AND
— PRÍNCIPE

FACTS AND FIGURES

OFFICIAL NAME: Democratic Republic of São Tomé and Príncipe.

CAPITAL: São Tomé.

LOCATION: Off African coast in Gulf of Guinea.

AREA: São Tomé—330 sq. mi. (855 sq. km.). **Príncipe**—42 sq. mi. (109 sq. km.). **Total:** 372 sq. mi. (964 sq. km.).

PHYSICAL FEATURES: Highest point—Pico de São Tomé (6,640 ft.; 2,024 m.). **Lowest point**—sea level.

POPULATION: 128,500 (1991; annual growth 3.0%).

MAJOR LANGUAGES: Portuguese (official), local languages.

MAJOR RELIGION: Roman Catholicism.

GOVERNMENT: Republic. **Head of state**—president. **Head of government**—prime minister. **Legislature**—National People's Assembly.

CHIEF CITIES: São Tomé, Santo António.

ECONOMY: Chief agricultural products—cacao, coffee, copra, palm oil, palm kernels, bananas. **Industries and products**—vegetable oils, lime, soap. **Chief exports**—cacao, copra, coffee, palm oil, coconuts. **Chief imports**—machinery, food, clothing.

MONETARY UNIT—Dobra.

São Tomé has an airport and about 155 mi. (250 km.) of asphalt roads. The capital and chief seaport of the province is the town of São Tomé. It lies in the northeastern part of the island and has a fine museum, several churches, and a broadcasting station. The country has elementary schools, several secondary schools, and a technical school. Portuguese is the official language.

The much smaller island of Príncipe lies 90 mi. (144 km.) northeast of São Tomé. Less heavily settled than São Tomé, it has an area of about 42 sq. mi. (109 sq. km.). Santo António, on the east coast of Príncipe, is the most important town on the island.

History and Government

São Tomé and Príncipe were uninhabited when they were first sighted by Portuguese navigators in the 15th century. They were settled by Portuguese and by Africans who were brought as slaves to work the sugarcane plantations. The islands became an overseas province of Portugal in 1522. When sugar declined in importance, the islands became a stopping point on the slave route between Africa and the Americas. With the ending of slavery in the 19th century, cacao and coffee were introduced, and remain the islands' chief products.

São Tomé and Príncipe remained a part of Portugal until independence in 1975. According to a new constitution adopted in 1990, a prime minister is head of government. The head of state is a president, who is limited to no more than two five-year terms. Members of the legislature also serve five-year terms. The nation's first direct multiparty elections were held in 1991. Manuel Pinto da Costa, the nation's president since 1975, did not run for reelection. The former ruling party, the Movement for the Liberation of São Tomé and Príncipe–Social Democratic Party (MLSTP-PSD) lost the presidential election and its legislative majority.

Reviewed by RAUL SERGIO PINTO BALDAIA
Former Chief of Cabinet, São Tomé and Príncipe

CHAD

Locked in the heart of Africa, far from the nearest seaport and without a railway to link it to the sea, lies the country of Chad. It stretches from the Sahara in the north to the savannas of tropical Africa in the south.

The country's population is distributed unevenly over a large area. The entire northern half of the country is desert and almost empty. The south, particularly the southwest where most of the cities are located, is the most heavily populated area.

THE PEOPLE

The people of Chad belong to a number of ethnic groups. In the north, where the population is mainly Muslim, the major groups include Arabs and Toubou. Groups in the non-Muslim south include the Sara, who make up the largest single group in Chad, the Massa, and the Moundan. Most of the non-Muslim population follows animistic beliefs, while a small percentage is Christian. People in the north speak Arabic dialects, and each of the groups in the south has its own language. French is the official language of the country.

Education

Although only a small percentage of the people have been taught to read and write the number of children who attend school increases each year. Instruction is in French, and the educational system is like the

People come from all over Chad to conduct business in N'Djamena, the capital.

After the harvest grain and other products are sold in town.

French system: primary school, followed by the lycée (secondary school), technical school, or teacher-training school. Lycées in the major cities include an Arab-French lycée in Abéché.

THE LAND

Chad occupies the eastern half of a vast interior African basin. The country slopes down from the Tibesti Massif in the north and the Ennedi Plateau in the east to the lowlands of Djourab north of Lake Chad.

Lake Chad, a large, shallow, freshwater lake, lies 925 feet (282 meters) above sea level at the meeting place of Chad, Niger, Nigeria, and Cameroon. The Shari and Logone are the two main rivers flowing into Lake Chad, but it has no visible outlets. The size of the lake varies greatly from season to season.

Cities

Chad remains essentially a rural country, with industries just beginning to develop in the cities. The capital and largest city, N'Djamena (formerly called Fort-Lamy), is situated in western Chad at the confluence of the Shari and Logone rivers. Sarh (formerly known as Fort-Archambault) and Moundou are the other main cities.

N'Djamena is a political and administrative center; the great distribution point for Chad's herders, fishermen, and farmers; and an important center of air traffic.

THREE REGIONS AND THREE WAYS OF LIFE

Chad spans three distinct climatic zones. These have helped shape three different ways of life.

Southern Chad

The south is a wooded savanna, with trees and tall grasses. During the rainy season in the summer between 35 and 47 inches (89–120 centimeters) of rain falls. Southern Chad is the region best suited to agriculture.

The traditional way of life is one in which members of a family live grouped around a patriarch, who is the oldest man in the family. A large family may occupy dozens of individual dwellings. These are usually houses with clay walls and cone-shaped straw roofs.

People live as settled farmers, raising food for their own use—millet, sorghum, peanuts, peas, and beans—and cotton, which is the country's main export. Rice-growing is increasing in the Logone River basin. Along the Chari and Logone rivers people catch fish for food. They also smoke and dry fish for marketing.

The sorghum and millet are planted in a different place each year to allow natural vegetation to restore needed elements to the soil. This vegetation is then removed by cutting and burning. Farm tools are limited mainly to hoes and small hatchets. Plows drawn by animals are also used in cultivating the land.

Sowing takes place at the beginning of the rainy season. Sorghum and millet harvested from October to December are stored in granaries of beaten earth or woven straw in the form of enormous bottles. The grain is crushed as it is needed and the flour is made into a *boule,* or ball, of boiled dough. This is eaten with a spice, fish, or meat sauce. Millet is also used to make *bil-bil,* a kind of millet beer.

Farmers in southern Chad use a simple cart to carry a bulky load.

Central Chad

Central Chad is open grassland, with a shorter rainy season and less rainfall than the southern zone. The central area receives between 10 and 35 inches (25–89 cm.) of rain a year. But farming is still possible. People raise peanuts and millet, and in the area around Lake Chad they raise wheat and corn. They also tap gum arabic from acacia trees. This is used in making candy, medicine, and some inks. Lake Chad is an important source of fish. However, the main activity is raising livestock. Most of Chad's nearly 4,500,000 cattle and 4,000,000 goats and sheep are in this zone.

The livestock farmers live as seminomads. Among the seminomads are some 50,000 Kreda, who are related to the vast Toubou family of northern Chad. The Kreda live along the Bahr el Ghazal around Moussoro. Their homes are movable tents made of woven palm fiber placed on a light wooden framework. Each Kreda encampment, or *ferik*, is made up of from five to 10 tents placed in a row.

During the dry season the Kreda stay along the banks of the Bahr el Ghazal, where they draw water from wells in goatskin bags. As soon as the rainy season starts, in June or early July, the people start south. A whole *ferik* moves together. At about the 13th parallel the Kreda sow millet, then move farther south with their herds until August. On the return north the older people stay and tend the millet fields, while the herds are settled once again along the Bahr el Ghazal. In October and November some of the adults go back to help with the harvest.

The Kreda take the products of their herds and their harvests to the regional market of Moussoro. There they buy what they need: cloth, tea, and salt.

Livestock is herded to market in N'Djemena, the center of Chad's meat industry.

FACTS AND FIGURES

REPUBLIC OF CHAD—is the official name of the country.

THE PEOPLE—are called Chadians.

CAPITAL: N'Djamena.

LOCATION: North central Africa. **Boundaries:** Libya, Sudan, Central African Republic, Cameroon, Nigeria, Niger.

AREA: 495,753 sq. mi. (1,284,000 sq. km.).

PHYSICAL FEATURES: Highest point—Emi Koussi (11,204 ft.; 3,415 m.). **Lowest point**—Djourab lowlands (509 ft.; 155 m.). **Chief rivers**—Shari, Logone. **Major lake**—Lake Chad.

POPULATION: 4,646,054 (latest estimate).

MAJOR LANGUAGES: French and Arabic (official), Sara, Sango, various local dialects.

MAJOR RELIGIONS: Muslim, African traditional religions, Christianity.

GOVERNMENT: Republic. **Head of state**—president.

CHIEF CITIES: N'Djamena, Sarh, Moundou.

ECONOMY: Chief minerals—petroleum, uranium, natron, kaolin. **Chief agricultural products**—cotton, gum arabic, livestock, peanuts. **Industries and products**—agricultural and livestock processing, natron. **Chief exports**—cotton, meat, fish, animal products. **Chief imports**—cement, petroleum, foodstuffs, machinery.

MONETARY UNIT: CFA franc.

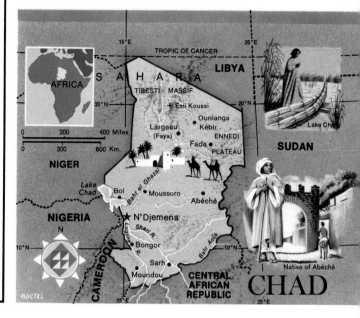

The Sahara Zone

The Sahara zone, north of the 15th parallel, has relatively few inhabitants. They live either as settled farmers in the oasis towns of Ounianga Kebir, Largeau (Faya), and Fada or as nomadic camel raisers. Some of the camel raisers have now added cattle to their herds. In the past, the great camel herders owned the lands around the oases, as well as saltworks, which were operated by slaves. Today the former slaves, who are called the Kamadja, raise date palms. They also extract natron, or carbonate of soda, a mineral salt, for profit. Natron, which is used in many industrial processes, is the only mineral now in production in Chad.

During the brief rains of August and September the camel raisers gather their herds near ponds and stream beds (wadis). In the dry season when the surface waters disappear, the herders dig wells that permit them to use the underground water in the wadi beds. From December on, the water supply declines, and the herders must move near sources of water in the Ennedi Plateau. The nomads live by selling the products of their herds and by transporting dates and natron to the market at Abéché.

ECONOMIC DEVELOPMENT

The cotton produced in Chad each year represents approximately one half of the country's export earnings. At harvesttime in November, the cotton markets create great activity in all of southern Chad. Cotton is ginned in the country's factories, and the balls of cotton fiber are exported to Europe. In addition, there is a weaving plant in Sarh, and at Moundou a plant has been built to press cottonseed, which formerly went to waste, into oil.

Livestock is Chad's second largest source of earnings. Slaughterhouses have been built in N'Djamena, and refrigerated meat is flown to markets in other African countries.

Efforts to introduce new crops are proving successful. The plains of the Logone, which flood each year, are admirably suited to rice growing. Already two rice-milling plants handle the production of the rice fields around Bongor and Lai. In the area around Bol on Lake Chad, dikes have been built to keep sections of the land from flooding. Wheat has been introduced as a commercial crop on the protected land.

The major handicap to the development of Chad, apart from the civil war that has ravaged the nation almost since independence, remains its distance from the sea. From N'Djamena to Douala, Cameroon, the nearest port, is a distance of about 1,200 mi. (1,900 km.). Furthermore, Chad has no railroad, and there are few paved roads outside of the towns. The two main supply routes of the country, through Cameroon from Douala and through Nigeria from Port Harcourt, are long and require costly transshipments.

Air transport, in contrast to surface transport, is well developed, and the country has a number of airports and landing strips.

HISTORY

According to legend, the earliest settlers of the Lake Chad basin were the Sao, who lived in organized towns and were skilled workers in terra cotta and bronze. In the 7th century desert nomads, known as Zaghawa, began to arrive in the region. In the 8th century one family of Zaghawa founded the state of Kanem.

Traders from North Africa, in search of slaves and gold, first brought the religion of Islam into the Chad basin. As early as the late 11th or early 12th century Kanem had a Muslim king. This state was the first of the African kingdoms—Kanem, Bornu, Baguirmi, and Wadai—that were to have power in the region until the 19th century.

In the 1890s, when the first French explorers went to the area, they found the local kingdoms weak. By 1913 the French had been able to gain control of all of present-day Chad. In 1920 it became a colony of French Equatorial Africa, and in 1946 an overseas territory of the French Republic. Chad proclaimed its independence in 1960, with François Tombalbaye as its first president. In 1963, however, Muslim rebels from the north began a prolonged armed revolt against the government.

Recent Events. Chad's 1962 constitution was suspended in 1975 when the government was overthrown in a coup and President Tombalbaye was killed. Military rule followed the coup until 1979, when the first of several coalition governments was set up in an attempt to bring the warring factions together. But civil war continued.

Late in 1980, Libya sent troops and tanks to Chad to aid then-President Goukouni Oueddei. After the Libyans withdrew in 1981 at the president's request, Oueddei was overthrown by his rival Hissène Habré. Libya backed Habré's opponents, while France supported Habré with weapons and troops. The Libyans were expelled from Chad, except for a disputed mineral-rich area called the Aozou Strip, in 1987. Libya and Chad signed a peace accord in 1989, although their competing claims to the Aozou Strip remained unresolved. Habré, elected president under a new constitution in 1989, was overthrown in 1990 by his former ally, Idriss Deby. Deby remained president under an interim national charter adopted in 1991 pending a planned transition to multiparty democracy.

JEAN CABOT, Département de Géographie, Université de Paris-Vincennes

The attractively designed presidential chalet is on the Ubangi River.

CENTRAL AFRICAN REPUBLIC

At the end of the dry season farmers in the Central African Republic gather together at the outskirts of their villages. They soon separate and go off to the surrounding fields. The men and women, working in swift co-ordination, soon have everything ready. They set fire to the yellowing grass and the dry brush. While the adults work, the children stand at various ends of the fields ready to trap any small animals that might come scurrying through the flaming brush. The people look about with satisfaction, for they know that the land will soon be cleared for planting. Each year this has been going on, for a long, long time.

THE LAND

The Central African Republic lies deep in the interior of Africa, just a short distance north of the equator. The total land area of this hot, tropical country is only slightly smaller than that of the state of Texas.

Plaza Edouard Renard runs through the heart of Bangui.

Formerly it was one of the four territories that made up the colony of French Equatorial Africa. In 1960 it became an independent African nation.

The country spreads out on a vast plateau between two extensive depressions of the African continent: the Congo and Chad basins. The average elevation of the rolling Ubangi-Chari plateau and smaller adjoining plateaus is from 2,000 to 3,000 feet (600–900 meters), but on the northeastern and central western margins, land rises to over 4,000 feet (1,200 m.). The countryside, in the main, is open savanna (land with tall or medium-height grass and scattered trees). But the southwestern section of the country has some areas of tropical rain forest.

Those streams that flow north drain land on a gentle slope to Lake Chad. Streams flowing south cut deep, narrow forested valleys into the surface of the plateaus, as they hasten toward the Ubangi River, the leading tributary of the great Congo. There are several noted stretches of rapids and falls.

The climate of the Central African Republic is tropical. There are two distinct seasons, a rainy one lasting from March to October and a dry one lasting through the rest of the year. The harvest rains fall during July, August, and September, while the driest months are January and February. During the dry months the grass turns yellow and the leaves shrivel and fall from the trees. In the wet season the ground is moist for days on end.

The country has an abundance of wildlife. Elephants, lions, buffalo, giraffes, hyenas, jackals, and many kinds of antelope still roam the open spaces. In order to protect the animals from hunters the government has established large game reserves. Chimpanzees, baboons, and some gorillas inhabit the rain forest in the southern part of the country. Crocodiles and hippopotamuses are found in the larger streams, such as the Ubangi and Chari rivers. Brightly colored birds, reptiles, and insects are seen throughout the land. Huge termite mounds of red and yellow earth are a familiar sight in the local landscape.

Cities. The capital and largest city of the country is **Bangui.** This city, once the French administrative capital for the territory of Ubangi-Chari, is located on the Ubangi River. It is the country's chief river port, major air terminal, and commercial center. **Berbérati, Bouar,** and **Bambari** are other important population centers. However, most of the people of the Central African Republic live in rural areas.

THE PEOPLE

The people of the Central African Republic are composed of many groups. The Banda, the Baya, the Mandjia, and the Bwaka are found in the western half of the country. Most of these people are farmers who work long hours in their fields. The chief crops grown by them for food are manioc (a starchy root), corn, sweet potatoes, yams, cooking bananas, and peppers. Cotton and coffee are cash crops that are shipped to foreign markets. Rice, peanuts, and tobacco are grown either for home consumption or for marketing. The fruit of the wild oil palm is gathered for processing into oil.

The Sara live in the north of the country. They raise grains, such as millet and sorghum, sesame, beans, peas, and squash; and they keep a small-size breed of horses. Many of the Sara men served with the French Army when the country was a French colony. Along the numerous streams of the south and west live the fishing and trading Banziri, Yakoma, and Sango. These people are extremely skilled in river navigation, especially in shooting the rapids in their dugout canoes.

At the end of the dry season, a farmer sets fire to the brush.

There has never been a census of the Central African Republic and sample surveys differ. Much of the east is thinly populated with about five persons to each square mile of land. The shadow of the slave trade that continued well into this century still hangs over the area. Arab, Nubian, and Egyptian raiders periodically devastated the region, carrying off slaves. Today, in some of the highlands, one can still see caves and caverns that served as hiding places for the people of the area. But the grim history of the people tells of the men, women, and children who were carried off and sold as slaves in Egypt, Arabia, Persia, and places as far away as America. The people of the northern part of the country at various times suffered the very same bitter fate at the hands of the Senoussi raiders from the oases of Libya.

Way of Life

Most of the people of the republic live in country areas in clusters of villages. The task of building the family dwelling falls upon the men. Traditional huts are mostly round, with walls of mud and sticks topped by a conical thatched roof. However, more and more, larger rectangular huts are being constructed. The walls are made of dried mud, grass mats, or planks. Roofs may be made of thatch or store-bought sheets of corrugated iron.

Preparing the family's food is a hard and time-consuming task for the women of the household. Manioc roots have to be soaked for a long while in stream water and then dried in the sun. They are then pounded into a flour that is used to make a porridge. The thick porridge, the mainstay of the people's diet, is eaten with a vegetable sauce called gombo and with meat or fish bits. Some chickens and little pigs may scurry about the village, but other sources of meat are not plentiful. Because of the tsetse fly, which thrives in this area and spreads the dreaded African sleeping sickness, there are few cattle. The people like to eat fish that is either dried or smoked. The fish are caught in the Ubangi River and its tributaries. Tropical fruits such as mangoes, papayas, and guavas are found in abundance on the trees that stand beside village huts. Beer is brewed from millet. Palm wine is prepared for special feasts.

Most men now wear Western-style clothes. Women wear gaily colored wraparounds, with jauntily knotted head kerchiefs. Ornaments of copper and iron wire worn around the neck, wrists, or ankles are still seen in the interior.

Before World War II most of the population lived dispersed through the countryside, in small clusters of huts in the forest or the grasslands, or in rows of huts lining the riverbanks. A village chief governed such a tiny community. The only fair-sized communities were Bangui, then the French administrative capital of Ubangi-Chari, and the towns of Bouar and Bambari. Since then Bangui has sprawled, amid profuse tropical vegetation, to contain 300,000 people. Bambari has about 42,000 residents and a dozen townships have at least 5,000 inhabitants. Country people have moved closer to the cities and now live in large village clusters around them. When the rainy season starts and farmwork beckons, they leave their homes for the outlying fields and stay away until the crops are harvested. Then they return and sell their produce in the city markets.

FACTS AND FIGURES

OFFICIAL NAME: Central African Republic.

NATIONALITY: Central African(s).

CAPITAL: Bangui.

LOCATION: Central Africa. **Boundaries**—Chad, Sudan, Zaïre, Congo, Cameroon.

AREA: 240,535 sq. mi. (622,986 sq. km.).

PHYSICAL FEATURES: Chief rivers—Ubangi, Chari.

POPULATION: 3,200,000 (1992: annual growth 2.6%).

MAJOR LANGUAGES: French, Sango (both official).

MAJOR RELIGIONS: Animism, Christianity, Islam.

GOVERNMENT: Republic. **Head of state**—president. **Head of government**—prime minister. **Legislature**—National Assembly.

CHIEF CITIES: Bangui, Berbérati, Bouar, Bambari.

ECONOMY: Chief minerals—diamonds, gold. **Chief agricultural products**—cotton, coffee, manioc, corn, millet, sorghum, bananas, rice, peanuts, tobacco. **Industries and products**—textiles, raw cotton, hides and skins, sawmills. **Chief exports**—cotton fiber, coffee, diamonds, tobacco, timber. **Chief imports**—machinery, cotton, textiles.

MONETARY UNIT: Franc CFA (African Financial Community).

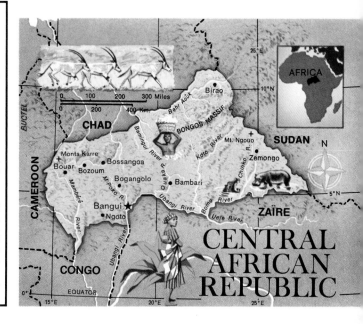

Education

This attraction of the cities has aided the government in its efforts to improve education, since most of the schools are located in urban areas. Village buses are used to bring children to elementary school. Secondary schools are few, but the number of students is increasing. Close to 60 technical and teacher training schools have been built. College-bound youths may attend the University of Bangui or may travel to Senegal to study at the University of Dakar. Some go to France for their studies. French has been the language of education and business since colonial times. Sango, a local language often used for communication between various groups, became an official language in 1991. Generally each small group has its own dialect.

ECONOMY

Diamonds and coffee now account for about half of the country's export trade. The chief customers for these products are France; some other Western European countries, such as Belgium; Japan; and the United States. Other exports are cotton, timber, oil palm kernels, and a small amount of gold. Major imports are machinery, cotton textiles, and motor vehicles.

Industrial development is only beginning. A textile plant near Bangui uses power from a nearby stream and some of the local cotton to produce cotton materials for clothing. Ginning plants scattered throughout the country process raw cotton. Hides and skins are tanned and made into shoes. Vegetable oils and soap are prepared, together with soft drinks and beer. There are several sawmills in the tropical forest areas.

There are no railroads in the country, and its waterways are only intermittently navigable. The river port of Bangui, the chief outlet for foreign trade, is 900 mi. (1,400 km.) from the Atlantic coast and can be reached only by a combination of river and rail transport through the Republic of Congo. Air transport is quite well developed.

Bales of cotton in Bangui's port await shipment to distant countries.

HISTORY

Little is known of the history of the country before the 19th century. It is believed that at one time groups of Pygmies lived in the southern section of the country. They later moved into the Congo region.

Late in the 19th century the French entered the area and set up military outposts. A trading station was established at Bangui. In 1903 the territory of Ubangi-Chari was created. Six years later this territory and the neighboring French colonies of Chad, Congo, and Gabon were joined to form French Equatorial Africa.

The period of French rule was marked in the late 1920s by conflict. But during World War II soldiers of the territory fought on the Allied side. On August 13, 1960, the territory gained full independence. David Dacko was elected president. In 1966 he was ousted by Army Colonel Jean Bedel Bokassa, who became president and suspended the constitution and dissolved the government. In 1976, he changed the country's name to the Central African Empire and named himself Emperor Bokassa I. His rule was marked by violence, and in 1979 he was deposed by David Dacko, who restored the name Central African Republic. After two years marked by a worsening economy, Dacko was again ousted, this time by General André Kolingba. The exiled Bokassa voluntarily returned in 1986 and was tried and convicted of murder and embezzlement. His death sentence was later commuted to 20 years of hard labor. Legislative elections under a one-party system were held in 1987. In the early 1990s the constitution was revised to legalize multiple political parties and allow the president to appoint a prime minister, but Kolingba resisted popular demands for further reforms.

IRENE S. VAN DONGEN, California State College, California, Pennsylvania

GABON

The gray freighter lies quietly at anchor in the sunny Port-Gentil harbor. Its hull rides high on the gently swelling water; the hold of the ship is empty, waiting for its cargo. Near the ship, bobbing on the surface of the sunlit water, are huge logs. They are about to be lifted by crane onto the freighter. These logs were cut from the okoume trees deep in the green forests of Gabon. They were cut with power saws and hand-saws and then floated down the river to the ocean port.

Soon the loading is finished. The ship weighs anchor and slowly steams out of the port on its way across a vast ocean. Thousands of miles away the cargo is unloaded and taken away by trucks. The wall of a house in a far-off country is later built of plywood—wood that came from the lofty okoume trees in a forest in the small African country of Gabon.

THE LAND

The Gabon Republic is situated on the western coast of Africa. It lies across the equator just below the bulge of the continent. The country is bounded on the north by Cameroon and Equatorial Guinea, on the east and south by the Congo, and on the west by the Atlantic Ocean. It has an area of 103,346 square miles (267,667 square kilometers) and a population of more than 700,000.

Gabon is covered almost entirely by a dense tropical rain forest. There are a few savannas, east of Franceville, south of Mouila, and along the lower course of the Ogooué River. Much of Gabon is low and marshy, but a broad plateau and several low mountain ranges rise in the north, southeast, and center of the country. Mount Iboundji, Gabon's highest peak, rises to a height of 5,165 feet (1,574 meters).

Logs await loading at harbor of Port-Gentil.

In many places the plateau and the mountain regions are cut by rivers, which form deep valleys and rapids. The Ogooué, Gabon's longest river, rises in the Republic of Congo, but its course is almost entirely through Gabon territory. The river enters the country just south of France-ville, flows in a broad arc through the center of Gabon, and then empties into the Atlantic at Cape Lopez. Cut by many rapids along its upper course, it is navigable for a distance of about 155 miles (249 km.) from N'Djolé to the Atlantic. The two major tributaries of the Ogooué are the Ivindo and the N'Gounié. Along the coast are a number of smaller rivers such as the Como.

Climate.   The Gabon Republic has the typical hot and humid climate of equatorial regions. On the average, temperatures range from 72 to 95 degrees Fahrenheit (22–35 degrees Celsius). There are four seasons in Gabon: A long rainy season from mid-January to mid-May; a long dry season from mid-May to September; a short rainy season from the beginning of October to mid-December; and a short dry season from mid-December to mid-January. Monsoons are common in the rainy seasons, and trade winds blow during the dry seasons.

Cities.   **Libreville**, Gabon's capital, is also the country's largest city and chief port. This community of 250,000 inhabitants lies on the coast, just north of the equator. The city is pleasantly laid out, with broad sunlit streets and modern buildings. Tourists who come to Libreville find excellent hotel accommodations.

Port-Gentil, with a population of 77,000, is the country's second largest city. It lies south of Libreville on the Atlantic coast. **Lambaréné**,

Libreville, a broad sunlit city, lies on the coast close to the equator.

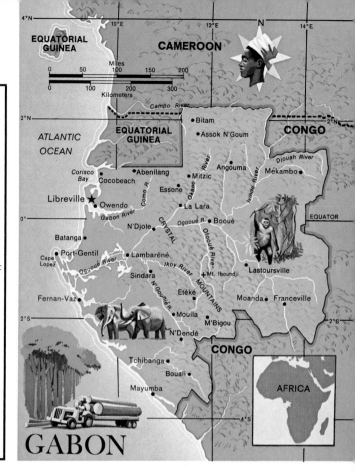

FACTS AND FIGURES

GABONESE REPUBLIC is the official name of the country.

THE PEOPLE—are called Gabonese.

CAPITAL: Libreville.

LOCATION: West central Africa. **Boundaries:** Cameroon, Congo, Atlantic Ocean, Equatorial Guinea.

AREA: 103,346 sq. mi. (267,667 sq. km.).

PHYSICAL FEATURES: Highest point—Mount Iboundji (5,165 ft.; 1,574 m.). **Lowest point**—sea level. **Chief rivers**—Ogooué, Ivindo, N'Gounié.

POPULATION: 1,206,000 (latest estimate).

MAJOR LANGUAGES: French (official), local languages.

MAJOR RELIGIONS: Roman Catholic, Protestant, animistic beliefs.

GOVERNMENT: Republic. **Head of government**—president. **Legislature**—one-house national assembly. **International co-operation**—United Nations, Organization of African Unity (OAU), Afro-Malagasy Organization of Cooperation.

CHIEF CITIES: Libreville, Port-Gentil, Lambaréné.

ECONOMY: Chief minerals—oil, manganese, uranium, iron. **Chief agricultural products**—cacao, coffee, manioc, bananas, rice. **Industries and products**—mining, petroleum refining, timber processing (plywood). **Chief exports**—petroleum, manganese, uranium, timber, cacao, coffee. **Chief imports**—machinery, textiles, vehicles, chemicals.

MONETARY UNIT: Franc CFA (African Financial Community).

the third largest community (although it has less than 25,000 inhabitants), has a fairly good port and storage facilities for the river traffic that passes through it. Lambaréné became world-famous because of Doctor Albert Schweitzer, the noted philosopher, physician, humanist, and winner of the Nobel peace prize, who maintained a hospital there for more than half a century.

THE PEOPLE

There are about 40 distinct ethnic groups in Gabon. The Fang are the most numerous and account for about one third of the country's population. Generally, they live in the northern part of the country and across the border in southern Cameroon and in Equatorial Guinea. The Fang have no king, and they are divided like most other Gabonese into smaller groups. Léon Mba, the first president of Gabon, was a Fang. Omar Bongo, who succeeded him, is a Batéké. Batéké live in southeastern Gabon and in neighboring land of the Congo. Other ethnic groups are the Omyéné, who live on the Atlantic coast, the Bakota in the northeast, the Bapounou in the southwest, and the Bandjabi in the south central region.

Way of Life

Although many of these peoples live far from one another and often have little contact, their cultures are not very different. Most live in small villages in forest clearings near the ocean or on the shores of one of the many rivers. Fish is therefore one of the most important foods of these people. Their diet also consists of manioc, bananas or plantains,

Workers tend an oil pump deep in the interior region of Gabon.

rice, and chicken and lamb. Manioc, part of the root of a plant, is probably the most important part of the diet of almost all rural Gabonese. The city-dwellers of Libreville and Port-Gentil have some canned foods and a more varied diet.

The people of Gabon are known for their beautiful sculptures of wood and stone. Many of their masks and statues, which express deep feelings and are styled in exquisite forms, are displayed in museums all over the world.

Education.   More than 80 percent of the country's school-age children are in public or private schools. School attendance is compulsory up to the age of 16. However, many of the primary school students do not go on to secondary schools. Although secondary schools are being built, there are still not enough to meet the country's needs. There is also a shortage of trained secondary school teachers. As to higher education, there is a technical institute at Libreville that trains executive personnel and technicians. The Oyem Agricultural School educates its students in the best and most modern agricultural techniques. Many of its graduates then go into the farm regions to instruct the farmers in the newest methods of farming. Gabon does not as yet have a university. A number of young Gabonese leave the country each year to study in universities abroad, most of them going to France. French is the official language of the country and is the language used in the schools.

Religion.   Christian missionaries settled in the area during the first half of the 19th century. They set up the country's first schools and began converting the people to Christianity. Today most Gabonese are either Roman Catholic or Protestant. Certain local religions that existed before the coming of the missionaries are still practiced, and new religions, which are mixtures of the old beliefs and Christianity, have appeared. Gabon also has many secret societies with their own dances, masks, and even languages.

ECONOMY

Most of the Gabonese people are engaged in some form of agriculture, with cacao and coffee the leading export crops. Timber from the country's forests provides another source of income. Since independence, the production of oil, manganese, and uranium has greatly increased Gabon's income. Oil provides about 70 percent of export earnings, and a major new field in southern Gabon was discovered in 1988. The country also has rich deposits of iron ore. The Trans-Gabon Railroad, inaugurated in 1986, opened the interior of the country.

HISTORY

Little is known of Gabon before the end of the 14th century. Around 1500, Portuguese sailors landed on the coast near the mouth of the Ogooué River. The name Gabon comes from the Portuguese word *gabão,* which means a Portuguese coat with sleeves and hood. The shape of a bay near the Atlantic Coast reminded the sailors of a *gabão.* Dutch, British, and French traders also visited Gabon in the 16th century.

Gabon first came under French influence as a result of treaties that were made with coastal chiefs in 1839 and 1841. In 1849 the French captured a slave ship and released the slaves at the mouth of the Como River. The freed slaves remained in Gabon, established a settlement, and named it Libreville, "city of liberation." A number of French explorers came to Gabon in the latter part of the 19th century and claimed more land for France. In due time the area became a French colony. It became part of a group of colonies set up in 1910 and called French Equatorial Africa. During the colonial period the French established the frontiers of the country and the internal administrative divisions as they now exist.

Gabon remained a French colony until 1958. At that time, as a result of a referendum, it became an autonomous republic of the French Community. Finally, on August 17, 1960, Gabon became independent, and Léon Mba was elected the country's first president. In 1967 Mba ran for a second term and, with his running mate, Albert (later Omar) Bongo, won the election. Later that year Mba died, and Bongo became the new president. Bongo, running unopposed, was elected to a fourth term in 1986. His Parti Démocratique Gabonais (PDG), or Gabonese Democratic Party, was the only legal political party in the country from 1968 to 1990, when the constitution was revised to introduce a multiparty system. The PDG managed to retain a bare majority when multiparty legislative elections were held in 1991. Multiparty presidential elections were scheduled for December 1992.

GOVERNMENT

Gabon has a one-house legislature whose members are elected to five-year terms. An elected president serves as head of state. A prime minister appointed by the president is head of government.

BRIAN WEINSTEIN, Howard University
Reviewed by THE PERMANENT MISSION OF THE REPUBLIC OF GABON
TO THE UNITED NATIONS

CONGO

The People's Republic of Congo is one of the most highly developed countries in Central Africa. Formerly it was part of French Equatorial Africa, and Brazzaville, its major city, was the capital of the colony. The People's Republic of Congo was often referred to as Congo (Brazzaville), to distinguish it from its larger neighbor, the former Democratic Republic of the Congo, which is now called the Republic of Zaïre. Several times a day ferry boats steam back and forth between Brazzaville and Kinshasa, the capital of the Republic of Zaïre, which stand on opposite banks of the Congo (Zaïre) River.

THE LAND

The Congo Republic lies astride the equator. It is a long, narrow country that runs from 5 degrees south of the equator to 4 degrees north. Generally, the country is divided into four major geographical regions. A low, treeless plain about 40 miles (64 kilometers) wide extends along the shore of the Atlantic Ocean for a distance of about 100 miles (160 km.). Inland from this coastal plain is the Mayombé Escarpment. Reaching an elevation of 2,600 feet (790 meters), in a series of folded ranges running parallel to the coast, the area is hard to penetrate. Dense vege-

Church of Saint Anne of the Congo, in Brazzaville. Eboué Stadium is at left.

tation that reaches jungle growth in places adds to the difficulty of crossing the area. The railroad must use 92 bridges and 12 tunnels in order to make its run from the coast to the interior. Farther inland are the Batéké Plateaus, which cover a small part of the country. The plateaus give way in the far interior of the country to a huge swamp area. This swamp is found alongside the Congo and Sanga rivers.

Climate. Due to its low elevation and its proximity to the equator, the country has a hot, humid climate. Temperatures average between 80 degrees Fahrenheit (27 degrees Celsius) and 90 degrees Fahrenheit (32 degrees C.) all year long, and there is very little seasonal change. Rainfall is heavy, except in the Batéké Plateaus, where there is a long dry season and lower annual rainfall.

Rivers. The mighty Congo, one of Africa's great rivers, runs for many miles along the eastern border of the country until it empties into the Atlantic Ocean. (See article on CONGO RIVER in this volume.) The country's second largest river is the Ubangi, a tributary of the Congo. Smaller rivers are the Niari, the Kouilou, and the Sanga. There are numerous rapids and falls in many of Congo's rivers. Rapids block navigation on the Congo River below the Brazzaville area. Some of the rapids and falls may soon provide sites for the development of hydroelectric plants. There are long navigable stretches on the Niari, Kouilou, and Sanga rivers.

Cities. **Brazzaville,** the nation's capital and largest city, is located on the Congo River, 320 miles (515 kilometers) inland from the Atlantic

Pointe-Noire has grown into one of the busiest seaports in equatorial Africa.

coast. Brazzaville is growing rapidly, as is **Pointe-Noire,** a major seaport on the Atlantic Ocean. Both are modern, progressive cities, with neat boulevards shaded by waving palm trees. The two cities are linked by the Congo-Ocean Railway. Before the building of this railway the interior of the country was virtually isolated. Other cities in the Congo, much smaller than Pointe-Noire, are Dolisie and Jacob.

THE PEOPLE

The Congo is not densely populated, but its population is highly diverse. There are about 15 distinct ethnic groups, divided into some 75 tribes, nearly all of them of Bantu origin. As is typical of many African states, almost half the population is under 15 years of age. Most of the people live in the southern third of the country, especially in the vicinity of Brazzaville and Pointe-Noire.

In the dense forest areas some Pygmies still cling to the ways of their ancestors. Along the coast the Vili group are the dominant people. Around Brazzaville it is the Bakongo who dominate. The Batéké and the M'Bochi live inland, and the Batéké are the larger of the two groups. All groups, aside from the Europeans and Pygmies, are of Bantu stock. Many Bantu dialects are spoken, but French is the official language of the country.

All Bantu have developed the dance as a form of expression for almost every important event from birth to death. People gather and clap hands in a rhythm while others keep the beat with bells, drums, horns, and flutes.

In the rural and forest areas, the people live mainly in homes that are made of wood or of clay blocks. In the city Western-type architecture, both old and modern, predominates. Most of the Congolese, especially those living in towns and cities, wear Western-style clothing.

More than half the people of the Congo Republic follow animistic beliefs. Most of the urban population is Christian, either Catholic or Protestant. Less than 1 percent is Muslim.

Education

The educational system of the Congo is patterned on that of France, and French remains the language of instruction. Education is free and compulsory between the ages of 6 and 16. The literacy rate is rising, and a large percentage of primary-school-age children attend school. A much smaller number of students go on to secondary school. The leading institution of higher education is Marien Ngouabi University in Brazzaville, established in the late 1960's. The Congo also has technical and vocational schools and teacher training institutes.

ECONOMY

Some 50 percent of the total population is engaged in traditional subsistence agriculture. There are thousands of small farms spread throughout the country, but their production is quite low. Generally the subsistence farmers use poor and outmoded techniques to grow their crops. Women are most often responsible for the farm work. They tend to think of farming as gardening, growing the products they need and stopping when they have enough. Cassava and yams are the staple food crops.

FACTS AND FIGURES

THE PEOPLE'S REPUBLIC OF CONGO—La République Populaire du Congo—is the official name of the country.

THE PEOPLE—are called Congolese.

CAPITAL: Brazzaville.

LOCATION: Central equatorial Africa. **Boundaries**—Cameroon, Central African Republic, Zaire, Cabinda (Angola), Atlantic Ocean, Gabon.

AREA: 135,000 sq. mi. (349,650 sq. km.).

PHYSICAL FEATURES: Highest point—2,600 ft. (792 m.). **Lowest point**—sea level. **Chief river**—Congo.

POPULATION: 1,694,000 (latest estimate).

MAJOR LANGUAGES: French (official), Bantu dialects.

MAJOR RELIGIONS: Christianity (principally Roman Catholic), traditional African religions, Islam.

GOVERNMENT: Republic. **Head of state**—president. **Head of government**—prime minister. **Legislature**—one-house National Assembly.

CHIEF CITIES: Brazzaville (422,400), Pointe-Noire (185,110).

ECONOMY: Chief minerals—petroleum, natural gas, potash, iron. **Chief agricultural products**—coffee, cacao, palm products, cassava, plantains, rice, peanuts, tobacco. **Industries and products**—food processing, tobacco, woodworking, metalworking, textiles, chemicals, oil refining, construction materials. **Chief exports**—petroleum, wood. **Chief imports**—machinery and vehicles, basic manufactured goods, foodstuffs.

MONETARY UNIT: Franc CFA (African Financial Community).

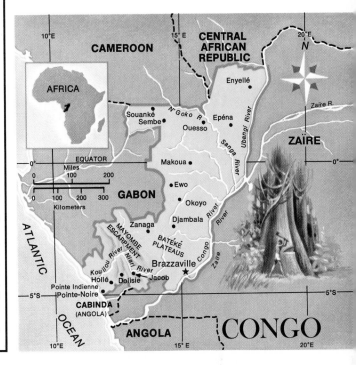

The modern and more developed sector of the country's farmland is in the Niari River valley. Here, vast sugarcane plantations produce more than 325,000 tons of sugar every year. The largest and most important sugar establishment in the entire region is the Sosuniari Plant, which processes the sugarcane of the Niari River valley. Other commercial products raised for export are palm nuts and groundnuts (peanuts), cacao, coffee, rubber, and tobacco.

The Congo Republic has more than 54,000,000 acres of forest land. Shipments of wood and forest products make up more than half of the country's total export trade. Five plants equipped with modern machinery produce veneers and plywoods. The most popular woods of the forest lands are okoume and limba. They have beautiful grains and make colorful wall panelings.

Mining is now the most dynamic sector of the Congolese economy. One of the largest potash mines in the world is located at Hollé. Hollé lies at the southern tip of the Congo, just a short distance from the major port of Pointe-Noire. The deposit of rich potash covers a vast area and is easy to work. Exports are mostly to France, where the potash is used as a fertilizer. Iron deposits have been discovered at Zanaga near the Gabon border and at Sembé, which is near the Cameroon border. But better rail facilities are needed to develop these potentially profitable deposits. Oil was discovered in 1960. However, it was not until the early 1970's that petroleum production began to transform the economy. The turning point was the discovery of huge offshore oil deposits totaling more than 500 million tons. Some natural gas is also extracted.

Manufacturing in the Congo Republic is done on a relatively small scale. There are factories that produce textiles, soap, tobacco, glass, cement, beer, and soft drinks. In addition to the Congo-Ocean Railway there are two rail transportation lines. One connects Pointe-Noire to

Brazzaville, a distance of 320 mi. (515 km.), and a branch of this line, called the Comilog Line, runs almost 170 mi. (275 km.) northward to the Gabon border. The development of the Comilog Line made it possible to tap the rich timber areas of the Batéké Plateaus.

HISTORY

Some 400 years ago a kingdom was established that became the largest in this part of Africa. Called the kingdom of Kongo, it stretched across the lower Congo River to present-day Angola. The kingdom reached its height of power and influence during the 16th century A.D. In the following century, because of internal political and economic problems and European involvement, it broke apart and eventually ceased to exist.

Portuguese explorers under the leadership of Diogo Cão visited the area in the late 15th century. French merchants set up trading and slave stations in the 17th and 18th centuries. By 1785 over 100 French ships sailed along the coast each year. As the European powers began to outlaw slavery, France used the area as a patrol base for its naval craft. French settlers moved into the territory to substitute other types of trade for slave trading.

In 1880 Pierre Savorgnan de Brazza, an Italian-born Frenchman, explored the region inland from the coast. He established a post that has since become the site of the modern city of Brazzaville. The treaties he signed with the Batéké rulers gave the French control over the entire area. In 1903 France gave territorial status and the name "Middle Congo" to the area. Middle Congo, along with the territories of Gabon, Chad, and Ubangi-Chari, became part of French Equatorial Africa in 1910. The office of governor-general of the new federation was located in Brazzaville. French Equatorial Africa lasted until 1958, when it was dissolved. The Congo became a fully autonomous member of the French Community and took the name of the Republic of Congo. It gained full independence on August 15, 1960. From 1970 to 1991, when the original name was restored, the country was called the People's Republic of Congo.

The Congo's first president, Fulbert Youlou, was forced to resign in 1963. His successor, Alphonse Massamba-Débat, established a Communist-style government, but was deposed by the military in 1968. A series of socialist military governments followed until 1979, when the legislature was restored and Colonel Denis Sassou-Nguesso became president. He was reelected in 1984 and 1989. The Congolese Labor Party was the sole legal political party until 1990, when other parties were permitted to register. A 1991 national congress stripped Sassou-Nguesso of most of his executive powers and appointed a prime minister as head of government pending a transition to multiparty rule. Sassou-Nguesso and his party were defeated in multiparty elections held in 1992.

GOVERNMENT

A new constitution approved by voters in 1992 created a semi-presidential system. A president, who is head of state, and members of the National Assembly are elected to five-year terms. Members of the Senate serve six-year terms. A prime minister, appointed by the president but responsible to the legislature, is head of government.

HUGH C. BROOKS, Director, Center for African Studies, St. John's University

A tree-lined boulevard in central Kinshasa.

ZAÏRE

Zaïre is truly the heart of Africa. It lies astride the equator and borders on nine different nations. Yet until the second half of the 19th century, most of this huge country was but a blank on a great many Western maps. Because a large part of the country is almost impenetrable rain forest, very few outsiders ever ventured there. But almost from the time Henry Morton Stanley, the famous explorer, came to the Congo (as it was then called) in the late 1870's, the area has been in the world's news. More recently, during the 1960's and 1970's, because of the military and political strife that involved the region, it became the focus of the attention of people all over the globe.

THE LAND

The Republic of Zaïre (formerly called the Democratic Republic of the Congo) lies in Central Africa. It has an area of 905,565 square miles

Kivu Falls in Kivu province are beautiful and spectacular.

(2,345,409 square kilometers). It is bounded on the west and on the north by Congo, the Central African Republic, and Sudan; on the east by Uganda, Rwanda, Burundi, and Tanzania. On the south it is bordered by Angola and Zambia.

The country has a vast, low-lying north central area, which is covered by a tropical rain forest. This area is surrounded by mountainous terraces in the west, and plateaus merging into plains in the south and southeast. In the northwest are vast and dense grasslands. The highest and most spectacular mountains are found on the Congo-Uganda border, along a north–south line known as the Great Rift Valley. It is here also that the country's major lakes—Albert, Edward, Kivu, and Tanganyika—are found. The two major mountain ranges in the area are the Ruwenzori and the Virunga. The Ruwenzori mountains are sometimes known by the poetic name Mountains of the Moon. Mount Margherita, the country's highest peak, rises to a height of 16,795 feet (5,119 meters). There are eight major volcanoes in the Virunga mountains, some of which are still active.

The country covers about two thirds of the drainage basin of the Congo River (called the Zaïre River in Zaïre). The river has a stable water level and some 1,700 miles (2,736 kilometers) are navigable throughout the year. The adequate water level is due to the fact that Zaïre straddles the equator, and one part of the country is always experiencing a rainy period. (See the article on CONGO RIVER in this volume.)

Climate. Although temperature in the Zaïre Republic is usually high, it varies a great deal according to rainfall and altitude. The annual mean temperature for the entire country is close to 80 degrees Fahrenheit

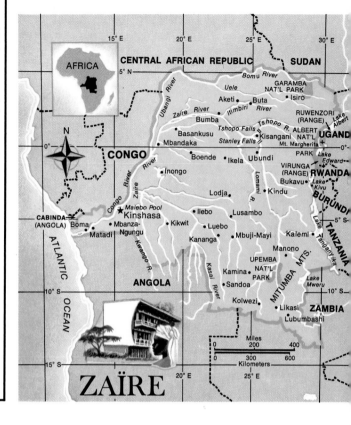

FACTS AND FIGURES

THE REPUBLIC OF ZAÏRE—La République du Zaïre—is the official name of the country. It was formerly called the Democratic Republic of the Congo, or Congo (Kinshasa).

THE PEOPLE—are called Zairians.

CAPITAL: Kinshasa.

LOCATION: Central equatorial Africa. **Boundaries**—Central African Republic, Sudan, Uganda, Rwanda, Burundi, Tanzania, Zambia, Angola, Congo.

AREA: 905,565 sq. mi. (2,345,409 sq. km.).

PHYSICAL FEATURES: Highest point—Mount Margherita (16,795 ft.; 5,119 m.). **Lowest point**—sea level. **Chief river**—Congo. **Major lakes**—Albert, Edward, Kivu, Tanganyika.

POPULATION: 31,250,000 (latest estimate).

MAJOR LANGUAGES: French (official), Lingala, Swahili, Kikongo, Chiluba.

MAJOR RELIGIONS: Roman Catholicism, Protestantism, traditional African religions, Islam.

GOVERNMENT: Republic. **Head of state**—president. **Legislature**—one-house National Legislative Council.

CHIEF CITIES: Kinshasa, Lubumbashi, Kisangani.

ECONOMY: Chief minerals—copper, cobalt, diamonds, zinc, uranium, manganese, petroleum, coal, tin. **Chief agricultural products**—cassava, corn, sugarcane, peanuts, rice, plantains, bananas, sweet potatoes, coffee, cotton, palm products. **Industries and products**—metal refining, food processing, textiles, footwear, cement, oil refining. **Chief exports**—copper, cobalt, diamonds, petroleum, coffee. **Chief imports**—consumer goods, foodstuffs, machinery and vehicles, fuels.

MONETARY UNIT: 1 zaïre = 100 makuta.

(27 degrees Celsius). Part of the Zaïre Republic is·in the Northern Hemisphere (north of the equator) and part of the country is in the Southern Hemisphere (south of the equator). Winter months in the Southern Hemisphere are from June to September. Since rainfall tends to "follow the sun," the equatorial belt in the center of the country has two periods of heavy rain as the sun "migrates" across the area in the course of a year. In the equatorial zone these two rainy periods almost overlap, so that there is hardly a dry season. The rainfall there averages about 60 inches (150 centimeters).

In the northern region the rainfall, averaging 60 to 80 inches (150–200 cm.), occurs mainly in the May–October period, with December and January almost dry. In the southern portion of the Congo (Zaïre) Basin, the rain averages 40 inches (100 cm.) and occurs between the months of September and May.

Animal Life. Spread over the length and breadth of the Zaïre Republic are many species of animals and a wide variety of birdlife. Reptiles and amphibians are found in great abundance throughout the entire region.

Gorillas and chimpanzees roam through the forest areas of the country. However, there are very few large animals that live on the ground in the dense, tropical rain forest region. Perhaps the strangest of these is the okapi, which looks like a mixture of a zebra and a short-necked giraffe. Elephants, lions, giraffes, leopards, antelope, hyenas, and rhinoceroses all live in the grasslands. The rivers and lakes of the Zaïre Republic abound in many varieties of fish, as well as the dreaded electric eel.

This sidewalk café will become much busier as evening falls in Kinshasa.

Cities

The capital city of **Kinshasa**, formerly known as Leopoldville, was founded on the site of a small fishing village. It now has a population of over 3,000,000. Kinshasa—the commercial, social, and industrial center of the country—lies on the Congo (Zaïre) River in the western part of the Republic. It is a city of broad, tree-lined streets, modern buildings, and a bustling, downtown commercial area. Its sidewalk cafés, hotels, and elegant shops give Kinshasa the look of a European capital. The city is also a center of higher education, with the Republic's oldest university, Lovanium, located in the suburbs.

Lubumbashi, formerly Elisabethville, is located at the southern end of the country in Katanga Province. The city has a population of over 450,000. It is a mining community and the principal distribution point in eastern Zaïre for industrial equipment. Situated across the border from Zambia, it is also the chief center of trade with that country and southern Africa. Other mining centers of the Zaïre Republic are Likasi, Kolwezi, and Mbuji-Mayi. **Matadi**, near the mouth of the Congo River, is the country's chief port. Lying about 220 miles (349 km.) southeast of the capital, it has up-to-date docking facilities that are being expanded. Another major city is **Kisangani**, formerly Stanleyville, located near Stanley Falls.

Places of Interest. Zaïre has three national parks, which attract many visitors each year. There are also many forest and game reserves. In the national parks—the Albert, the Garamba, and the Upemba—the traveler can admire at close range the many different kinds of animals and plants of the country. Along the course of the mighty Congo (Zaïre) River, there are a number of magnificent waterfalls. One of the best-known is the Tshopo Falls at Kisangani.

THE PEOPLE

The original inhabitants of the Zaïre region were probably the Pygmies who settled in great numbers over large portions of the country. But with the passage of time, other peoples came into the region and gradually drove the Pygmies into the rain forest areas. Today the Pygmies make up only a small part of the total population of the region. Pygmies are short—the average adult male is only 4 feet 9 inches tall—and their skin is a light yellowish-brown. They are found mostly in the Ituri Forest and live by hunting, trapping, and gathering wild foods. Pygmies live in small shelters and move to new encampments from time to time. They have an exceedingly simple social life and are a generally peaceful people. They trade their forest products with their Negro neighbors for agricultural produce.

Except for the Pygmies and the small number of Europeans, the rest of the inhabitants of the country are Negroes. Most of them belong to a single branch of the Negro family known as Bantu—although not all members of this group live in the Zaïre Republic. Other branches of the Negro family, such as the Sudanese and the Nilotes, are found only in the northern and eastern fringes of the country, where they probably arrived at a fairly recent date.

The Europeans helped run the economy of the region before it became independent. Most of these Europeans were Belgians. Before independence there were over 100,000 Europeans settled in the area. Today, because of political and economic reasons, that number has dwindled to a little more than 50,000.

Language. By far the greatest number of Zaïrians speak one of the many Bantu languages, which are found from Cameroon to South Africa. These languages are all somewhat related and this allows for some degree of understanding among the various peoples who speak them. Other Zaïrians, approximately 10 percent, use Sudanese languages. The Pygmies no longer have a language of their own and speak the language of their Negro neighbors.

French was first introduced into the country by the Belgians. Today, it is the official language and the only one commonly spoken in the Zaïre Republic. But it is spoken only by those Zaïrians who have had some education.

Education. Nearly all Zaïrian children receive some kind of schooling—though perhaps no more than 2 or 3 years. However, many children now get secondary school education, and a few eventually enter one of the country's three universities. All education beyond the early grades is given in French. The country also has technical and teacher training institutions. The literacy rate is estimated at over 40 percent, relatively high by African standards.

Religion. About 25% of the people follow traditional animistic religious beliefs. Roman Catholic and Protestant missionaries, however, have long been active in the territory. Today, it is estimated that some 45 percent of the population is Catholic and about 30 percent is Protestant. Less than 1% of Zaïrians are Muslims.

Way of Life

The people of Zaïre have two major tasks to face. They must keep their country together, and they must do away with poverty, disease, and ignorance. The first problem is not an easy one to solve. The country has greater social, cultural, ethnic, and religious unity than most other African countries, and the people generally think of themselves as Zaïrians in relation to the outside world. But at home these very same people feel that the family, the clan, and the group are their most important ties.

The family is strongly organized, usually under the authority of the oldest male. It includes not just the parents and children but also the grandparents, uncles, aunts, and cousins. This type of family organization is generally known as an extended family.

A Zaïrian relies on the members of his extended family in most circumstances of life, and they, in turn, will expect similar loyalty. A somewhat simpler form of this same kind of solidarity exists among members of the same clan. Members of a clan are people who claim descent from a same, but often quite distant, ancestor. These people settle in the same hamlet or in a section of a large village.

Beyond the clan, there is the ethnic group. This is simply the largest group to which people traditionally feel a tie of allegiance. Some modern groups like the Bakongo (who number over 1,000,000 in the country) are the result of the clustering of several smaller groups into a larger one. People can feel that they belong to a group even though they never had common political institutions. A common language, or common traditions, for example, can be their bond.

On the other hand, groups who once belonged together may split off and become quite hostile to each other. As a matter of fact, hostility

Women carry produce outside of their village in the eastern highlands.

is often the greatest between once closely related groups such as the Baluba and the Lulua, or the Lunda and the Tshokwe.

But, most important, a man's feelings toward his group can change when he leaves his village. As he meets people from other groups, he may become more aware of his own identity. He may also feel closer to the people of the same region even though they are not members of his own traditional group. This is important because most Zaïrians have, at one time or another, left the village of their birth. Something like one out of every four Zaïrians now lives more or less permanently away from his original home. These people left their villages searching for a better life and seeking employment in cities, in mines, and on plantations. Many times, the pressures of city life bring about a breakdown in the traditional pattern of family life.

Considering the vast area of the country, a population of 17,000,000 people is relatively small. But much of the soil of the country is poor. Like the soil of many equatorial lands, it is subject to erosion and to the formation of laterite—a kind of red, rocklike crust that lacks minerals necessary for plant growth. Where the land is good, as in parts of the southern savanna or in the eastern lake area, population density is quite high, and land for farming is in great demand. The two major areas of population concentration, excluding the cities, are the eastern Kivu region and a belt extending almost due east from the mouth of the Congo (Zaïre) River to the upper Lomami River.

Farming. The traditional farming methods used by the Zaïrians depend a great deal upon the environment. Farmers have cleared areas

A village nestles before the rising outlines of the Ruwenzori mountains.

The Kolwezi open-pit copper mines are some of the most productive in Katanga.

in the tropical forest where they grow a variety of root crops. The yield is enough for a relatively small group, yet the task of clearing the forest is a huge one and requires all available manpower. The size of a forest community, therefore, hinges upon a delicate balance between the people and their environment.

In the savanna, on the other hand, farming can be practiced more extensively. Farmers are able to produce enough grain crops so that part can be stored for future needs or bartered for other goods. The land can support a larger community and the production of a surplus makes it possible for specialized skills to be developed.

ECONOMY

Zaïre is the most richly endowed country in tropical Africa and, comparatively, one of the most economically advanced. However, the people do not get their full share of their country's wealth because it was developed by and still remains in the control of non-Africans.

The Zaïre Republic exports, among other agricultural products, coffee, cotton, palm oil, and lumber. Its chief wealth, however, comes from beneath the soil. Over two thirds of the country's exports are in the form of minerals. The land of Zaïre produces cobalt, industrial diamonds, copper, and tin. It is also a leading producer of a variety of minerals needed by space and electronics industries, such as manganese, columbo-tantalite, wolfram, cadmium, and germanium. Uranium for the first atomic bomb came from the Zaïre Republic. Gold is mined in the northeast. The country's impressive potential for hydroelectric power has been only partly developed. Zaïrian industries manufacture textiles, soap, margarine, shoes, house paints, plastics, hardware articles, chemicals, and many other products. Most of this advanced economic activity, however, continues to depend upon non-African technicians and, even more importantly, upon foreign investments and foreign buyers. This is why many Zaïrians feel that they will not be masters in their own country until they learn to exploit and control its wealth by themselves.

Transportation. Certainly one of the most notable things about the country is its sheer size. It is the third largest state in Africa. Great distances are compounded by the lack of good transportation facilities, especially decent roads, and by the fact that most urban centers are situated far from the center of the country. Of Zaïre's 10 largest cities, seven are located on or near its borders. Except where interrupted by rapids, the Congo (Zaïre) River, as well as its many tributaries, permits navigation. The country's railroads were built at points where navigation was impossible. This combined use of the railroad and the river is still the major form of inland transportation, especially for goods. An increasingly large portion of passenger travel is now done by air. Passenger transportation by trucks or buses is not nearly as common as it is, for example, in West Africa, but it is steadily increasing.

HISTORY

In the 1st century A.D., Bantu-speaking people invaded the Zaïre region and conquered the Pygmies. They came in waves, possibly from the southeastern part of what is now Nigeria. A few centuries later, most of them had reached the Congo River Basin, where they farmed and worked metals. The early Negro settlers were probably pushed into the forest regions by later-arriving peoples. The whole process was a slow and a very intricate one. Several states emerged in the southern savanna between the 13th and 19th centuries. The best-known of these was the kingdom of the Kongo, from which the river and later the country took their names.

The kingdom of the Kongo, which was on the Atlantic coast, was first visited by Portuguese navigators in 1482. In the years that followed, other European countries sent ships to the Kongo's shores. Because of political pressures, within the country and from foreign interference, the kingdom of the Kongo finally fell apart in the late 17th century.

Other states included the small kingdom of the BaKuba, famed for its artistic achievements, and the far-flung and loosely structured Luba and Lunda empires. The land of these empires embraced portions of present-day southern Zaïre, Angola, and Zambia. In the northern savanna belt, the Azande and Mangbetu states were the most notable. Unlike their counterparts in West Africa, these Central African states had few direct contacts with the outside world until the Portuguese, later followed by other Europeans, set up trading posts.

There was little penetration into the interior of Central Africa by Europeans between the 15th and 19th centuries. As in other parts of Africa, Europeans were content to stay on the coast and let the flow of goods come to them from the interior through local traders. The Europeans dealt not only with goods but also with slaves. The slave trade reached its peak during the first half of the 19th century, when some 150,000 slaves were being shipped each year, mostly to the Americas.

Systematic European exploration of Central Africa began in the mid-19th century. Among the explorers who ventured into the area were

David Livingstone, Richard F. Burton, and John H. Speke. One of the best-known of the explorers was Henry Morton Stanley. Stanley crossed Africa from Zanzibar to the Atlantic Ocean, exploring Lake Tanganyika and Uganda, and tracing the course of the Congo River. King Leopold II of Belgium hired him to open up the vast territory that now forms the Republic of Zaïre. Stanley set up posts and signed treaties with African chiefs on behalf of an organization sponsored by the King. At the Berlin Conference (1884–85), which resulted in the partition of the African continent among European nations, the country was placed under Leopold's, not Belgium's, personal sovereignty. It was given the name of the Congo Free State. Leopold's emissaries evicted Muslim traders from the eastern section of the Congo Free State and secured control of mineral-rich Katanga in the southeast, but their harsh and brutal actions caused such an international scandal that Leopold eventually had to surrender control of the region to Belgium in 1908. Large cities grew up and roads and railroads were developed, but all of this was organized primarily to serve Belgian needs. Yet, for a variety of reasons, few Belgians settled permanently in the area and most of the land remained in African hands. From the mid-1950s, Africans began to demand self-rule and set up various political parties. The Belgians, confident that they would retain economic control, agreed to give over political power. Joseph Kasavubu and Patrice Lumumba became, respectively, president and prime minister of the Democratic Republic of the Congo on June 30, 1960.

As often happens with new nations, independence was followed by years of inner turmoil. The worst threat to the new state was the attempt of its richest province, Katanga, to break away from the Congo. Under the leadership of Moïse Tshombe and with the help of European businessmen, Katanga seceded. Lumumba asked the United Nations for aid, and soldiers from several countries were sent to try to reunite the country.

Tshombe resisted the efforts to end Katanga's secession, and fighting broke out between the United Nations and Katangese forces. Lumumba was removed from office. Later, he was imprisoned and then killed by his political opponents. In 1961 a new government was formed, with Cyrille Adoula as prime minister. Katanga was brought under the control of the central government in 1963 and Tshombe replaced Adoula as prime minister in 1964, but civil strife continued.

Army commander General Joseph Mobutu (now Mobutu Sese Seko) seized control in 1965. The Constitution of 1967, which gave the Congo a presidential form of government, was amended in 1970 to make President Mobutu's Popular Movement of the Revolution the only legal political party. In 1971 the country's name was changed to Zaïre. Shaba Province (formerly Katanga) was invaded in 1977 and 1978 by Zaïrian exiles who were repulsed by French and Belgian paratroopers sent to aid Mobutu. As Zaïre's standard of living declined, however, calls for Mobutu's resignation mounted. Economic discontent sparked a week of rioting and looting in September 1991 that led to the virtual collapse of the modern economy. A national conference began meeting sporadically in July 1991 to draft a new constitution and schedule multiparty elections. In August 1992 it named one of Mobutu's chief opponents as prime minister of a transitional government, but Mobutu remained in power and said the conference's decisions were only advisory.

EDOUARD BUSTIN, Boston University

CONGO RIVER

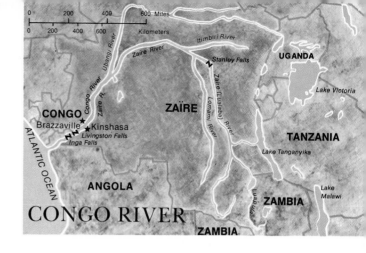

At evening a hush comes across the waters and the sun streaks a darkening sky. The jungle leans close, a tangle of deepening green. The wet, rounded backs of hippopotamuses glisten in the fading light. Crocodiles lie fierce and old in a dark mudbank. Suddenly the scream of an animal shatters the silence and echoes across the wide river, from shore to shore. Then all is silent.

The river flows on, broad and serene, as it has done from the very beginning of time. Here and there a wave ripples, then smooths out. The water is flat and quiet again. Suddenly the sun drops and disappears and the night sweeps in, covering the wet, glistening backs and wiping them out in blackness. Even the crocodiles are gone. Only the hushed sound of the flowing water remains.

This is the Congo.

Yet this is not the Congo. For the Congo has other faces and other moods and other characters.

The Giant

The Congo is one of the giant rivers of the world. It is the second longest river in Africa—only the Nile is longer. The Congo is about 2,900 miles (4,700 kilometers) long and drains an area of some 1,450,000 square miles (3,800,000 square kilometers). Kisangani, Mbandaka, Kinshasa, Brazzaville, Boma, and Matadi are some of the important cities that line its banks.

Rising in the Katanga Plateau near the Zambia-Zaïre border, the river cuts through the center of equatorial Africa in a winding, twisting course, until it reaches the brilliant sunlit waters of the Atlantic Ocean. There, unlike the Nile and other large rivers of the world, it does not slow down to form a delta. The river has cut a deep, wide canyon beneath the sea. The Congo rushes on through this canyon into the ocean, forming a swath of muddy water that extends for a distance of many miles. Then, some 100 miles (160 km.) out from the shore, the muddy water that was once part of a vast and majestic river filters away into a vaster ocean.

The giant is known by many names. At its head it is known as Luapula, and elsewhere as the Lualaba. In Zaïre it is the Zaïre River. There are other names for its tributaries, names that sound like soft melodies, but all the smaller rivers flow into the one great river.

At different stages of its long, winding, westward drive to the sea, the Congo shows different traits and characteristics. It is a wide, serene river—at one place 9 full miles (14 km.) from shore to shore. It is a

Dugout boats on that part of the Congo called the Zaïre River.

narrow, plunging river; a deep river; a shallow, sluggish, muddy one. It is a river broken by many rushing cataracts. The well-known waterfalls include Livingstone Falls, Inga Falls, and Stanley Falls. The cataracts and waterfalls of this river are a huge source of hydroelectricity. Some of this energy is already being used for mining, smelting, and refining of metals.

The Congo is a river of many islands. Many of these islands are small and bare—nothing more than sandbars. Others are large and lined with old trees. The largest island of all, Nsumba, is 50 miles (80 km.) long and almost 5 miles (8 km.) wide. All in all, the Congo has more than 4,000 islands scattered along its course.

The River Highway

The Congo is the highway of Central Africa. The people of the villages that dot its banks use dugouts to travel up and down the river. The people of the port cities, such as Kinshasa, Brazzaville, Kisangani, and Mbandaka, use modern steamers for their travels. The merchants use freighters to send timber, rubber, and palm produce along the river to the ocean and from there to the world. All through the year the Congo is open to shipping.

History

A Portuguese navigator, Diogo Cão, discovered the mouth of the Congo in 1482. Cão called the river Zaïre—the Portuguese corruption of a local word, zadi, meaning "great water" or "big water." The river later came to be known as the Congo after the powerful kingdom of the Kongo, which flourished in present-day Angola, Congo, and Zaïre in the 16th and 17th centuries. But centuries passed before the famous English explorer, Henry Morton Stanley, began his expedition. Stanley traveled the entire length of the river. That trip, which began in 1874 and ended in 1877, opened the Congo. From then on, it played a significant role in the modern history of Central Africa.

Reviewed by AUGUSTIN N. LEKONGA, First Secretary
Permanent Mission of the Republic of Zaïre to the United Nations

ZAMBIA

Kabwe today is a modern mining center in Zambia, with all the atmosphere of the 20th century. But some 50,000 years ago, in a cave near Kabwe, the following scene could well have taken place.

It was raining and the day was cold, with a coldness that penetrated to the very bones. But inside the cave the men were warm. They listened to the driving rain and gathered about the burning branches, huddling close to the flames. These hardy people had learned how to use one of man's greatest resources, fire. This was a new tool for man to master and to use, in turn, to master his environment.

From the traces of life they left—not only at Kabwe, discovered in 1921, but also at Kalambo Falls, in the Gwembe Valley, and around Kalomo, we know that generations of Stone Age men camped in the area. These were the forerunners of modern man in Africa.

THE LAND

The Republic of Zambia, a land of great natural wealth, lies in south central Africa. A landlocked country, it is bordered on the north by the Republic of Zaïre and by Tanzania, on the east by Malawi, on the south

This office building in Lusaka has shops and cafés on its street floor.

by Mozambique, Zimbabwe, and Namibia (South-West Africa), and on the west by Angola. Most of the cities of Zambia are quite small. The major ones are Lusaka, Kitwe, Ndola, Chingola, Luanshya, Kabwe (formerly Broken Hill), and Livingstone. **Lusaka,** the capital, is Zambia's largest city and major center of commerce and transportation. Its main business section is dominated by modern buildings, busy traffic, and during the height of the day, crowded intersections.

For the most part, Zambia is a rolling plateau country 3,000 to 5,000 feet (900–1,500 meters) above sea level, with fairly good soil for agriculture in many areas. One section, called the Eastern Highland, averages 6,000 feet (1,800 m.) above sea level. The highest point in Zambia, about 7,000 feet (2,100 m.), is in the Muchinga Mountains in the northeast part of the country.

Climate

Even though it is within the tropics, Zambia has cooler average temperatures than many other parts of tropical Africa. This is because of the general height of the country's plateau. Zambia's winter, which is a cool, dry season, runs from April to August. A warm, wet summer season extends from September to March. Annual rainfall is 50 inches (130 centimeters) or more in the northern part of the country but decreases to 20 to 30 inches (50–80 cm.) in the south.

THE PEOPLE

Countless people have passed over the hills and plateaus of Zambia. In early times it was the Pygmy, who hunted game and picked the

Tourists and Zambians alike enjoy the sun at the Inter-Continental Hotel in Lusaka, one of the finest hotels in south central Africa.

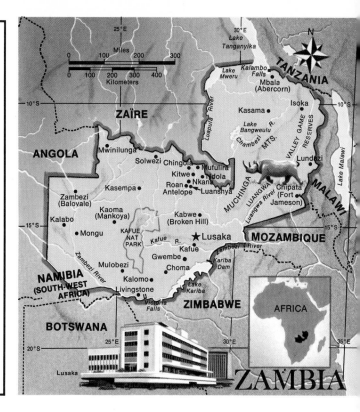

FACTS AND FIGURES

OFFICIAL NAME: Republic of Zambia.

NATIONALITY: Zambian(s).

CAPITAL: Lusaka.

LOCATION: South central Africa. **Boundaries**—Tanzania, Zaïre, Malawi, Mozambique, Zimbabwe, Botswana, Namibia, Angola.

AREA: 290,585 sq. mi. (752,615 sq. km.).

PHYSICAL FEATURES: Highest point—7,123 ft. (2,171 m.). **Lowest point**—1,150 ft. (351 m.). **Chief river**—Zambezi.

POPULATION: 7,875,448 (1989).

MAJOR LANGUAGES: English (official), Bemba, Lozi, Nyanja, Tonga, Luvale, Lunda.

MAJOR RELIGIONS: Roman Catholicism, Protestantism, Islam, traditional African religions.

GOVERNMENT: Republic. **Head of state**—president. **Head of Government**—prime minister. **Legislature**—one-house national assembly. **International cooperation**—United Nations, Organization of African Unity (OAU), Commonwealth of Nations.

CHIEF CITIES: Lusaka, Kitwe, Ndola.

ECONOMY: Chief minerals—copper, coal, zinc, lead, cobalt. **Chief agricultural products**—sugar cane, corn, cassava, millet, peanuts, tobacco, cotton. **Industries and products**—copper refining, textiles, mining, sawmilling, cement making, beverage making. **Chief exports**—copper, lead, zinc, cobalt, tobacco. **Chief imports**—manufactured goods, machinery, chemicals.

MONETARY UNIT: Kwacha.

fruits and grains of the area. Much later, in about the 13th century, the Bantu, a larger, better-organized group, appeared. The term Bantu is a linguistic one and applies to all people living east and south of Nigeria who speak a form of this language. These Bantu were a pastoral people, grazing their cattle and periodically planting a crop.

The lands of Zambia are grass covered, and the Bantu quickly spread over the entire area. Some groups settled in different sections. In time they developed different ways of speaking—that is, variants of the Bantu language—different ways of worship, and different ways of governing themselves. From this, various ethnic groups developed.

Some, like the Lozi, settled around the Zambezi River north of Victoria Falls some 200 years ago. It is a rich area, and the cattle are healthy. In fact, it is one of the few areas in Zambia not bothered by the tsetse fly, which brings disease to the cattle. Others, like the Bemba in the north, are farmers and do not raise cattle. These people live in villages scattered throughout the country, some 15 to 20 mi. (24–32 km.) apart. In areas where the annual rainfall is over 50 in. (130 cm.), the soil is so poor that the Bemba must continually search for good land. They practice *chitemene*, or slash-and-burn agriculture. The brush and other growth are burned until the ground is completely cleared for planting. Then the ash from the fire is mixed with the soil as a form of fertilizer. By this method the Bemba are able to get a good crop for 3 or 4 years. Then they move on and repeat the process.

Today more than 70 different ethnic groups live in Zambia. The principal groups are the Bemba, the Tonga, the Ngoni, and the Lozi of Barotseland. They have learned to adjust to the land and work out a reasonably good way of life. In times of drought or disaster, many people go hungry, but generally they are able to feed themselves on a subsistence level.

Education

About 80 percent of the children of Zambia receive primary education. About 26 percent of these children go on for a secondary school education. The Zambian government, which took over all education in 1964, is doing its best to bring more students to secondary schools and beyond. In 1966 the University of Zambia was opened in Lusaka. This was the first university ever to be established in the country. It offered courses in the social sciences, natural sciences, and education. The initial enrollment was a little over 300 students, but within a few years the number had increased to more than 1,000. There were more than 4,500 students in the late 1980s. Other institutions of higher learning include a college of agriculture and two technical schools.

ECONOMY

Although the country is not rich from an agricultural point of view, it is very rich in minerals. Zambia is one of the world's largest producers of copper. Minerals account for 90 percent of the country's exports, and of all minerals, copper is by far the most important.

The copper belt in the north central part of the country is one of the

Copper ingots are loaded onto freight cars for shipment overseas.

The floodgates of Kariba Dam are often opened during the rainy season.

richest mineral areas in all Africa. The mines—huge industrial complexes—were founded by British and American capital, but the government now owns 60 percent. They yield some 500,000 tons of copper per year. Smelters and refineries are located at Mufulira, Nkana, Ndola, and Roan Antelope. Ndola is a manufacturing center, producing equipment for the mines and some consumer goods. Kabwe is the center for lead and zinc production.

About half of Zambia's population live in urban areas. The largest of these is Lusaka, the capital, but about 20 percent of the people live in the five big towns of the copper belt. Although mining is central to the nation's economy, the industry has been suffering from falling world prices and underinvestment. Shortages of raw materials, spare parts, and fuel have led to declines in production.

Kariba Dam

A major source of electric power for the mines is supplied by Kariba Dam, one of the great dams of the world. Astride the mighty Zambezi River, the dam rises to a height of 420 ft. (128 m.). The lake formed by the dam is among the largest of all man-made lakes and has an area of some 2,000 sq. mi. (5,180 sq. km.). The cost of building the Kariba Dam was enormous—more than $250 million was spent before the project was completed.

HISTORY AND GOVERNMENT

From artifacts that have been dug up and studied, leading anthropologists believe that the country now known as Zambia was inhabited some 500,000 years ago. However very little is known of the type of men who lived and hunted in the area. And very little is known of Zambia's early history until the coming of the first Europeans in the 15th century.

Two Portuguese explorers, crossing between Angola and Mozambique, were probably among the first Europeans to venture into the country. But it was David Livingstone, the missionary explorer, who was the first European to have a great impact upon the area. During his exploration between 1851 and 1873 he discovered Victoria Falls. He died in 1873, about 70 mi. (115 km.) southeast of Lake Bangweulu.

Another European important in Zambia's history was Cecil John Rhodes. Rhodes had made a fortune in the diamond fields of South Africa, but he missed out on the gold mines in the Transvaal. He kept looking to the north, searching for a new source of minerals to make him even more powerful financially. Also, he had the dream of British holdings running through the continent of Africa from the Cape of Good Hope to Cairo.

In 1888 he signed agreements with local chiefs for mineral rights in what is now Zambia. To explore and develop the area he created the British South Africa Company, which the British Government chartered, giving him full economic and political control over the country. In fact, this company ran the territory for the British Government until 1924. In that year the government assumed control and named the area the Protectorate of Northern Rhodesia, after Cecil John Rhodes.

In 1953 Northern Rhodesia (now Zambia), Southern Rhodesia (now Zimbabwe), and Nyasaland (now Malawi) formed the Federation of Rhodesia and Nyasaland. The African majority opposed the federation because it was dominated by whites. In 1962 Nyasaland withdrew, and the federation was dissolved December 31, 1963.

In January 1964, elections were held in Northern Rhodesia under a new constitution that provided for internal self-government. On October 24, 1964, Northern Rhodesia became independent under the name of Zambia.

Zambia is an independent republic within the Commonwealth of Nations. The president and the members of the one-house National Assembly are elected for 5-year terms. Zambia was a one-party state from 1972 until 1990, when popular discontent fueled by a decline in the standard of living led to the reintroduction of a multiparty system. Multiparty presidential and legislative elections were held in 1991. Kenneth David Kaunda, who had been president of Zambia since independence, and his party, the United National Independence Party, were defeated. Zambia's new president, Frederick Chiluba, ended the nation's 27-year state of emergency and worked to rebuild the economy.

PLACES OF INTEREST

Victoria Falls, discovered in 1855, is one of the great tourist attractions in Zambia. Every year thousands of visitors travel to see the awesome beauty of these falls, which are twice as high as the famous Niagara Falls in the United States. Another popular attraction is Kafue National Park, one of the largest game reserves in Africa. Kariba Dam and its huge lake is another area of great interest to travelers and vacationers from many parts of the world.

HUGH C. BROOKS, Director, Center for African Studies, St. John's University
Reviewed by EMBASSY OF ZAMBIA, Washington, D.C.

Fishermen in dugout canoes on Lake Malawi.

MALAWI

Malawi is a beautiful country of high mountains, sparkling lakes, and lush green fields. Its name reaches back into the country's early history. Sometime about the 16th century, a people drifted into the area of present-day Malawi. They slowly settled there and took on the name "Maravi." This name—"Malawi" is the modern spelling—means "land of flames." Some historians say the word originated when this people saw the waters of Lake Malawi glimmering red in the sunset. Others say the word comes from a reference to the glow of an iron furnace. Iron smelting was an important occupation of the early peoples who wandered about the territory.

THE LAND

The Republic of Malawi, formerly known as Nyasaland, is located in southeast Africa. It is bounded by Zambia on the northwest, Tanzania on the northeast, and Mozambique on the south, southeast, and southwest. It has a total land area of 45,747 square miles (118,484 square kilometers) and a rapidly growing population.

Because of its beautiful scenery, its mountains and its lakes, Malawi has been called the Switzerland of Africa. Part of the Great Rift Valley runs through the country from north to south. Lake Malawi, once known as Lake Nyasa, lies in this deep trough. The towering plateaus on both sides of the trough are a majestic sight. Mount Mlanje, rising to nearly 10,000 feet (3,000 meters), is the highest point in Malawi. It has become a great attraction for tourists and mountain climbers.

Malawi is a tropical country, but because much of the land is mountains and plateaus it has a fairly pleasant climate. Generally the tempera-

A quiet afternoon in an outlying area of Blantyre.

tures range from 65 to 85 degrees Fahrenheit (18–30 degrees Celsius) and sometimes there is even frost. However, it does get quite hot in the Shire River valley area. The country has a single rainy season, which lasts from November to April.

Cities. Because it is a landlocked country, Malawi has no ocean port of its own. The nearest ports are Sofala and Nacala in Mozambique. The present capital of the country is **Lilongwe.** A growing city of about 105,000 located in the central agricultural region, it became the seat of government in 1975. Formerly **Zomba** had been Malawi's capital. In the Shire Highlands are **Blantyre** and **Limbe,** which have been united to form the country's major commercial and industrial center. They were amalgamated in 1959 for pupuses of local government. Today, this city, called Blantyre, has a population of over 230,000. Blantyre, the main shopping area of Malawi, has fairly busy streets, department stores, modern office buildings, and factories.

THE PEOPLE

Most of the people of Malawi are Africans of Bantu origin, some of whom came into the area at various times between the 16th and 19th centuries. The chief groups are the Chewa, Lomwe, Ngonde Yao, Ngoni, and Tumbuka. There are also some thousands of Europeans and Asians, and a small number of people of mixed origin. Most of the Europeans live in the larger towns and work for the government, the Christian missions, industry, and the tea plantations. The Asians are also town-dwellers and work in small shops.

Because there are not enough jobs to go around in Malawi, thousands of Malawians leave the country to work in the copper mines of Zambia and Zimbabwe or on the farms and in the mines of South Africa. They generally stay away for intervals of 2 to 3 years. The money they send back home makes an important contribution to the economy of Malawi.

The two main languages spoken in Malawi are Chichewa and Chitumbuka. Chitumbuka is the language of the northern region of the country, while Chichewa is that of the southern region. However, English and Chichewa are the two official languages of Malawi. English is used in administration, in the courts, in official publications, and in schools.

A large proportion of the people follow animistic beliefs. The rest of the indigenous population of the Republic of Malawi are either Christians or Muslims.

Education. Because Malawi needs many trained people to help build the country and solve its pressing problems, education is of the utmost importance. Every effort is being made to get all the children of school age into the classroom. More and better-equipped schools are being built each year. About three out of every five children of primary school age in Malawi actually do go to school. However, the proportion is much lower for secondary school, and few Malawians attend college. A high point in Malawi's educational development was the opening of the University of Malawi in 1965. The university's first chancellor was the president of the country, Dr. H. Kamuzu Banda.

ECONOMY

Malawi is an agricultural country with many severe problems. Only about 10,000 square miles (26,000 sq. km.) of the total land area are suitable for agriculture. The average population density is 118 persons to the square mile, or 45 to the square kilometer. Only three African countries, Burundi, Nigeria, and Rwanda, have higher densities. All this means that Malawi's small land area has to provide for a very large population. This calls for better methods of cultivation, an increased use of effective fertilizers, better marketing facilities, and greatly improved communications and means of transportation. Fortunately, the country's arable land is extremely fertile.

In the old days, maize, cassava, millet, beans, pumpkins, yams, groundnuts (peanuts), tomatoes, and rice were grown for local consumption. The economy was a moderately self-sufficient one. But today the old crops are simply not large enough to keep the economy going. Cash crops like tobacco, cotton, groundnuts, and tea, among others, have to be encouraged and developed. These crops must be sold abroad in order to bring much-needed money into Malawi.

Shortly after independence the Young Pioneer movement was organized by the government. This movement was aimed at educating Malawi's youth in improved methods of agriculture. Government leaders viewed the Young Pioneer training centers as extremely important to the country's economic prospects. The Young Pioneer movement helped to bring about the new emphasis in agriculture on the growing of cash crops. After a training period of 14 months, the youths were sent to the villages to introduce the new ways of farming to the people.

Most of the crops for export are grown on large estates, which occupy about 15 percent of the total land available for cultivation. The remainder of the farmland is worked in small plots under the overall control of the traditional village leaders, or headmen. In normal years Malawi is self-sufficient in food production. When a drought occurs, food is imported.

The government still plays an active role. The Farmers Marketing Board, a government agency, has opened branches throughout the country to help farmers sell their produce.

A few small industries have been started in Blantyre. Clothing, ceramics, cement, alcoholic beverages, and soft drinks are manufactured. The only industry outside the city is the sugar factory at Chikwawa, on the Shire River near the sugar plantations.

HISTORY

Very little is known of the early history of Malawi. At one time migrant peoples began moving into vast areas of Africa south of the equator. They were called Bantu, which designates people who speak a common language. So the people who settled in Malawi, in Zambia, or in South Africa, for example, may be called Bantu-speaking peoples. The Maravi, from whom Malawi takes its name, were one such group. The Maravi crossed into Zambia and Tanzania from the southern Congo sometime during the 16th century. Their direct descendants, the Chewa, now live in the central and southern regions of Malawi. During the 17th and 18th centuries Portuguese explorers made a number of trips across the southern end of the country. However, these explorers established no lasting settlements, and today there are very few traces left of their expeditions.

Malawi's modern history began in 1859. In September of that year David Livingstone, the famous explorer, first came upon what is now known as Lake Malawi. He called the huge lake, third largest in all Africa, Lake Nyasa. Livingstone's discovery and further explorations opened the

Schoolchildren performing gymnastics during Republic Day celebrations.

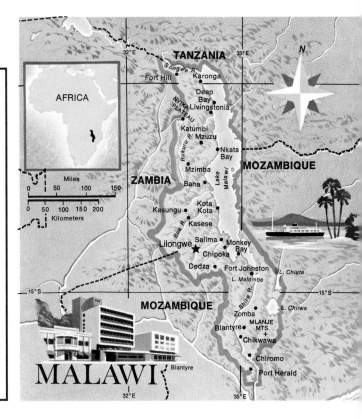

FACTS AND FIGURES

OFFICIAL NAME: Republic of Malawi.

NATIONALITY: Malawian(s).

CAPITAL: Lilongwe.

LOCATION: Southeast Africa. **Boundaries:** Tanzania, Mozambique, Zambia.

AREA: 45,747 sq. mi. (118,484 sq. km.).

PHYSICAL FEATURES: Highest point—Mount Mlanje (9,843 ft.; 2,952 m). **Lowest point**—121 ft. (37 m.) above sea level. **Major lake**—Malawi.

POPULATION: 8,700,000 (1992; annual growth 3.5%).

MAJOR LANGUAGES: English and Chichewa (official), Chitumbuka.

MAJOR RELIGIONS: Traditional African religions, Christianity, Islam.

GOVERNMENT: Republic. **Head of government**—president. **Legislature**–National Assembly.

CHIEF CITY: Blantyre.

ECONOMY: Chief agricultural products—maize, cassava, millet, beans, pumpkins, yams, groundnuts, tomatoes, tea, sugarcane, rice, tobacco, cotton. **Industries and products**—clothing, ceramics, cement, alcoholic and soft drinks. **Chief exports**—tobacco, tea, sugar, coffee, groundnuts. **Chief imports**—metals, machinery, construction materials, fuels, fertilizers.

MONETARY UNIT: Kwacha.

way for British penetration into the territory. Livingstone was a Scottish missionary, and he was revolted by the conditions of the slave trade then in existence in the area. After his death a number of missions were established in the country. For many years these missions helped educate the people of Malawi. Declaring that its purpose was to end the slave trade and to uplift the people, the British Government in 1891 set up a protectorate, later to be called the Nyasaland Protectorate.

The British control of Nyasaland was challenged at times. In 1915 troops crushed a revolt by a group calling for national freedom. In 1953 Nyasaland was joined with Northern and Southern Rhodesia in the Federation of Rhodesia and Nyasaland. This federation lasted for some 10 years, until it was finally dissolved at Nyasaland's request. On July 6, 1964, the country gained full independence as Malawi, with Dr. H. Kamazu Banda as its first prime minister. In 1966, under a new constitution, Malawi became a one-party republic with Banda as president. The constitution was amended in 1970 to name Banda president for life. Despite unprecedented demands for Banda's resignation and for democratic reforms, one-party legislative elections were held as scheduled in 1992.

GOVERNMENT

Malawi is an independent republic within the Commonwealth of Nations. The head of state and government is the president, and the Malawi Congress Party is the only legal political party. Most members of the National Assembly are directly elected, although the president may appoint an unlimited number of additional members.

BRIDGLAL PACHAI, University of Malawi

Rocky hills called "ambas" dot Ethiopia's plateau.

ETHIOPIA

Ethiopia, once known as Abyssinia, is an ancient land in eastern Africa whose history was long shrouded in mystery. On early Greek and Roman maps all of Africa below Egypt and the Sahara had the word "Ethiopians" emblazoned across it. But in time Ethiopia came to be the name of an increasingly powerful country located in the highlands of East Africa where the Blue Nile has its source.

THE LAND

Ethiopia lies on the horn of East Africa, with Sudan on the west and the Red Sea on the northeast. To the east and southeast are Djibouti (formerly the French Territory of the Afars and the Issas), and Somalia. To the south lie Kenya and another segment of Somalia.

Ethiopia's heartland is the East African rift plateau, or Ethiopian highlands. This is one of Africa's loftiest regions, so Ethiopia is sometimes called the Tibet of Africa. The plateau is generally between 3,000 and 10,000 feet (900–3,000 meters) high, and mountains thrust above it to more than 14,000 feet (4,300 m.).

Africa's Great Rift Valley slices through the plateau in a southwesterly direction. Both parts of the plateau, on either side of the Rift Valley, are slashed and scored by plunging smaller valleys walled in by mountainsides and cliffs. But even where the land is level, the strange-shaped

The famous Blue Nile Falls are also called Tisisat, or "smoke of fire."

ambas rear up out of it. These flat-topped pinnacles have for centuries provided refuges for people wishing to withdraw from the surrounding plateau. Kings have fled to *ambas* when besieged and have also exiled enemies atop them. *Ambas* have made homes for monasteries too.

Surrounding the plateau are four hot lowland regions. In the north, near the Red Sea, the Rift Valley widens to form the deserts of the Danakil Plains. The Danakil Plains are among the hottest spots on earth and are below sea level in some places. To the southeast of the highlands are the semiarid grazing lands of the Ogaden, inhabited by nomadic Somalis. To the west, bordering Sudan, is a narrow strip of lowland inhabited by peoples related to the Sudanese.

Of Ethiopia's many rivers, the most famous is the Blue Nile (called the Abbai in Ethiopia). It rises in the highlands of Gojjam province in northwestern Ethiopia and flows into Lake Tana. After issuing from the lake's southeastern corner, the river spills over the great Blue Nile (Tisisat) Falls and follows a serpentine course westward into Sudan. It joins the White Nile at Khartoum, and the combined stream flows northward as the Nile, Africa's greatest river.

Climate

Ethiopia lies near the equator. In the lowlands temperatures often reach 100 degrees Fahrenheit (38 degrees Celsius) or more. But the high plateau, which covers about two thirds of the country, is temperate, with bright sunshine and cool and bracing air. The warmest and sunniest period is from October through January. The rainy season is from mid-

June to mid-September. Ethiopia's summer rains are highly erratic. In some years they fail to come at all or come in amounts insufficient to support farm crops and grazing lands. These failures often cause widespread hunger and suffering and force hungry refugees to migrate in search of food and water. Occasionally, as in the early 1970's and again in the 1980's, there may be year after year of drought. When this happens, thousands of hungry people flock to food relief camps, and many more, unable to reach the camps, die of starvation. It is estimated that more than 1,000,000 Ethiopians perished in the first half of the 1980's.

Cities

In the plateau's invigorating climate, Ethiopia's main cities have flourished. Here the ancient capital of **Aksum** held sway. And here, south of Aksum (only a village today), is the modern capital of **Addis Ababa** ("new flower"), founded in 1887. Rapidly growing in population, Addis Ababa has a university, hospitals, modern hotels, Ethiopia's main banking institutions, and a large number of Ethiopian Christian churches. Here too are the former royal palace and its gardens, the busy boulevards, government ministries, foreign embassies, and the impressive Africa Hall, which houses the United Nations Economic Commission for

Addis Ababa, Ethiopia's capital, is the country's most modern city.

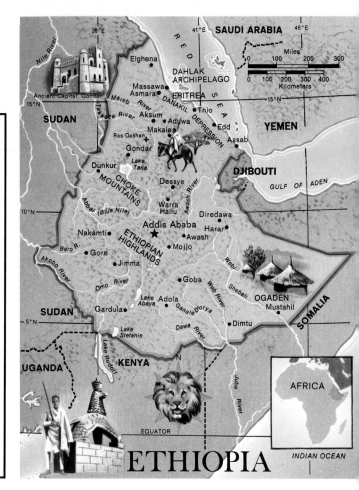

FACTS AND FIGURES

OFFICIAL NAME: People's Democratic Republic of Ethiopia.

NATIONALITY: Ethiopian(s).

CAPITAL: Addis Ababa.

LOCATION: Eastern Africa. **Boundaries**—Red Sea, Djibouti, Somalia, Kenya, Sudan.

AREA: 471,776 sq. mi. (1,221,900 sq. km.).

PHYSICAL FEATURES: Highest point—Ras Dashan (15,158 ft.; 4,620 m.). **Lowest point**—Lake Karum, in Danakil depression, 381 ft. (116 m.) below sea level. **Chief rivers**—Blue Nile (Abbai), Awash, Omo, Takkaze, Webi Shebeli. **Major lake**—Tana.

POPULATION: 53,191,127 (1991; annual growth 3.1%).

MAJOR LANGUAGES: Amharic (official), Tigrinya, Orominga, Arabic.

MAJOR RELIGIONS: Muslim, Ethiopian Orthodox, animistic beliefs.

GOVERNMENT: Republic. **Head of state**—President. **Legislature**—Council of Representatives.

CHIEF CITIES: Addis Ababa, Asmara, Diredawa.

ECONOMY: Chief minerals—potash, salt, gold, copper, platinum. **Chief agricultural products**—coffee, grain, livestock, sugar refining. **Industries and products**—cement, sugar refining, cotton textiles, food processing. **Chief exports**—coffee. **Chief imports**—petroleum products, vehicles, machinery, electrical equipment, metals, foodstuffs.

MONETARY UNIT: Birr.

Africa and where the Organization of African Unity (OAU) has its head-quarters and yearly meetings. There is also a national library in Addis Ababa and an archeological museum of considerable interest. High-rise buildings give "Addis" an aura of modernity.

In other parts of the highlands, the cities of Gondar, Makale, Dessye, Diredawa, Jimma, and the walled city of Harar (long a Muslim center) have grown up. **Asmara,** the capital of Eritrea, lies on a northern spur of the plateau. The only important cities not located in the highlands are the ports of Assab and Massawa on the Red Sea coast in Eritrea. As part of a 1991 accord giving Eritrea the right to hold a referendum on independence in 1993, Assab was to become a free port, which would give Ethiopia an outlet to the sea even if Eritrea voted for independence. Some 70 percent of Ethiopia's imports and exports pass through Assab.

THE PEOPLE

Ethiopia is one of the five most populated countries in Africa. But population experts can only guess at the actual number of people since no nationwide census has ever been taken. Sometimes their estimates can vary by as much as 5 million people. All agree, however, that the population, despite famines and civil strife, is expanding rapidly. This is pushing the predominantly rural and agricultural Ethiopians to cut down the forests and to farm drought-prone lands in their search for more food and farmland. Many are also migrating to the cities, where now only about 11 percent of the people live, in search of a better life.

Islamic-style gateway to the town of Agordat in Eritrea.

Ethiopia's population is a mix of more than 70 ethnic groups. These are separated from each other by traditional hostilities, language, religion, and way of life. Governing such a mix of different peoples is difficult. Although the coalition government that took power in 1991 planned to divide Ethiopia into self-governing regions and to grant "nationalities" within these regions the right to control their own affairs, there were fears that ethnic rivalries would lead to renewed civil war and the eventual dissolution of the nation. The situation was complicated by a huge influx of refugees fleeing civil wars in neighboring Sudan and Somalia.

The Amharas and the Tigrais of the central highlands have traditionally dominated Ethiopia in the past. Together, the two groups make up about 45 percent of the population. They live mainly as farmers but have only primitive tools, like those used in medieval Europe, with which to work the land. Christianity is their religion.

Long ago, the Amharas and the Tigrais were one people speaking the same ancient language, Ge'ez. Over time, the people divided into two separate groups and the language branched off in three separate directions. The original language, Ge'ez, survives today in the services and prayers of the Ethiopian Church. In the Tigrais' area, Ge'ez developed into Tigre and Tigrinya, and in the Amharas' area, into Amharic.

The Falashas, also called "Black Jews," of Ethiopia are an unusual Hamitic group. Their religion reflects an ancient form of Judaism, to which they were attracted more than 2,000 years ago. They are relatively small in number (about 30,000) and traditionally lived north of Lake Tana. By 1992, almost all of the Falashas had been airlifted to Israel.

The Oromo are Ethiopia's single largest ethnic group. Called Gallas by the Amharas, they make up about 40 percent of the population and live mainly in the south. The Oromo, who have their own language, entered the plateau from the south in the 15th and 16th centuries. Their arrival was more an armed migration than an invasion, for they adopted the customs of the groups they vanquished and did not impose their own. The Oromo in Shoa, Addis Ababa's province, for example, have intermarried with Amharas, adopted Christianity, and taken up Amhara customs. Other Oromo generally follow animist beliefs or Islam.

Very different are the Somalis and the Danakil or Afars. They inhabit arid regions in the east and southeast and share a nomadic pastoral tradition. The two peoples look very much alike, are both Muslim, but are enemies by tradition. The Somalis, related to Somalis in neighboring Somaliland, are the more numerous and live mainly in Ogaden province. To survive in the Danakil Plains, the Danakil stand ready to defend each of their water holes to the death—whether their rights be challenged by outsiders or by other, rival, Danakil. Some of the Danakil are engaged in a salt-cutting industry in the Danakil depression and have long traded the salt with the Amharas and other peoples of East Africa.

Border Peoples. A mix of smaller ethnic groups live along the border with Sudan. Many such groups are settled farmers. The Abigars and Annuaks in the southwest are cattle herders. In the past these border peoples were the object of slave raids by the highland Ethiopians.

Way of Life

Family life in Ethiopia varies greatly from one ethnic group to the next. In prerevolutionary Ethiopia (before 1974), Amhara traditions, as-

An outdoor market in Gondar, a city in the northwestern highlands.

Orphaned children gather for a meal in Eritrea, Ethiopia's northernmost province.

sociated with the Emperor and ruling classes, were often imposed on other societies. After the 1974 revolution, the government launched a program to end the old powers of the nobility. It also disestablished as the official state religion the Ethiopian Orthodox Christianity associated with the long-dominant Amharas. In so doing, the new government encouraged a feeling of pride in being Ethiopian, of whatever origin, as opposed to ethnic pride in being Amhara, Oromo, Somali, Afar, or some other ethnic group.

Food. Ethiopia's staple bread dish is *injera,* a large flat pancake made from teff, a cereal grain. The *injera* covers the whole top of the small table it is served on. *Wat,* a spicy sauce sometimes made with meat, is ladled right onto the *injera,* which is then torn off in bits and eaten with the *wat.* An Ethiopian barley beer called *talla* is usually drunk with this meal. On festive occasions a stronger drink called *tej,* made of fermented honey, is served.

Religion. Today, approximately 45 percent of the population, mostly the Amharas and Tigrais, are Christians. Their church, the Ethiopian Orthodox Christian Church, traces its development to the 4th century A.D. It was closely tied to the Egyptian (Coptic) Church until 1950 and shares its doctrine that Christ's divine and human natures are one. At the same time it differs significantly from the Christian churches emanating from Rome and Constantinople in that many ancient Judaic customs are preserved. These include circumcision, the Saturday Sabbath, and the distinction between clean and unclean food. Lay clergy called *dabtaras,* who are like Judaic cantors, chant the liturgy and do the ritual dances that mark important feast days.

The Ethiopian Church clergy was very numerous (some say 20 percent of all men in the country), poorly educated, and conservative. But the revolutionary government in power since 1974 seized all church lands for redistribution to community groups and has encouraged clergymen to seek other occupations.

Islam is the religion of another 40 percent of all Ethiopians. Its followers, known as Muslims, maintain close ties with neighboring Arab and other Islamic societies in the Red Sea and Persian Gulf areas. Long under Amharic domination, Ethiopia's Muslim peoples actively seek greater political self-determination. Among such groups are the dissident Somali and the Arabic-speaking peoples of Eritrea.

Far less numerous, accounting for less than 10 percent of all Ethiopians, are isolated local groups who practice animistic religions. Such groups were often visited by Catholic and Protestant missionaries anxious to convert them to Christianity.

Health

Disease is one of Ethiopia's great human problems. Trachoma, dysentery, bilharziasis, tuberculosis, typhus, malaria, leprosy, and syphilis are all common diseases. Unless these are controlled they will continue to keep the life expectancy of the average Ethiopian down to 45 to 50 years. Lack of basic sanitation causes a death rate of 50 to 60 percent in infants under the age of 2½ years.

The Ethiopian Government has turned to the World Health Organization, UNICEF, Sweden, the United States, and West Germany for assistance in improving health conditions. A public-health college and training center has been established at Gondar. A medical school has been founded at the National University in Addis Ababa. In rural areas, health centers have been set up and pilot projects in water supply and sanitation are also under way.

Education

Fewer than 40 percent of adult Ethiopians are literate. For years schooling was available only to the wealthy and in the Amharic language. This earlier neglect of education has left modern Ethiopia with a severe shortage of the engineers, teachers, technicians, and other skilled personnel needed to modernize the country. Some improvements were made after the 1974 revolution, but there is a great shortage of schools. Only about 35 percent of all children have elementary schools to attend, and only about 12 percent are able to attend high school. Those who do have schools available are now offered instruction in one of at least nine local languages and find that their schooling emphasizes agriculture, crafts, and other practical subjects.

ECONOMY

Ethiopia is one of the world's poorest countries. Most of the people earn a minimal living as farmers or nomadic herders. Nearly everyone lives in extreme poverty, and they are unable to survive droughts and other setbacks without outside assistance. The revolutionary government that seized power in 1974 blamed this widespread poverty on faulty economic planning and misplaced priorities in prerevolutionary days. They nationalized all farmland and organized farmers into communal production groups. Opposition to these policies contributed substantially to the armed struggle that eventually led to the government's downfall in 1991.

Agriculture

Grains are Ethiopia's chief food crop. Teff, a grain used to make the nation's staple bread, is the chief grain, along with wheat, barley, maize, sorghum, and millet. Pulses, including chick peas, beans, and lentils, are other leading crops and the principal source of protein in the Ethiopian diet. Various oils, derived from oilseeds and peanuts, are used for cooking. Ensete, or false banana, is a nutritious staple food raised in the southern highlands along with taro, yams, and sweet potatoes.

In good years coffee accounts for as much as 75 percent of all export earnings. Coffee bushes grow wild in some parts of the country and are also cultivated for greater yields. Other useful commercial crops are cotton, which helps support the nation's infant textile industry, and sugarcane. Cattle, sheep, and goats, tended mainly by nomadic herders, provide important exports of livestock and hides.

Modern manufacturing contributes little wealth to Ethiopia's economy. Most manufactures are for local use, and very little is exported. The principal manufactures are processed sugar and other foods, cigarettes, cotton textiles, shoes, matches, and a few glass, metal, and petroleum

Many Ethiopian farmers work the land with simple tools, such as ox-drawn plows.

products. Several hydroelectric plants—on the Awash River and Blue Nile in the highlands—provide small amounts of electricity, but most of the country's abundant water resources are undeveloped. Also undeveloped are most forestry and fishing resources.

Mining
Salt is the only mineral produced in large amounts in Ethiopia, most coming from arid Eritrea. Other minerals include gold and platinum and as yet undeveloped resources of iron ore, copper, and potash.

WILDLIFE
The lion, the symbol of Ethiopia, is scarce today. What lions remain roam the southeastern part of the plateau. The leopard population is also in real danger of extinction. It is against the law to shoot leopards, but they are still killed for their high-priced pelts.

Near Awash, not far from Addis Ababa, visitors can see small herds of gazelles, zebras, oryx (a deerlike animal), greater kudus, lesser kudus, and a small type of gazelle called the dik-dik. In the second park, at Omo in the southwest, there are larger herds of plains animals.

In the tropical southwest, elephants, rhinoceroses, and hippopotamuses are found, and the Baro River in Ilubabor province teems with crocodiles. Tropical birds abound in these humid regions, while farther north in some of the Rift Valley lakes are thousands of pink flamingos.

Hyenas scavenge through city streets by night all over Ethiopia. The ease with which these animals wander into the towns gives some idea of how close urban life in Ethiopia still is to the wilderness. Hyenas plagued even Addis Ababa until the coming of neon lights in the 1960's.

HISTORY
Semitic peoples migrated to Ethiopia from southwestern Arabia sometime in the first 1,000 years B.C. They founded the kingdom of Aksum in the highlands after conquering the Hamitic peoples already living there (the Hamites had probably displaced a Negro population in an early day).

In the 4th century A.D., Christianity was brought to Ethiopia by two young Syrian Christians, and close ties were later set up with the Egyptian Christian Church. But after the rise of Islam in the 7th century, the Arabs conquered all of North Africa, isolating the Christian kingdom of Aksum.

A kaleidoscope of kingdoms rose and fell during the 1,000 years of Ethiopia's isolation. One, the Zagwe dynasty (1137–1270), left a fascinating legacy in the 11 rock-hewn churches of Lalibala, built as a "new Jerusalem." These churches, the remains of ancient Aksum, and the castles of King Fasiladas at Gondar (dating from the 17th century) are the major monuments left today from Ethiopia's turbulent history.

Modern Period
Ethiopia's modern history was ushered in by Menelik II, who became emperor in 1889. This monarch traced his ancestry back to Menelik I, legendary child of King Solomon and the Queen of Sheba. Menelik II ended the age-old rivalries among local rulers and gave Ethiopia a strong central government. He defeated an invading Italian army at Aduwa in 1896, allowed the French to start the building of a railroad between Addis

Ababa and the port of Djibouti in French Somaliland (now Djibouti), and laid the groundwork for a modern army.

Menelik died in 1913, and in 1916 his daughter Zauditu was proclaimed empress. Her second cousin Ras Tafari Makonnen was made regent. When Zauditu died in 1930, Ras Tafari claimed the throne and took the title Emperor Haile Selassie I. Both before and after his coronation, Haile Selassie saw to it that Ethiopia passed anti-slavery laws. Under his influence also, Ethiopia opened its doors wide to Western influences and took its first steps toward democracy in the Constitution of 1931.

The Italian invasion of 1935–36 forced Haile Selassie to leave the country. In 1941 the British drove the Italians out of Ethiopia and restored him to his throne. In 1952 the coastal territory of Eritrea, which had been

Church of St. George, Lalibala, hewn from solid rock in the shape of a cross.

The castle of King Fasiladas at Gondar was built in the 17th century.

under separate Italian rule since 1889, was federated with Ethiopia and annexed, despite some opposition, in 1962.

Recent Events.   In subsequent years, Haile Selassie was criticized for being slow to introduce land reform and full political democracy. Famine increased the widespread unrest, and in 1974 the army deposed the Emperor and took control of the country. Parliament was dissolved, and the monarchy was abolished. In the 1980s Ethiopia became, at least in theory, a Soviet-style Communist state.

The revolutionary government, led by Lieutenant Colonel Mengistu Haile Mariam, established close ties with the Soviet Union in 1976. Many civilians objected to these ties, but their opposition was put down by the military during the late 1970s. Fighting intensified in Eritrea, where secessionists sought to establish a separate state, and in Ogaden, where ethnic Somalis sought a closer association with neighboring Somalia. A severe drought in the early 1980s caused widespread famine, resulting in a major international relief effort and giving rise to a disastrous government campaign to force millions of peasants to relocate in new villages. By 1990, there were an estimated 21 regional insurgencies. Mengistu fled the country in May 1991 and a rebel coalition government headed by Meles Zenawi of the Tigrayan Ethiopian People's Revolutionary Democratic Front was established pending multiparty national elections planned for 1993. Eritrea set up its own provisional government pending a scheduled 1993 referendum in which it was expected to vote for full independence.

WILLIAM H. LEWIS, George Washington University

DJIBOUTI

About a third of the way down the east coast of Africa lies the Great Horn. There, just before this landmass juts out into the sea, is the country of Djibouti (formerly the French Territory of the Afars and the Issas). Except for its location, this tiny, sun-parched country might have existed unnoticed by any but its immediate neighbors. Because it faces the Gulf of Aden, however, guarding the southern entrance to the Red Sea, Djibouti has been for thousands of years a focal point of trade between Europe and Asia.

In ancient times the country exported frankincense and myrrh, which the Gospels say the Three Wise Men brought to the infant Jesus. Salt was traded for its weight in gold. Now, however, Djibouti depends almost entirely on transit trade and related activities such as ship and railroad repair work to sustain the life of its people.

The Land. Djibouti covers 8,494 square miles (22,000 square kilometers) on the northeast coast of Africa. It is bordered on the north, west, and south by Ethiopia, on the southeast by the Somali Republic, and on the east by the Gulf of Aden. Most of the land is desert, particularly in the lowland interior. The country is characterized by three fairly distinct landforms. From a low-lying coastal plain the land rises to a series of mountain ranges that reach about 5,000 feet (1,520 meters) at their greatest height. There are small areas of forests on the mountain slopes. Just

Farmers sell their produce at the market in Djibouti.

FACTS AND FIGURES

OFFICIAL NAME: Republic of Djibouti.

NATIONALITY: Djiboutian(s).

CAPITAL: Djibouti.

LOCATION: East coast of Africa. **Boundaries:** Ethiopia, Red Sea, Somalia.

AREA: 8,958 sq. mi. (23,200 sq. km.).

PHYSICAL FEATURES: Highest point—Gouda Mountains (6,594 ft.; 2,010 m.). **Lowest point**—sea level. **Major lakes**—Abbe, Assal.

POPULATION: 346,300 (1991; annual growth 2.6%).

MAJOR LANGUAGES: French, Arabic (both official), Afar, Somali.

MAJOR RELIGION: Islam.

GOVERNMENT: Republic. **Head of state**—president. **Head of government**—prime minister. **Legislature**—Chamber of Deputies.

CHIEF CITIES: Djibouti, Dikhil, Ali-Sabieh.

ECONOMY: Chief agricultural products—dates, garden vegetables, livestock. **Industries and products**—transit trade, ships' supplies, meat-packing, construction plants, hides, milk products, bottled mineral water. **Chief exports**—hides and skins. **Chief imports**—machinery and electrical equipment, cotton goods, sugar, flour, chemicals.

MONETARY UNIT: Djibouti franc.

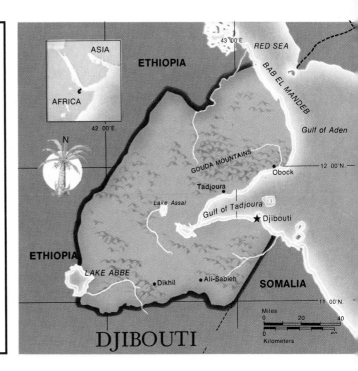

DJIBOUTI

beyond the mountains, the terrain is marked by high plateaus and sunken plains. Here and there the desolate landscape is dotted with sparse patches of grass and occasional scraggly shrubs, which provide meager forage for the herds of nomadic tribesmen.

Djibouti is a land of intense heat. The average temperature is over 85° F. (32° C.). The soil produces little, and the country has no permanent streams or freshwater lakes, so that irrigation is a major problem. In addition, rainfall is too erratic to be beneficial. Less than 5 in. (12.7 cm.) falls annually in the coastal areas. In the highlands, where there is a little farming, rainfall is more than 20 in. (51 cm.) annually.

Djibouti has no useful natural resources, little arable land, and almost no manufacturing. About half the people are nomads who eke out a living raising cattle, sheep, donkeys, and camels. Only a very small number of people work the land for its limited yields. The country's economic mainstay is the port of Djibouti. Because it is a free port, no customs duties are paid. Djibouti also owes much of its importance to its location on the waters leading to and from the Suez Canal. The city is a port of call for ships using the canal. Many of the city's people work on the docks and in ship-repair yards. Another important source of income is the railroad linking Ethiopia with the port of Djibouti. The port is Ethiopia's main outlet to the sea. Most of Ethiopia's imports and exports pass through Djibouti by way of the railroad.

The French military garrison, which remained in Djibouti after independence, also provides some revenue. In addition, France contributes an annual subsidy to keep the economy going.

The People. There are some 346,000 people in Djibouti. According to French Government estimates, the Afars, who are related to the Ethiopians, form the bulk of the population. The Issas, a Somali group with strong ties to the neighboring Somali Republic, are less numerous. It is difficult to determine the exact population figures because many Afars and Issas are nomads. Their search for pasture for their herds often takes them across the borders of the country. The coming of independence has had little effect on the nomadic people's way of life.

In addition to the two major population groups, there are also some Europeans, chiefly French, and Arabs in the coastal towns. Except for the Europeans, almost all of the people are Muslims. Languages spoken include French, Afar, Somali (spoken by the Issas), and Arabic.

Nearly half the population lives in **Djibouti.** Other population centers include **Tadjoura** on the gulf of the same name, **Dikhil** and **Ali-Sabieh** in the south, and **Obock** on the east coast.

History and Government.   Almost since the dawn of history Djibouti has been a starting point for migrations between Africa and Asia. Its closeness to the Middle East made it one of the first African areas to be dominated by the conquering Arabs. Between the 8th and 10th centuries, Arab warriors converted most of the people to Islam. For many centuries the area existed in isolation. In 1862, however, tribal chiefs at Obock ceded that territory to France. French control was extended south to Djibouti in succeeding years, and France was thus able to dominate shipping through the Suez Canal, opened in 1869. Djibouti became the administrative capital in 1896, and soon after, the boundaries of the French colony were defined and the area was given the name French Somaliland. In 1917, the Franco-Ethiopian Railroad, from the Ethiopian capital of Addis Ababa to Djibouti, was completed. In 1949 Djibouti became a free transit zone, greatly enhancing its commercial importance.

Internal self-government was granted to the territory in 1957, when the Territorial Assembly was established. As a result of the 1958 referendum the Territory became part of the French Republic, entitled to elect one deputy and one senator to the French legislature. In 1967, in a referendum on the question of independence, the Territory voted to remain part of the French Republic. That same year, the name of the Territory was changed from French Somaliland to the French Territory of the Afars and the Issas. Ten years later, however, the people voted for independence, which was declared on June 27, 1977. The government consists of a directly elected president and legislature and an appointed prime minister. In 1981, Djibouti became a one-party state.

Two problems facing Djibouti are the lack of a true economic base upon which to develop the country and continued tensions between the Afars and the Issas. In the 1980s and early 1990s, refugees fleeing ethnic violence in Ethiopia and Somalia imposed an economic burden on Djibouti and increased social tensions there. An Issa group in northern Somalia is seeking union with Djibouti, while northern Afar rebels demanding a greater role in Djibouti's Issa-dominated government have allied themselves with Ethiopian Afars demanding autonomy. In November 1991, the Afar Front for the Restoration of Unity and Democracy (FRUD) launched open war against the government. France sent a peacekeeping force to Djibouti and pressured President Hassan Gouled Aptidon, who had served as president since independence, to implement political reforms to avert civil war. In 1992, as FRUD and other rebel groups gained control of much of the country, Gouled introduced a draft constitution that restored multipartyism but retained a strong presidency. The opposition considered his proposed reforms inadequate, and strife continued.

Reviewed by PRESS AND INFORMATION SERVICE OF THE FRENCH EMBASSY, New York

Once-peaceful Mogadishu was devastated by civil war in the early 1990s.

SOMALIA

As the shadows lengthened across the Somali plain, the caravan arrived at the watering place. The men and women of the caravan had traveled many miles in hot, dusty weather, and the well was their meeting place. Men in white togas met with hearty greetings, women gathered in small groups to chat, children ran from group to group, and animals restlessly awaited their turn at the water trough. People looked forward to evening, when they would sit around a fire and describe their adventures in the bush and exchange news with relatives from the city.

By the early 1990s, however, such peaceful scenes had become rare in Somalia, which was torn by a civil war between rival clans. Fierce fighting and disrupted food deliveries led to widespread starvation among Somali refugees. In December 1992, the United Nations approved a military intervention by a U.S.-led multinational force to protect the delivery of relief supplies to Somalia.

THE LAND

The Somali Democratic Republic, or Somalia, as it is also called, is located in eastern Africa. Its northern coast faces the Gulf of Aden, and its eastern coast overlooks the Indian Ocean. Kenya, Ethiopia, and Djibouti are the three bordering countries.

Larger in size than France, Somalia has an area of 246,200 sq. mi. (637,657 sq. km.). **Mogadishu** (Mogadiscio), on the coast near the Equator, is the capital and chief port. Other important cities are Hargeisa, Merca, Berbera, and Kismayu. Three important regional capitals are Burao, Belet Uen, and Galkayu.

White stone buildings stand along the waterfront of Mogadishu.

The chief rivers are the Webi Shebeli, which runs through the central part of Somalia, and the Juba, which flows in the southern region. Both rivers have their sources in neighboring Ethiopia. They rise in that country's highands and then flow southward across Somalia.

Somalia has a dry tropical climate with an annual rainfall of under 20 inches (50 centimeters). A large part of the land is arid semidesert. There are mountains in the northern part of the country. The southeastern region is low and flat.

Somalia has a coastline of some 1,600 miles (2,600 kilometers) but there are no major natural harbors. Because of offshore coral reefs, travelers and goods on modern oceangoing vessels must be carried ashore in launches. Major improvements in the ports of Mogadishu, Berbera, and Kismayu are being carried out. Dhows, long sailing vessels with triangular sails, are quite active in coastal waters and across the Gulf of Aden to the city of Aden. Today, they are increasingly being replaced by less colorful but more practical power boats. The country has no railroads.

During its long history, the Somali region has been called by many names. In ancient times it was said to be the land of God. At another time it was known as the land of milk and myrrh. *Somal* means "milk of the cow or goat," and the favorite food of the Somalis, especially the herdsmen, is milk. Myrrh and frankincense grow in the northern part of the republic and, indeed, the myrrh and frankincense the Three Wise Men carried to Bethlehem may have come from this region. It may be that Somalia was the Land of Punt mentioned in ancient Egyptian writings. Today, the region is called the Horn of Africa, and if you turn the map of Africa sideways, so that east is north, you may be able to see why. From this perspective the part that juts out into the Gulf of Aden and the Indian Ocean resembles a rhino's horn.

FACTS AND FIGURES

OFFICIAL NAME: Somali Democratic Republic.

NATIONALITY: Somali(s).

CAPITAL: Mogadishu (Mogadiscio).

LOCATION: Northeastern Africa. **Boundaries**—Gulf of Aden, Indian Ocean, Kenya, Ethiopia, and Djibouti.

AREA: 246,200 sq. mi. (637,657 sq. km.).

PHYSICAL FEATURES: Highest point—8,250 ft. (2,515 m.). **Lowest point**—sea level. **Chief rivers**—Webi Shebeli, Juba.

POPULATION: 8,248,133 (1989).

MAJOR LANGUAGES: Somali, Italian, English, Arabic.

MAJOR RELIGION: Islam.

GOVERNMENT: Republic. **Head of government**—president. **Legislature**—People's Assembly.

CHIEF CITIES: Mogadishu (377,000), Hargeisa (70,000), Kismayu (70,000), Merca (60,000), Berbera (55,000).

ECONOMY: Chief minerals—iron ore, tin, limestone, sandstone. **Chief agricultural products**—bananas, sugar, maize, cotton, peanuts, sesame, sorghum, cattle, camels, goats, sheep. **Industries and products**—food processing, soap, canning, textiles, leather. **Chief exports**—bananas, hides and skins, wood, cotton, fish, oil seeds and kernels. **Chief imports**—machinery, chemicals, petroleum products, cloth, and grain.

MONETARY UNIT: 1 Somalo, or Somali shilling = 100 cents.

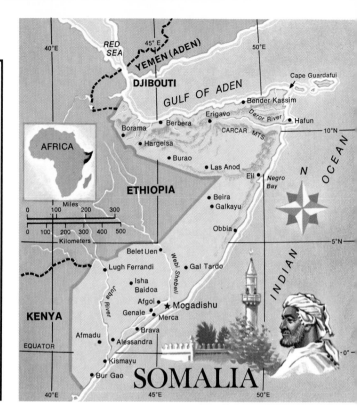

THE PEOPLE

The Somalis who live in the republic have strong ties with other Somalis who live in the neighboring countries of Ethiopia, Kenya, and Djibouti. Many Somalis in these three countries hope that someday the territories in which they live will be incorporated in the Somali Republic.

Although Somalis vary in physical appearance (tall, short, dark, light) the typical Somali is dark-skinned with dark, almond-shaped eyes and thick curly hair. Some men and boys in the urban areas wear Western-style clothing, but young boys and many men in the countryside wear the traditional *futa*, or toga. Women and girls wear sarongs made of many yards of colorful cloth, wrapped around the body and tied at the right shoulder, leaving the left shoulder bare. In the cities, as well as in the interior, the women carry their babies in slings on their backs. The women and girls wear scarves over their heads, while the men and boys wear turbans or Muslim caps of woven or embroidered material.

Way of Life

The occupations of the Somalis and their way of life are largely determined by the climate, which is dry and tropical. Wherever there is enough water and arable land, the people plant gardens. In the southern part of the republic, near the Webi Shebeli and Juba rivers, are banana and sugarcane plantations. There are also farms that grow sesame, sorghum, peanuts, cotton, fruits, and vegetables.

Most Somalis, about 70 percent of the population, are shepherds, with herds of camels and cows and flocks of sheep and goats. These shepherds live on their home grazing grounds part of the year. During the dry seasons, they round up their herds and flocks and travel to more distant areas. Each clan has its own traditional lands. In the past, wars

The marketplace in Genale is often crowded with shoppers.

often broke out when one clan trespassed upon the territory of another. Even today the clans guard their traditional wells and grazing areas.

Family Life

A typical pastoral group consists of an extended family—perhaps as many as 150 persons. Since the Somalis are Muslims, men may have as many as four wives, although few can afford this many. In an extended family, one might find a grandfather and his wives, several of his sons and their wives, and all the grandchildren. Married daughters live with their husbands' clan groups. The men and older boys herd the camels, and the women, girls, and smaller boys take care of the cows, sheep, and goats. The women and girls are also the camp makers.

Wherever the extended family stops to pasture the animals, the women set up temporary beehive huts of woven straw mats spread over a frame of curved branches. When the group moves on, the women dismantle the huts and pack them on the camels.

Education and Culture

The Somalis have a large oral tradition. Legends and songs are passed by word of mouth from one generation to another, and much of the nation's history is recorded in poems that have never been written down.

Since the Muslim religion frowns on the reproduction of the human figure in art forms, the Somalis, unlike many other Africans, do not make masks. The designs they use to decorate clay pots, woven baskets, wooden dishes, combs, spoons, and other objects are geometrical figures and lines. In recent years, Somali stamps have won several international prizes for their extraordinary beauty.

Because so large a part of the population is on the move most of the year, only a small number of boys and girls—those who live in the settled areas—go to school regularly. There is a university in Mogadishu, and in other towns throughout the nation there are elementary and vocational schools and a few secondary schools. Since the northern part of the republic was governed by Great Britain and the southern part by Italy, English, Italian, and Arabic are national written languages. The Somali language is spoken throughout the land, but until relatively recently no official written version existed. In 1974, however, a uniform written Somali language was adopted by the government.

HISTORY AND GOVERNMENT

Some Somalis believe that their ancestors came to Africa across the Gulf of Aden from Arabia sometime around the 7th century. It is known that Arabs migrated to the area, intermarried with the local inhabitants, who were primarily nomadic shepherds, and introduced the Muslim faith. This was the beginning of the Somali nation. It was a nation of shepherds, divided into a number of clans, each claiming an Arab migrant as its founder. Over the centuries the clans spread over the semiarid steppes in search of water and grazing lands and developed a common language and culture.

The modern history of Somalia began with the British and Italian colonization in the mid-1880s. Zeila, Berbera, and the area around them were governed by the British as British Somaliland from the 1880s to 1960. Much farther down the coastline, from Cape Guardafui to Kenya, is a stretch of land that was an Italian colony, Italian Somaliland. During World War II and immediately after it was occupied by the British. After the war the colony became a United Nations trust territory administered by Italy. The Somali in British Somaliland began to agitate for independence, achieving it in June 1960. In July the trust territory became independent, and the two new states joined to form the Somali Republic.

The Somali Republic was a parliamentary democracy until 1969, when, after the assassination of the president, the armed forces seized power. A military junta led by Mohammed Siad Barré, who became president, declared the country a socialist state named the Somali Democratic Republic. In 1977–78 Somalia unsuccessfully invaded Ethiopia's Ogaden region, an area long inhabited by Somali clans. A new constitution was approved in 1979, and parliamentary elections were held.

Armed opposition to the dictatorial Siad Barré began in 1988, and he was forced to flee the country on January 27, 1991. Since that time, the country has been engulfed in civil war. Northern Somalia proclaimed its independence as the Somaliland Republic in May 1991, two rival groups battled for control of Mogadishu, and various factions fought each other in other parts of the country. Due to drought and strife, much of the nation's livestock died and farmers were kept from planting their crops. As international organizations negotiated to end the fighting and distribute food aid, it was feared that as many as one-third of all Somalis might die of disease and starvation by the end of 1992.

MARGARET F. CASTAGNO; ALPHONSO A. CASTAGNO, Director
African Studies Center, Boston University

Reviewed by ABDURAHMAN HUSSEIN MOHAMOUD, Counselor
Embassy of the Somali Republic, Washington, D.C.

KENYA

Kenya is named after its most famous mountain, Mount Kenya, which towers above the surrounding countryside. The Kikuyu, who live near the mountain, call it Kirinyaga. Their neighbors, the Kamba, call it Ki-nyaa. Both names mean "the place where there are ostriches." The mountain is usually covered by clouds, but at certain times of the year the thin jagged finger of its peak can be seen for many miles.

THE LAND

Kenya is located in East Africa, and the equator divides the country into two almost equal parts. Kenya is bounded on the south by Tanzania, on the west by Uganda, on the north by Sudan and Ethiopia, and on the

Nairobi, the capital of Kenya, is one of the most cosmopolitan cities in Africa.

Vendors with colorful baskets of flowers can be found on many Nairobi streets.

east by Somalia and the Indian Ocean. The total area of the country is 224,960 square miles (582,646 square kilometers).

Despite Kenya's location on the equator, there are great variations of vegetation and climate in the country. The main geographical divisions in Kenya are the coastal belt; the highlands and Great Rift Valley; and the dry scrublands and savanna grasslands, called the bush, which make up the largest sector of the country.

The Coast.   The Kenya coast has long stretches of white sand lined with palm trees. Not far offshore in the blue Indian Ocean is a coral reef that can be seen at low tide. The beaches inside the reef and the excellent deep-sea fishing outside the barrier make the coastal region of Kenya an attractive place for tourists and vacationers.

The Bush.   Within 20 miles (32 kilometers) of the coast and stretching to the north and west is the most typical of Kenyan landscapes, the bush. The bush is a large expanse of low thorn trees and scrub brush dotted with baobab trees. A large, leafless tree, the baobab is shaped like a bottle. This is the kind of vegetation that covers most of Kenya. Because of the poorness of the soil and the lack of rainfall, the bush has been inhabited mainly by animals, hunters, and the nomadic peoples who roam with their herds of cattle. With little agricultural potential, it is increasingly being used for game parks and animal preserves.

Kenya's two important rivers, the Tana and the Athi, flow eastward through the bush to the Indian Ocean. Oil prospecting is being undertaken along the Tana River. Since Kenya has no petroleum, the discovery of oil would make the bush country much more valuable.

The Highlands.   Most of Kenya's people live in the southwest. This is a region of high plateau and mountains, with more rainfall and better soil than the rest of the country. Mount Kenya, rising from the plateau to a height of 17,040 feet (5,193 meters), is the second highest mountain in Africa. (Kilimanjaro in Tanzania is the highest.) The Aberdare Range ex-

The modern harbor in Mombasa is equipped to handle large oceangoing ships.

tends south and west from Mount Kenya, and the mountains are covered by a thick bamboo forest.

The Great Rift Valley. The eastern arm of the Great Rift Valley stretches throughout the length of Kenya. It is a continuation of a gigantic valley that runs from Syria through the Red Sea and then south through Africa to Mozambique. In Kenya the valley is shallow and wide in the north, but grows steeper and narrower as it traverses the plateau country to the south. The length of the valley is broken up by a series of lakes, including Lake Rudolf in the north, and lakes Nakuru and Naivasha near Nairobi.

West of the Great Rift Valley, on the Kenya-Uganda border, stands Mount Elgon. It is a large solitary mountain, whose slopes are covered with excellent agricultural land. Southwest of Mount Elgon is Lake Victoria, which Kenya shares with Uganda and Tanzania. Kenya's only large port on the lake is Kisumu. From the shores of Lake Victoria a hilly region known as Nyanza rises toward the plateau country.

THE CITIES

Nairobi. Kenya's capital city, Nairobi, lies at the southern edge of the high plateau country. It is often said that Nairobi has one of the finest climates in the world, and this is a valid claim. It is the altitude of 5,500 feet (1,650 m.) that makes Nairobi so delightful. Most days are warm, but at night the temperature drops to about 45 degrees Fahrenheit (7 degrees Celsius), and one must sleep with blankets. Nairobi has sun for so many hours each day that residents call it the Garden City in the Sun.

Nairobi's name comes from a Masai word meaning "a cold stream." The site of the city was chosen in 1900 because it was the last level

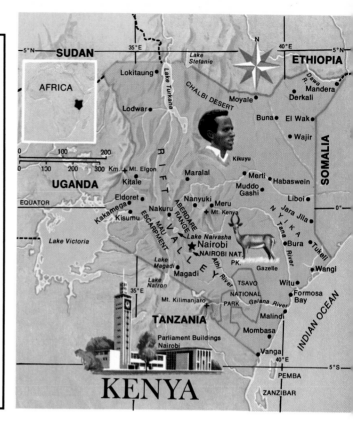

FACTS AND FIGURES

OFFICIAL NAME: Republic of Kenya.

NATIONALITY: Kenyan(s).

CAPITAL: Nairobi.

LOCATION: East coast of Africa. **Boundaries**—Ethiopia, Somalia, Indian Ocean, Tanzania, Uganda, Sudan.

AREA: 224,081 sq. mi. (580,367 sq. km.).

PHYSICAL FEATURES: Highest point—Mount Kenya (17,040 ft.; 5,193 m.). **Lowest point**—sea level. **Chief rivers**—Tana, Athi. **Major lakes**—Victoria, Turkana, Naivasha.

POPULATION: 24,346,250 (1989).

MAJOR LANGUAGES: Swahili (official) English, local languages.

MAJOR RELIGIONS: Christianity, traditional African religions, Islam.

GOVERNMENT: Republic. **Head of government**—president. **Legislature**—one-house National Assembly. **International cooperation**—United Nations, Commonwealth of Nations, Organization of African Unity (OAU).

CHIEF CITIES: Nairobi, Mombasa.

ECONOMY: Chief minerals—soda ash, fluorspar, limestone. **Chief agricultural products**—livestock, sisal, coffee, tea, cassava, sweet potatoes, corn, millet, beans, peas, nuts, fruits, sugar, cotton. **Industries and products**—food processing, livestock products, oil refining, cement. **Chief exports**—petroleum products, coffee, tea. **Chief imports**—crude petroleum, machinery, automobiles, appliances, iron and steel, chemicals.

MONETARY UNIT: Kenya shilling.

ground before the railroad entered the high rugged mountain country to the north. Today Nairobi is a mecca for tourists and the starting point for most safaris, whether for hunting, bird-watching, or photography. In Kenya the word "safari" means any kind of trip.

Mombasa.   The major city of the coast area is Mombasa, a busy tropical port. The city is built around the large modern harbor of Kilindini. Ships from all over the world come here with goods for much of East Africa, since Mombasa is also the harbor for Kenya's landlocked neighbor to the west, Uganda.

THE PEOPLE

Kenya has an interesting and diverse population. Among the largest groups are the Kikuyu, the Luo, the Luhya, and the Masai. There are also small communities of Europeans, Asians, and Arabs.

The Kikuyu.   Just north of Nairobi is the home of the Kikuyu people. Their land is marked by a series of hills, ridges, and valleys centered around Mount Kenya. Traditionally, the mountain was sacred to the Kikuyu, who believed that their god, Ngai, resided on the mountaintop.

The Kikuyu are excellent farmers who grow coffee, tea, and pyrethrum (a source of insecticides) to sell. They grow sweet potatoes and other vegetables for their own use. The Kikuyu also keep large herds of goats and sheep. Kikuyu women and girls work on the small plots of land around their homes. The traditional round Kikuyu houses, together with their small plots of land, are known as *shambas. Shamba* was originally a Swahili word meaning "garden." Although agriculture is still their main occupation, many Kikuyu now commute to work in Nairobi's factories and stores.

The Luo.   The Luo live mainly on the shores of Lake Victoria and in the Nyanza region. They are good fishermen and earn money from a tasty fish called *tilapia,* which they sell to markets all over Kenya. The Luo are also farmers. Although their land is not as fertile as that of the Kikuyu, it is one of the best corn-growing regions in Kenya. The Luo also grow millet and other cereals, and they keep cows and goats that provide both meat and milk.

The Masai. Perhaps the most striking of the African people of Kenya are the tall, stately Masai. The Masai are nomads, who live and travel with their large herds of cattle in the open grassland to the south and west of Nairobi. They destroy their houses, which are made of clay and cow dung, as they move with their cattle to better grazing land. The Masai traditionally wore skins, but their togalike outfits are now made from sheets and blankets. For many years after the Europeans arrived in Kenya, the Masai would not abandon their traditional ways and adopt Western modes of life. Now, however, they are beginning to change, as many of the other African peoples have done.

The Europeans. The European population, particularly the British, has played an important part in Kenya's history. Europeans first settled in Kenya in large numbers in the early 1900s. The majority of the settlers became farmers in an area that was called the White Highlands. This is a fertile agricultural region in the plateau country, which the British government restricted for the use of the settlers. In 1960 the White Highlands were opened to Kenya's African citizens. After independence some of the Europeans remained in Kenya and became citizens.

The Asians. In Kenya there is yet another group that is important to the nation. This is the Indian population, or Asians, as they are called in Kenya. The first large group of Asians arrived in Kenya in 1895, just as work was beginning on the railroad that runs through the heart of Kenya, from Mombasa to Kisumu. Many of these men stayed on after the completion of the railway, and many others came later because of the promise of better jobs and a richer life. Most of the Asians came from areas near Bombay, India. Yet the Asian community is made up of a great variety of peoples: tall, bearded Sikhs in turbans; followers of the Aga Khan, who are known as Ismailis; and members of many of the Hindu castes. In Kenya the Asians became shopkeepers, artisans, clerks, and lower-echelon government workers.

After Kenya became independent the majority of Asians chose to retain British passports rather than become citizens of Kenya. In 1967 Kenya passed a new immigration law in order to promote Africanization of Kenya's economy. According to this law non-Kenyans, including European and Asian residents, must obtain work permits and cannot be employed unless there are no Kenyan citizens available or unless their employment is considered valuable to Kenya. After this law went into effect there was an outpouring of Asian emigrants to Britain. By 1979 the number of Asians in Kenya had fallen to 80,000, compared to 180,000 in 1968.

The Arabs. Merchants from Arabia have been trading with Kenya for many centuries, and Arabs have lived in Mombasa and other smaller Kenyan coastal cities for hundreds of years. Arabian sailors still come to Kenya in dhows, large wooden boats, which sail down the Indian Ocean from Arabian ports, mainly Aden and Oman. When the northeast monsoon wind blows down the Indian Ocean from December to March

Dancers participate in one of Kenya's many traditional festivals.

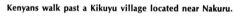

Kenyans walk past a Kikuyu village located near Nakuru.

each year, the dhows come to Kenya. They return to Arabia during April and May, when the wind shifts and blows from the south.

Language and Religion

In May, 1970, the government declared Swahili to be the national language of Kenya. Swahili is a combination of several Bantu languages and Arabic. It has absorbed many words from Portuguese and English, as well as from Urdu, a Persianized form of Hindustani. English and Hindustani are also spoken by many Kenyans, and there are also several common African languages, including Kikuyu, Luo, Luhya, and Masai.

The majority of Kenyans are animists, but many other variations of religious beliefs are also represented. The Arabs and the Somali people in the northeast are Muslims, as are some of the Asians. Most of the Asians are Hindus. Europeans and some Africans are members of the Roman Catholic Church or of various Protestant sects.

Education

Under British rule the pace of education for Africans was very slow. But as independence drew near, steps were taken to improve the system. The number of primary and secondary schools increased dramatically,

Muslims from all over Kenya worship in the magnificent Khoja mosque in Nairobi.

Workers pick tea leaves on a plantation in Kenya.

and some private schools previously closed to Africans were integrated. In 1974 education for the first several grades was made free, the first step in a government policy of free universal education. The University of East Africa was organized in 1956, with headquarters in Uganda and branches in Tanzania and Kenya. However, in 1970 the University of East Africa was dissolved and each of the three countries now maintains its own university. Young Kenyans attend the University College of Nairobi, the country's major institute, as well as travel abroad in large numbers for a university education.

Kenyan students must learn Swahili, the country's official language. In many Kenyan primary schools English is taught along with the vernacular languages, such as Kikuyu, Luo, and Masai.

ECONOMY

Most Kenyans are farmers, and the Kenya Government is working hard to expand the production of the nation's major crops. The most important crops, and Kenya's leading exports, are coffee and tea. Livestock raising and dairying are also important to the economy and are being encouraged by the government.

After agriculture Kenya's major industry is tourism. The location of the country, its extremely pleasant climate, and the magnificent game parks are attractions for a growing number of tourists from all over the world. Several large new hotels have been built around Nairobi to serve the tourists, and more hotels and other facilities are planned.

Kenya has almost no important mineral resources, although some soda ash and cement are produced for export. Manufacturing still plays a small role in the economy. Most manufacturing involves the processing of agricultural commodities. An oil refinery has been constructed at Mombasa, and further heavy industry is planned.

Animals roam freely in Tsavo National Park, a game sanctuary near Nairobi.

PLACES OF INTEREST

Every year thousands of people visit Kenya's game parks to see the many herds of elephants, buffalo, rhinoceroses, leopards, zebras, wildebeests, giraffes, ostriches, gazelles, and lions. Tsavo National Game Park between Nairobi and Mombasa is one of the largest game preserves. But perhaps the most interesting preserve is Nairobi National Park, located just a few miles outside the capital. Photographers must be careful when they take pictures of animals here, for the skyscrapers of the city can be seen in the background and often spoil a picture.

Other tourist attractions in Kenya include the Kenya National Museum in Nairobi, Dr. Leakey's archeological excavations at Gamble's Cave in the Great Rift Valley, and Fort Jesus in Mombasa. Fort Jesus, which was originally built by the Portuguese, has now been restored and also serves as a museum.

HISTORY AND GOVERNMENT

Africans were living in Kenya thousands of years ago. The famous 20th-century anthropologist Dr. Louis S. B. Leakey discovered remains indicating that the first beings we can truly call men evolved in East Africa.

The first written records we have of Kenya, however, date only from about the 7th century A.D., when Arab traders settled along the coast. Among the towns built by the Arabs are Mombasa and Malindi. The first Europeans to arrive in what is now Kenya were the Portuguese. Vasco da Gama landed at Malindi after rounding the Cape of Good Hope in 1498. The Portuguese built forts and trading posts along the coast, but these lasted only a little over 200 years. By 1740 the Arabs had forced the Portuguese out.

In the 19th century American ships began to call at Kenyan ports. The British also became interested in the area, mainly because of their efforts to end the slave trade between East Africa and Asia. British administration in the area was first under the control of the Imperial British East Africa Company. In 1895 the British Government assumed responsibility for what are now Kenya and Uganda and named the area the East Africa Protectorate. In the same year the British began construction of a railway from Mombasa to Uganda.

In 1920 Kenya and Uganda were separated and what is now Kenya became the Kenya Colony and Protectorate. The "Protectorate" in the name referred to a 10-mi. (16-km.)-wide coastal strip that was leased from the Sultan of Zanzibar, the area's nominal ruler. When Kenya became independent, this strip became an integral part of the country.

In October 1952, the British government declared a state of emergency in Kenya because of the Mau Mau crisis. Mau Mau was a secret organization composed mainly of Kikuyu people, and its aim was to drive the European settlers out of the territory and gain independence. During the emergency, Jomo Kenyatta, the Africans' chief spokesman, and several other political leaders were jailed. Kenyatta was not finally freed until 1961. After his release he resumed control of the African freedom movement. On December 12, 1963, Kenya became independent, and one year later it became a republic. Kenyatta became the first prime minister and then the first president of the republic.

After Independence

Kenya's constitution provides for a popularly elected president, who normally serves a five-year term. The one-house National Assembly consists of 170 members, of whom 158 are elected by universal suffrage and 12 are appointed by the president. There is only one legal political party, the Kenya Africa National Union, originally headed by Kenyatta.

Since independence Kenya has faced many problems, including difficulties caused by the government's program of Africanization of Kenyan life. Also in the first years of independence, Kenya and the Somali Republic (now called Somalia) almost went to war over the wanderings of the nomadic Somali people across the Kenya-Somalia border. Both countries felt entitled to rule the Somalis and their territory, but the Somalis resisted efforts by the government of Kenya to exercise authority over them. In 1967 both governments agreed to seek peaceful ways of resolving the problem. Another problem arose in July 1969, when Tom Mboya, the minister for economic planning and development, was assassinated in Nairobi. The murder of Mboya reawakened racial tensions in Kenya, because Mboya was a Luo and his assassin was a Kikuyu. Kenyatta, a Kikuyu, eased some of the tension by grooming a non-Kikuyu, Daniel arap Moi, for the presidency.

Kenyatta died in August 1978. He was succeeded by the vice-president, Daniel arap Moi, who was then elected president in his own right. Kenya officially became a one-party state in June 1982. About two months later, an alliance of junior military men, urban laborers, and university students tried to topple the government. President Moi survived the coup attempt and reorganized the air force to root out dissidents. President Moi was reelected without opposition in 1983 and 1988. But deteriorating economic conditions gave rise to increasing unrest. In December 1991, under pressure from international aid donors, the constitution was revised to allow multiple political parties.

JACK H. MOWER, School of Advanced International Studies, Johns Hopkins University
Reviewed by EMBASSY OF KENYA TO THE UNITED STATES
and PERMANENT MISSION OF KENYA TO THE UNITED NATIONS

Village huts dot the rolling green plains of Uganda.

UGANDA

"Where is the source of the Nile?" This question fascinated 19th-century European explorers in Africa. Years passed, lives were lost, and a great deal of money was spent before the answer was found—Lake Victoria in Uganda. When John Hanning Speke and James Grant discovered the source of the White Nile in 1862, they also guaranteed a continuing European interest in Uganda. In addition to affecting Uganda's history, this European interest in the Nile and Uganda's position in relation to the river eventually changed the whole course of East African history.

THE LAND

Sir Winston Churchill once called Uganda a fairy tale. Great lakes, one of the world's major rivers, snowcapped mountains, and an enormous valley are all found in Uganda. What is lacking is a seacoast—Uganda is landlocked in the center of the East African plateau.

Along the border with Zaïre, the deep trough of the Great Rift Valley cuts through Uganda. A number of lakes, including Edward, Albert, and George, dot the floor of the valley. Between lakes Edward and Albert, the Ruwenzori mountains rise to heights of over 16,000 feet (4,900 meters) along the Great Rift Valley scarp. It is thought that the Ruwenzori are the fabled Mountains of the Moon that ancient geographers often mentioned. Along the Rwanda border the Virunga range (Mufumbiro Mountains), which contains some still active volcanoes, rises to heights of over 14,000 feet (4,260 m.).

Stretching north and east from the Great Rift Valley and the mountains, most of Uganda is a plateau ranging from 3,000 to 5,000 feet (900–1,500 m.). This altitude gives Uganda a pleasant climate, with little variation in temperature during the year. Throughout the southern portion of the country rainfall is usually plentiful the year round, but in the north much less rain falls and there is a dry season during June and July.

Lake Victoria, the source of the White Nile, dominates southeastern Uganda. With an area of 91,134 square miles (236,036 square kilometers), it is second in size only to Lake Superior in North America. The Nile leaves Victoria at Jinja and flows west through Lake Kyoga to Lake Albert. This stretch of the river is known as the Victoria Nile, and on its journey to Lake Albert it drops over 130 feet (40 m.) through a spectacular gorge at Murchison Falls. Once it leaves Lake Albert and turns north toward the Sudan, the river becomes known as the Albert Nile. (An article on the NILE RIVER appears in this volume.)

North of Lake Victoria on the Uganda-Kenya border, Mount Elgon, a solitary extinct volcano, rises to a height of 14,178 feet (4,321 m.). The slopes of Mount Elgon are among the most fertile agricultural lands in Uganda.

Cities.   A growing number of rural Ugandans are leaving the countryside for the city, but urbanites are still a minority in Uganda. The capital city, **Kampala**, like Rome, is said to stand on seven hills. With a population of over 500,000, Kampala is the largest city in Uganda and a center for commerce and manufacturing as well as government. The city was also the traditional capital of the kingdom of Buganda.

Just a few miles from Kampala, along the shore of Lake Victoria, is **Entebbe**, the old British colonial capital. Uganda's international airport is located at Entebbe. **Jinja**, the second largest city in Uganda, lies on the banks of the Victoria Nile. Jinja has become a growing industrial center since the inauguration of the Owen Falls Dam in 1954.

Kampala, Uganda's capital, is one of East Africa's pleasantest cities.

THE PEOPLE

The population of Uganda is over 98 percent African and includes Bantu, Nilotic, Nilo-Hamitic, and Sudanese peoples. Asians, mostly merchants of Indian and Pakistani extraction, were once important in the commercial sector of the country. In 1972, however, under government order, most of the Asians, especially non-citizens, were expelled from Uganda. A few Europeans and Americans still remain in the country, most of them temporarily in Uganda on contract as technical assistants and advisers to the government and to educational institutions.

The Nile River acts as a dividing line between the Bantu and the Nilotes and Nilo-Hamites. The Bantu generally are found south of the river and the other groups to the north.

The Bantu

Among the Bantu, the Baganda are the largest group, making up about 16 percent of the total population. They live in the area around Kampala and Entebbe, along Lake Victoria. For centuries Baganda society was organized into a kingdom called Buganda. The kingdom was ruled by a *kabaka* (king). Local chiefs were appointed by the *kabaka* and acted as an advisory council, or parliament, known as the *lukiko*. The *kabaka* was also assisted by a *katikiro,* or prime minister. Some clans had hereditary duties—such as keeping watch over the fire that burned outside the *kabaka's* palace throughout his reign. Most of the people were peasants who farmed the fertile land of the kingdom. Under British colonial administration, Buganda was permitted to keep its monarch and its traditional institutions. But in 1966, after a long conflict between the central government of Uganda and the kingdom, the *kabaka* was forced into exile, and Buganda was divided into a number of districts ruled directly by the central government.

As in the past, most of the Baganda today are farmers, living in isolated family homesteads rather than villages or towns. The traditional Baganda house is shaped like a beehive, with a thatched roof, but houses of mud bricks with metal roofs are increasingly popular. Long, colorfully patterned cotton dresses are the usual garb of Baganda women, while the men wear either long white robes or Western-style clothing.

Bananas are the principal food crop and are cultivated mostly by the women. In addition to being the staple food, bananas are often used to make a type of beer and to distill a unique drink—*waragi*—also called banana gin. Coffee and cotton, the cash crops, are cultivated by the men, but at harvesttime the whole family works to gather the crop.

Other important Bantu peoples in Uganda include the Banyoro, the Batoro, and the Banyankole. Like the Baganda, these peoples had established kingdoms in precolonial times. The Banyoro, the Batoro, and the Banyankole are mostly farmers. The Banyankole also raise long-horned cattle famous throughout Africa.

Nilotes and Nilo-Hamites

The Karamojong are a Nilo-Hamitic people who live in the dry savanna of northeastern Uganda. Cattle are wealth to the Karamonjong. Therefore the number of cows in a herd, rather than their quality, is important. A Karamojong man may be called by the name of his favorite cow, and he often trains the horns of this cow to grow in decorative

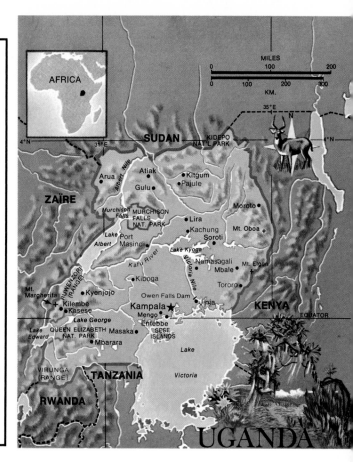

shapes. A man spends most of his time looking after his cattle, often talking and singing to them. Women raise grain and other foods to supplement the basic diet of milk and blood from the cattle. The Karamojong usually slaughter cattle for meat only on special occasions.

Cattle form the major portion of the bride price, which a man must pay in order to obtain a wife. But the payment of cattle does not mean that a man is buying a wife. It is an act that ties the two families together, and it ensures that all the kin will have an interest in keeping the marriage stable.

The great majority of the other Nilotes and Nilo-Hamites in northern Uganda are also herders whose lives are centered around their cattle. Unlike their Bantu neighbors to the south these herders have never been organized into highly centralized kingdoms. In addition to the Karamojong, other important groups living in northern Uganda include the Acholi, the Alur, the Teso, the Langi, and the Lugbara.

WAY OF LIFE

Education. School attendance is not compulsory, and most students must pay fees. Primary schooling lasts 7 years, and over half of all primary-school-age children now attend classes. Secondary schools are divided into four categories: grammar schools, technical schools, farm schools, and primary-teacher-training schools. The grammar school course lasts 6 years and is designed as preparation for a university education.

Makerere University College is the oldest institution of higher education in East Africa. For several decades Makerere has been serving

Young boys, on their way home from school, stop to watch friends play soccer.

Kenya, Uganda, Tanzania, Malawi, Zambia, and other neighbors. Students from Rwanda, Burundi, the Sudan, and Nigeria also came to Makerere. Overseas students included Europeans, North Americans, and Japanese.

Religion. About 50 percent of the Ugandans are Christians—almost equally divided between Roman Catholics and Protestants. There is also a significant Muslim minority. The remainder of the people follow traditional religions. Many of these religions are animistic, and they often involve some form of ancestor-worship.

Economy. The economic legacy of the rule of Idi Amin in the years from 1971 to 1979 was chaos. In the early 1980's the country had no functional economy. Uganda, however, is potentially rich. Its location at the head of the Nile has important economic implications. The Owen Falls Dam is one of the keys to Uganda's industrial development. The power generated at Owen Falls has supplied much of Uganda's electrical needs, and surplus power had been exported to Kenya. A textile plant and a brewery were among the industries attracted to Jinja after the dam was built.

Nevertheless, Uganda is basically an agricultural country. The major cash crops have been coffee and cotton, which accounted for the bulk of the country's exports in 1970. Uganda had been the largest producer of coffee in the Commonwealth of Nations. In many African countries white settlers introduced plantation farming of cash crops. But in Uganda white settlement was discouraged and little plantation farming developed. Almost all of the coffee and cotton was grown by Africans. However, the Asians traditionally handled the processing of the crops. Tea, sugar, and peanuts were also cash crops.

The most common food crops are bananas, maize, sweet potatoes, and millet. The bananas grown are of two types: the familiar edible fruit and the plantain, or cooking banana. The raising of livestock, mainly cattle, sheep, and goats, is concentrated in the northeastern Karamoja

Water from the Victoria Nile gushes through the Owen Falls Dam at Jinja.

area and in the southwest. Because one seventh of the country's total area is open water, fishing has always been an important part of the Ugandan economy. A sizable proportion of the catch is exported to the other East African countries. Recently fish farming has been encouraged by the government.

Copper is Uganda's major mineral resource. The copper mines at Kilembe in the Ruwenzori began operations in the 1950's. The development of the copper industry was aided by the extension of the railway to Kasese in western Uganda.

Workers in a cotton field. Cotton is one of Uganda's chief crops.

Before the 1970's tourism was a good source of income for Uganda. Thousands of tourists came each year to visit the game parks. But after Idi Amin took power in 1971, tourism declined because people feared the violence that had spread over Uganda. Under the present anarchic conditions there is no tourist industry.

In 1952 the Uganda Development Corporation was founded by the government to promote economic development. The corporation financed projects in mining, hotels, fisheries, and agriculture. Its activities nearly ceased during the 1970's when Amin was in power, and there has been no success in reviving it.

Until 1977 Uganda, Kenya, and Tanzania were members of the East African Community. This body had preserved a long tradition of cooperation among the three countries in the fields of transportation, postal services, tax collection, finance, and education. About 1977 the Community disbanded for political reasons.

HISTORY AND GOVERNMENT

The earliest inhabitants of Uganda were probably Pygmoid peoples who lived by hunting and gathering. During the first millenium B.C. Cushites from southern Ethiopia migrated into present-day Uganda. Centuries later they were followed by the Bantu who, according to one important theory, spread out over most of central and southern Africa from the Congo. The Bantu absorbed the Cushitic peoples they encountered in Uganda and adopted a great deal of their culture. By the 14th century the Cwezi kings of Kitara ruled over many of the Bantu people in what is now western Uganda. Toward the end of the 15th century Nilotic Luo invaders from the north entered Uganda and overthrew the rulers of Kitara. Over the centuries the invaders adopted the language and culture of the Bantu people they had conquered. Eventually other kingdoms such as Bunyoro, Ankole, Buganda, and Toro were established. Bunyoro, based on the old Kitara kingdom, was the most powerful state in the 16th and 17th centuries. In the 18th century Buganda began to battle against Bunyoro for dominance in the area.

Arab slavers and traders visited Uganda in the 1840's. They made a number of Muslim converts among the Baganda, and some Arabs served as advisers to the Kabaka of Buganda, Mutesa I. The search for the source of the Nile brought John Hanning Speke and James Grant to Uganda in 1862. Sir Samuel Baker, another English explorer, visited Uganda in 1864, and he discovered Lake Albert. He named the lake after Prince Albert, Queen Victoria's husband.

The first foreigners to arrive in the land were impressed by the sheer complexity of the early kingdoms of Uganda. In Buganda, Mutesa I was in turn impressed by the technology of the foreigners, particularly that of the Europeans. When Henry Morton Stanley, the explorer-journalist, visited Buganda in 1875, Mutesa accepted his suggestion that Christian missionaries be invited to enter the country. But extreme rivalry soon developed between the Protestant, Catholic, and Muslim factions in Buganda. When Mutesa died in 1884, he was succeeded by his son, Mwanga. Shortly thereafter Mwanga began to persecute the Christians. This persecution marked the beginning of a decade of civil and religious strife within Uganda.

At the Berlin Conference of 1884–85 the European powers agreed on a plan of dividing Africa among themselves. In the late 1880's Britain and Germany agreed to divide East Africa. Kenya and Uganda were given to the British, and Tanganyika was given to Germany. In 1894 a British protectorate was established in Buganda. The British and the Baganda then joined forces to extend British control to the rest of present-day Uganda.

In 1900 an agreement was signed between Britain and the kingdom of Buganda. As a result of the agreement Buganda retained a semi-independent status. The British later made similar agreements with the kingdoms of Bunyoro, Toro, and Ankole and the district of Busoga.

Throughout the 1950's Buganda opposed British efforts to create a strong central government in Uganda. However, in 1962 a new constitution granted federal status to Buganda and the other kingdoms. When Buganda accepted the constitution the path was cleared for independence. On October 9, 1962, Uganda became an independent member of the Commonwealth of Nations. A governor-general represented the British Queen and acted as head of state.

Shortly after independence the office of governor-general was abolished and the Kabaka of Buganda, Sir Edward Mutesa, became the first president. Conflict soon developed between President Mutesa and the prime minister, Dr. Apolo Milton Obote. In 1966 the conflict led to a battle in which the President's forces were defeated. Milton Obote took over the presidency and a new constitution was adopted. All the kingdoms were abolished and the country was divided into 18 districts administered by the central government. In January, 1971, Uganda's Army ousted Obote. Major General Idi Amin became president of Uganda.

Recent Events.   Following the 1971 coup, Idi Amin set aside the 1967 constitution, dissolved the National Assembly, and made himself head of state and head of government with the title President-for-Life. During the next 8 years Amin's secret police murdered at least 300,000 people, most of them Christians. During Amin's rule, many Ugandans fled into exile in neighboring Tanzania, including former president Obote. Tourists ceased to visit the country's famous game parks, and many sectors of Uganda's economy were badly damaged. But the high price of Ugandan coffee (the chief export) on the world market shored up the Amin regime.

Then in late 1978 some army units in southern Uganda mutinied, and Amin sent loyal troops to quell the rebellion. The fighting spilled over into neighboring Tanzania, where Amin's troops seized about 1,125 square kilometers (700 sq. mi.) of land. Tanzanian forces, helped by the Ugandan rebels, responded by invading Uganda in April, 1979. They took Kampala, and Amin fled into exile. The Tanzanian Government was criticized by the Organization of African Unity (OAU) for invading Uganda, but it replied that Amin's troops had invaded Tanzania first.

After several transitional governments, Obote returned to power as president following elections held in 1980. Opposition to his regime, however, led to Obote's downfall. In 1985 he was again removed from office by the military. At the same time, Uganda was faced with the threat of civil war between guerrilla forces opposed to the government and government troops. In 1986 the military government was overthrown by the National Resistance Army (NRA), the largest guerrilla force, and the NRA leader, Yoweri Kaguta Museveni, became president of Uganda.

ALI A. MAZRUI, Makerere University College, Kampala, Uganda

The beauty of Lake Kivu attracts many tourists.

RWANDA

The flag of Rwanda tells a great deal about the country and its people. The flag has three vertical stripes of equal width, one red, one yellow, and one green. In the center of the yellow stripe there is a large black R. The red, which is nearest the mast, represents the blood and toil expended for Rwanda's liberation. The yellow symbolizes the peace and quiet of a people released from a long and crushing bondage. It tells of the freedom from the contempt and debasement of the feudal and colonial regimes. The green means trust and hope in the future.

THE LAND

Rwanda is a small country that lies south of the equator in the eastern lake region of Africa. It is bordered by Uganda to the north, Tanzania to the east, Burundi to the south, and the Republic of Zaïre to the west. Composed of rugged mountains and a gently rolling plateau, the country covers an area of approximately 10,169 square miles (26,338 square kilometers). It is a land of beautiful lakes, valleys, and snowcapped mountains. The highest mountains in the west and the northwest were formed by volcanoes. To the west lies Lake Kivu, one of the most beautiful lakes in Africa. The land rises sharply from Lake Kivu to an average height of about 10,500 feet (3,200 meters) above sea level. The Virunga range in northwest Rwanda rises to well over 14,000 feet (4,270 m.). Its highest peak, snowcapped Mount Karisimbi, towers 14,780 feet (4,505 m.) over the surrounding countryside.

Several rivers flow through the country. The most important include Akanyaru and Ruzizi in the south, the Nyawarongo in the center, and the Kagera in the east.

Kagera National Park, which covers a huge area in the northeastern part of Rwanda, attracts tourists from all over. The park has herds of streaked zebras, antelope of many species—including the unique and beautiful impala—massive but fleet-footed buffalo, lions, leopards, bush cats, hippopotamuses, crocodiles, and an extraordinary variety of birdlife.

Climate. Rwanda has a mild and somewhat temperate climate. There are two dry seasons, one from December to January and one from June to September. The country's two wet seasons are from mid-September to November and from February to May. Average annual rainfall ranges from 40 inches (102 centimeters) in the northeast to 60 inches (152 cm.) in the southwest.

Towns. There are few large towns or villages in Rwanda. Most of the population live in self-contained compounds throughout the country. The most important towns are **Kigali**, the capital; Butare, the leading cultural and scientific center; and Gisenyi, Kibuye, and Cyangugu, three resort towns on famous Lake Kivu.

THE PEOPLE

Rwanda is one of the few African countries where all the people speak a common native language. This language, Kinyarwanda, and French are the official languages of the country.

There are three major ethnic groups in Rwanda: the Hutu, the Tutsi, and the Twa. The total population of the country is about 5,300,000. The Hutu, who constitute about 90 percent of the population, and the Tutsi,

A young woman of Rwanda on her way to market.

who make up 9 percent, are mostly farmers. The Twa, who are less than 1 percent, were hunters in their early history. Today, while some Twa have become farmers, others still carry on their traditional activities of hunting, fishing, and gathering for subsistence. The remainder of the population are Europeans or Asians. Some of them are farmers who raise tea, pyrethrum (which is used for making insecticides), and plants that yield geranium oil, used in making perfume. Some work in the mining industry. Other Europeans are missionaries representing the various Christian churches.

The Hutu generally raise enough food for both their families and the local markets. A number of them grow coffee, beans, peas, sorghum, millet, cassava, potatoes, and plantains.

The Tutsi ruled the country from the 16th century until 1959. No one knows for certain the exact date of their arrival in the region. For hundreds of years the Tutsi dominated the country and treated the Hutu as servants. In 1959 bloody civil strife broke out between the two groups. Hundreds of Hutu and Tutsi were killed and many of the Tutsi left the country. Today, some of the educated Tutsi who remained in Rwanda hold administrative, teaching, and clerical positions.

The Rwandese dress is very simple. The women wear a pagne—which is like a sari—tied at the waist, a blouse, and another pagne draped over them. The men used to wear a pagne from the waist down and a shirt, but now more and more people wear dresses and suits of the Western world.

Economy

The majority of the Rwandese people are farmers. They grow coffee, peas, beans, cotton, sorghum, millet, cassava, and pyrethrum. Coffee is the country's chief export. Rwanda has very little industry. Furniture, shoes, and blankets are made for use in the country. European companies operate tin and wolfram mines in the north central highlands and along the southern border. Tin and wolfram account for about one third of the country's exports.

HISTORY

Rwanda was first inhabited by the Twa, Pygmies who seldom reached a height of more than 5 feet (1.5 m.). They lived in the forests and were hunters and food gatherers. Today some of the Twa still carry on their traditional way of life in the mountains of the Virunga range.

The Hutu came into what is now Rwanda some centuries after the Twa. They were hunters and farmers. During the 16th century, the Tutsi, a warrior group with large herds of cattle, invaded the country from somewhere in the north. The Hutu, who were then spread out over most of the country, could not defend themselves against the powerful Tutsi. Subsequently each one of them agreed to serve a Tutsi chieftain. In return, the Tutsi chieftain, or lord, agreed to protect his Hutu servant and give him the use, but not the ownership, of cattle. Cattle was the Tutsi's source of wealth and the most important status symbol. Through this agreement, the Tutsi were able to dominate the territory for many centuries.

European explorers came into the territory during the 19th century. One of the most noted was John Speke, a British explorer who reached

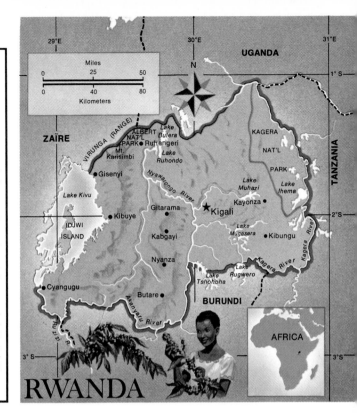

FACTS AND FIGURES

OFFICIAL NAME: Republic of Rwanda.

NATIONALITY: Rwandan(s).

CAPITAL: Kigali.

LOCATION: East central Africa. **Boundaries:** Uganda, Tanzania, Burundi, Zaïre.

AREA: 10,169 sq. mi. (26,338 sq. km.).

PHYSICAL FEATURES: Highest point—Mount Karisimbi (14,780 ft.; 4,505 m.). **Lowest point**—sea level. **Chief rivers**—Kagera, Akanyaru, Ruzizi, Nyawarongo. **Major Lake**—Kivu.

POPULATION: 7,903,000 (1991; annual growth 3.8%).

MAJOR LANGUAGES: Kinyarwanda and French (both official).

MAJOR RELIGIONS: Christianity, animistic beliefs, Islam.

GOVERNMENT: Republic. **Head of state**—president. **Head of government**—prime minister. **Legislature**—National Development Council.

CHIEF CITY: Kigali.

ECONOMY: Chief minerals—tin, wolfram. **Chief agricultural products**—coffee, beans, peas, sorghum, millet, cassava, pyrethrum. **Industries and products**—food processing, handicrafts. **Chief exports**—coffee, tea, tin, wolfram, pyrethrum. **Chief imports**—textiles, foodstuffs, machinery, transport equipment, fuel, electrical equipment, mineral products.

MONETARY UNIT: Rwanda franc.

RWANDA

what is now Rwanda about 1858. He was followed by the German explorer, G. A. Von Götzen, who discovered Lake Kivu in 1894. In the last decade of the 19th century, Rwanda, with Burundi to the south, became a German colony called German East Africa.

Germany lost all of its African territories after World War I, and Belgium acquired the region under the name of Ruanda-Urundi. From 1919 Ruanda-Urundi was a League of Nations mandate. In 1946 it became a United Nations trust territory. In 1959, the Hutu rose up against the Tutsi. Many Tutsi fled to neighboring countries. A U.N.-supervised referendum on the future of the region was held in 1961. On July 1, 1962, Ruanda-Urundi gained independence as two separate nations—Rwanda and Burundi. (A separate article on BURUNDI appears in this volume.)

There was further violence in 1963 and again in 1973, when Rwanda's first elected president, Grégoire Kayibanda, was overthrown in a military coup led by Major General Juvénal Habyarimana. Habyarimana remained president after the adoption of a new constitution in 1978. After an invasion by Rwandan refugees from Uganda in 1990, the government agreed to stop labeling citizens as Hutu or Tutsi on their national identity cards. The constitution was revised to create a multiparty political system in 1991, but anti-government rebel activity continued.

Government

Rwanda is a republic. An elected president serves as head of state. Since 1991, a prime minister has served as head of government, and future presidents are limited to two 5-year terms. Members of the unicameral legislature are also elected to 5-year terms. In an effort to reduce communal tensions, political parties must be non-tribal and Rwanda-based.

EDOHO BASSEY EDOHO, State University of New York at Albany

Barundi gather at a cotton market.

BURUNDI

Burundi is an independent African nation with a long history as a feudal state. From the end of World War I until independence in 1962, Burundi and its northern neighbor Rwanda formed a single Belgian-ruled territory known as Ruanda-Urundi. Burundi is one of the smallest and most densely populated of all African countries. The people, like those of Rwanda, represent three major ethnic groups. They also represent two contrasting attitudes: a demand for change and resistance to change.

THE PEOPLE

Burundi's people are crowded into a small area—about the size of the state of Maryland. The Barundi, or people of Burundi, consist of the Tutsi (or Watusi), who are cattle raisers; the Hutu, who are farmers; and the Pygmies, who live as hunters and fishermen. Both the Tutsi and the Hutu are part of the vast population south of the Sahara who speak one of hundreds of Bantu languages and have similar cultures. The Pygmies are culturally different from these two groups, and their original language is lost in history. The Pygmies today speak the language of the Bantu among whom they live.

The Tutsi are as tall as the Masai of Kenya and Tanzania and may come from the same northeast African stock. A few Tutsi are over 7 feet (2 meters) tall. For centuries, aided by their military and political skills, they have dominated their neighbors. Yet the Tutsi make up only 15 percent of the population.

The Hutu are the largest group. Between 80 and 85 percent of Burundi's people are Hutu farmers. Pygmies, who were the earliest inhabitants of the region, are today only a small fraction of the population.

The Feudal System.   In an unknown time Bantu farmers, ancestors of the Hutu, invaded the area of present-day Rwanda and Burundi, where Pygmies had long lived as hunters and gatherers. Waves of these Hutu came, and they increased, spreading throughout the region. Several hundred years ago the ancestors of the Tutsi streamed into the area from northeast of Lake Victoria, bringing cattle with them and subduing the people already in the country. The Tutsi organized a feudal state that was well established by the 15th century.

At the top of the feudal system in traditional Burundi was a king (*mwami*) who was treated as divine. Under him was a group of princes who were feudal lords over the people. Under each lord (*ganwa*) were sub-chiefs, and each sub-chief ruled over his own sib, or clan. Beneath all of these were the commoners of the Tutsi and Hutu. The Pygmies occupied a position below both groups. The Tutsi called the Pygmies Twa, or "inferiors."

The Way of Life.   Centuries of contact and dependence on one another have bound all of Burundi's people together and brought interchange of many kinds. In all three groups newly married couples go to live with the husband's family. Parents and children, grandparents, uncles, aunts, and cousins live in a common area of residence.

Houses of the Tutsi and Hutu are beehive-shaped structures of thatch

The Burundi landscape.

on a framework of poles. Frequently the houses have brick foundations. The Pygmies build houses of the same shape, but are less concerned with fine finish, since they may use the houses for only a short time.

The Hutu provided their Tutsi overlords with the produce of their fields and gardens. The Tutsi lived mainly on butter, milk, and blood drawn from their live cattle. The Hutu received from their rulers some of these products. Both Tutsi and Hutu obtained from the Pygmies wild meat from the forest and fish from the streams. The Pygmies, in turn, obtained bananas and plantains by barter from the Hutu.

The religious traditions of the Tutsi and Hutu also became mixed. Both groups revered one they called Kiranga or Ryangombe, who acted as a mediator between them and Imana, the creator. Today more than half of the Barundi are Christians, mostly Roman Catholics, and there are some Muslims. The Pygmies generally worship the spirit of the forest.

The two main languages of the country are Kirundi, a Bantu language, and French. Schoolchildren are taught in both languages. More than 465,000 students attend primary and secondary schools. There is a university in Bujumbura, the capital.

THE LAND

Burundi lies along the Great Rift Valley of eastern Africa. From Lake Tanganyika in the southwest, which is about 2,534 feet (772 m.) above sea level, the land rises to more than 8,000 feet (2,440 m.). Then it slopes down gradually to about 4,000 feet (1,220 m.) in the east and south. The Ruzizi River runs along the western boundary and the Malagarasi along the eastern boundary. Both rivers flow into Lake Tanganyika.

Although the country is near the equator, the temperature is moderately cool because of the high altitude. Rainfall, which averages nearly 50 inches (127 centimeters) a year, is heaviest from February through May and lightest from June through August.

The few forests that have not been cut down are found near streams, which are well distributed throughout the country. In the rich soil along the banks of the streams, elephant grass grows to a height of 16 feet (5 m.) or more. The rest of the land is largely savanna. In many areas overgrazing has stripped bare old grasslands and caused soil erosion. Only two fifths of the land can be used for cultivation, and the wildlife population has shown a decrease.

Close to the head of Lake Tanganyika is the capital and largest city, **Bujumbura.** A second urban center is Kitega.

THE ECONOMY

Most people live by farming, raising food for themselves and their families. Their crops include bananas, cassava, beans, maize, sorghum, peanuts, and sweet potatoes. Coffee is the main cash crop and the country's major export. Cotton is also grown and exported, and tea plantations are being developed. In the higher lands people keep livestock—cows, goats, sheep, and some pigs. In some of the low-lying land in the west the presence of the tsetse fly makes cattle raising impossible. (The tsetse fly causes diseases in cattle and human beings.) The government is trying to build up fishing as an industry. Lake Tanganyika is the main source of fish. In the cities there is some light manufacturing, largely of clothing, food products, and building supplies.

FACTS AND FIGURES

OFFICIAL NAME: Republic of Burundi.

NATIONALITY: Burundian(s).

CAPITAL: Bujumbura.

LOCATION: East central Africa. **Boundaries**—Rwanda, Tanzania, Lake Tanganyika, Zaïre.

AREA: 10,745 sq. mi. (27,830 sq. km.).

PHYSICAL FEATURES: Highest point—8,809 ft. (2,685 m.). **Lowest point**—2,534 ft. (772 m.). **Chief rivers**—Ruzizi, Akanyaru, Malagarasi, Ruvuvu. **Major lakes**—Tanganyika, Rugwero, Tshohoha.

POPULATION: 5,831,233 (1991; annual growth 3.2%).

MAJOR LANGUAGES: Kirundi and French (official), Swahili.

MAJOR RELIGIONS: Christianity, traditional African beliefs, Islam.

GOVERNMENT: Republic. **Head of state**—president. **Head of government**—prime minister. **Legislature**—National Assembly.

CHIEF CITIES: Bujumbura, Kitega.

ECONOMY: Chief minerals—nickel, uranium, rare earth oxide, peat, cobalt, copper, platinum. **Chief agricultural products**—coffee, cotton, tea, manioc, yams, corn, sorghum. **Industries and products**—blankets, shoes, soap, food processing. **Chief exports**—coffee, tea, hides and skins. **Chief imports**—petroleum products, foodstuffs, consumer goods.

MONETARY UNIT: Burundi franc.

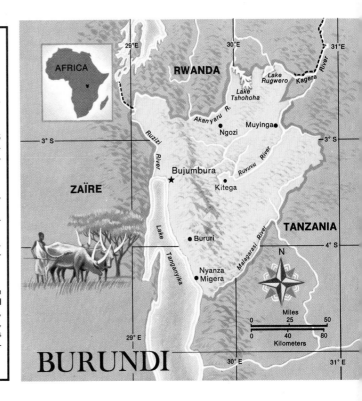

BURUNDI

HISTORY AND GOVERNMENT

For centuries the Tutsi dominated the Hutu, and both groups took advantage of the Pygmies. The missionary David Livingstone and the explorer Henry Stanley passed south of Bujumbura after their meeting in 1871. They interested missionaries in the welfare of the people.

In the last decade of the 19th century Germany took Burundi, along with Ruanda and Tanganyika, as part of German East Africa. World War I brought the end of German colonies, and in 1919 Belgium was given the region known as Ruanda-Urundi under a League of Nations mandate. The Belgians supported the dominant Tutsi. After World War II the area became a United Nations trust territory, administered by Belgium. In 1961, under United Nations supervision, the people voted for their own separate governments, from which evolved, on July 1, 1962, the two independent nations of Burundi and Rwanda. (A separate article on RWANDA appears in this volume.)

Recent Events. Burundi was a constitutional monarchy under its *mwami*, or king, Ntare V, until 1966, when Prime Minister Michel Micombero deposed the *mwami* and established a republic with himself as president. In 1976, Micombero was overthrown in a military coup led by Colonel Jean-Baptiste Bagaza, who assumed the presidency. He was overthrown by Major Pierre Buyoya in 1987.

Burundi was a one-party state from 1981 to 1992, when a new constitution establishing a non-ethnic multiparty political system was adopted. It provided for direct elections of a president and members of the legislature to five-year terms. Legislative elections were scheduled for late in 1992, with presidential elections planned for 1993.

CHARLES EDWARD FULLER, Chairman, Sociology and Anthropology Department
St. John's University

Mount Kilimanjaro soars above the surrounding plains.

TANZANIA

For most of the people of Tanzania, everyday life is concerned with farming and village affairs. Small settlements dot the fertile sections of the country, and families walk out daily to cultivate their fields or to pasture cattle. On Mount Kilimanjaro the people grow coffee and bananas. In Sukumuland, the countryside is covered with cotton. The Masai seldom grow crops. Their wealth comes from herding. Tanzania has very few areas of dense tropical vegetation. The lack of water in some areas, especially during the summer, and the presence of the tsetse fly, which spreads sleeping sickness, make much of the rolling savanna country uninhabitable. In areas such as the Serengeti Plains, there are major resorts of abundant wildlife, but little room for man.

THE LAND

The name Tanzania is actually a short one for the former United Republic of Tanganyika and Zanzibar. Tanganyika lies on the east coast of Africa, just south of the equator, while Zanzibar is made up of several small coral islands about 25 miles (40 kilometers) offshore in the Indian Ocean. The republic was created in April, 1964. It took its present name in October of the same year. Tanzania has an area of 364,900 square miles (945,087 square kilometers).

Climate

Tanzania has a tropical climate, but the heat is tempered on the islands by steady sea breezes and on the mainland by the high altitudes.

The port of Dar es Salaam is one of the busiest in East Africa.

Some parts of the country get up to 120 in. (305 cm.) of rain a year, while the eastern and northern sections of the central plateau receive less than 20 in. (51 cm.) of rain.

CITIES

Dar es Salaam, capital and largest city of the country, is located on the coast of the mainland and was established in the 1860s. Dar es Salaam, whose name means "haven of peace," is a modern city with an international airport, railroad terminal, and excellent harbor. The harbor, a sheltered and beautiful one, is one of the busiest in all of East Africa. Not far from the harbor is Independence Avenue, where many of the banks, foreign embassies, and commercial firms are located.

Dar es Salaam was founded by the Sultan of Zanzibar as a summer residence, and it is now an important commercial and business center. A recently established oil refinery has helped to make the city the leading industrial center of the country, producing textiles, furniture, paint, and soft drinks for sale at home and abroad.

Another main port city is **Tanga,** which is also on the mainland coast, north of Dar es Salaam. One of the country's major cities, **Zanzibar Town,** is located on the island of Zanzibar. This bustling city is a processing and shipping center for the clove industry.

In 1973 the government announced that the capital would be moved inland to **Dodoma.** The move was still in progress in the early 1990s.

THE PEOPLE

There are over 120 ethnic groups in Tanzania, most of whom speak Bantu languages and have some social and cultural features in common. Swahili is now spoken everywhere, but each group has its own structure

Travel by automobile can be quite hazardous in the old city of Zanzibar.

and language, as well as customary laws that define, among other things, kinship and wrongdoing. Some of the communities had chiefs in the past, while others were governed by councils of elders or heads of clans.

Until quite recently, each cluster of villages or ethnic groups ran most of its own affairs. Custom decreed most daily activities. For example, a young Masai boy was expected to become a cattle herder at the age of 6 or 7. He was promoted in his teens to a junior warrior and left his family to live with a regiment of his fellows. His sister spent her

Women walk to market while the men tend their cattle herds.

time at home until she married—cooking, making clothes of skins and leather, and helping move the family *manyatta,* or homestead, when seasonal pasture changed.

Just 60 miles or so away from the Masai are the people of the Chagga tribe. There on the slopes of Mount Kilimanjaro, a Chagga youth is trained as a farmer, growing coffee and bananas. His family's holdings are irrigated by an elaborate system of water channels running all over the mountain slopes. Land is so fully occupied and planted that there is little room for cattle pasture. Cows are kept in their byres, or cattle barns, and grass for their feed is carried up the mountains from plains several miles distant. For his dinner the young Chagga has a stew made from bananas, sometimes spiced with beans or meat.

A Changing World

But Tanzania, like many other African countries, is changing. Most Tanzanians still live in a rural environment, and many young Masai and Chagga continue their traditional activities. The traditional patterns are breaking up, however, and more and more Masai, Chagga, and young people of other ethnic groups and other areas of the country are attending primary, secondary, and trade schools. Some are even going to college, where they are taught in English and Swahili.

Increasing numbers of rural families are moving to the growing urban centers such as the capital, Dar es Salaam. Here rural Africans come upon Western industry, entertainment, and customs. A poor family lives in the slums, drinks tea, and listens to Swahili radio broadcasts of soccer games on Saturday afternoons. Families with larger incomes, in which the father is a teacher or a doctor or a government employee, have more elaborate housing, wear European-style clothing, and often own an automobile. In Dar es Salaam the rural African meets and mingles with Asians and Europeans who have settled in the city.

The majority of Tanzanians follow animistic beliefs, but there are large numbers of Muslims and Christians. Close personal connections exist between the people of the city and those of the country.

Legends and folklore are remembered and kept alive. On the national holiday of Saba Saba Day (July 7) dancers from almost all parts of the country come to Dar es Salaam to perform. Saba Saba means the 7th day of the 7th month. The holiday celebrates the founding of the Tanganyika African National Union (TANU), the chief political party of the country. Many of the folk dances and songs that are performed on Saba Saba Day are taught in the schools. A number of folktales and local histories have been translated and published in Swahili and English.

Education

Education is free at all levels in Tanzania, although it is not compulsory. Most of the schools are run by the government and some are conducted by missions that receive grants. Because of the shortage of school buildings and teachers, only a little more than half of Tanzania's children enter primary schools. A small percentage of the youth attend secondary and trade schools. Those who want to get a higher education usually attend the University of Dar es Salaam. Other Tanzanian youths leave the country to study at universities in other parts of the world.

Cloves, one of Tanzania's major products, are left to dry in the sun.

ECONOMY

The economy of Tanzania is based largely on agriculture. Over 90 percent of the people are engaged in farming. Tanganyika is the world's largest producer of sisal, a fiber used in the making of rope, twine, and other similar products. Zanzibar produces most of the world's cloves. Other important agricultural products of Tanzania include coffee, cotton, tobacco, coconuts, bananas, and corn.

Gold and diamonds are the two most important minerals mined in Tanzania. Diamonds make up about one third of the country's mineral output. The Williamson diamond mines, located at Mwadui, in north central Tanzania, are considered one of the most important diamond deposits in the world. Small quantities of salt, mica, and tin concentrate are also exported. Most of Tanzania's industry is devoted to the processing of raw materials for export and local use.

HISTORY

Tanzania has a long history, though many of its chapters are completely unknown. Recent excavations in Olduvai Gorge in northern Tanganyika indicate that the earliest known man, *Homo zinjanthropus,* lived there more than 500,000 years ago. Ancient Greek sailors sailed along the East African coast. Tradition maintains that in the 8th century seven brothers from Arabia arrived, introduced the Islamic religion, and founded seven trading cities. Archeological studies confirm that there were Arab cities on the coast by the 10th century. In 1499 Vasco da Gama stopped off at Zanzibar for water and fresh provisions on his way to

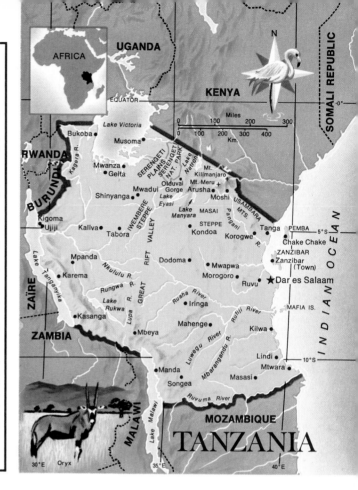

India. For the next 2 centuries the Portuguese Empire controlled many of the East African trading cities.

The Portuguese did not venture inland, however, and it was not until the 19th century that Europeans traveled there. Johannes Rebmann, a missionary, first saw Mount Kilimanjaro in 1848. Most Europeans did not believe his statement that a mountain in the heart of Africa was snow-covered.

During much of the 19th century, Zanzibar was a powerful Arab sultanate that controlled the ivory and slave trade on the mainland. However, as a result of slave raiding and local warfare, strong African societies began to disintegrate. It was at this time that various European powers became involved in the scramble for Africa. Great Britain declared a protectorate over Zanzibar, though retaining the Arab sultan as head of the government, while Germany took control of mainland Tanganyika.

Some steps were taken to modernize both Tanganyika and Zanzibar, although the countries remained separate. Slavery was abolished, schools were built by missionaries and by the government, and roads and railroads were constructed. After the defeat of Germany in World War I, Tanganyika was made a mandate of the League of Nations, administered by the British. In 1946 it became a trust territory of the United Nations, under British administration.

In the 1950's Africans in both countries began to press for political representation and independence. In Tanganyika, Julius K. Nyerere founded the Tanganyika African National Union (TANU) in 1954. After winning a series of elections with little opposition, he led the country

Ngorongoro Crater, a refuge for wildlife, is a major tourist attraction.

to independence in 1961. Zanzibar was granted political independence by the British in December 1963. A revolution a month later led to the overthrow of the Arab sultanate and the establishment of a republic. In April 1964, Tanganyika and Zanzibar joined to form the United Republic of Tanganyika and Zanzibar. The name was later changed to the United Republic of Tanzania.

Nyerere, who was the first president of Tanganyika, became the first president of Tanzania when Tanganyika and Zanzibar were united. He retired in 1985 and was succeeded by one of his vice presidents, Ali Hassan Mwinyi. Mwinyi, who began to modify the government's former strict socialist economic policies, won election in his own right in 1990.

GOVERNMENT

Tanzania is a republic. An elected president, assisted by two appointed vice presidents, serves as chief executive. The legislative body is the National Assembly. Tanzania was a one-party state from 1965 until 1992, when multiparty politics were legalized. Zanzibar has its own constitution, which provides for an elected president and legislature.

PLACES OF INTEREST

Serengeti National Park is one of the many reserves that Tanzania has established to protect and show off its abundant wildlife. This huge park of over 5,000 sq. mi. (13,000 sq. km.) of open plain and savanna is one of the finest of its kind in all of Africa. Another lovely wildlife park is Lake Manyara in the Great Rift Valley. Other places of interest include Ngorongoro Crater and the nearby Olduvai Gorge where *Homo zinjanthropus* was found. But perhaps the most thrilling sight for visitors is snowcapped Mount Kilimanjaro, the highest point in Africa.

MARGARET L. BATES, Smith College

SEYCHELLES

The tiny Republic of Seychelles is made up of more than 100 islands and islets scattered over 150,000 square miles (400,000 square kilometers) of the western Indian Ocean. The islands have a total land area of 108 square miles (280 sq. km.). Some of them are rocky and mountainous and others are coral islands only a few feet above sea level. The mountainous group contains most of the population, while the coral group has few permanent inhabitants. Over 80 percent of the island republic's people live on Mahé, the largest island, whose area is 56 square miles (145 sq. km.).

The climate of Seychelles is subtropical, with trade winds blowing for most of the year. Rainfall is about 90 inches (200 centimeters) a year at sea level and much more on the highlands.

The People

The vast majority of Seychellois are descendants of the original French settlers and the African slaves they imported. There are also a few British settlers and a number of Chinese and Indians, most of whom are merchants and shopkeepers. One quarter of the country's population lives in **Victoria**, which is on the northeastern side of Mahé Island. Victoria is the capital and chief port of the Seychelles.

Most of the people speak Creole, a French dialect, though some

The city and harbor of Victoria, on Mahé, largest island of Seychelles.

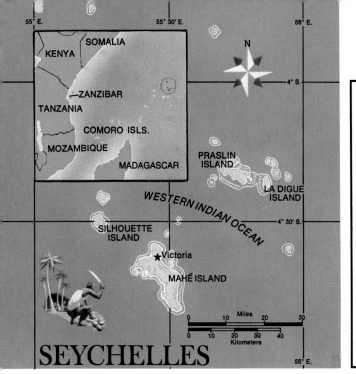

SEYCHELLES

FACTS AND FIGURES

OFFICIAL NAME: Republic of Seychelles.

NATIONALITY: Seychellois.

CAPITAL: Victoria.

LOCATION: Western Indian Ocean.

AREA: 171 sq. mi. (444 sq. km.).

PHYSICAL FEATURES: Highest point—Morne Seychellois (2,993 ft.; 912 m.). **Lowest point**—sea level.

POPULATION: 68,932 (1991; annual growth 0.9%).

MAJOR LANGUAGES: Creole, (official), French, English.

MAJOR RELIGIONS: Roman Catholic, Protestant.

GOVERNMENT: Republic. **Head of state and government**—president. **Legislature**—National Assembly. **International co-operation**—United Nations, Commonwealth of Nations, Organization of African Unity (OAU).

ECONOMY: Chief agricultural products—coconuts, cinnamon, vanilla beans, patchouli oil. **Industries and products**—processing of copra, cinnamon, and foodstuffs; tourism; construction; fishing. **Chief exports**—cinnamon, patchouli oil, copra, vanilla, guano. **Chief imports**—rice, sugar, cloth, food.

MONETARY UNIT: Seychelles rupee.

speak French and English. Rice is the staple food and constitutes one of the republic's chief imports. Inshore fishing provides most of the fish consumed. Vegetables and many tropical fruits are grown.

ECONOMY

Most Seychellois earn their living by working on coconut plantations. Copra (dried coconut) is the country's chief export, followed by cinnamon, patchouli oil, and vanilla. Patchouli oil is used in making perfume. A few proprietors hold most of the agricultural land. Although unemployment was once a problem in Seychelles, it has now largely disappeared due to growth in the tourist and construction industries.

HISTORY AND GOVERNMENT

The islands were uninhabited when the French first settled there in 1770. The settlers named the islands after Vicomte Moreau de Séchelles, a minister of finance to the French king Louis XV. The colonists imported African slaves to cut the timber, capture tortoises, and plant spice gardens. In 1794 the British took over Seychelles.

Throughout the 19th century Seychelles was administered as a part of Mauritius, which was also a colony of Great Britain. The British brought to Seychelles large numbers of Africans liberated from slave ships. In 1903, Seychelles was separated from Mauritius, becoming a British Crown Colony. Seychelles gained its independence in 1976, with James Mancham as its first president. Mancham was overthown in 1977 in a coup led by France-Albert René, who assumed the presidency. In 1979 Seychelles became a one-party state under a new constitution, with a president as head of state and government and a largely elected National Assembly. René was elected president in 1979 and reelected in 1984 and 1989. Multipartyism was reintroduced in 1992, and legislative and presidential elections were planned by year's end.

BURTON BENEDICT, University of California at Berkeley; author, *People of the Seychelles*

ANGOLA

The evening sun of southern Africa sinks into the Atlantic Ocean and bathes the coast of Angola, a former overseas province of Portugal. Its last rays touch a black African returning to his home after a long day's work. As he walks, he thinks about his life. He remembers his boyhood in the school, run by Portuguese, in his village. He reflects that there was a time when the most he could have hoped was that his sons might some day become clerks under the Portuguese administration.

Change came in 1975 when Angola achieved independence. Now children would go to schools run by Angolans. And fathers could hope that a son might become head of a company, or even a government official.

Before 1975 several hundred thousand Portuguese lived in Angola. They ruled the province. They gave Portuguese names to towns, built cities like those in Portugal, and controlled the economy.

When European countries were being forced to give up control of their African colonies, Portugal managed to retain its territories on the continent. But in 1961 guerrilla war broke out in northern Angola, and the movement for independence had begun.

Hardly had freedom been won when fighting flared among rival Angolan groups. Civil war erupted, and foreign nations became involved. Angola had achieved independence, but it faced many problems.

THE LAND

Angola is a huge almost square chunk of land on the western coast of Africa. With a total area of 481,351 square miles (1,246,700 square

The São Miguel fortress in Angola was used as protection against pirate raids.

kilometers), Angola was Portugal's largest overseas province. On the north and northeast, it is bounded by the Republic of Zaïre, on the southeast by Zambia, and on the south by Namibia (South-West Africa). Cabinda, a tiny enclave separated from Angola by the Republic of Zaïre, is a district of Angola.

A low strip of land ranging from 20 to 100 miles (32–160 kilometers) in width runs along the coast. Most of the interior of Angola consists of the Benguela highland, a vast plateau with altitudes averaging between 3,000 and 6,000 feet (910–1,830 meters). The highest point in the country (8,270 ft.; 2,520 m.) is located in the Bié Plateau. The plateau gradually levels off in the north to the Congo River basin and in the south it meets the Kalahari Desert, which covers most of southwest Africa.

Rivers. The interior plateau of Angola is drained in the north by the mighty Congo River and in the south by the Cubango, which forms part of the boundary between Angola and Namibia (South-West Africa). The great Zambezi River, which travels about 1,600 miles (2,575 km.) across southern Africa before draining into the Indian Ocean, flows through the extreme eastern part of Angola.

Climate. The climate of Angola ranges from tropical in the Congo Basin of northern Angola to arid in the extreme south. Because of its altitude, the interior plateau has a temperate climate, with alternating rainy and dry seasons. The driest and coolest months in the country are June through September; the hottest and wettest are October through May. Rainfall averages as much as 60 inches (152 centimeters) in the northeast but decreases considerably in the south and southwest.

Cities. Situated along the Atlantic Ocean, **Luanda,** the capital, is the largest city of Angola. Founded by the Portuguese in 1575, it is one of the oldest European settlements in all of Africa south of the Sahara. Many of its buildings date from the 17th and 18th centuries, when Luanda served as the key point of the slave trade between Africa and Brazil. Today, the city is a modern administrative center with wide boulevards, large hotels, shops, and office buildings.

Luanda, Angola's capital, commands a panoramic view of the Atlantic coastline.

Luanda's improved harbor and dock facilities can handle large foreign ships.

Lobito, a modern and cosmopolitan city, is the major port of Angola and the terminus of the trans-African Benguela Railway. Its port is one of the most modern and best equipped in southern Africa. An oil refinery and several industries, such as shipbuilding and metalworking, are located in Lobito.

Huambo (formerly called Nova Lisboa) is the principal agricultural center of the country. It also has considerable commercial activity, shipping wheat, rice, maize, fruits, and hides and skins to Angola's busy ports. Situated in the interior region, Huambo has modern public buildings, churches, a radio transmitter, and an airstrip.

Other important cities include Benguela, Moçâmedes, Malange, and Cabinda, the leading town in the Cabinda enclave.

THE PEOPLE

More than three quarters of the population of Angola belongs to various Bantu groups. The Ovimbundu, the largest of the groups, occupy the somewhat densely populated center of the country. The Kimbundu, the second largest group, live farther north. The Bakongo inhabit the most northerly areas near the borders of the Congo and Zaïre. The remainder of the population is made up of people of mixed Portuguese and African ancestry, and a small number of Bushmen and Hottentots. Almost the entire Portuguese population left the country at the time of independence and civil war.

The Ovimbundu are famous in Africa as traders, and they, of all the native population of Angola, have taken most readily to European culture. The Ovimbundu live in an area rich in iron ore and are noted for their skill as ironworkers as well as for their work in pottery, basketry, leatherworking, and wood carving.

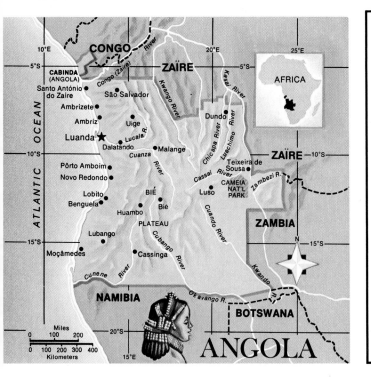

FACTS AND FIGURES

OFFICIAL NAME: People's Republic of Angola (República Popular de Angola).

NATIONALITY: Angolan(s).

CAPITAL: Luanda.

LOCATION: West coast of southern Africa. **Boundaries**—Congo, Zaïre, Zambia, Namibia, Atlantic Ocean.

AREA: 481,351 sq. mi. (1,246,700 sq. km.).

PHYSICAL FEATURES: Highest point—Bié Plateau (8,270 ft.; 2,520 m.). **Lowest point**—sea level. **Chief rivers**—Congo, Cubango, Zambezi.

POPULATION: 8,533,989 (1989).

MAJOR LANGUAGES: Portuguese (official), many local languages.

MAJOR RELIGIONS: traditional African religions, Roman Catholicism, Protestantism.

GOVERNMENT: Republic. **Head of state**—president. **Legislature**—one-house National People's Assembly.

CHIEF CITIES: Luanda (1,200,000), Lobito, Huambo.

ECONOMY: Chief minerals—petroleum, diamonds, copper, phosphates. **Chief agricultural products**—coffee, sisal, cassava, maize, plantains, yams, cotton. **Industries and products**—petroleum refining, food processing, cement, textiles. **Chief exports**—crude petroleum and petroleum products, coffee, diamonds. **Chief imports**—machinery, foodstuffs, raw materials.

MONETARY UNIT: 1 kwanza = 100 lwei.

The Kimbundu, because of their closeness to Luanda, have also become largely Europeanized. Many have left their traditional homelands and moved to Luanda where they hold jobs in many of the business establishments, government offices, and industries. But those Kimbundu who inhabit the interior regions, far from the urban centers, still engage in agricultural activities—mostly subsistence farming.

The Bakongo can be found along the northern coastal region of Angola. These people are a branch of the large Kongo family that spills over several borders in central Africa. The Bakongo of Angola are basically farmers who cultivate corn, sweet potatoes, peanuts (groundnuts), and beans. Fishing and hunting also play an important part in their economy. The Bakongo also excel in sculpture and music. These people, more than any other group in Angola, were the most involved in the independence movement that kept the north in a state of guerrilla warfare from 1961 until independence was granted.

Religion. Approximately half of the Bantu peoples of Angola have been converted to Christianity, both Roman Catholicism and Protestantism. The remainder of the people hold animistic beliefs. Many of the traditional Bantu religions have lost most of their force in their pure form, but some practices combining Christianity and certain aspects of the traditional religions are widespread.

Education. Until independence, Angola's educational system was based on that of Portugal. Many of the elementary schools were run by the Roman Catholic Church. In areas where schools were available, attendance began at the age of 6 and generally continued for only 4 years. Some advanced schooling, both academic and technical, was offered. The University of Angola, in Luanda, and a few Catholic seminaries and teacher training schools provided higher education.

Vendors at a rural train stop sell refreshments to the passengers.

In 1976 the Ministry of Education announced plans for an expanded school construction program and a new educational system. By 1982 some 1.5 million students attended primary and secondary schools.

Although Portuguese is the official language of the country, Bantu languages, chiefly Ovimbundu and Kimbundu, are spoken by most of the population.

ECONOMY

Before the 1970s, the economy of the country was largely sustained by a single crop—coffee. Other traditional Angolan products of importance have been diamonds from a huge mining complex in the northeast, fish products, sisal (from which rope is made), timber, sugar, corn, cotton, and bananas. Since 1973, crude oil has been the chief export. Angola now ranks second to Nigeria in sub-Saharan Africa in oil production. The state oil company and several foreign companies extract petroleum from fields along the Atlantic coast, mostly off the enclave of Cabinda. The country also has excellent hydroelectrical potential as well as substantial actual production.

Most of the people raise food crops for their own consumption or for the local market. Subsistence agriculture is still the single most important economic activity.

Much of Angola's industry is involved in the processing of local foodstuffs, such as coffee and sugar, and the production of vegetable oils. Textile factories use cotton that is grown locally. In addition, beverages and tobacco products make an important contribution to the economy. Other products include cement, tires, and paper.

Continuing guerrilla warfare and the flight of skilled technicians following independence disrupted Angola's economy and brought the country almost to a halt. The post-independence civil war (1975–91) further devastated the economy. Free-market reforms were adopted in 1990.

HISTORY

In the 14th and 15th centuries, the Bantu peoples of central Africa moved into the southern part of the continent, occupying lands that previously had only a sparse population of Hottentots and Bushmen. The Bantu established several important kingdoms in the area that includes present-day Angola. The three major kingdoms were Luba, Lunda, and the great Kongo Kingdom. In the 16th century central Angola was invaded by the Jagas, a fierce warlike people. The Jagas were not a culture group or a tribe as such, but rather a warrior people. The Jagas settled in the highland region and gradually were assimilated into the larger population of Kimbundu and Ovimbundu peoples.

The first European to reach Angola was Portuguese navigator Diogo Cão, who sighted the mouth of the Congo River in 1482. He later explored inland and came into contact with the Manikongo ("king of the Kongo"). Later these kings were converted to Christianity, and the Kongo became a vassal state of the Portuguese king. From the 16th to the 19th century, the Portuguese in Angola remained in fortified coastal ports.

In the mid-19th century the English became interested in expanding their African empire. Fearing the loss of their foothold in Africa, the Portuguese began to explore and conquer the interior of Angola. In 1891 a treaty with the British set Angola's present boundaries, and by 1918 the last interior regions were brought under Portuguese control. After World War II Angola became an overseas province of Portugal.

In 1961 armed revolts against Portuguese rule broke out in northern Angola. Portugal sent troops to fight the insurgents and instituted economic and political reforms, but the fighting continued. In 1974 a group of military officers overthrew the government of Portugal. The new leaders in Lisbon granted Angola its independence, to become effective late in 1975. An interim body including representatives of the three Angolan liberation groups was formed to govern the country. As independence neared, rivalry among these groups led to civil war. When the Portuguese withdrew in November 1975 one of these groups, the Popular Movement for the Liberation of Angola (MPLA), seized power with the aid of Soviet arms and Cuban troops before elections could be held. Its leader, António Agostinho Neto, became president of the Marxist government. Upon Neto's death in 1979, he was succeeded by José Eduardo dos Santos.

Civil war continued between the MPLA and the National Union for Total Independence of Angola (UNITA), led by Jonas Savimbi and supported by the U.S. and South Africa. In a December 1988 accord, Angola, Cuba, and South Africa agreed to a timetable for the withdrawal of Cuban forces, the ending of South African support for UNITA, and independence for neighboring Namibia (gained in March 1990). The last Cuban troops left Angola in May 1991. The MPLA abandoned Marxist-Leninism in 1991, and the MPLA and UNITA signed a peace accord calling for a UN-monitored cease fire on May 31. In multiparty elections held in September 1992, the MPLA captured a legislative majority. Dos Santos won 49.6 percent of the presidential vote versus Savimbi's 40.1 percent; a runoff election was scheduled as Savimbi threatened renewed civil war.

NORMAN A. BAILEY, The City University of New York

Windhoek, the capital and chief city.

NAMIBIA

On March 21, 1990, the Republic of Namibia became the world's newest independent nation, ending 75 years of South African rule. Representatives of more than 30 countries attended a midnight ceremony at the sports stadium in Windhoek, the capital, in which the South African flag was hauled down and the new blue, red, green, and gold flag of Namibia was hoisted. Independence followed an election supervised by the United Nations and the drafting of a constitution. The constitution established a multiparty democratic system and guaranteed an independent judiciary and such fundamental human rights as freedom of speech and freedom of the press. Namibia, formerly known as South-West Africa, has accepted an invitation to join the London-based Commonwealth of Nations.

THE LAND
Namibia stretches a distance of about 1,000 mi. (1,600 km.) along the Atlantic coast of southern Africa. The total land area is 318,000 sq. mi. (823,620 sq. km.). This includes the enclave of Walvis Bay, which is part of the Cape Province of South Africa but which Namibia claims as its own. Also included is a strip of land in the extreme northeast called the Caprivi Strip. It extends some 300 mi. (480 km.) to the Zambezi River, and at its widest point measures 60 mi. (97 km.). Administration of this narrow piece of land was taken over by South Africa in 1939.

A large plateau runs north-south through the center of the country. With an average elevation of 3,600 ft. (1,100 m.), the plateau is the most populous region of the country. Just north of Windhoek, the plateau merges into the Kaokoveld Hills. Brandberg (8,550 ft.; 2,606 m.), an isolated mountain peak in the Kaokoveld chain, is the new nation's highest point.

The Namib Desert, for which Namibia is named.

To the west of the plateau lies the Namib Desert, which runs along the entire west coast of the country. The Kalahari Desert dominates the land southeast of the plateau.

The rivers in Namibia that provide much of the year-round water supply are the Orange, which runs along the border with South Africa, the Cunene in the extreme north, and the Zambezi and Okavango in the Caprivi Strip. The Fish River, a tributary of the Orange, has cut a canyon some 20 mi. (30 km.) long and 2,000 ft. (600 m.) deep.

Climate. In general Namibia has an extremely hot and dry climate. Most of the precipitation occurs in the summer months (October through April). There are frequent periods of drought even in the summer, however, and when rain does fall, it comes in torrents with the water running off so rapidly that little is left to soak into the ground.

Cities. Windhoek, the capital, is the hub of Namibia's transport network. It is the industrial, commercial, and distributing center of the country. On the three hills overlooking the city rise three large castles constructed in medieval style. These castles and the city's main thoroughfare, Kaiser Street, are a reminder of the country's status as a German colony during the late 19th and early 20th centuries.

Lüderitz, a port city on the Atlantic coast, is a popular vacation resort. Lüderitz is also an important industrial center, particularly for the processing of rock lobster and fish meal.

Keetmanshoop lies in the center of the karakul sheep-raising country in the southern part of the territory. It is here in Keetmanshoop that the engineering shops for the country's railroads are located.

Swakopmund is a seaside resort area on the Atlantic Ocean, across a river from Walvis Bay. Because of its ideal climate, Swakopmund becomes the capital of Namibia each year during the hot summer months of December and January.

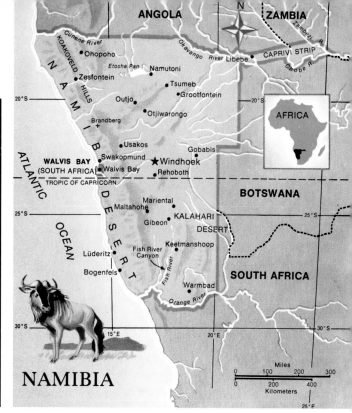

FACTS AND FIGURES

OFFICIAL NAME: Republic of Namibia.

NATIONALITY: Namibian(s).

LOCATION: Southwest Africa. **Boundaries**—Angola, Zambia, Botswana, South Africa, Atlantic Ocean.

CAPITAL: Windhoek.

AREA: 318,000 sq. mi. (823,620 sq. km.).

PHYSICAL FEATURES: Highest point—Brandberg (8,550 ft.; 2,606 m.). **Lowest point**—sea level. **Chief rivers**—Orange, Cunene, Okavango.

POPULATION: 1,372,475 (1989).

MAJOR LANGUAGES: English (official), Afrikaans, German, Ovambo, Herero.

MAJOR RELIGIONS: Protestantism, Roman Catholicism, traditional African religions.

GOVERNMENT: Republic. **Head of state and government**—president. **Legislature**—National Assembly.

ECONOMY: Chief minerals—diamonds, uranium, copper, lead, silver, zinc, salt. **Chief agricultural products**—goats, sheep, cattle, maize, millet. **Industries and products**—mineral and food processing, fishing. **Chief exports**—diamonds, minerals, fish products. **Chief imports**—manufactured goods, foodstuffs, fuel.

MONETARY UNIT: South African rand.

NAMIBIA

THE PEOPLE

Most Namibians are of black African ancestry. Namibians of European origin include Afrikaners and those of German heritage. Another important minority consists of the Coloureds—people of mixed ancestry. The largest African group, the Ovambo, live on a northern reserve along the Angola border. They engage in agriculture and animal raising. Quite a few of the Ovambo form the bulk of the labor force for the local diamond mines and the farms and ranches owned by the Europeans.

Two other important African groups are the Damara and the Herero, both of whom are primarily cattle breeders. At one time, the Herero were a very large and powerful group. However, they, more than any other people in Namibia, resisted the German occupation of the territory in the late 19th and early 20th centuries and were almost annihilated. The Herero women dress as the early German missionaries taught them —turbans, beautifully designed blouses with leg-of-mutton sleeves, and voluminous skirts.

The Bushmen live in the desert areas of Namibia. These fascinating people have retained their primitive nomadic way of life and generally roam the Kalahari Desert in search of animals, berries, and roots for food. They are a small people, averaging just over 4 ft. (1.2 m.) in height.

The Hottentot, or Nama, as they are also known, live on several small reserves in the southern part of the country. Some Nama work on farms and ranches or hold jobs in nearby towns. Together with the Bushmen, these people are known as Khoisan.

Education. Namibian children between the ages of 7 and 16 are required to go to school. Virtually the entire adult European population is literate; about 4 out of 10 Africans can read and write. A postsecondary academy was opened in the early 1980s.

Language. Afrikaans (a language based on Dutch) and English are the principal languages of the country, but German is widely used among members of the European community. The Africans speak mainly their traditional languages.

Religions. Formerly, the African population followed tribal religions. Most black Namibians have now converted to Christianity.

ECONOMY

Because of the arid conditions throughout much of the country, most Africans engage only in subsistence agriculture and the grazing of farm animals. South of Windhoek it becomes so dry that farming is almost impossible and only sheep and goats can be grazed. The skins from the karakul sheep in this area are sold for Persian lamb fur coats.

North of Windhoek cattle become more important and are the mainstay of the economy. In some valleys farms have been laid out, and windmills pump water from beneath the surface of the dry land. The government is in the process of building a dam and irrigation works on the Cunene River, which will help put agriculture on a more solid basis and also provide much-needed hydroelectricity.

Diamonds, Namibia's most important export, are to be found under the sands of the Namib Desert. Offshore, additional diamonds are mined by a kind of seagoing vacuum cleaner that sucks them up from the ocean floor. Most of the diamonds are of gem quality. Other important minerals found in Namibia are lead, zinc, and copper.

Fishing is one of the major industries. Fish, particularly pilchards, and rock lobsters are processed for export at the canneries in Walvis Bay and Lüderitz.

HISTORY AND GOVERNMENT

Long before recorded history the Bushmen and Hottentots lived in the area now known as Namibia. Over the centuries many other African groups moved into the territory.

The first European to visit the area was the Portuguese navigator Diogo Cão, who landed on the sandy coast of southwestern Africa in 1484. During the centuries that followed, missionaries and merchants from Europe began to arrive in the region. In 1884, Germany proclaimed a protectorate over the territory. The area was gradually enlarged, and in 1892, the colony of German Southwest Africa was formed.

In 1915, near the beginning of World War I, German troops were forced to surrender the territory to invading South African troops. In 1920 the territory was made a League of Nations mandate under South African administration. The United Nations voted in 1966 to eventually assume control of the area, which it renamed Namibia, but South Africa continued its rule. The South-West African People's Organization (SWAPO), supplied with Soviet and Cuban arms, then began guerrilla warfare to win independence. SWAPO refused to participate in 1980 elections for bodies representing each of the 11 officially designated population groups in the territory. In December 1988, South Africa agreed to give up Namibia as part of a settlement that provided for the withdrawal of Cuban troops from Angola. SWAPO won a majority of seats in elections held in November 1989 for a constituent assembly, and SWAPO leader Sam Nujoma was chosen the nation's first president.

HUGH C. BROOKS, Director, Center for African Studies, St. John's University

The National Assembly in Gaborone, the capital.

BOTSWANA

Botswana is a new African nation with old as well as new problems and a great dream. Formerly the British protectorate of Bechuanaland, Botswana has been independent since 1966. It is a black nation that at independence was all but surrounded by white-dominated nations. It had just had a 5-year drought. Many predicted that Botswana would collapse and fall under South African domination. Instead, Botswana stands with strength, holding its principles of racial equity and justice.

THE PEOPLE

The Batswana (people of Botswana) number 800,000. The population is mainly Bantu but includes Bushmen and whites. The Tswana, a branch of the Sotho peoples of southern Africa, are the main Bantu group.

The Bushmen, estimated at 29,000, include many who claim Bantu relationships. Bushmen live as hunters and gatherers, most of them depending on the plant and animal life of the Kalahari Desert for their food. Their nearest neighbors are Tswana Kgalagadi, who live on the desert margins. This Bantu group borrowed the hunting and gathering ways of the Bushmen and added the cultivation of crops.

In the Okavango Basin, Bushmen and Bantu from central Africa live by fishing. The Bantu also do some farming in the swampland. Their neighbors, the Tawana, a segment of the Tswana, mix cattle herding with an increasing amount of farming, learned from the swamp farmers.

Elsewhere the people are all Tswana. Unlike most Bantu, the Tswana build large towns. People live in the center, farm in a circle up to 20 miles (32 kilometers) out from the center, and herd their cattle from that distance to about 50 miles (80 km.) from the center.

A Botswana village.

A small European population, estimated at about 5,000, has for 35 years increasingly integrated with the blacks.

More than a third of the Batswana read and write Setswana, a Bantu language, and more than a fourth read and write English. Bushmen use their "click" (Khoisan) language, which has a number of clicking sounds, but many Bushmen know Setswana.

Unlike most African nations, Botswana has more literate women than men. Boys often miss school to herd cattle. However, more men than women attend higher classes. There is a campus of the University of Botswana and Swaziland at Gaborone.

Way of Life. European dress is almost universal. Two kinds of head-gear are popular: funnel-shaped straw or reed hats and fur caps, Daniel Boone style. Children under 8 may wear aprons of dangling orange strings tipped with glass beads.

Food is a mixture of European and Tswana. Breakfast cereals, ice cream, tea, coffee, and hard liquors take their place with traditional foods. These include steamed mush, made of pounded or ground grains, such as millet, sorghum, and corn. Stewed wild or domestic meat mixed with tasty vegetables is another favorite dish. A brew of lightly fermented grain is popular. People drink milk, but prefer it when it is curdled.

The Bushman's shelter is a loosely made lean-to of grass. Tswana build sturdy round or oblong houses. Heavy upright poles are set in the ground, and branches placed horizontally are tied to the poles. Clay is plastered onto the branches, inside and out, and painted. Round houses are fitted with conical roofs, oblong houses with long, peaked roofs. Both kinds are covered with thick thatch of grass. Around the Tswana house is a veranda of clay or cement, and around this a fence of sticks or a hedge of cactus. Wealthier Africans and Europeans have brick or cement houses with metal or tile roofs.

FACTS AND FIGURES

REPUBLIC OF BOTSWANA is the official name of the country.

THE PEOPLE—are called Batswana.

CAPITAL: Gaborone.

LOCATION: Southern Africa. **Boundaries:** Zambia, Zimbabwe, South Africa, Namibia.

AREA: 224,711 sq. mi. (582,000 sq. km.).

PHYSICAL FEATURES: Highest point—5,922 ft. (1,805 m.). **Lowest point**—1,800 ft. (549 m.). **Chief rivers**—Okavango, Chobe, Shashi, Limpopo, Molopo, Nosob, Botletle. **Major lake**—Ngami.

POPULATION: 1,169,000 (latest estimate).

MAJOR LANGUAGES: English (official), Setswana.

MAJOR RELIGIONS: Christian, animistic beliefs.

GOVERNMENT: Republic. **Head of government**—president. **Legislature**—national assembly. **International cooperation**—United Nations, Commonwealth of Nations, Organization of African Unity (OAU).

CHIEF CITIES: Gaborone, Francistown, Selebi-Phikwe.

ECONOMY: Chief minerals—diamonds, nickel, copper, coal, asbestos, manganese, gold, soda ash, salt. **Chief agricultural products**—corn, sorghum, millet, cotton, peanuts. **Industries and products**—cattle herding, meat, hides. **Chief exports**—diamonds, textiles, hides and skins, canned meat. **Chief imports**—manufactured goods, cereals, textiles, sugar.

MONETARY UNIT: Pula.

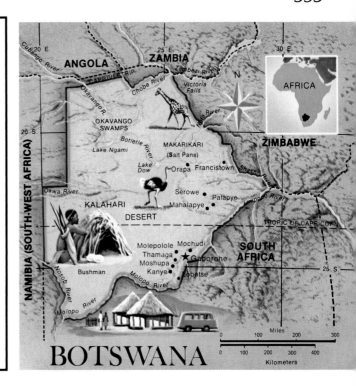

BOTSWANA

THE LAND

Botswana is landlocked more than 300 miles (480 km.) inland from the Atlantic and Indian oceans. The Republic of South Africa, with the Caprivi Strip and Namibia (South-West Africa), encircles all but the northeastern boundary. This is closed by Zimbabwe. One small point in the north touches Zambia.

Botswana's 231,804 square miles (600,372 square kilometers) form a sloping table. Its eastern edge averages over 3,000 feet (915 meters) above sea level. The east is a savanna region, with grasses, bushes, and trees. The land slopes down to about 1,800 feet (549 m.) above sea level in the west, passing through a region of steppes to true desert.

Rainfall ranges from a high of about 25 inches (64 centimeters) in the east to less than 10 inches (25 cm.) in the west. The rains come in the hot season, from November to May. Few rivers run except during the rains. Two constantly flowing rivers come from Angola through the Caprivi Strip. They are the Cubango, which becomes the Okavango, and the Cuando, which becomes the Chobe.

Natural Resources.   Botswana has great mineral wealth: coal, asbestos, manganese, and gold. Soda ash and salt abound in Makarikari Salt Pans. Late in the 1960's rich deposits of diamonds, nickel, and copper were found in the northeast.

In northern forests teak and other hardwoods are found. Large herds of elephant, wildebeest, buffalo, and zebra move with African antelope and other wild game throughout the north.

Cities.   Nearly half the population live in towns of over 5,000 people. The largest cities are **Gaberone,** the capital, with a population of over 54,000, and Francistown and Serowe, with populations of more than 30,000. Kanye and Lobatse are also leading cities. The major industrial plants, for the slaughtering and canning of beef, are in Lobatse.

ECONOMY

Diamonds, first discovered in Botswana in 1967, gave the country one of the world's greatest rates of economic growth in the 1980s. By 1990, it produced more diamonds by value than any other nation. Diamonds provide about 75 percent of all export income; the country also has valuable deposits of copper-nickel, uranium, and chromite.

Mining employs only a small portion of the labor force, however, and many of Botswana's people do not share in its mineral wealth. Agriculture, particularly cattle-raising, still provides the living for about 85 percent of the population, and unemployment is high. The chief food crops are corn and sorghum; cotton and peanuts are also grown. Agriculture was adversely affected by a severe drought from 1981–87, although government aid programs kept people from starving. Traditionally, many men from Botswana worked in mines and on farms in neighboring South Africa, but this source of jobs is declining. The safari and tourist industries and the sale of local handicrafts provide some additional income. Botswana's manufacturing sector is small, and the government is seeking foreign investment to reduce the dependence on diamonds and create jobs.

Botswana, Lesotho, Namibia, Swaziland, and South Africa are joined in a customs union. Land-locked Botswana is heavily dependent on South Africa to transport its imports and exports. It is a member of the Southern African Development Co-ordination Conference (SADCC), founded in 1979 in an effort to reduce the region's economic dependence on South Africa.

HISTORY AND GOVERNMENT

Historians believe that Tswana cattlemen moved south into present-day Botswana about 1,000 years ago, wedging themselves between the Bushmen to the west and the earlier cattlemen, the Nguni, to the east. The Tswana gradually took over highlands from below Victoria Falls to what is now Lesotho. Between 1702 and 1778 the Boers, who came north from Cape Town, South Africa, found Bantu tribes in battle. After the establishment of its first mission in 1820, the London Missionary Society under Robert Moffat tried to help settle wars among Tswana and between Tswana and Nguni. In 1837 the Boers drove out the Nguni but were then a threat to the Tswana. Advised by the missionaries, the Tswana chiefs asked the British for help. In 1885 the Bechuanaland Protectorate was formed. It continued until Botswana became a free nation on September 30, 1966. The first elected president was Sir Seretse Khama, who was succeeded, upon his death in 1980, by Vice President Quett Masire.

The Botswana Constitution gives rights of citizenship to residents of all races. It provides for a national assembly to be elected every five years. This body elects the president, who appoints the vice president from among the members of the National Assembly.

Botswana lies in a part of Africa where European (white) dominance has lasted the longest but is now on the wane. South Africa, Botswana's main trading partner, previously tried to influence Botswana's policies. But the government of Botswana resisted such pressures and steered an independent course.

CHARLES EDWARD FULLER, Chairman, Sociology and Anthropology Department
St. John's University

Victoria Falls, on the northern border of Zimbabwe.

ZIMBABWE

Inland in southern Africa, north of the Limpopo River and south of the Zambezi, lies Zimbabwe, a beautiful country. It is named Zimbabwe for an ancient African city, now in ruins. It was formerly named Rhodesia, for the British colonizer Cecil Rhodes.

THE LAND

The Limpopo River forms much of the country's southern border, separating it from the Republic of South Africa. On the northern border is the turbulent Zambezi River, whose magnificent Victoria Falls stretches for more than a mile across to Zambia, to the north. In the early 20th century a railway bridge was flung across the Zambezi at the first gorge below the falls. The train passes so near the falls that passengers can feel their spray.

Zimbabwe shares its northeastern and eastern borders with Mozambique. Since Zimbabwe is landlocked, ports in Mozambique provided access to the ocean. This access was lost when Mozambique closed its border with Zimbabwe in the period 1975 to 1979.

The Veld Country   Most of Zimbabwe is a plateau, and the high veld ("veld" means "grassland" in Afrikaans) is its heartland. A traveler reaching this high country can gaze over an expanse of softly rolling green land. As the dry season (April to October) comes on and the tall veld grasses change from green to brownish-yellow, the plateau looks like a rippling sea of gold.

Harare, formerly Salisbury, the capital of Zimbabwe.

Outcrops of granite rock called kopjes dot the plateau. In fact, the Matopo Hills in the west are almost entirely granite. Other mountains—the Manica, the Vumba, the Inyanga, and the Chimanimani—lie in the Eastern Highlands region near the Mozambique border.

Apart from a few peaks in the Eastern Highlands, the high veld is the loftiest land in Zimbabwe. Comprising one-fourth of the land area, the high veld has an altitude of between 4,000 and 6,000 ft. (1,220–1,830 m.) and stretches northeast to southwest across the middle of the country. It has a temperate climate.

North and south of the high veld the land drops away to the middle veld, where elevations are between 2,000 and 4,000 ft. (610–1,220 m.). There the land is more eroded and the climate hotter. The low veld is the term used for the Limpopo and Zambezi river valleys and for a wide floodplain in the southeast. These areas are below 2,000 ft. (610 m.).

Climate. Most of the country is rather dry, especially the west. There are four seasons. The cool season begins in May. Days are warm and sunny, but at night there is frost. At the end of August the cool season ends and the hot season begins. The hottest period is in mid-October. In November the main rainy season starts, lasting till March. Between March and May comes the post-rainy season, when just enough rain falls to ripen crops.

Cities and Places of Interest. The gleaming white buildings of **Harare** (formerly Salisbury), the capital city, jut up suddenly from the Mashonaland plateau. Harare was founded at Fort Salisbury in 1890 by white settlers from South Africa. The city grew slowly at first, but by the 1980s was a major metropolitan center. Tobacco curing and food processing are important industries. Furniture, building materials, and fertilizers are leading products. Of more interest to visitors, however, are the handsome government buildings and the University of Zimbabwe.

The Acropolis, a hilltop fort at Zimbabwe, was built by the Bantu centuries ago.

In the western part of the high veld is **Bulawayo,** the second largest city and the main commercial center. It is the hub of a highway network and the main junction of the country's railway lines. The city manufactures metal products, tires, and farm equipment.

Northwest of Bulawayo are the Khami Ruins, remains of stone buildings and terraces constructed by the Rozwi, a Bantu people.

Other important cities in Zimbabwe include Chitungwiza, Gweru (formerly Gwelo), and Mutare (formerly Umtali). A lovely small city, Mutare lies in a valley encircled by the Manica and the Vumba mountains. To the north, in the Inyanga Mountains, is the country's highest peak, Mount Inyangani (8,517 feet; 2,596 m.). In the Inyanga are Bantu ruins covering between 2,000 and 3,000 square miles (5,180–7,770 sq. km.).

Zimbabwe, or Great Zimbabwe, near Fort Victoria, is the country's major Bantu ruin and the largest royal temple-fort complex in black Africa. The site was probably occupied as early as A.D. 500. But the buildings there today were built by successive Bantu groups between the 11th century A.D. and 1800. It has three main parts: the Temple, whose high walls enclose two cone-shaped towers; the Acropolis, a fortified hill; and the Valley of Ruins, an area of walled enclosures.

THE PEOPLE

The vast majority of the country's people are Bantu. This majority increased in the early 1980's as a growing number of whites of European ancestry left the country. The Bantu are black Africans who are a mixture of Hamitic and Negroid strains. The main Bantu groups are the Mashona and the Matabele (or Ndebele).

The Mashona, who live in the north and east, are the larger group. Their forebears seem to have been in this part of Africa since between A.D. 1000 and 1400. The Matabele, who live in the south and west, are the smaller group. After they entered the country, about 1837, they dominated the Mashona. The Mashona speak Shona, and the Matabele speak Ndebele. Both are Bantu languages.

The European residents in Zimbabwe make up less than 2 percent of the population. They live mainly in the high veld. The term "European" is used simply to mean "white." Many whites are immigrants from South Africa, of either English or Afrikaner (early Dutch settler) background. The language of the whites is English, and the vast majority are Christians. The whites continue to dominate the economy but have given up their hold on the government.

Two other important groups are the Coloureds and the Asians. In southern Africa the word "Coloured" is used to mean anyone of mixed descent. It is never used of a full-blooded Bantu. The Asians, who are Indians, Chinese, and Japanese, are primarily merchants.

Way of Life

There are essentially three life styles in Zimbabwe. The traditional life of the nearly two-thirds of the Bantu who live on Tribal Trust Lands (government lands set aside for the Bantu); the life mode of the more than one-third of the Bantu who work in the white society; and the life style of the whites.

Tribal Life. The Bantu village has from 6 to 50 small huts, or *kaias,* usually grouped around a cattle kraal, or pen. The cattle are the villagers' most valuable possessions. The basic Bantu social unit, the clan, is the basis also of the village. All the villagers are related to each other. Though many Bantu on the Trust Lands have become Christians, the greater number still practice ancestor-worship.

When a Bantu couple marry, their relatives help build their small, round house. The walls of the *kaia* are made of a mixture of mud, clay, and grasses plastered over a framework of poles. The cone-shaped thatched roof is made from sheaves of veld grasses. If the husband

A rural Bantu village in Zimbabwe.

FACTS AND FIGURES

OFFICIAL NAME: Republic of Zimbabwe.

NATIONALITY: Zimbabwean(s).

CAPITAL: Harare.

LOCATION: Southern Africa. **Boundaries**—Mozambique, South Africa, Botswana, Zambia.

AREA: 150,806 sq. mi. (390,580 sq. km.).

PHYSICAL FEATURES: Highest point—Mount Inyangani (8,517 ft.; 3,596 m.). **Lowest point**—Limpopo River valley (660 ft.; 201 m.). **Chief rivers**—Zambezi, Limpopo. **Major lakes**—Kariba.

POPULATION: 10,119,037 (1989).

MAJOR LANGUAGES: English (official), ChiShona, Si Ndebele.

MAJOR RELIGIONS: Christianity, traditional African religions.

GOVERNMENT: Republic. **Head of state**—president. **Legislature**—parliament.

CHIEF CITIES: Harare, Bulawayo, Chitungwiza.

ECONOMY: Chief minerals—coal, chrome, asbestos, gold, nickel, copper. **Chief agricultural products**—tobacco, corn, tea, sugar, cotton, livestock. **Industries and products**—mining, steel, textiles, chemicals. **Chief exports**—tobacco, asbestos, cotton, copper, tin. **Chief imports**—machinery, petroleum products, wheat, transportation equipment.

MONETARY UNIT: Zimbabwe dollar.

marries other wives, as some rural Bantu still do, each wife has her own *kaia*. The Matabele *kaias* are sometimes square and decorated with geometric designs. In some areas, brick houses are replacing *kaias*.

When children are born they are loved by all their many relatives. At 7 a boy begins to help guard the sheep and goats. The girls learn to make clay pots and jugs and to carry them on their heads. Boys of 10 begin to help tend cattle. The girls of 10 learn household duties. The men tend the cattle, while the women grow maize (corn).

Because the poor Bantu lands cannot always yield enough food, the father must sometimes leave home to work in the city or on the big white-owned farms. Sometimes whole families go.

Townships. The Bantu who work for white farmers or mining companies rent some of their employer's land and build homes on it. But the Bantu flocking to the cities for jobs live in "native townships," set up outside the city. Life in the townships is hard for the newly arrived Bantu, who often do not know English.

"European" Life. Those white people who have chosen to remain in Zimbabwe generally live the good life. Many have modern, Western-style houses, often with pretty yards and swimming pools. Both houses and grounds are cared for by Bantu servants. Zimbabwe's constitution guaranteed the whites a certain number of seats in parliament; these provisions could not legally be changed until 1987, when the white seats were eliminated.

Education

The University of Zimbabwe, located in Harare, opened its doors in 1955 and has always been a multiracial institution. The 20 or so teachers colleges have been multiracial by law only since 1979. Indeed, before 1979 there were two separate educational systems below the university level—one for Africans and one for Europeans. But in 1979, when a limited form of black majority rule came to Zimbabwe, eight statutes barring racial discrimination went into effect. One of these prevents segregation in public education.

ECONOMY

Zimbabwe has two distinct economic systems. One is the family farming economy of the tribal Bantu. The other is the modern economy built and run by the whites. Maize (corn) is the chief crop of the tribal farmers. They also grow some beans and rice, and keeping cattle provides them with milk.

The separation of the two economies derives from a policy of land division between the races. The law under which this was done, the Land Apportionment Act of 1930, was repealed in 1978. But when the act was in force, it gave 42 percent of the land to the Bantu and 48 percent of the land to the whites. The whites got the fertile cool land of the high veld, near to the railways and the highways. The Bantu areas tended to be in the hotter middle and low velds, where the land is poorer and far from the highways and the rail lines.

About one third of the Bantu work in the white-run economy as miners, farm workers, or factory hands. In the past it was rare for a Bantu to advance from laborer to foreman. The average white still earns about ten times what the average Bantu earns in a year.

Minerals.   Gold has first place among the country's minerals. Others are asbestos, chrome ore, coal, iron, copper, and nickel.

A Sunday afternoon soccer match in Harare.

Bulawayo's wide streets were designed for the many-teamed ox wagons of the 1890's.

Agriculture. Tobacco remains the country's leading export. Other important products of the high veld farms and ranches are maize (corn) and cattle. In the 1950's sugar and cotton began to be grown in the low veld, and sugar became a major export. Citrus fruits, tea, wheat, sorghum, millet, rice, peanuts, and cassava are also grown.

Industry. Heavy industries include metals, building materials, and farm machinery. Flour milling, sugar refining, textiles and clothing, engineering, fertilizers, and paper are all important, too.

The manufacturing of consumer goods increased sharply after 1965, when the country claimed independence without Britain's permission. Britain and the United Nations, thinking the country to be in rebellion, asked other countries to stop trading with it. The people responded by starting over 1,000 industries to make their own goods.

The economic sanctions, in effect until 1980, reduced export markets. Tobacco, the major export, was hurt most. The government had farmers reduce the crop. Sugar also was hurt badly. Sanctions made most farmers diversify their crops, with cotton a favorite substitute.

HISTORY AND GOVERNMENT

Iron Age people who were probably Bantu began to enter what is now Zimbabwe from regions to the north between about A.D. 500 and 1000. The Stone Age Bushmen who had lived in the area before were gradually absorbed or pushed out.

Shona-speaking Bantu groups came in from the north between about 1000 and 1400. One group, the Karanga, founded the Monomotapa kingdom in the mid-15th century. It lasted for 200 years, though after 50 years its southern half split away under a clan called the Rozwi.

The Rozwi overthrew the Monomotapa kingdom just before 1700.

The Rozwi stayed powerful for over 100 years but were declining when the Matabele came in 1837. Led by Mzilikaze, the Matabele soon dominated the whole country from the western region around their capital, Bulawayo. This area came to be called Matabeleland.

The English Arrive.   Lobengula, Mzilikaze's son, was king of the Matabele in the late 1880s. At this time Cecil Rhodes, who dreamed of extending British power from "the Cape to Cairo," set his sights on the region now called Zimbabwe. In 1888 Rhodes' agents obtained from Lobengula mineral rights in the area. Rhodes went to England and set up the British South Africa Company (B.S.A. Company).

To solidify the company's claim, Rhodes sent the Pioneer Column, made up of 180 white settlers, 117 ox wagons, and 500 police guards, into Mashonaland in 1890. Setting out from South Africa, the column crossed into what is now Zimbabwe in June. It skirted Matabeleland and arrived in Mashonaland in August, setting up a base camp called Fort Victoria. The column then pushed north to found Fort Salisbury in September. Farmers followed them, settling along the same route.

Wars between the Bantu and the settlers broke out in 1893 and 1896. The first crushed the Matabele and opened Matabeleland for settlement. These wars left a lasting scar on race relations in the country.

In 1895 the name Rhodesia was adopted by the B.S.A. Company for Mashonaland and Matabeleland. But they later came to be known as Southern Rhodesia instead to distinguish them from Northern Rhodesia on the other side of the Zambezi. The B.S.A. Company governed Southern Rhodesia until 1923, when it became a self-governing colony under white rule. In 1953 Southern Rhodesia joined with Northern Rhodesia and Nyasaland in forming the Federation of Rhodesia and Nyasaland. This federation ended in 1963.

The Road to Majority Rule.   When the federation was dissolved, Northern Rhodesia and Nyasaland became independent as Zambia and Malawi. Southern Rhodesia now became known simply as Rhodesia. Britain, which still retained authority, refused to grant independence to Rhodesia without a promise of majority rule. But no such promise was forthcoming. In 1965 the white-ruled Rhodesian Government unilaterally declared its independence from Great Britain. Britain looked on the declaration as illegal. In 1970 Rhodesia became a republic.

In 1978 Prime Minister Ian Smith and three black nationalist leaders agreed on a new constitution giving voting rights to blacks and safeguards to whites. In 1979 Bishop Abel Muzorewa became the first black prime minister of the country, renamed Zimbabwe Rhodesia. But militant black nationalists of the Patriotic Front continued to oppose the government, and there was international pressure for a settlement that would include all groups. Britain brought all parties together late in 1979. A cease-fire agreement was reached and a new constitution drafted. In 1980 new elections were held, and Robert Mugabe, leader of the Patriotic Front, became prime minister of the new nation of Zimbabwe. Mugabe won re-election in 1985. Two years later, Zimbabwe converted to a presidential-style form of government, with Mugabe as president. He was re-elected without opposition in 1990, when his Zimbabwe African National Union won 116 of 120 parliamentary seats. Soon after, the government released all of the 250 political prisoners it was holding.

HIBBERD V. B. KLINE, Jr., The University of Pittsburgh

Maputo is Mozambique's capital city.

MOZAMBIQUE

Late in the 15th century the Portuguese navigator Vasco da Gama reached Mozambique's palm-bordered white beaches. For nearly 500 years the association of this African land with Portugal was unbroken, until 1975 when Mozambique achieved independence. Mozambique stretches in a long, narrow strip along the Indian Ocean, on the southern coast of East Africa. Excellent natural ports rim its shoreline. In the past 30 years or so these have been developed, and a network of railroads has been built to serve them. A number of landlocked nations lying inland in southern Africa customarily send export products by rail across Mozambique to the Mozambican ports. Here the goods are transferred to ships and carried to markets all over the world. In recent years, however, the ports and railroads have deteriorated, partly because of civil war.

THE LAND

Mozambique appears on the map rather like an elongated Y, with the Zambezi River cutting through from the sea to the center of Africa just below the fork of the Y, where the most southern part of Lake Malawi begins to form the country's border.

Mozambique's climate is marked by two seasons: a wet, warm season from October to March and a dry, cooler season from April to September. A number of rivers and streams run across the northern and central parts of the country, and rainfall is heaviest in the north. Much of the south is extremely dry.

The country falls roughly into three physical regions. Along its extended coastline there is a region of sandy lowlands. The lowlands

Village women walk to market along a country road.

extend inland along the fertile and productive banks of the Zambezi, the Save, the Limpopo, and the other rivers that empty into the sea. Cashew trees and coconut palms flourish in the lowlands. Rice and other food crops are grown in the marshes.

In the interior, the land rises, forming plateaus that range in elevation from 500 to 2,000 feet (150–610 m.). Farther inland are mountain ranges. Tea estates have been developed near the Malawi frontier. In the north, between Lake Malawi and the coastal strip, is a high, rocky plateau. Cotton is grown in this area. Although the area around Maputo in the south is most heavily populated, the north is gaining importance in the economy as a result of cotton production.

An intensive search for valuable natural resources has revealed tantalite (used in making steel), beryl, copper, and bauxite, among others. There is some coal mining in the plateau region, and extensive deposits of natural gas have been discovered offshore.

The country has vast amounts of timber. Among the woods of commercial value are ebony, mahogany, African teak, African sandalwood, and ironwood. A wealth of animal life makes Mozambique a place of special interest to photographers, hunters, and tourists. In Gorongoza National Reserve thousands of animals, including elephants, lions, and buffalo, roam freely.

Cities

Maputo, the capital, is an extremely elegant and cosmopolitan city that lies in the southernmost part of the country. Maputo is not only Mozambique's largest city but also its chief port. Moreover, Maputo is

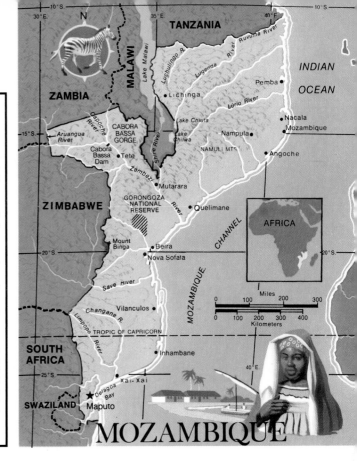

FACTS AND FIGURES

OFFICIAL NAME: Republic of Mozambique.

NATIONALITY: Mozambican(s).

CAPITAL: Maputo.

LOCATION: Southeastern coast of Africa. **Boundaries—** Tanzania, Indian Ocean, Mozambique Channel, South Africa, Swaziland, Zimbabwe, Zambia, Malawi.

AREA: 309,494 sq. mi. (801,590 sq. km.).

PHYSICAL FEATURES: Highest point—Mount Binga (7,993 ft.; 2,436 m.). **Lowest point—**sea level. **Chief rivers—**Zambezi, Save, Limpopo, Lugenda.

POPULATION: 14,275,301 (1989).

MAJOR LANGUAGES: Portuguese (official), various African languages.

MAJOR RELIGIONS: traditional African religions, Christianity, Muslim.

GOVERNMENT: Republic. **Head of state—**president. **Legislature—**People's Assembly.

CHIEF CITIES: Maputo.

ECONOMY: Chief minerals—coal, natural gas, copper, bauxite, titanium. **Chief agricultural products—**prawns, cotton, cashew nuts, sugar, copra, timber. **Industries and products—**food processing, chemicals, petroleum products, beverages, textiles. **Chief exports—**prawns, cashew nuts, shrimp, sugar, cotton. **Chief imports—**petroleum products, machinery, transportation and military equipment.

MONETARY UNIT: Metrical.

the head of the rail system that serves the economic heart of Southern Africa.

Beira in the narrow waist of the country, is the second largest port and is also an important rail center. The harbor is being rehabilitated and efforts have been made to restore the war-damaged rail lines. Beira handles cargo to and from central Africa. Other port cities are Nacala, Mozambique, Quelimane, and Inhambane. Tete and Mutarara, on the Zambezi River, are important inland cities.

THE PEOPLE

Most of the people of Mozambique are Africans, largely of Bantu stock. The population also includes some European settlers as well as Asians (Indians, Pakistanis, and Chinese) and people of mixed race. The country's official language is Portuguese. The Africans speak Bantu languages. The main religion of the European population is Roman Catholicism. Many of the Africans are Catholics; some are Protestants; and others follow traditional religions. And in the northern regions of Mozambique there are many Muslims.

Way of Life. There was a sharp contrast between two ways of life in Mozambique. There was the Portuguese world of the old coastal cities and the newer towns of the interior. The houses, parks, squares, and gardens still show a strong Portuguese influence. And then there was, and still is, the world of the small villages and the countryside, where traditional African life goes on in its own quiet rhythm.

Houses in the small villages are usually made of mud and straw and have cone-shaped thatched roofs. Most families plant crops that will supply them with food. Maize grows well in the sandy soil of southern and central Mozambique and is the main crop. Maize, ground into meal, then boiled and pressed into a ball, is a staple food. For people who live along streams and lakes or along the coast, fish and shellfish are a major part of the diet. Women and young boys help fish. Fishing is usually done with a simple hook and line or a bamboo rod.

Education. Formerly, only a very small percentage of Mozambique's African population could read and write. Before independence, Portugal began a program of educational reform. The new government in Mozambique has also emphasized education, especially literacy training. Today, it is estimated that one-third of adult Mozambicans can read and write, and hundreds of thousands are enrolled in literacy classes.

Education is compulsory in principle between the ages of 7 and 14. About half of all children of primary school age actually do go to school, and the number of children enrolled in school has risen each year. Mozambique's leading institution of higher education, now called Eduardo Mondlane University, was established in 1963 and is located in Maputo.

ECONOMY

The export of agricultural products is a major source of national income. Prawns are now the foremost export. After prawns, the most important exports are sugar, cashews, cotton, coconut products, sisal (used in making rope), and tea.

The total value of exports is the equivalent of many millions of dollars less per year than the cost of the goods Mozambique imports— petroleum products and machinery, mainly. Another source of national income is the money that migrant workers send home to their families from neighboring countries. Tourists who came to Mozambique's fine beaches also contributed substantially to the economy, but tourism is no longer encouraged. Drought, war, and economic mismanagement have taken a heavy toll on the crop yield, and food is scarce. In the late 1980's, Mozambique needed international food aid to combat wide-spread famine.

Portugal, under its third (1968–73) development plan, invested the equivalent of hundreds of millions of dollars in Mozambique. A number of projects to expand agriculture and industry and the transportation system and port facilities were undertaken.

One of the most important projects was a program to build an enormous hydroelectric station. The project involved damming the Zambezi River at the foaming cataracts of the Cabora Bassa Gorge, northwest of the city of Tete. Completed in 1975, the 500-foot-high (152 m.) dam and generating station is the largest in Africa. Its manmade lake is 150 miles (241 kilometers) long. The hydroelectric station provided the electric power for the station as well as a surplus for export until 1985, when sabotage shut down its operation.

HISTORY

On his first voyage to India (1497–98) the Portuguese explorer Vasco da Gama found Arab settlements along the entire African shore of the Indian Ocean. For centuries the Arabs had controlled the trade in African gold to India. Sofala, near present-day Beira, was the center of this trade.

Da Gama made a strong show of force against the Arabs. By the

Gorongoza National Reserve is the home of thousands of birds and animals.

turn of the century Portuguese trading posts and forts at the mouths of major rivers were regular ports of call on the new route to India. By 1510 hardly a town along the coast failed to recognize European authority. Thousands of pounds of ivory were bought and carried away each year in Portuguese ships, and the slave trade flourished as the labor needs of Brazil, Portugal's colony in South America, grew.

By 1700, however, Portugal had lost much of its eastern empire to the Dutch and English, and trade through Mozambique's ports had fallen off sharply. Mozambique entered a period of decline that was to last 200 years.

The country's present borders were agreed on at the Berlin Conference (1884–85), when the European powers carved Africa into spheres of influence. A later treaty between Great Britain and Portugal further defined the boundaries. Lisbon's dream of a vast African kingdom extending from the west to the east coast of the continent clashed with British ambitions in central and southern Africa. That is why Portuguese Mozambique on the Indian Ocean and Portuguese Angola on the Atlantic Ocean were separated by a wedge of British territory. This former British territory now consists of the countries of Zimbabwe, Malawi, and Zambia and the Transvaal region of South Africa.

Mozambique Under Portuguese Rule

While under Portuguese rule, Mozambique was considered to be an overseas province of Portugal. The country's affairs were administered by a governor-general appointed in Lisbon. Portugal's policy was the same in Mozambique as it was in the other African territories that were still under the Portuguese flag. The stated aim of this policy was to weld the entire population into a single cultural, economic, and political community. In theory, the factors that should have knit the people of Mozambique together were the Portuguese language, the Roman Catholic religion, and a strong pride in Portuguese culture. As events proved, however, these factors were not enough to maintain Portuguese rule forever.

Beginning in 1960 the Portuguese made an effort to make their form of colonialism more acceptable to an increasingly uneasy African population. Before 1961 a code known as the *indigenato* prescribed the steps by which an African could achieve the legal status and privileges of a fully assimilated Portuguese citizen. In 1961 the code was replaced by new legislation. In theory this gave all Africans equal civil rights and job opportunities with the Portuguese.

However, Africans critical of Portugal's policy saw the entire situation quite differently. Having watched the departure of all the other major colonial powers, they dismissed as a myth the idea that Africans could or should be turned into Portuguese. Rule of one people by another is intolerable in the 20th century, African critics said.

The Nationalist Movement and Independence

In 1964 an armed rebellion against Portuguese rule was launched by a union of Mozambican nationalist movements called Frelimo, from *Frente de Libertaçao de Moçambique* (Mozambique Liberation Front). As the years passed, more and more Africans gave their support to what was called the liberation movement. The money to equip the Frelimo military force came mostly from the independent African states.

Frelimo conducted its underground military and civic action campaigns within Mozambique from headquarters in neighboring Tanzania. The force was active throughout the northern third of Mozambique. To counter the revolt, Portugal increased its military force in Mozambique and built new communications facilities and airfields. Frelimo's first leader, Eduardo Mondlane, was assassinated in Tanzania in 1969. His successor, Samora Machel, continued the war against the Portuguese.

The strain of the war finally became too much for Portugal. In 1974 the Portuguese government was overthrown, and the country's new leaders acknowledged the right of Mozambique to independence. A transitional government made up of both Portuguese and Mozambicans governed the country until June 25, 1975, when it became independent.

Mozambique's first constitution stated that Frelimo is the "directing power of the state and society" of the People's Republic of Mozambique. Machel, the president of Frelimo, was also the president of Mozambique until his death in a plane crash in 1986. He was succeeded by Joaquim Chissano. After Mozambique gained independence, it came under attack from a rebel group, the Mozambique National Resistance Movement (Renamo), which was aided first by the white government of Rhodesia (now Zimbabwe) and then, until recently, by South Africa. By 1992, more than 1 million Mozambicans had died in the war. More than 5 million more were refugees and the economy was in ruins.

In 1990 the government approved a new constitution providing for a multiparty system, direct presidential and legislative elections, and a free-market economy, and the country was renamed Republic of Mozambique. In 1991 Renamo agreed to recognize the government's legitimacy and to begin operating as a political party after the signing of a general peace accord. In August 1992, as the devastation caused by the civil war was compounded by severe drought, the government and Renamo signed a tentative agreement calling for a cease-fire and democratic elections. The cease-fire became effective on October 4, 1992.

HELEN KITCHEN, Former Editor in Chief, *Africa Report*

Rice fields in the central plateau region of Madagascar.

MADAGASCAR

The island country of Madagascar has been called "the land of the living fossils" because of its many unusual plants and animals. Throughout the rest of the world they are found only in fossil form. The country abounds in birds, animals, and insects; but perhaps its most unusual inhabitant is the lemur, a primate now found almost exclusively in Madagascar. These agile little creatures are related to, and resemble, the monkey in general form and habits. Their large eyes glow palely at night as they jump from tree to tree in the forests. The Malagasy, as the people of Madagascar are called, revere the lemurs, and some of the people believe that the souls of the dead inhabit them.

Madagascar is also the land of the chameleons. About two thirds of those found in the world inhabit this country. Many species of birds living in Madagascar are to be found nowhere else, and this colorful land is ablaze with ancient varieties of flora that disappeared long ago from all other parts of the world.

THE LAND

Madagascar is composed of one large island and a number of minor adjacent islands. The main island is the fourth largest island in the world. It lies in the Indian Ocean about 250 miles (400 kilometers) across the Mozambique Channel from the southeast coast of Africa. The geographic and climatic conditions differ considerably in each of the six major regions of the island.

Perhaps the richest agricultural region of the country is in the northwest. Because of the soil deposited by the great rivers in this area, the land is suitable for growing rice, tobacco, peanuts, cassava, and cotton.

The east coast is a true rain forest, with an annual rainfall of about 110 inches (280 centimeters). Vegetation thrives in the warm and humid climate of this region. Coffee, rice, cloves, and vanilla are the principal export crops, while many tropical fruits and vegetables are sent to the markets.

The central plateau, with an altitude averaging 3,300 feet (1,000 meters), has a temperate climate. The plateau slopes sharply off to the east coast and less sharply to the west. On the plateau the growing of rice, coffee, and corn is possible because of the cool climate and rainy season. The area is also well suited for raising cattle.

The south is a semidesert of forbidding character. During the annual dry season some of the rivers of this region become mere trickles of water. However, during the rainy season some of the rivers turn into raging torrents that cut off all communication. Irrigation projects have made it possible to extend the cultivation of corn and sisal. The area is also used for the grazing of cattle and, in the most arid parts, goats.

The west is a region of gradual slopes, dropping to a fairly wide, flat plain near the sea. Because of adverse weather conditions—heavy rains alternating with extreme aridity—and badly eroded land, the interior area is almost uninhabited. The coastal plain, however, has a Mediterranean-type climate and is watered by four major rivers: the Betsiboka, Tsiribihina, Mangoky, and Onilahy. Most of the area was once used for grazing cattle, but in the past century rice growing has been introduced in the marshy areas near the rivers. Some attempts at vegetable farming have been successful.

The north is an area of high mountains, including the Tsaratanana Massif, the highest range in the country. It reaches an altitude of 9,450 feet (2,880 m.). The region has great forests as well as rich, well-watered plains. The chief agricultural products are sugarcane, coffee, vanilla, pepper, and rice.

CITIES

Antananarivo is the capital and also the largest city of Madagascar. It has a population of over 520,000. The narrow streets and hillsides of Antananarivo are lined with rows of brightly painted houses. In one part modern French shops and hotels give the streets a European atmosphere. A short distance away is the great Zoma market. Every Friday people from the central plateau region make their way to the Zoma to sell their vegetable products and handicrafts in the marketplace.

Principal port cities include Toamasina (Tamatave), Antsiranana (Diégo-Suarez), and Toliary (Tuléar).

THE PEOPLE

The inhabitants of this island nation refer to themselves as Malagasy. Although the origin of the Malagasy people is not historically documented, the evidence of language and customs indicates that the an-

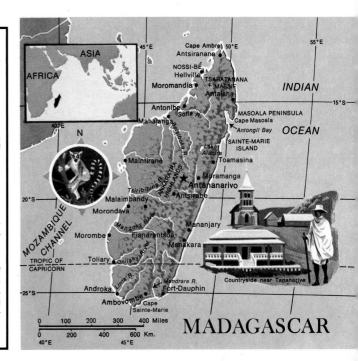

FACTS AND FIGURES

DEMOCRATIC REPUBLIC OF MADAGASCAR is the official name of the country.

THE PEOPLE—are called Malagasy.

CAPITAL: Antananarivo.

LOCATION: Off southeastern coast of Africa.

AREA: 226,657 sq. mi. (587,041 sq. km.).

PHYSICAL FEATURES: Highest point—Tsaratanana Massif (9,450 ft.; 2,880 m.). **Lowest point**—sea level. **Chief rivers**—Betsiboka, Tsiribihina, Mangoky, Onilahy.

POPULATION: 9,985,000 (latest estimate).

MAJOR LANGUAGES: Malagasy, French.

MAJOR RELIGIONS: Animistic beliefs, Christian.

GOVERNMENT: Republic. **Head of state**—president. **Head of government**—prime minister. **Legislature**—National People's Assembly. **International co-operation**—United Nations, Organization of African Unity.

CHIEF CITY: Antananarivo.

ECONOMY: Chief minerals—chromite, graphite. **Chief agricultural products**—rice, cassava, sugar, vanilla, coffee, corn, sisal, tobacco, livestock. **Industries and products**—processing of hides, meats, and sugar, cloves and clove oil. **Chief imports**—food, fuel, machinery, motor vehicles, chemical products, cotton textiles.

MONETARY UNIT: Malagasy franc (FMG).

cestors of the present Malagasy people came from somewhere in Indonesia, probably as traders.

Later migrations from Africa are certain as well. Many of the peoples play the *jejo vaotavo*, an instrument of African origin. It is a long, thin piece of wood with strings stretched along it and a calabash, or gourd, at one end. The presence on Madagascar of the zebu, the humpbacked cow of Africa, is also evidence of the migration of people from that continent. It is thought that some of the Africans came as slaves, brought by Arab traders from about A.D. 900 on. According to legends of several groups, many Arabs were present on the island. The Arabs seem to have been traders who set up their trading posts in areas with natural harbors. Antaimoro (people coming from the Moors), descendants of the Arabs, wrote in Arabic script and knew the Koran by A.D. 1600. Arabic influence spread rapidly across the island, leaving its cultural marks. The names for the days of the week and months of the year show Arabic influence. Everywhere on the island, especially in the south, one can see dances resembling those of the Turkish whirling dervishes and hear music with Arabic influence.

For the most part, Madagascar is a melting pot of races and cultures. However, the majority of the Malagasy peoples can be classified into eight important groups. The largest of these is the Merina community. Together with the Betsileo group, they constitute about one third of the country's population. Both groups live in the high plateau area in the central highlands. The majority of the rural Merina and Betsileo are engaged in the production of rice and the raising of livestock. The Merina also play an important role in the civil service.

The Betsimisaraka are found on the east coast of Madagascar. These people are skillful weavers who use reeds and creepers to make mats, clothing, and fishing and hunting nets. They cultivate rice and raise domestic animals.

The great Zoma open-air market in Antananarivo is a center of activity.

The Antandroy, Bara, and Mahafaly reside in the plains of the semi-arid south. They are basically cattle herders and depend on fishing and, to a lesser extent, farming, for their daily existence. Traditionally, the men usually do the herding and fishing, while the women tend the small gardens.

The Sakalava are found along the west coast of Madagascar. They are primarily cattle herders who also depend on fishing and agriculture for their livelihood. Rice is their most important crop.

The Tsimihety are farmers and herders who live in the mountainous region of the north. However, in recent years they, like many of the other groups, have begun to migrate to different parts of the island.

Most Malagasy men and women wear the *lamba*, a huge shawl. Some Merina wear ordinary unbleached muslin *lambas*, although others of this group wear brightly colored shawls, woven of heavy wool in a technique called strip-weaving. The Sakalava *lambas*, called *lamba-hoany*, are dyed in bright colors, often red. Those worn by the Bara are generally bright blue. The Betsimisaraka of the east coast usually wear woven raffia slip-on coats. Many of the people in the major cities wear Western-style clothing.

The staple diet of most Malagasy consists of rice, *brettes* (a green vegetable similar to spinach), and cassava. Those who can afford it have meat or fish with their rice. In the southern desert region corn (maize) is the staple grain.

Villagers, wearing "lambas," walk along a street in a small town near Antananarivo.

Bricks, used in the construction of houses, are left to dry in the sun.

Religious practices are centered around the worship of ancestors. Some of the people of Madagascar believe in the transmigration of souls —that is, that dead ancestors are born again as animals, such as crocodiles, snakes, or lemurs. Where these beliefs are held, such animals are greatly respected.

About 40 percent of the population is Christian; half of these are Roman Catholic and half are Protestant. There is also a sizable Muslim community.

All of the people of Madagascar share a common language— Malagasy. Along with French it is the official language of the country. Malagasy is written in roman letters. It has a soft sound and flows gently from the tongue. Malagasy contains many colorful phrases. The sun, for example, is called the "eye of the day."

Approximately 50 percent of the nation's children attend primary school. Some students go on to the secondary and technical schools on the island. Madagascar also has teacher training centers and agricultural schools. There is a university in Antananarivo.

Way of Life

The Malagasy share a great many things in common. While funeral customs differ from group to group, all the people of Madagascar believe that a dead person must be buried with great ceremony and that there must be some lasting evidence of his passing. The Merina built great tombs for their kings. The Betsileo hid their kings' bodies, covered with molten gold, in caves. The Mahafaly of the southern desert region build rectangular tombs about 4 or 5 feet (1.2–1.5 m.) high. On the tombs they place carved poles called *aloalo,* which depict events in the life of the dead person. The Sakalava bury their dead in cemeteries. Each grave is surrounded by a fence with carvings at the four corners and halfway between the corners. The Bara raise a large cross and cover the crosspiece with the horns of bulls that were eaten at the funeral.

The funeral is a scene of feasting, singing, and dancing. Some groups have funeral ceremonies that run as long as 30 days, although the government has recently decreed that no funeral may be more than 4 days long.

Family life in all of Madagascar is very close, and older people are treated with respect. Each village is run by a council. Older men are deferred to, and their opinions are held in high regard. The Malagasy believe that as a man grows older, he grows wiser; as such, his opinion is more valuable than that of a younger person. Public speaking, called *kabary,* is considered a great art. Especially prized is the recitation of proverbs (*hainteny*) and other wise sayings. Men of political ambition must be adept at public speaking and must learn many proverbs by heart.

The houses of the Malagasy are built of either packed earth or wood and are generally rectangular. In the rain forest of the east coast, houses are raised on stilts to avoid flooding. In the dry southern desert, where wood is scarce and flash storms cause severe flooding, houses are often temporary brush structures. The central plateau houses of the Merina and Betsileo are permanent dwellings. Formerly, they were made of planks; now sunbaked bricks or stamped earthen walls are more popular. These houses are usually three stories high with the first two floors divided into two rooms. The kitchen is located on the third floor. In

Many shops in Toamasina are owned by members of the Chinese community.

some parts of the country, houses are prefabricated, except for the frame. This type of construction arises from the belief that evil spirits try to get into houses to make the children sick. When a new house is being built, the spirits hover about, waiting to enter. For this reason, the frame is built and left standing for as long as a year while the walls and roof are made in secret. On the day when the diviner has determined that the spirits have become bored with waiting, the people rush at the frame from all four sides, holding the prefabricated walls. Soon the house is complete, the doors and windows are shut, and the spirits are left outside.

The Malagasy are famous for their outrigger canoes, which were probably introduced by early Indonesian traders. The people of the west coast use outriggers for fishing among the reefs, while the residents of the east coast have adopted the Arab dhow.

Ironworking seems to have been known to the Malagasy before the advent of Europeans, as were the arts of toolmaking, strip-weaving, pottery-making, cattle breeding, goldsmithing, and papermaking.

Madagascar has small but important communities of Europeans, Indians, and Chinese. The Europeans are active in commerce and industry centered around Antananarivo, while the Chinese own and operate small shops in Toamasina on the east coast of the island. The Indian population lives on the west coast of Madagascar. Like the Chinese, these people tend small businesses.

ECONOMY

The economy of Madagascar is based primarily on agriculture. Agricultural production accounts for 90 percent of exports and provides

By their home in the rural village of Anosibe, women thresh
rice and pound cassava in preparation for their evening meal.

jobs for 85 percent of the population. The variations of soil and climate
throughout the country lend themselves well to the raising of many
different crops.

Rice is grown on over half of the cultivated acres and is the most
important food crop. A variety of high quality rice has been developed,
primarily for export. The most important cash crops are coffee, vanilla,
sugar, sisal, and tobacco. Coffee is the leading export. Madagascar produces about two thirds of the world's vanilla.

There are more cattle than people on the island. But cattle are
looked on as a status symbol rather than a source of income. Hogs,

sheep, and goats are also raised by the people. Poultry is abundant on the island, and fish are an important source of protein.

Madagascar has very little industry. Most manufacturing involves the processing of agricultural products.

Graphite, of which Madagascar is the world's largest producer, and mica are the only minerals that are mined in quantity. However, there are small deposits of coal, uranium, gold, nickel, bauxite, and precious stones. In 1980, the president announced the discovery of some oil.

HISTORY

Madagascar is first mentioned by Arab trade documents of the 10th century and seems to have been the southern end of the Arab trade route at that time. There is speculation that the island of the great roc, the legendary bird of great size mentioned in tales of Sinbad, may have been Madagascar. The first European contact dates from 1500, when Diogo Dias, a Portuguese sea captain, sighted the southeastern coast of Madagascar upon rounding the Cape of Good Hope. Once the island became known in Europe, Dutch, Portuguese, French, and English traders attempted to set up colonies or trading posts and oust the Arabs. Only the French succeeded in establishing a colony.

During the 16th and 17th centuries Malagasy kingdoms began to emerge. Most prominent were the Sakalava, Betsimisaraka, Betsileo, and Merina. By 1800, Andrianampoinimerina, king of the Merina, succeeded in uniting his people and paved the way for his son, Radama I, to attempt to conquer the island. Radama took control of most of Madagascar and subdued the Betsileo and Sakalava kingdoms, but he died before the empire could be consolidated.

During this time, British and French influence remained strong on the island. France finally won the struggle for control, forcing a protectorate on Queen Ranavalona III in 1885. In 1896 France took over the island completely on the pretext that the Malagasy could not govern themselves. Madagascar gained autonomy within the French Community in 1958 and won full independence in 1960. Its first president, Philibert Tsiranana, was ousted by the military in 1972. Didier Ratsirika, who had become head of the military government in 1975, was elected president under a new socialist constitution later that year. He was re-elected in 1982 and 1989. Late in 1991, after demands for political reforms, Ratsirika was stripped of many of his powers. A transitional government was installed pending elections under a new constitution.

GOVERNMENT

Under the socialist constitution approved in 1975, the name of the country was changed to the Democratic Republic of Madagascar. The country was a one-party state from 1975 to 1990. A president elected for a seven-year term was chief executive. There was an advisory Supreme Revolutionary Council and a directly elected legislature, which were dissolved in November 1991 pending the creation of a third republic. The president remained head of state and commander of the armed forces in a transitional government, but a prime minister from the opposition became head of government. A national forum met in 1992 to draft a new constitution under which democratic elections would be held.

NORMA McLEOD, Tulane University

The rugged and dramatic landscape just outside of Port Louis.

MAURITIUS

Mauritius is a land of variety. Europeans, Africans, Indians, and Chinese walk along the streets of Port Louis, the capital. Women can be seen dressed in saris or the latest Western fashions. Men may wear business suits, a dhoti, or the oriental pajama, while on their heads are fezzes, Gandhi caps, or wide-brimmed straw hats. The languages heard on the city's streets include Creole, which is a French dialect, French, English, two dialects of Chinese, and six Indian languages. The theme of variety and contrast is repeated in the buildings and in the beliefs of the people. There are Hindu temples, Muslim mosques, Roman Catholic and Anglican churches, and Chinese pagodas. In the country districts there are stately French colonial mansions and thatched huts, modern sugar factories and ramshackle wooden shops.

The very countryside reflects the diversity of the island. Bare black peaks, weirdly shaped, rise from glittering green fields of sugarcane. Shimmering white beaches are fringed with coconut palms and casuarina trees, while a blue sea breaks on the reefs offshore. Rushing rivers and dense vegetation contrast with dry regions dotted with aloe plants, whose tough fibers are used for making sugar bags. And all this is found on a small and isolated island.

THE LAND

Mauritius is an island that lies in the Indian Ocean about 20 degrees south of the equator. It has an area of 720 square miles (1,865 square kilometers) and a population of about 1,000,000. The population of

The Place St. Louis in Port Louis, capital city of Mauritius.

Mauritius is increasing by nearly 3 percent per year and may reach 2,000,000 by the end of the century. With more than 1,000 persons per square mile, overpopulation is the country's most serious problem.

Port Louis, the capital of Mauritius, has a population of over 135,000. It is situated on the northwest coast of the island and has an excellent mile-long harbor. Almost all of the trade of Mauritius passes through Port Louis. The town of **Curepipe**, which is the next largest community in Mauritius, is located in the center of the island.

Mauritius has a central plateau that reaches a height of 2,200 feet (670 meters). The land slopes gently to the north but drops sharply to the southern and western coasts. Coral reefs surround the island on all sides but the south. There are a number of peaks and craters created by volcanic action that ceased about 100,000 years ago. To this day 70 percent of the surface of the island is covered with lava from 2 to 20 inches (5–50 centimeters) thick. Before a farmer can plant, he must first clear his fields of volcanic rocks.

Dependencies

Mauritius has a number of island dependencies. The most important is Rodrigues, a volcanic island of 40 square miles (100 sq. km.) some 350 miles (560 km.) east of Mauritius. Most of its 21,000 inhabitants are Creole farmers and fishermen.

Agalega consists of two small islands totaling 27 square miles (70 sq. km.). It lies 580 miles (930 km.) north of Mauritius, and its 400 people work in coconut groves and copra manufacturing.

The Cargados Carajos archipelago consists of 22 tiny islands totaling only about ½ square mile (1.3 sq. km.). Its chief island, St. Brandon, is a fishing station.

Climate

The climate of Mauritius is subtropical, with temperatures ranging from 44 to 96 degrees Fahrenheit (7–35 degrees Celsius). The central plateau is a region of mists and rainfall that may reach 200 inches (500 cm.) a year. The southwest coast gets only 35 inches (89 cm.) a year. There are two seasons, summer and winter. Summer lasts from November to April, when the southeast trade winds blow. These winds sweep heavy rains onto the central plateau but leave the northern coast warm and dry. Sometimes during the summer there are devastating cyclones that are the terror of the islanders. In recent years the island has had cyclones that severely damaged installations and ruined crops. Winter, extending from the month of May to the month of October, is a period of calms and gentle southeast winds.

ECONOMY

Three geographical factors are responsible for the lack of greater social and economic development in Mauritius: its small size, its few natural resources, and its extreme isolation. Located 500 miles (800 km.) east of Madagascar, Mauritius is 1,551 miles (2,496 km.) from Durban, South Africa; 2,094 miles (3,238 km.) from Colombo, Ceylon; and 3,182 miles (5,120 km.) from Perth, Australia.

Because it has few natural resources, Mauritius depends on agriculture. About 90 percent of the arable land is planted with sugarcane. Sugar and its by-products account for 98 percent of exports. Tea production is being expanded and there are some small manufacturing industries, but more than half the food supply must be imported. Rice is the largest import both in quantity and value.

THE PEOPLE

Today most big sugar millers are Mauritians of French descent. Most of the big sugar planters are of either French or Indian descent. Most

There are stands of sugarcane like this one throughout Mauritius.

FACTS AND FIGURES

OFFICIAL NAME: Republic of Mauritius.

NATIONALITY: Mauritian(s).

CAPITAL: Port Louis.

LOCATION: Indian Ocean east of Madagascar.

AREA: 790 sq. mi. (2,045 sq. km.); with dependencies.

PHYSICAL FEATURES: Highest point—2,711 ft. (826 m.). **Lowest point**—sea level.

POPULATION: 1,081,000 (1991; annual growth 0.8%).

MAJOR LANGUAGES: English (official), Creole, Indian and Chinese dialects.

MAJOR RELIGIONS: Hinduism, Christianity, Islam.

GOVERNMENT: Republic. **Head of state**—president. **Head of government**—prime minister. **Legislature**—one-house Legislative Assembly.

ECONOMY: Chief agricultural products—sugar, tea, tobacco. **Industries and products**—food processing, garments and textiles, chemicals, metal products, tourism. **Chief exports**—textiles, sugar, tea, molasses. **Chief imports**—machinery, foodstuffs, petroleum products.

MONETARY UNIT: Mauritius rupee.

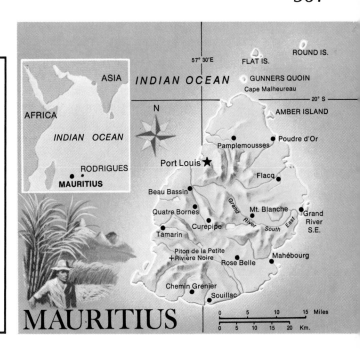

MAURITIUS

shopkeepers are of Chinese origin, and most laborers are of Indian origin. The Creoles, who are of mixed African, European, and Indian origin, are artisans, clerical workers, civil servants, and fishermen.

However, Mauritian society is not so rigidly made up as this would suggest. Many Mauritians of Indian origin have entered the professions and the civil services. Others have become planters raising vegetables. Some Mauritians of French descent have gone into government or business in Port Louis. There are a few British sugar planters, and a number of Chinese run large wholesale firms or have entered the professions.

About 40 percent of the population live in five main towns, which stretch up the hill toward the central plateau from Port Louis. The rest live in villages ranging in size from a few households to over 9,000 inhabitants. Most villages contain members of all ethnic groups except Europeans, who live on sugar estates or work in towns. Most large villages have a medical dispensary, a village hall, and various religious buildings and shops. Schooling in Mauritius is free but not compulsory, and most large villages have a primary school. More than 80 percent of the adult population is literate.

Customs

Each community has distinctive religious festivals. The Hindi-speaking Hindus make an annual pilgrimage to a sacred lake in the center of the island to collect holy water. They are dressed entirely in white and may carry elaborately decorated shrines. The Tamil-speaking Hindus walk barefoot over burning embers or climb ladders whose rungs are swords with the cutting edges turned upward. They do this to fulfill vows made to various deities.

The Muslims have an annual parade in Port Louis to commemorate the martyrdom of two Muslim saints. They build elaborate floats that are driven through the city's streets. At their New Year, the Chinese set off firecrackers and march and dance in a large, colorful parade. The

Roman Catholics celebrate many saint's days with processions and make an annual pilgrimage to the tomb of a French missionary who converted many slaves to Catholicism.

HISTORY

Originally, Mauritius was an uninhabited island. All Mauritians are the descendants of immigrants who arrived on the island after the 16th century. The island may have been known to Arab and Malay sailors in the Middle Ages, but the first Europeans to visit it were the Portuguese in the 16th century. They did not attempt to settle, but merely used the island to provision their ships.

In 1598 the Dutch visited the island and named it after their ruler, Prince Maurice of Nassau. In 1638 they established a settlement that lasted until 1710. It was about this time that the dodo, the famous flightless bird of Mauritius, became extinct.

In 1715 the French claimed the island, renaming it Ile de France. The first settlement was set up in 1722. Large numbers of slaves were imported from Africa and Madagascar. They were used to work on the plantations that were established all over the island. Attempts were made by the French to produce coffee, cloves, indigo, and sugar. Only sugar, however, could withstand the terrible cyclones that plagued the island, and sugar became the chief crop. During the war between Britain and France in the 18th and early 19th centuries, the Ile de France was an important base for French naval operations. In 1810, the British sent a large force of ships and men and captured the island.

By the terms of the Treaty of Paris in 1814 the island was formally ceded to the British, who renamed it Mauritius. The treaty also provided that the inhabitants be allowed to retain their religion, laws, and customs.

Thus the Roman Catholic Church, the French civil code, and the French language and culture were given official sanction. They have remained prominent features of Mauritian society to this day. Although English is the official language, French may also be used in the Legislative Assembly, which is the governing body of the island.

A new era began in the history of Mauritius when slavery was abolished in 1833. The freed slaves left the plantations and became artisans or small farmers. The planters were faced with a serious shortage of field labor. They turned to India as a source of workers. Between 1837 and 1907 nearly 450,000 Indians were brought to Mauritius. In the 19th and 20th centuries Chinese traders also arrived on the island.

GOVERNMENT

Mauritius became independent within the Commonwealth of Nations on March 12, 1968. Until 1992, it was a constitutional monarchy with the British monarch, represented by a governor-general, as the formal head of state. It is now a republic, headed by a president elected by the legislature. A prime minister is the head of government. Most members of the Legislative Assembly are popularly elected. Mauritius's first prime minister, Sir Seewoosagur Ramgoolam, retired in 1982. His successor, Anerood Jugnauth, retained the post in successive elections.

BURTON BENEDICT, University of California at Berkeley
Author, *Mauritius: Problems of a Plural Society*

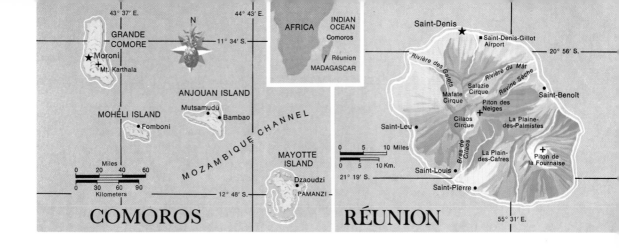

COMOROS

This nation of islands lies in the Indian Ocean at the northern entrance to the Mozambique Channel, which separates East Africa and the island of Madagascar. There are four main islands—Grand Comore, Mayotte, Anjouan, and Mohéli—plus a number of smaller islets. Together they have a total land area of 838 square miles (2,171 square kilometers).

The Land. Picturesque beaches and mangrove swamps line the coastlines of the islands. In the interior, mountain peaks contrast dramatically with deep valleys and steep-sided ravines. The islands are thickly forested in places, and are everywhere covered with lush green vegetation. Mount Karthala, on Grande Comore, is the highest point in the islands. An active volcano, it rises to a height of about 8,120 feet (2,475 meters). Its crater, one of the world's largest, measures nearly 2 miles (over 3 kilometers) in diameter.

Moroni, on Grande Comore, is the capital and largest city. About 15,000 people live in this city of narrow, winding streets, tree-shaded public squares, and white buildings. Dzaoudzi, which lies on an islet just off Mayotte island, was the capital until 1962.

The People. The Comoros' population of about 270,000 is a mixture of Arabs, Africans, and people from the island of Madagascar. Arabic and Swahili are the chief languages. The major religion is Islam, although there is a minority of Roman Catholics, most of whom live on Mayotte. Subsistence agriculture is the primary occupation of the people. Rice, cassava, corn (maize), sweet potatoes, and eggplant are the main food crops. The most important commercial crops are vanilla, perfume plants, coconuts, spices, sisal, sugarcane, and coffee.

History. The Comoros were known to sailors in ancient times. Later the islands came under Arab influence. The Portuguese discovered the Comoros in the 16th century and were followed by the French. It was not until the 19th century, however, that the islands became a French protectorate. The islands became an overseas territory of France in 1946. They were granted internal self-government in 1968. In a referendum held in 1974, most Comorians voted for complete independence, and independence was declared in 1975. The people of Mayotte, however, had voted to remain part of France, a decision upheld in a 1976 local referendum.

Reviewed by HUGH C. BROOKS, Director, Center for African Studies, St. John's University

RÉUNION

Réunion is an island in the Indian Ocean, lying to the east of the nation of Madagascar. Politically, it is an overseas department of France. Geographically, it is part of the Mascarene Islands, a group that also includes Mauritius and Rodrigues. (A separate article on MAURITIUS appears in this volume.)

The Land. Réunion is oval in shape and about 969 square miles (2,510 square kilometers) in area. It is volcanic in origin. One of its most striking sights is Piton de la Fournaise ("furnace peak"), a still-active volcano, which from time to time sends streams of lava down the mountainside into the sea. Much of the island consists of rugged mountains and high plateaus, surrounded by a narrow coastal plain. The highest point is Piton des Neiges ("snowy peak"), which rises to a height of over 10,000 feet (about 3,070 meters).

Parts of the island are thickly forested, although there has been widespread cutting of trees for lumber, and there are areas of fertile lowland that are extensively cultivated. A number of swift streams run from the interior; they sometimes overflow and destroy crops.

The climatic conditions vary according to location and altitude. The coastal regions have a tropical climate, but temperatures are more moderate in the mountainous interior. Rainfall is much heavier on the eastern side of the island than on the drier western part. The coastal areas are subject to occasional destructive hurricanes.

The capital and largest city of Réunion is **Saint-Denis**, which has a population of about 100,000. Other important cities are Saint-Louis and Saint-Pierre. There is air service between Gillot airport, near Saint-Denis, and Madagascar.

The People. The population of Réunion is about 500,000. The people are descendants of the first French settlers, Africans, Malays, Chinese, and Indians. French and a creole dialect are the major languages. The creole dialect is a mixture of French and African Bantu languages. Most of the people are Roman Catholics, but there are smaller numbers of Muslims and Hindus.

The majority of the people are farmers, and the economy of the island is essentially agricultural. Sugar is the most important crop, and much of the cultivated land is occupied by sugarcane plantations. Sugarcane processing and rum distilling are important local industries. Other crops include perfume plants, vanilla, coffee, tobacco, and manioc.

History. Although probably known to earlier explorers, Réunion was first visited by European navigators when the Portuguese explorer Pedro Mascarenhas discovered the island in the early 16th century. At the time it was uninhabited. The French landed and claimed the island in the 17th century, but permanent settlers did not arrive until some years later. Réunion became an overseas department of France in 1946. It is governed by a prefect, who is assisted by a secretary-general. There is an elected 36-member representative assembly called the General Council. Réunion is also represented in the French National Assembly and the Senate.

Reviewed by HUGH C. BROOKS, Director, Center for African Studies, St. John's University

SWAZILAND

Swaziland is a small inland country located near the southern tip of Africa. On the north, west, and south the country is bounded by the Republic of South Africa. On the east it is bounded by South Africa and Mozambique. Swaziland has only two cities of more than a few thousand people. Mbabane, the capital and largest city, is a major trade center. Swaziland's second-largest city, Manzini, is also a commercial center and is located near an international airport.

THE LAND

Despite its small size, Swaziland is divided geographically into three markedly different regions. The mountainous high veld, or high grassland, in the west consists of broken and rugged country averaging about 4,000 feet (1,200 meters) above sea level. Slopes are often too steep for cultivation and grazing is often poor, but the terrain is excellent for timber plantations. The middle veld, with an average elevation of 2,000 feet (600 m.) has good soil and plentiful rainfall. In the east the low veld is gently undulating, averaging about 1,000 feet (300 m.) in elevation. Bush-type vegetation is common and cattle ranching is extensive in the region.

Five rivers, the Lomati, Komati, Usutu, Umbeluzi, and the Ngwavuma flow from west to east. They cut their way across the entire country into Mozambique and then empty into the vast Indian Ocean. The development of irrigation projects along these rivers is particularly important to the agricultural growth of the country.

The rugged western region of Swaziland.

Swazi schoolchildren at recess.

Climate. The high veld has a humid, near-temperate climate with an average annual rainfall of 40 to 75 inches (100–190 centimeters). The middle veld is subtropical and drier, with 30 to 45 inches (80–110 cm.) of rain, while the low veld is almost tropical and has between 20 and 30 inches (50–80 cm.) of rain annually. Temperature ranges are greatest in the low veld and smallest in the high veld.

THE PEOPLE

About 97 percent of the people are Swazi, a Bantu group. There are about 10,000 whites (approximately half from South Africa), a few Asians, and 800 Eurafricans (people of mixed ancestry). There are about 8,000 to 10,000 Swazi working in the mines of neighboring South Africa. As conditions of living improve in Swaziland, fewer people find it necessary to work as migrants abroad.

Except for those who live in Swaziland's few modern towns, the majority of the people continue to follow a traditional way of life. Family homesteads are scattered throughout the countryside. Men wear the traditional attire of a cloth draped over the right shoulder and under the left armpit and a loincloth on top of which must be worn loinskins. On their arms and legs are bracelets and anklets. Yet the new is starting to blend into Swaziland's life, for these same men ride bicycles or drive automobiles.

The women in the countryside dress in bright cloths draped around them as skirts and cloaks. Some wear Western-style dresses. Small boys carrying long sticks herd the family cattle. They also sell brightly decorated handicraft items to tourists and city-dwellers. Everywhere the new and the old are beginning to stand in contrast.

FACTS AND FIGURES

KINGDOM OF SWAZILAND is the official name of the country.

THE PEOPLE—are called Swazi.

CAPITAL: Mbabane.

LOCATION: Southwest Africa. **Boundaries**—Mozambique, South Africa.

AREA: 6,704 sq. mi. (17,363 sq. km.).

PHYSICAL FEATURES: Highest point—6,000 ft. (1,829 m.). **Lowest point**—980 ft. (299 m.). **Chief rivers**—Lomati, Komati, Usutu, Umbeluzi, Ngwavuma.

POPULATION: 650,000 (latest estimate).

MAJOR LANGUAGES: English and siSwati (both oficial).

MAJOR RELIGIONS: Christianity, traditional African religions.

GOVERNMENT: Constitutional monarchy. **Head of state**—king. **Head of government**—prime minister. **Legislature**—two-house parliament.

CHIEF CITIES: Mbabane (42,000), Manzini (31,000).

ECONOMY: Chief minerals—asbestos, coal, iron. **Chief agricultural products**—cotton, sugarcane, maize, citrus fruits, pineapples. **Industries and products**—food processing, wood pulp, fertilizer. **Chief exports**—sugar, wood pulp, asbestos, canned and fresh fruit. **Chief imports**—manufactured goods, machinery and vehicles, fuels, chemicals, foodstuffs.

MONETARY UNIT: 1 lilangeni = 100 cents.

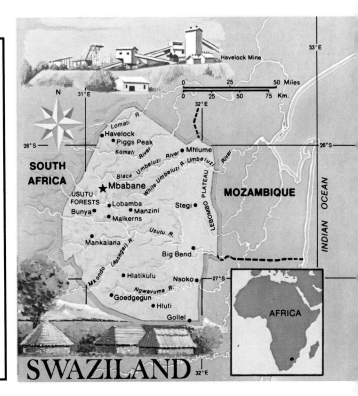

SWAZILAND

Lobolo. Swaziland is a polygynous society, and most Swazi men, like their King, have many wives. But all men, including the King, must pay lobolo to the bride's family. This entitles the man to give his surname to the wife's children. Otherwise, it is believed, a child would have to carry two family names. Although a few Swazi denounce lobolo as old-fashioned, most defend it as an important aspect of traditional values.

Religion. Although about 60 percent of the Swazi are Christian, approximately 40 percent of the adults still hold traditional beliefs. They acknowledge a creator or supreme being named Mkhulumngcandi. However, they do not believe that the creator concerns himself much with man's daily affairs. Instead the Swazi very often turn to their deceased ancestors to intercede with Mkhulumngcandi for their safety, health, and well-being.

Language and Education

The Swazi language, siSwati, is spoken by most of the people of the country. For business and governmental purposes, however, both English and siSwati are the official languages. Illiteracy has been a serious obstacle to the country's development culturally, economically, and politically. But this handicap is being overcome. Adult education has been encouraged, and it is now estimated that about 60 percent of Swaziland's adult population can read and write in English or siSwati.

About 75 percent of all children between the ages of 5 and 14 are in school. When Swaziland was a British protectorate, little effort was made by the government to develop a public education system. Even today, most schools are operated by churches, but they do receive financial assistance from the government.

A sawmill and chipboard factory in the Piggs Peak district in the northwest.

Education is highly valued, and there is keen competition among students to enter the few secondary schools available. Students who perform well are able to attend the University of Botswana and Swaziland, which has a campus at Kwaluseni. The university is operated cooperatively by the two small countries. There is also an agricultural college at Luyengo.

ECONOMY

Swaziland is rich in minerals and produces asbestos and iron ore in abundance. A large asbestos mine near Piggs Peak, in the north, produces Swaziland's second most important export. An iron mine in the northwest yields about 2,000,000 tons a year, and since 1967 iron ore has been the chief export. A railway was completed in 1964 that made it possible to export iron ore to Mozambique for shipment to Japan. Coal, gold, and tin are mined in small quantities. Swaziland has valuable timber plantations and produces such cash crops as cotton, tobacco, rice, and vegetables. Much of Swaziland's timber is used in the making of paper pulp. Two large mills process most of the sugar crop and help make sugar the country's third largest export.

HISTORY

The Swazi people trace their origins to the main body of the Bantu migrants who reached southeast Africa (Mozambique) in the 15th or 16th century. About 1750 they crossed into the area of present-day Swaziland. At first they were merely a number of small clans who joined under the leadership of the Dlamini clan. In the 1840's they were led by King Mswati, and perhaps they took their name from him. The Swazi were in constant conflict with the strong Zulu people who lived south of their area. King Mswati sought protection from the British, but this was refused. Under a convention signed in 1894 by Britain and South Africa, the Swazi were handed over to be protected by Paul Kruger's South African Republic, against their wishes.

After the Anglo-Boer War of 1899–1902, the British Government took over full administrative responsibility for Swaziland. The Swazi king, who was then called paramount chief, and his council were permitted to exercise authority only over Africans. In 1903 Swaziland became a British protectorate and in 1907 a high commission territory. Britain governed Swaziland through a resident commissioner who in turn was responsible to the British high commissioner in South Africa. In 1964 Swaziland received its first constitution, which the Swazi did not like, and the Swazi elected a legislative council.

A new constitution came into force in 1967 that gave Swaziland internal self-rule, recognized King Sobhuza II as king of Swaziland, and provided for a parliament composed of a house of assembly and a senate. In 1968 Britain granted Swaziland its independence, with King Sobhuza II as head of state. Under a new constitution proclaimed in 1978, there is a two-house parliament limited to debating government proposals and advising the king. The king appoints ten members of each house and the prime minister and cabinet.

Sobhuza II

King Sobhuza II died on August 21, 1982, in Mbabane. There was probably no other country in Africa that depended so much on its traditional ruler as Swaziland. Sobhuza II played an important role in the modern history of his nation. He was installed as paramount chief in 1921 under the British protectorate and ruled thereafter. According to Swazi custom Sobhuza married a number of wives from various places in the country each year, thereby fostering a sense of national solidarity and assuring male issue. Nobody knows for certain the number of wives the King took, but there were at least 50. The King was seen as the head of a homogeneous society sharing a common culture and language.

In addition to the modern capital of Mbabane, the village of Lobamba remained the traditional capital. There in his village, Sobhuza seemed an embodiment of ancient majesty. It was in Lobamba that great religious rituals and dances were held once a year. The Incwala, or "first fruits dance," was held annually in December or January. This colorful affair centered around the King and the Queen Mother, drawing thousands of Swazi in traditional garb.

The Future

As Swaziland began its early years of existence as an independent state, King Sobhuza and other Swazi political leaders realized that traditional ways of life must be sacrificed in part to modern ideas of nationalism and technology. But the King, like many of his people, was convinced that to make changes too rapidly would be harmful. The King hoped to integrate the traditional and popular Swazi customs with the good customs of the Europeans. "We should take the good from each and match them to produce the best."

These words might well serve as a motto for Sobhuza's successor. For nearly 4 years after Sobhuza's death the throne remained vacant, while the people of Swaziland waited for Crown Prince Makhosetive, one of 70 sons of the old king, to come of age. The 18-year-old prince was installed as King Mswati III in 1986.

RICHARD P. STEVENS, Director, African Studies Program, Lincoln University

A village of rondavels in the Maluti Mountains.

LESOTHO

A land of towering mountains and tranquil valleys, Lesotho has rugged scenery, a colorful way of life, and charm, which create an atmosphere difficult to find in most 20th-century societies. Landlocked Lesotho is one of the few independent countries of the world that exist as an enclave—a country entirely enclosed within the boundaries of another. This gives its giant neighbor—the Republic of South Africa, which borders Lesotho on all sides—the power to control Lesotho's foreign trade and blockade its borders.

THE LAND

The Kingdom of Lesotho is located in the southern part of the African continent. About one quarter of the country—the western part—is lowland, varying from 5,000 to 6,000 feet (1,500 to 1,800 meters) in height. This is the country's chief agricultural zone. The rest of the country is made up of highlands, which rise to over 11,000 feet (3,400 m.) in the Drakensberg range.

Climate. Rainfall is variable and averages approximately 28 inches (100 centimeters) over the greater part of the country. Most of it occurs between October and April, but normally there is no month that has less than ½ inch (1.3 cm.) of rain. Unfortunately, most of this water is lost to Lesotho in the form of runoff. The farmer needs rain that comes in steadily soaking showers, at intervals suited to the growth of the staple crops. But in Lesotho too often the rain comes in short, heavy storms. The water is wasted and the soil eroded. Occasionally, there are severe droughts that cause great damage to the crops. In the lowlands the temperatures vary from a maximum of 90 degrees Fahrenheit (32 degrees Celsius) or more in the summer to a minimum that rarely drops below 20 degrees F. (−7 degrees C.) in winter. In the highlands the range is much wider, and winter temperatures below zero are common.

THE PEOPLE

More than 99 percent of the people in Lesotho are black Africans of Bantu stock. They are referred to as Mosotho (singular) or Basotho (plural). Europeans form a tiny minority of about 2,000, and Asians a smaller minority of about 800. Most of the people live in small villages in the western lowlands. There are no large urban centers in Lesotho. The largest community in the country is Maseru, Lesotho's capital, which is connected by air, rail, and bus to South Africa.

The Basotho speak a language called Sesotho. The official languages are English and Sesotho. English is the language of instruction from the secondary school level upward, and Sesotho is used in primary schools.

Lesotho has one of the highest literacy rates in Africa. More than 60 percent of the people read and write either English or Sesotho. Most of the country's schools are run by religious missions, but they do get government subsidies. The National University of Lesotho is at Roma.

About 70 percent of Lesotho's people are Christian. The rest of the people follow traditional animistic beliefs.

A Basotho wears the same type of hat his ancestors wore years ago.

Way of Life

Most of the people of Lesotho are either farmers or herders. All land in the country traditionally had been handed out by the chieftainship—a bureaucracy of headmen, subchiefs, and chiefs, at the top of which was the paramount chief, now the king. But it is only the use of the land, not the ownership of the land, which is given out. Therefore, no one legally owns land in Lesotho. In theory, each family receives land according to the size of the family and its need. This did not encourage careful farming, and soil erosion became a serious problem in mountain areas. In 1979, in order to encourage better farming techniques, the government allowed the king to grant 99-year leases on some farmlands.

Most Basotho families do not eat balanced diets, and many suffer from diseases associated with malnutrition. In many Lesotho families, the women and children live at home together while the men are away working in South Africa's mines and factories. The money these migrant workers send back to their families in Lesotho is an important part of the country's national income.

Although the traditional folk art of the Basotho has been neglected, the government and private organizations are now encouraging its revival. Today the Basotho have little in the way of traditional clothing except for the distinctive conical hat, woven from grass. Often a masterpiece of craftmanship, the Basotho hat appears as the national symbol on the country's flag. Most Basotho men, women, and children also wear a colorful blanket over their Western-style clothing. The blanket serves as a protection against the hot sun and cold nights, the winter winds and snow. The Basotho house (rondavel), usually a circular structure of stone with a thatched roof, is also a distinctive feature of Lesotho culture.

ECONOMY

Lesotho is one of the poorest and least-developed countries in the world. It has no manufacturing industries and depends heavily on maintaining friendly relations with neighboring South Africa. All imports and exports of landlocked Lesotho move through South Africa, and money sent home by some 200,000 Basotho workers, mostly men, employed in South Africa accounts for much of the nation's limited income. Other sources of income are foreign aid and a negotiated share of customs revenues collected by South Africa. Leading economic activities within the country are subsistence herding of sheep, goats, and cattle and producing small crops of maize, millet, sorghum, wheat, and vegetables. The tourism industry, based on a national park at Sehlabathebe, is developing. Wool, mohair, wheat, and live cattle are the country's principal exports. Diamonds are sometimes mined in the region north of Mokhotlong when world prices for the gems are high.

HISTORY

The emergence of the Basotho as a unified people dates from 1818. At that time, Chief Moshoeshoe gathered together the widely scattered clans and brought them under his rule. Later on, in mid-century, a series of wars began between the Basotho and the Boers of the Orange Free State, now part of the Republic of South Africa. As a result of these battles, the Basotho lost a large part of their territory. Chief Moshoeshoe saw the threat of his country being dominated by the neighboring Boer

FACTS AND FIGURES

OFFICIAL NAME: Kingdom of Lesotho.

NATIONALITY: Mosotho (singular), Basotho (plural).

CAPITAL: Maseru.

LOCATION: Southern tip of Africa. **Boundaries:** surrounded by South Africa.

AREA: 11,761 sq. mi. (30,460 sq. km.).

PHYSICAL FEATURES: Highest point—11,425 ft. (3,482 m.). **Lowest point**—4,700 ft. (1,433 m.).

POPULATION: 1,801,000 (1991; annual growth 2.6%).

MAJOR LANGUAGES: Sesotho, English, (both official), Zulu, Xhosa.

MAJOR RELIGION: Christianity.

GOVERNMENT: Constitutional monarchy. **Head of state**—king. **Head of government**—chairman, military council. **Legislature**—Parliament (dissolved 1986).

CHIEF CITY: Maseru.

ECONOMY: Chief mineral—diamonds. **Chief agricultural products**—corn, wheat, pulses, sorghum, barley. **Chief exports**—wool, mohair, wheat, cattle, vegetables, hides. **Chief imports**—corn, building materials, clothing, vehicles, machinery, petroleum, oil and lubricants.

MONETARY UNIT: I Loti (plural, maloti) = 100 lisente.

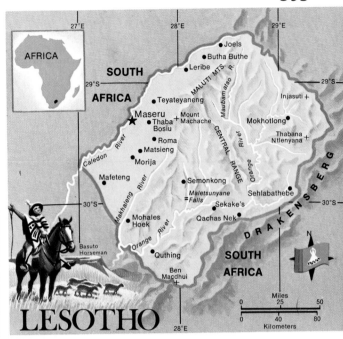

LESOTHO

republic. He asked Britain to protect his country, then known as Basutoland. In 1871 the territory was transferred to the Cape Colony without the agreement of the Basotho. After various disturbances, the country was restored to direct British control.

From 1884 to 1959 legislative and executive authority over Basutoland was vested in a British High Commissioner. In 1959, Basutoland was granted its first constitution. This was done because of a growing nationalist sentiment and Basotho fears that South Africa might acquire the territory. A new constitution, establishing Lesotho as a constitutional monarchy governed by a paramount chief, an elected National Assembly, and an appointed Senate, went into effect in 1965. Full independence as the Kingdom of Lesotho was attained on October 4, 1966.

Moshoeshoe II, paramount chief since 1960, was proclaimed king, and Leabua Jonathan, as leader of the National Assembly, became the first prime minister. Jonathan refused to accept defeat in the 1970 elections, suspended the constitution, and began ruling by decree. King Moshoeshoe II was arrested and exiled; when allowed to return in late 1970, he was forbidden to participate in politics. Jonathan appointed an Interim National Assembly in 1973, but his autocratic rule was not popular. He also angered the South African government by backing the black nationalist cause there. In early 1986, a 20-day blockade of Lesotho's borders by South Africa created great hardship and led to Jonathan's overthrow in a coup led by General Justin Lekhanya, who was more sympathetic to South Africa. In November 1990 Lekhanya dismissed King Moshoeshoe II; the former king's eldest son became King Letsie III. Lekhanya was overthrown in April 1991. Moshoeshoe II returned from exile in 1992, but was barred from resuming the throne before November elections to return the country to civilian rule under a new constitution.

RICHARD P. STEVENS, Lincoln University; author, *Lesotho, Botswana, and Swaziland*
Reviewed by J. L. MASITHELA, First Secretary
Embassy of the Kingdom of Lesotho to the United States, Washington, D.C.

Johannesburg, the commercial center of South Africa.

SOUTH AFRICA

The Republic of South Africa is one of the richest countries in the world. In 1867 an African boy playing on the banks of the Orange River discovered a beautiful pebble, later identified as a diamond. This discovery of diamonds changed the history of South Africa. Thousands of people poured into the territory to settle and strike it rich.

In 1884 gold was discovered in the area that is now the city of Johannesburg. Once again hopeful adventurers came into South Africa seeking fortunes. The wealth that the diamond fields had produced was invested in the development of the gold mines. Eventually the profits from the mines were used to develop industries. Without the immense wealth created by the discovery of gold and diamonds, the country might still be poor.

THE LAND

The Republic of South Africa, lying at the southern tip of the African continent, is bordered on the northeast by Swaziland and Mozambique, on the north by Botswana and Zimbabwe, and on the northwest by Namibia, which it ruled until 1990. To the west is the Atlantic Ocean and to the east the Indian Ocean.

Devil's Peak towers high over the coastal city of Cape Town.

South Africa is made up of four provinces: the Cape of Good Hope, Natal, the Orange Free State, and the Transvaal. In addition, 13 percent of the land had been set aside by the white-dominated government to form 10 "homelands" for South Africa's black majority. In 1990, however, the government agreed to abandon the controversial homelands policy as part of a broader political settlement. Even the four homelands that had been declared "independent" were to be reintegrated into South Africa.

The Plateau

Most of South Africa is a plateau with an altitude of 3,000 to 6,000 ft. (900 to 1,800 m.). In the southwest the plateau is mostly arid steppeland with short, scattered grasses. Isolated rocky hills, called kopjes, sometimes rise as high as 100 ft. (30 m.) above the surrounding land. In this region lie the Great and Little Karoos, which are dry scrublands.

The plateau rises toward the north and east, where increased rainfall produces lusher grasses and scattered trees. This region is known as the High Veld. The Witwatersrand ("ridge of white waters"), also known as the Rand, runs across the veld through Johannesburg. It is the richest gold-producing area in the world and the center of the country's famous gold-mining region. In the northern Transvaal the plateau descends toward the valley of the Limpopo River. The vegetation here is more tropical and dense than in the High Veld.

The Great Escarpment

The plateau area of South Africa is walled off from the coastal regions by a series of mountains called the Great Escarpment. The escarpment reaches its highest point in the east in the Drakensberg ("dragon's mountains"). A number of peaks in the Drakensberg, including the Giant's Castle and Mont-aux-Sources, are over 10,000 ft. (3,000 m.).

The Coastal Regions

The Namib Desert of Namibia, formerly South-West Africa, extends into the Republic of South Africa along the Atlantic coast. Farther south, around the Cape of Good Hope, long, narrow mountain ranges separate the escarpment from the sea. Between the ranges are sheltered valleys that are used for farming. Farther east, high cliffs alternate with narrow beaches and rolling hills. Only along the northeastern coast is there any extensive lowland plain.

Rivers

Two major rivers drain the South African plateau—the Orange and the Limpopo. The Orange has its source high in the Drakensberg and flows west across the veld. The Limpopo rises in the western Transvaal and flows north along the Botswana border. In this area it is sometimes called the Crocodile River.

Another important river is the Vaal, a tributary of the Orange, which forms the boundary between Transvaal and the Orange Free State.

Climate

Because South Africa lies below the equator, the winter months are June, July, and August. In winter the plateau is cool and sunny during the day. At night temperatures sometimes drop to the freezing level. Summer on the plateau is warmer, although because of the high altitude it never gets too hot. Most of the rain in the plateau region falls during the summer.

The Cape area has a Mediterranean climate. During the winter it is cool and rainy. In the summer it almost never rains, and the days are hot. Along the west coast there is little rainfall at any time of year, and the cold Benguela Current makes temperatures here among the lowest in South Africa. Along the eastern coast the warm Indian Ocean currents create a subtropical climate. Summer is warm and humid, while winters are mild and pleasant. Most of the rain falls during the summer months.

Cities

South Africa has many cities with populations over 100,000. The leading cities include Johannesburg, Cape Town, Pretoria, Bloemfontein, and Durban. Port Elizabeth and East London are important Indian Ocean ports, and Kimberley is the center of the diamond industry.

Johannesburg.   Located in the rich Witwatersrand, Johannesburg is the largest city in the republic and South Africa's leading mining, industrial, and commercial center. The original 19th-century gold mines are near what is now the center of the city. All around Johannesburg are the white and yellow hills of the mine dumps.

Today the streets of Johannesburg are lined with modern apartment buildings, offices, and factories. South Africa's stock exchange and the

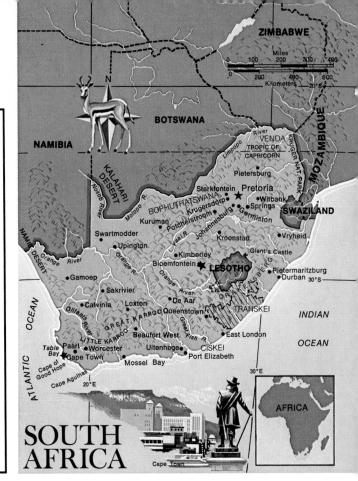

FACTS AND FIGURES

OFFICIAL NAME: Republic of South Africa.

NATIONALITY: South African(s).

CAPITAL: Pretoria (administrative), Cape Town (legislative), Bloemfontein (judicial).

LOCATION: Southern tip of Africa. **Boundaries**—Namibia, Botswana, Zimbabwe, Mozambique, Swaziland, Lesotho, Indian Ocean, Atlantic Ocean.

AREA: 471,444 sq. mi. (1,221,040 sq. km.).

PHYSICAL FEATURES: Highest point—Champagne Castle (11,073 ft.; 3,376 m.). **Lowest point**—sea level. **Chief rivers**—Orange, Limpopo.

POPULATION: 41,700,000 (1992; annual growth 2.6%).

MAJOR LANGUAGES: English, Afrikaans (official), various African languages.

MAJOR RELIGIONS: Christianity, Hinduism, Islam.

GOVERNMENT: Republic. **Head of state**—president. **Legislature**—three-house Parliament.

CHIEF CITIES: Cape Town, Durban, Johannesburg, Pretoria.

ECONOMY: Chief minerals—gold, chromium, antimony, coal, iron, manganese, diamonds. **Chief agricultural products**—corn, wheat, sugarcane, tobacco, fruits, livestock. **Industries and products**—mining, automobiles, metalworking, machinery. **Chief exports**—gold, coal, diamonds, corn, uranium. **Chief imports**—machinery, automobile parts, petroleum products, textiles, chemicals.

MONETARY UNIT: Rand.

headquarters of the South African Broadcasting Corporation are in the city. Johannesburg is also the site of the University of Witwatersrand.

Cape Town. This is South Africa's oldest city. It lies on the Atlantic coast between Table Bay and Table Mountain. On the slopes of the mountain is the Groote Schuur Estate, which Cecil Rhodes, former prime minister of the Cape Colony and British colonizer, left to the country. The estate includes Groote Schuur ("great barn"), the home of the prime minister when the South African Parliament is in session; the University of Cape Town; and Groote Schuur Hospital, scene of the world's first human heart transplant.

Cape Town is the seat of the South African Parliament. The Parliament buildings stand in the center of the city facing the Botanical Gardens. Nearby is the Castle, a fort that was constructed in the late 17th century to protect the harbor. The fort, built in the shape of a five-pointed star, now houses offices of the South African Defense Ministry.

Pretoria. About 40 mi. (58 km.) north of Johannesburg is Pretoria, the administrative capital of the Republic of South Africa and the capital of the Transvaal province. The city is famous for its jacaranda trees, which bloom in October and November. On a hill overlooking Pretoria are the Union Buildings, which were constructed after the four provinces were joined to form the Union of South Africa in 1910. They stand in terraced gardens and house government offices.

Durban. The Republic's largest port, Durban has in recent years become an important manufacturing and industrial center. South Africa's

The beach and pool area of Sea Point, a modern resort suburb of Cape Town.

Statue of Paul Kruger, president of the former Transvaal Republic, in historic Church Square, Pretoria. Nearby are many government buildings.

Durban is South Africa's chief seaport and a major commercial center.

sardine industry is centered in Durban. The Indian Ocean beaches around Durban are popular holiday resorts. West of the city is the Valley of the Thousand Hills, which is considered one of the most beautiful places in South Africa.

Bloemfontein. Located in central South Africa, Bloemfontein is the capital of the Orange Free State and the seat of the nation's Supreme Court and of the University of the Orange Free State. Bloemfontein is also an important industrial and trade center.

THE PEOPLE

South Africa has a diverse population. About 76 percent of the inhabitants are Africans; about 13 percent are whites, or Europeans; 8 percent are Coloureds (mixed African and other races); and about 2.5 percent are Asians. The Europeans, although in the minority, rule the country with a policy of segregation called apartheid.

Africans

The black Africans in the Republic of South Africa speak related Bantu languages. About 50 percent are also literate in either English or Afrikaans, South Africa's two official languages. The largest black group is the Nguni, to which the Zulu (South Africa's largest black community), Xhosa, and Swazi peoples belong. Archeological discoveries and written records tell us that the Nguni inhabited South Africa as early as 1500, long before most white settlers arrived. The Nguni settled along the east coast between the Drakensberg and the Indian Ocean, where they still mainly live today. The second largest black group are the Sotho, to which the Northern Sotho, Southern Sotho, South Ndebele, North Ndebele, and Tswana belong. Together, the Nguni and Sotho constitute over 90

South African children at play in a segregated nursery school.

percent of all South Africa's blacks. Smaller black groups are the Venda and the Shangana-Tsonga.

Under apartheid, South Africa's white-dominated government created ten separate "homelands," also known as "black states" or "bantustans," for the African majority. The homelands occupied about 13 percent of South Africa's total land area and were located in areas that were poorly endowed with soils, water, minerals, or other resources. All black Africans, even those who had lived in the "white" cities for many years, were considered citizens of the homeland designated for their particular ethnic group. Four of these homelands were granted "independence" by the South African government—Transkei in 1976, Bophuthatswana in 1977, Venda in 1979, and Ciskei in 1981. No country except South Africa recognized their independence. The South African government later said that the homelands would be reintegrated into South Africa as part of a broad political settlement that would give blacks a role in the national government. The main laws underpinning the apartheid policy, which was widely condemned inside and outside South Africa, were repealed in 1991. These laws included the Land Acts of 1913 and 1936 and the Group Areas Act of 1966, which had specified where blacks could live. In 1992, there were negotiations to determine the political structure of a post-apartheid South Africa.

The Europeans

There are actually two European, or white, communities: the Afrikaners and the English. The Afrikaners are descended from the original settlers who arrived with the Dutch East India Company in 1652. They were later joined by German Protestants and French Huguenots who were fleeing religious persecution in Europe. The English are descended from the settlers who arrived in the early 19th century after the British took over the rule of the Cape.

Most of the Afrikaners were traditionally farmers who lived an isolated life on the veld. What contact they had with other families came every 4 months when the kirk (church) would hold a communion service. All the families in an area would trek to the meeting place, unhook their wagons in a circle, visit with their neighbors, and then hold a church service. They were rugged people, fiercely independent, who worked long hours to eke out a meager living from the poor soil.

Afrikaners gradually turned in upon themselves and let the world pass them by. When social conditions changed, they were not prepared to change with them. The Dutch Reformed Church, to which most of the Afrikaners belong, has in the past lent support to a doctrine of racial superiority, viewing the Africans as sons of Ham, who have been cursed and cast into barbarism and who are therefore inferior to Christian white men. Although most Afrikaners now live in the cities and towns, they have retained many of their traditional attitudes. They have generally supported the National Party, the architect of the apartheid policy.

Afrikaners speak a distinctive language, Afrikaans, which was developed from the 17th-century Dutch spoken by the first settlers. Now many German, French, English, and African words have come into the language, and it is no longer a dialect of the Dutch but rather a separate language.

The English began to enter South Africa after the area came under British control in 1814. But it was not until the late 19th century, when gold and diamonds were discovered, that large numbers of English arrived. Since then most of them have lived in the cities, working in mining, industry, and commerce. Many of the English belong to the Anglican Church, various Protestant groups, and the Roman Catholic Church. There is also a sizable Jewish community. The English-speakers are more likely than the Afrikaners to vote for the more liberal opposition parties. There are separate Afrikaans and English schools, separate newspapers, and a generally separate cultural life.

The Coloureds

The Coloureds, or people of mixed descent, live mostly in the Cape region. They are descended from African and Malay slaves, Bushmen and Hottentots, and Europeans. The Malays constitute an important separate community within the Coloured group. Most of them are Muslims who are descended from slaves brought originally into the country from Dutch possessions in Malaysia. The majority of the Coloureds speak Afrikaans and belong to the Dutch Reformed Church.

The Asians

There is a small Asian minority in South Africa, mostly in the Natal province. The Asians are almost all Indians, although there is a very small Chinese community. The majority of the Indians are Hindus. A smaller number are Muslims. The Indians first came to South Africa in the late 1800s as indentured laborers in the Natal sugar fields. Many of them now live in the cities, where they are engaged in small businesses. One of the leaders of this small community was the Indian lawyer Mohandas Gandhi. He arrived in South Africa in 1893 and began a prosperous law practice. But Gandhi was distressed by the lowly position and bad treatment of the Indians. He began a program of civil disobedience to change the condition of the Indians of South Africa. Gandhi won some reforms from the government before he returned to become a political and spiritual leader in India.

Education

South Africa has many schools, colleges, and universities. Under apartheid, there was separate education for each racial group, but modest moves to integrate some public schools began in 1991, and nonwhites are gradually being admitted to formerly all-white universities. Education is free and compulsory for whites and Coloureds between the ages of 6 and 16 and for Indians between 7 and 15 years. Free and compulsory education for blacks is being phased in slowly, although many black children still do not attend school.

ECONOMY

Until the discoveries of diamonds and gold in the late 19th century, South Africa was a poor agricultural country. But the vast amount of its mineral wealth has encouraged the development of both industry and agriculture. Industry has now surpassed mining as the major sector in the South African economy.

Industry

The area around Johannesburg is the largest industrial center in the country. The factories of the Rand produce almost any item a person could want—stoves, automobiles, shoes, paper products, aspirin, and clothing. Many European and American companies have opened branches to serve the rich South African market. Durban, Cape Town, and Port Elizabeth are also major industrial centers. Among the most important industries are iron and steel, food processing, textiles, chemicals, and machinery.

Diamond Mining. Diamonds were formed millions of years ago in South Africa in volcanic throats, or pipes, called kimberlite or blue ground. Kimberlite deposits occur in a belt from the Orange Free State through Pretoria all the way up to Lake Victoria in East Africa. But less than 25 of the 150 pipes discovered contain diamonds. At first the diamonds were just dug out of large pits. "Just" may not be the correct word, because even in the richest diamond areas, tons of earth must be sifted to find one diamond. The biggest of the pits in South Africa, the Great Hole, is at Kimberley. As the pits got deeper and more miners worked on individual claims, such chaos developed that the industry almost collapsed. At this point, a young man who had left England to grow cotton in Natal came to Kimberley. He organized the mines into one of the world's most efficient organizations. The man was Cecil John Rhodes, later to become prime minister of the Cape Colony. The organization he founded was called De Beers, after one of the farms in Kimberley where diamonds were first found. Today, De Beers still controls the output of South African diamonds and the sales of rough uncut stones at Kimberley.

Gold. About one-third of the world's supply of gold comes from gold-mining industries located in South Africa. The miners at first discov-

Workmen at the Kimberly mines sift through dirt in search of diamonds.

Workers are searched before leaving the diamond mines at the end of the day.

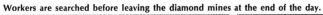

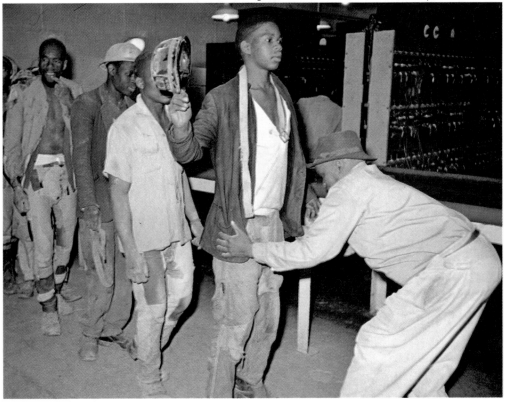

ered that the reef, or gold-bearing rock seam, extended 25 mi. (40 km.) east of Johannesburg to the town of Springs and 25 mi. (40 km.) west to the town of Krugersdorp. This is the Witwatersrand, or the Rand, the greatest gold-producing area in the world.

In the 1930s the gold reef was discovered to extend farther west, and after World War II mines were developed in the Orange Free State across the Vaal River. These mines are now producing more gold than the older ones around Johannesburg. Today mining is taking place down to 2 mi. (3.4 km.) below the surface.

To develop the gold mines, black Africans were recruited and trained to operate drills, push mine carts, and do the thousands of odd jobs necessary in such a large enterprise. Only non-Africans were permitted to hold more skilled jobs before 1985, when restrictions on the kinds of jobs blacks could hold in mining and industry were removed.

Other Minerals. Just to the east of the Rand at Witbank is the richest coal deposit on the African continent. Coal from Witbank has been brought to Pretoria since the 1930s to fuel the blast furnaces that help South Africa produce several million tons of steel per year. The iron ore used by the steel mills is mined in the Cape and the Transvaal. Most of the coal is burned to produce electric power that is sent to factories and mines. In the area just south of Johannesburg a new coalfield has been developed, and the government has built a factory to convert the coal into oil.

The other important minerals found in the republic include antimony, uranium, chromium, copper, manganese, platinum, asbestos, and vanadium.

Agriculture

Over half of South Africa receives less than the minimum amount of annual rainfall needed for growing crops, and many areas that receive more rain are too hilly to farm. Nevertheless, South African farmers generally grow enough food to make the country self-sufficient and a surplus for export. In 1992, however, severe drought destroyed about 75 percent of the maize harvest and made food imports necessary.

The Karoos and southwestern plateau are too dry to use for anything but the raising of sheep. South Africa has nearly 30 million sheep, most of which are raised for wool. Today the country ranks as one of the five leading wool-producing nations in the world. Farther west, where the land gets too dry even for sheep to graze, goats are raised. Angora goats yield leather and mohair, of which South Africa is the world's leading producer.

The African people raise a lot of cattle, mostly for prestige rather than yield, and often there are too many on the land. The animals are usually of poor quality and tend to overeat the grasses. This in turn causes erosion, and the soil wastes away. Many of the African groups look upon cattle as a source of wealth. The more cattle one owns, the richer one is. It doesn't matter whether the cattle are fat and free of disease—any will do. Some beef cattle and dairy cows are raised near the cities and irrigated river areas, while other cattle and oxen are used to pull wagons and help plow. The hides of some cattle are tanned and used to make shoes.

Most of the land that is wet enough to be farmed is planted in maize (corn), commonly called mealies in South Africa. Maize production is centered south of Johannesburg in the Transvaal and the Orange Free State. Another important crop is wheat, which is grown by irrigation in many areas. A severe drought in the early 1990s made it necessary for South Africa to import large quantities of grain to feed its people.

There are outstanding vineyards in the Hex River valley near Cape Town. Fresh grapes are also exported to Europe. Other major crops are citrus fruits, tobacco, sugarcane, and cotton.

South Africa is one of the leading fishing nations in the world. Rock lobster, or crayfish, and fish meal are important exports.

HISTORY

Little is known about the history of South Africa before the arrival of the first European explorers in the 15th century, despite the discovery of fossils of the early ancestors of humans at Sterkfontein—fossils similar to those found at Olduvai Gorge in Tanzania.

The first European knowledge of southern Africa came with Bartholomeu Dias' discovery of the Cape of Good Hope in 1488. Dias was followed in 1497–98 by Vasco da Gama, who sailed around the Cape and discovered and named the Natal region. But the Portuguese never explored or settled what is now the Republic of South Africa. In the 17th century the Dutch and the British began to compete for trading supremacy in the Far East. Since the voyage from Europe to the Far East was a long one, it was necessary to have stations where the ships could stop and restock food. In 1652 the Dutch East India Company decided to establish a refreshment station on Table Bay at the northern end of the Cape peninsula. Three shiploads of settlers were sent out under the leadership of Jan van Riebeeck. Upon landing the Dutch built a fort. They planted gardens and raised animals to provide meat for the sailors on the long voyage to the East Indies. Many of the Dutch settlers began moving away from the fort and settled down to raise cattle or trade with the Africans. Soon their numbers were increased by French Huguenots fleeing France during the late 17th century in search of religious freedom.

As the Europeans grew in number, they began to move farther from Cape Town and control by the Dutch East India Company. The farther they moved, the more they came in conflict with the Africans. Both groups were seeking the same thing: land and water for their cattle.

During the Napoleonic Wars, England acquired the Cape Colony from the Dutch. In 1815 the Congress of Vienna formally confirmed the British possession of the Cape. During the 1820s more and more British immigrants began to move into the Cape Colony. The Dutch people (called Boers, from the Dutch word for "farmer") resented the British settlement, and soon the two European groups came into conflict. In the 1830s Dutch discontent reached its peak, and many of the Boers decided to leave the Cape. Beginning in 1835 and lasting until 1838, hundreds of wagons left the Cape and rumbled eastward and northward. This migration came to be called the Great Trek. It was not a single movement. There were innumerable groups of Dutch who followed their wagon-train leaders and eventually established independent republics, including the Orange Free State and the South Africa Republic (Transvaal).

In 1899 difficulties between the Boers and the British reached a climax, and war broke out. In May 1902, the Boers surrendered to the

British forces. Britain granted the Boer states self-government, and in 1910, the Orange Free State, Transvaal, and the two British colonies of Cape of Good Hope and Natal formed the Union of South Africa.

During World War I, South Africa fought with Britain against Germany. After the war the League of Nations gave South Africa a mandate over the former German protectorate of South-West Africa (now called Namibia). In 1966 the United Nations voted to end the mandate, but South Africa refused to recognize the vote. (An article on NAMIBIA, independent since 1990, appears in this volume.)

In 1948 the National Party, led by Dr. Daniel François Malan, came to power. Under his guidance, the country embarked upon a policy of apartheid, or separate development of the races. From 1953 to 1989 the National Party held power in 10 consecutive parliamentary elections.

In 1958 the National Party chose Hendrik F. Verwoerd as prime minister. Verwoerd strengthened the laws of apartheid. The government hoped eventually to establish 10 "independent homelands" for the Africans where they could develop separately.

The white minority population of South Africa voted in October 1960 to remove their country from British control, and on May 31, 1961, South Africa was established as a republic.

A new constitution went into effect in 1984, which provided for some political representation for South Africa's Coloureds and Indians. Blacks, however, were still denied national political rights, although they could choose local officials in the "homelands." From 1984 to 1986, demonstrations against apartheid swept through many of the black townships, causing the government to declare a state of emergency. After National Party leader Frederik W. de Klerk succeeded P. W. Botha as state president in 1989, however, the government reversed course. In 1990 it lifted the state of emergency except in Natal. The African National Congress (ANC) and other banned groups were legalized and many imprisoned black nationalists, including ANC leader Nelson R. Mandela, who had been in jail since 1964, were released. In 1991 the main laws underpinning apartheid were repealed. A March 1992 whites-only referendum endorsed the continuation of talks between the government and black leaders designed to shape a post-apartheid government that would include all races. These talks were suspended by the ANC in mid-1992 after charges that white security forces were implicated in the ongoing political violence between the ANC and its chief rival, the Zulu-based Inkatha. Broad agreement on many aspects of a negotiated transfer of power had already been reached, however, and hopes for a peaceful shift to majority rule remained.

GOVERNMENT

The constitution that came into force in 1984 replaced the previously all-white parliament with one composed of three houses: the House of Assembly, with 178 white members; the House of Representatives, with 85 Coloured members; and the House of Delegates, with 45 Indian members. Blacks had no representation. The constitution also provided for a state president who served as both head of state and government. The state president was to be elected by a white-dominated electoral college whose members were drawn from the three houses of parliament.

HUGH C. BROOKS, Director, Center for African Studies, St. John's University

ILLUSTRATION CREDITS

The following list credits, according to page, the sources of illustrations used in volume 1 of LANDS AND PEOPLES. The credits are listed illustration by illustration—top to bottom, left to right. Where necessary, the name of the photographer or artist has been listed with the source, the two separated by a dash. If two or more illustrations appear on the same page, their credits are separated by semicolons

4 Robert Amon
5 Editorial Photocolor Archives, N.Y.
6 Jere Donovan
8 H. von Meiss—Photo Researchers
9 Alpha
10 Walter Hortens
12 Linda Bartlett; Marc & Evelyn Bernheim—Rapho Guillumette Pictures
13 Freelance Photographers Guild; Marc & Evelyn Bernheim—Rapho Guillumette Pictures
15 Jeppesen Maps—The H.M. Gousha Company
17 Editorial Photocolor Archives, N.Y.
19 Editorial Photocolor Archives, N.Y.
20 George Buctel
21 United Nations
23 Marc & Evelyn Bernheim—Rapho Guillumette Pictures
25 Linda Bartlett; Editorial Photocolor Archives, N.Y.
27 Michael A. Vaccaro
29 Michael A. Vaccaro
30 Charles Shapp
32 Picon—FPG; Marc & Evelyn Bernheim—Rapho Guillumette Pictures
33 Michael A. Vaccaro
34 Byron Crader—Lenstour Photos
36 Marc & Evelyn Bernheim—Rapho Guillumette Pictures
38 Marc & Evelyn Bernheim—Rapho Guillumette Pictures
39 Editorial Photocolor Archives, N.Y.
45 Marc & Eveyln Bernheim—Rapho Guillumette Pictures
46 Courtesy of the Brooklyn Museum, Gift of Mr. and Mrs. Gustare Schindler
47 Marc & Evelyn Bernheim—Rapho Guillumette Pictures
48 Marc & Evelyn Bernheim—Rapho Guillumette Pictures; Victor Englebert—De Wys, Inc.
51 Courtesy of the Brooklyn Museum, Gift of A. & P. Peralta-Ramos; Marc & Evelyn Bernheim—Rapho Guillumette Pictures
52 Marc & Evelyn Bernheim—Rapho Guillumette Pictures
53 Jacques Jangoux
55 Wesley McKeown
56 J. Jung—Alan Band Associates
58 Dick Huffman—Monkmeyer Press Photo Service
59 Mulvey-Crump Associates, Inc.
60 Dick Huffman—Monkmeyer Press Photo Service
61 Editorial Photocolor Archives, N.Y.
62 Mulvey-Crump Associates, Inc.
63 Carl Frank
64 Carl Frank
65 Carl Frank
66 Editorial Photocolor Archives, N.Y.
69 Editorial Photocolor Archives, N.Y.
71 Alan Band Associates
72 Editorial Photocolor Archives, N.Y.; Alan Seiden
73 Allen Seiden
75 George Buctel
76 Editorial Photocolor Archives, N.Y.
77 Editorial Photocolor Archives, N.Y.
78 De Wys, Inc.
79 Editorial Photocolor Archives, N.Y.
81 Philcarol—Monkmeyer Press Photo Service
82 Editorial Photocolor Archives, N.Y.
85 Mulvey-Crump Associates, N.Y.
86 Editorial Photocolor Archives, N.Y.
89 Editorial Photocolor Archives, N.Y.

90 Walter Hortens
91 Editorial Photocolor Archives, N.Y.
92 Editorial Photocolor Archives, N.Y.
94 Editorial Photocolor Archives, N.Y.
95 Peter Turner
97 Peter Turner
98 Mulvey-Crump Associates, Inc.
99 Michael A. Vaccaro
100 Michael A. Vaccaro
103 Michael A. Vaccaro
104 Peter Turner
105 Latham—Monkmeyer Press Photo Service; Michael A. Vaccaro
106 Michael A. Vaccaro; © Gerling/Alpha
108 Michael A. Vaccaro; Harrison Forman
109 Louis Jefferson—Monkmeyer Press Photo Service
110 Michael A. Vaccaro
112 Omar Bessim—Monkmeyer Press Photo Service
114 Peter Turner
116 Harrison Forman
120 Wesley McKeown
121 Editorial Photocolor Archives, N.Y.; Harrison Forman
122 Michael A. Vaccaro
123 Michael A. Vaccaro
124 Marc & Evelyn Bernheim—Rapho Guillumette Pictures
125 Patrick Morin—Monkmeyer Press Photo Service
126 © F. Jackson—Bruce Coleman, Inc.
127 Mulvey-Crump Associates, Inc.
128 © W. Campbell—Sygma
129 Marc & Evelyn Bernheim—Rapho Guillumette Pictures
131 Harrison Forman
132 Editorial Photocolor Archives, N.Y.
133 Frank Schwarz—Lee Ames Studio
134 De Wys, Inc.
135 De Wys, Inc.
137 Frank Schwarz—Lee Ames Studio
138 De Wys, Inc.
140 Victor Englebert
141 Editorial Photocolor Archives, N.Y.
143 George Buctel
144 Wesley McKeown
145 Wendy Watriss
146 Harrison Forman
147 United Nations
148 Marc & Evelyn Bernheim—Rapho Guillumette Pictures
149 George Buctel
151 Victor Englebert
153 Frank Schwarz—Lee Ames Studio
154 Marc & Evelyn Bernheim—Rapho Guillumette Pictures
155 Harrison Forman
156 Enrico Ferorelli
157 George Buctel
158 Harrison Forman
159 Harrison Forman
160 Harrison Forman
161 Enrico Ferorelli
163 Frank Schwarz—Lee Ames Studio
164 Kay Honkanen—Ostman Agency
166 A. Fessore—PIX, Inc.
167 Mulvey-Crump Associates, Inc.
168 G. Marshall Wilson—DPI
169 Ronnie Brathwaite
170 Ronnie Brathwaite
171 Mulvey-Crump Associates, Inc.
173 Amy Joof
174 Howard Cagle—Photo Researchers
175 Mulvey-Crump Associates, Inc.
177 Don Carl Steffen—Rapho Guillumette
179 Frederick Ayer III—Photo Researchers

180 Jacques Jangoux
181 Monkmeyer Press Photo Service
183 George Buctel
184 Jacques Jangoux
185 Jacques Jangoux
186 Marc & Evelyn Bernheim—Rapho Guillumette Pictures
188 Editorial Photocolor Archives, N.Y.
189 Walter Hortens
190 Editorial Photocolor Archives, N.Y.
191 Miriam Wolford
192 George Buctel
193 Monkmeyer Press Photo Service
194 Jacques Jangoux
196 Jacques Jangoux
198 © John Elk III—Bruce Coleman Inc.; Marc & Evelyn Bernheim—Rapho Guillumette Pictures
199 George Buctel
200 Marc & Evelyn Bernheim—Rapho Guillumette Pictures
201 Dr. Edward H. Schiller
202 Harrison Forman
203 Jacques Jangoux
207 Marc & Evelyn Bernheim—Rapho Guillumette Pictures
208 Editorial Photocolor Archives, N.Y.
209 United Nations
210 Marc & Evelyn Bernheim—Rapho Guillumette Pictures
211 Frank Schwarz—Lee Ames Studio
212 Gil Ross
213 Marc & Evelyn Bernheim—Rapho Guillumette Pictures
215 Frank Schwarz—Lee Ames Studio
217 Bruno Barbey—Magnum Photos
218 George Buctel
219 Wendy Watriss
220 Harrison Forman
221 Harrison Forman
222 Shell International Petroleum Co., Ltd.
224 Wendy Watriss
226 Harrison Forman
227 Harrison Forman
229 Wendy Watriss
230 Miriam Wolford
232 Editorial Photocolor Archives, N.Y.
233 United Nations
234 United Nations
235 Walter Hortens
238 George Buctel
239 George Orick
240 Frank Schwarz—Lee Ames Studio
241 Peter Turner
242 Peter Turner
243 Peter Turner
244 Peter Turner
245 George Buctel
247 Editorial Photocolor Archives, N.Y.
248 Editorial Photocolor Archives, N.Y.
249 Harrison Forman
251 George Buctel
252 Editorial Photocolor Archives, N.Y.
253 De Wys, Inc.
254 De Wys, Inc.
255 Mulvey-Crump Associates, Inc.
256 Editorial Photocolor Archives, N.Y.
258 De Wys, Inc.
259 De Wys, Inc.
261 Frank Schwarz—Lee Ames Studio
263 Editorial Photocolor Archives, N.Y.
264 Peter Turner
265 Frank Schwarz—Lee Ames Studio
266 Fujihira—Monkmeyer Press Photo Service
268 International Foto File
269 Jacques Jangoux
270 Fujihara—Monkmeyer Press Photo Service

273 Wesley McKeown
274 International Foto File
275 Editorial Photocolor Archives, N.Y.
276 Harrison Forman
277 George Buctel
278 Editorial Photocolor Archives, N.Y.
279 Peter Fraenkel—Ostman Agency
281 Tiers—Monkmeyer Press Photo Service
282 Tiers—Monkmeyer Press Photo Service
284 Tiers—Monkmeyer Press Photo Service
285 Frank Schwarz—Lee Ames Studio
286 Peter Turner
287 Victor Englebert
288 © William W. Bacon III—Photo Researchers
289 George Buctel
290 Peter Turner
291 © F. Jackson—Bruce Coleman, Inc.
292 © Sygma
293 Marc & Evelyn Bernheim—Rapho Guillumette Pictures
294 © W. Campbell—Sygma
296 Victor Englebert
297 Victor Englebert
298 Patrick Morin—Monkmeyer Press Photo Service
299 Mulvey-Crump Associates, Inc.
301 © Peter Menzel/Stock Boston
302 Ewing Galloway
303 Frank Schwarz—Lee Ames Studio
304 Ewing Galloway
306 E. Streichan—Shostal Associates
307 Harrison Forman
308 Editorial Photocolor Archives, N.Y.
309 George Buctel
311 Gosta Glase—Ostman Agency; Harrison Forman
312 Harrison Forman

313 Harrison Forman
314 Harrison Forman
316 Warren Slater—Monkmeyer Press Photo Service
317 Marc & Evelyn Bernheim—Rapho Guillumette Pictures
319 Walter Hortens
320 Marc & Evelyn Bernheim—Rapho Guillumette Pictures
321 B. Frodin—S. E. Hedin; Janet Zobel
324 Vivian M. Peevers—Peter Arnold
325 Robert Amon
327 George Buctel
328 Sipahioglu/Martel—C.I.R.I.
329 Sipahioglu/Martel—C.I.R.I.
331 Frank Schwarz—Lee Ames Studio
332 Dr. C. J. Chafaris
333 Harrison Forman
334 Harrison Forman; Gloria Karlson
336 Harrison Forman
337 George Buctel
339 Linda Bartlett
340 Mulvey-Crump Associates, Inc.
341 B. Frodin—S. E. Hedin
342 B. Frodin—S.E. Hedin
343 Editorial Photocolor Archives, N.Y.
344 Frank Schwarz—Lee Ames Studio
345 Monkmeyer Press Photo Service
347 Alan Band Associates
348 Editorial Photocolor Archives, N.Y.
349 Frank Schwarz—Lee Ames Studio
351 Goiffon—FPG
352 Goiffon—FPG
353 George Buctel
355 Peter Turner
356 John Havergal—Alan Band Associates
357 W. W. Howells
358 Harrison Forman

359 George Buctel
360 Jana Latta
361 Editorial Photocolor Archives, N.Y.
363 Harrison Forman
364 Peter Turner
365 Mulvey-Crump Associates, Inc.
367 Peter Turner
369 Lelieve—De Wys, Inc.
371 George Buctel
372 Picou—De Wys, Inc.
373 Jamet—De Wys, Inc.; Editorial Photocolor Archives, N.Y.
375 Warren Slater—Monkmeyer Press Photo Service
376 Editorial Photocolor Archives, N.Y.
378 S. E. Hedin
379 Robert Amon
380 Graham Norton—PIX, Inc.
381 George Buctel
383 Mulvey-Crump Associates, Inc.
385 Editorial Photocolor Archives, N.Y.
386 Richard Weiss
387 George Buctel
388 Richard Weiss
390 George Behrman
391 Tony Carr—Alan Band Associates
393 Frank Schwarz—Lee Ames Studio
394 Editorial Photocolor Archives, N.Y.
395 Linda Bartlett
397 Mulvey-Crump Associates, Inc.
395 Editorial Photocolor Archives, N.Y.; Harrison Forman
399 Alan Band Associates
400 Dr. Edward H. Schiller
403 Editorial Photocolor Archives, N.Y.; Harrison Forman

Cover photo: © Gerald Del Vecchio/Tony Stone Worldwide